D0598245

English
Provincial Cooking

English
Provincial Cooking

Elisabeth Ayrton

HARPER & ROW, PUBLISHERS

NEW YORK

Cambridge
Hagerstown
Philadelphia
San Francisco

London
Mexico City
São Paulo
Sydney

1817

Editor	Art Editor	Photographs
Rachel Grenfell	**Val Hobson**	Tony Copeland
Assistant Editor	Assistant Art Editor	Index
Gillian Abrahams	**Ingrid Mason**	Anne Hardy
Executive Editor	Production	Map
Alexandra Towle	**Martin Elliott**	Gillian Chapman

ENGLISH PROVINCIAL COOKING. Copyright © 1980 Mitchell Beazley
Publishers, Limited, Great Britain
Text copyright © 1980 by Elisabeth Ayrton
Photographs copyright © 1980 by Mitchell Beazley Publishers, Ltd, Great Britain

All rights reserved. Printed in Italy. No part of this book may be used or reproduced
in any manner whatsoever without written permission except in the case of brief
quotations embodied in critical articles and reviews. For information address
Harper & Row, Publishers, Inc., 10 East 53rd Street, New York, N.Y. 10022.

FIRST U.S. EDITION
ISBN: 0-06-010157-1
LIBRARY OF CONGRESS CATALOG CARD NUMBER: 79-2612

80 81 82 83 84 10 9 8 7 6 5 4 3 2 1

Contents

Introduction

The marked differences in the traditional cooking of the several regions of England are not always realized or expected by those who search for local specialities when they visit different parts of the country. Today many English hotels and inns serve a certain number of traditional dishes, but these are generally the roasts and pies which have been made all over the country since the Middle Ages. To enjoy the cooking of one region and to appreciate its differences from that of any other part of the country, it is necessary to be welcomed at several private households, preferably of different spending levels, scattered over England. Since this is not easy to arrange, I have tried, in this book, to give recipes which exemplify the culinary traditions of each region and, where possible, to explain and describe their origins.

England has an overall temperate climate, unlike France, whose cool north and Mediterranean south have resulted in the splendidly varied cooking of her provinces. The differences in the cooking of the English provinces have for the most part a less obvious explanation and we must look back in time to see how they often came from the land itself and the main occupations of the ordinary people.

The Romans conquered a wild Celtic Britain where the food of the tribes, from the chiefs to their lowest-ranking followers, was meat or fish, boiled or roasted or eaten raw, and various forms of porridge, roots and berries. The rations of the Roman legionaries were also mainly a form of porridge, but their commanders and the civil officers sent to govern the new Roman province of Britain introduced their own rather elaborate and sophisticated cuisine to those British chiefs and princelings who were prepared to learn Roman ways.

Eight centuries after the Romans were forced to recall their legions, their culinary influence remained. The proof of this lies in the accounts of medieval feasts, for the dishes that are described are very similar to the recipes given in the only surviving Roman cookery book, written by the great first-century gourmet and cook Apicius. Even today the lineage of some of our dishes can be traced back to Apicius' recipes, but in the Middle Ages the use of stuffings and forcemeats, pottages and ragouts, the many dishes composed of different meats and birds, finely chopped, highly spiced and seasoned, moistened with rosewater or milk of almonds, and with mushrooms, truffles, artichoke bottoms, cockscombs and ox palates, sweetbreads and lambs' tongues added, had remained so close to Roman culinary practices that they would have been recognized and appreciated by the provincial governors and garrison officers who had lived in Britain centuries earlier.

In the Dark Ages, which followed the departure of the legions, however, Britain was subjected to frequent invasions from Germany and further north. Angles, Saxons, Jutes and Frisians all landed in south-east England and succeeded in obtaining and holding land. Naturally, therefore, the different customs and tastes which each of these half-civilized, agricultural tribes brought with them affected the way of life in the areas where they settled and intermarried with the British. Some of the traditional dishes of Kent, which was settled by the Jutes and which rapidly became extremely prosperous, are entirely different from any to be found elsewhere in England. Some Kentish dishes, however, derive directly from the exceptionally fine fruit, particularly cherries and plums, grown in the Weald of Kent, and make use of fruit served hot where most other districts serve it cold.

The new settlers and the Britons alike were subjected to frequent and destructive raids by the Vikings, some of whom established settlements. They introduced the dried and salted "stockfish", which, in later centuries, carried all but the very wealthy through so many meatless Lents as well as fish days, which were imposed by the Church and which meant that no meat or poultry could be served on almost half the days of the year. Because it is not generally realized, it should perhaps be emphasized here that, in the sixteenth century, meatless days were imposed on the whole country by the Government as well as by the Church. This was, in fact, a kind of tax intended to encourage fishermen. Those who broke the law were heavily fined and any infringement might be reported by an inspector claiming hospitality as a guest or by a disloyal servant. Only the sick and, in certain circumstances, small children were exempt, as they were considered to need meat for health reasons.

This rather curious restriction seemed more natural in the sixteenth century than it does to us today because everyone was quite used to religious fasts. Fridays throughout the year and the whole of Lent were meatless, but the additional government restriction meant that there was no meat, poultry or game on anyone's table, be they noble or common, rich or poor, from Thursday until Sunday.

The variations of English cookery fall naturally into seven major regions: East Anglia and the Eastern Counties, The North, The Midlands, The West Country, The South and South East, The Home Counties, and London. Within these regions certain dishes are particular to one county or area.

This book is really a selective history and geography in terms of the cookery of England which in no way attempts to be definitive. It is a personal cookery book and readers will, no doubt, know of local dishes with long pedigrees which are not included. In some instances this is likely to be because the dish seems to have no place in our eating habits today; in others, certain of the ingredients called for in the original recipe may be unobtainable and substitutes would radically alter the character of the dish. Also, I do not doubt that there are many excellent, traditional dishes which I have not discovered.

Since 1967 several English county boundaries have been changed and the counties of Rutland and Huntingdon included in Leicestershire and Cambridgeshire respectively. New counties such as Avon and West

Midlands have been made and certain counties divided, as in the case of Yorkshire. County boundaries may change but regional traditions do not, and, therefore, this book adopts a middle course, treating the North of England as a whole and Yorkshire as a single great county, as it used to be. This simplifies the regions described but does not make it difficult to find the places mentioned.

The very interesting culinary traditions of Scotland, Ireland and Wales, differing from each other as well as from all parts of England, are not described in this book since these three countries of the British Isles deserve to be treated separately in terms of their cookery and not as regions of England.

Scottish baking is world famous, as are many Scottish dishes of meat and fish, and certain Scottish cheeses. Only in Wales is it possible today to eat laver, the seaweed which grows in many coastal areas and which once was much more widely collected and cooked. Ireland is known for her ways with potatoes, but has many other traditional recipes for pork and salmon, fine trout and good bread.

It is interesting to find the wide differences in traditional cookery between Wales and Scotland and the adjoining counties. The basic reason is that Roman civilization never spread north of Hadrian's Wall nor very far into Wales. Food remained primitive for much longer than in England. Records show that on some of the Scottish islands beef was being boiled in the hide as late as the sixteenth century, because the islanders were *"destitute of vessels of metal or earth"* according to a contemporary traveller. Boiling in the hide involved skinning and gutting the animal. The carcass was then hacked into joints and the hide slung on four poles to form a kind of shallow trough, half-filled with water, which was heated with pot-stones – these were stones which were heated red hot in the hearth fires and dropped into the trough to bring the water to the boil. To keep the water at boiling point, one or two stones would have been added at regular intervals. The joints were cooked in the boiling water and the liver and kidneys were toasted on sticks over the fire.

Exceedingly primitive cookery of this kind was well demonstrated by an archaeological experiment carried out in Ireland in 1952. A site was discovered where a cooking trough had been sunk in a peat bog, the water level being high enough to prevent water seeping from the trough, which was lined with wood and slabs of stone. There was a hearth at each end and many pot stones were found. A second pit formed a sunken oven, heated by inserting burning brushwood. To keep the oven hot it was necessary to cover it with red-hot stones, which were replaced as they cooled.

To test the efficacy of the trough and the oven Professor O'Kelly and his helpers prepared two ten-pound joints. The one to be boiled was wrapped in straw, the other left as butchered. Both were deliciously and cleanly cooked in a little over three hours, red-hot stones being continually added. The laborious process provided a meal for about 20 men. Neither trough nor oven would have taken much larger joints.

These methods of cookery continued to be used in hunting camps and temporary settlements, perhaps rather as we build a barbecue, as late as the tenth century AD and in Ireland possibly as late as the sixteenth century. It is of great interest that several early Irish poems refer to "a *roasting and a boiling"* in describing certain heroic meals and also mention a hut of wood, with a roof of sedge, erected as a meat store, presumably for the extra meat which hunters would take home. At the site where Professor O'Kelly carried out his experiment, the post holes of a hut were found, with additional holes for a meat rack and a butcher's block. Such cooking arrangements must also have existed in England.

The easiest cooking method, before any kind of pot had been introduced, was to hold pieces of meat on a green stick over a fire. It is clear that this was not satisfactory – the meat must have been partly burnt and partly raw – and that immense trouble was taken, as it has been in primitive societies all over the world, to find methods of cooking whole animals and large joints. It was easy to sling a whole carcass on a pole supported on a framework, but it was difficult to cook the inside while keeping the outside from charring and any but a very young animal would probably have been very tough indeed.

The pot was needed and the pot was invented. The first pots were of clay, which could be stood in the ashes at the side of the fire. Later the cauldron was introduced, made of bronze and, later still, of iron. A metal cauldron could be very large indeed and separate joints of meat could be hung from the rim, sealed jars of meat or vegetables stood in the bottom and a bag of peas or a pudding in a cloth tied to one handle, all immersed in the boiling water. Such a cooking arrangement was used in many a cottage throughout the British Isles until the nineteenth century.

Only with the introduction of the clay pot and the cauldron could any form of broth or gravy be made fit to eat. In cold, wet Britain all forms of porridge and pottage became warming staples, and with the Roman conquest, herbs and spices, worts (which meant any form of cabbage), turnips and other vegetables were cooked with the meat, which was often stuffed. The Romans introduced small iron grills to stand over hot coals, flat pans for frying and deeper ones for braising. The way was open for real cookery and real cookery began.

Since many of the recipes given in this book originated in the Middle Ages or even earlier, it may be of interest to describe briefly the elaborate serving of meals not only to royalty but to all the great nobles of England when they dined in full state in castle or manor.

Until the fourteenth century, prince, duke or earl would dine at the high table, usually raised on a dais at one end of his Great Hall, at the same time as the rest of his household, who were seated strictly according to rank. Trestle tables were set up for the meal and taken down afterwards. The taking down was called "drawing the boards". The kitchen, usually at the end of a short passage leading off the hall, was further separated from the diners by an elaborately carved and panelled screen. The Great Chamber was often above the hall, and here the earl and his family and any noble guests would withdraw at the end of the meal. In the fourteenth century, they began to withdraw in order to partake of the last course, the banquet, in the greater privacy of the Chamber. In the fifteenth century it became the custom for the lord to dine in the Chamber while the rest of his household dined in the hall, and this practice, which probably started in the royal palaces, became widespread. Queen Elizabeth I, as she grew older, almost always ate in her privy chamber, although the traditional accompanying ceremonial was most carefully preserved. We are told that at Nonsuch Palace in 1599, the table was prepared in her Presence Chamber with every formality. Forty yeomen of the guard brought in the immensely varied first course, which was tasted for poison (this is described in various household regulations as "taking sayes", from the old French word *assayer*, meaning to try). Wine was poured and a glass was put at the head of the table, where the Queen should have been sitting. In fact she was seated at a smaller but equally elaborately arranged table in her privy chamber and when she had been served in her absence in the outer chamber, a choice selection of the foods she was known to like was brought to her. This ritual was performed for each of the three courses of the meal.

The preparations for serving dinner to an earl in the Great Chamber of his castle were extremely elaborate. Mark Girouard, in his book *Life in the English Country House*, points out that the serving of the main meal of the day was the chief opportunity in daily life for demonstrating the position which a nobleman was able and entitled to keep. The preparations for dinner in Chamber and Great Hall usually began shortly after ten in the morning, although the cooking of the dishes had in general been going on since dawn or even earlier. The trestle tables were set up by the grooms of the chamber. The high table for the earl was placed on a carpet, at the foot of the great canopied state bed, which at this time was still part of the furnishing of the Great Chamber although it was usually completely out of use.

Two yeomen laid the cloth on the table, first genuflecting and kissing their hands towards the earl's seat. The yeoman of the cellar and his helpers prepared the cupboard, which was literally "a board for cups", although later it became an elaborately carved oak cupboard. It was loaded with gold and silver plate, some for use and some for show. Wine, brought in by the yeoman of the cellar, and beer, brought by the yeoman of the buttery, were poured into gold or silver ewers. The great salt was brought by the yeoman usher and set a little to the left of the earl's place, where his knife and spoon were laid under a special fold in the table cloth known as the "state". The origin of this was presumably to protect the cutlery from dust or from being smeared with poison.

The earl's gentlemen, the sewer, the carver and the cupbearer came in at this point in the preparations. They had their hands washed and were provided with towels and napkins by the yeomen of the ewery. The carver cut all the loaves on the earl's table and tasted them – again a precaution against poison which remained as part of the ceremonies. When the bread had been tried, the tablecloth was unfolded from over the earl's spoon and knife and the first course could be served. A procession went down through the hall and past the screen to the great serving dresser in front of the kitchen, where more sayes were taken, and returned, to be met by the marshall with his staff of office. Everyone in the hall stood up and removed his hat as the procession went through to the Great Chamber, where the dishes were arranged by the sewer and the carver took further sayes from the roasts. At this point the earl was told that he was served. When he and those who were to dine with him reached the Great Chamber they washed their hands in bowls of water, the earl's silver bowl being held by a gentleman on his bended knee. The earl was helped into his great chair and the other guests were placed at his table, the highest ranking above the salt on the earl's right (these places being known as "the reward"), the rest below the salt, their places being referred to as "the board's end". A Latin grace was said and the earl, all honour duly paid to him, could begin his lukewarm dinner.

Recipes for the preparation of two traditional foods which have always been important in England have been omitted because today very few people have time or space to prepare their own hams and cheeses. Hams bought cooked or cured and ready to cook are much the same all over the country, but certain specialist shops still offer York, Suffolk, Bradenham (the name of the district which once produced the finest Wiltshire hams) and standard Wiltshire hams. Wiltshire gammon and bacon can still often be bought in the West Country. Gloucestershire and Buckingham hams, now unobtainable, were highly regarded in the nineteenth century because the pigs in these areas had been fed on beech mast, which gave the hams a nutty flavour.

There are various methods of curing hams. In some areas they are thickly covered with dry salt, usually with saltpetre and bay salt added, and are rubbed and turned daily. In other areas a pickle is used. Some, such as Suffolk hams, are sweet-cured, using sugar, honey or treacle with the salt and saltpetre. Juniper berries, bay leaves and spices are often added. When the hams are withdrawn from the salt or pickle they are washed, dried and, in most cases, smoked, preferably over oak sawdust. In the past, on small farms they were simply hung in the chimney, on iron hooks that can often be seen today, and smoked over the fire. The variation in temperature, which did not occur in a proper smokehouse, only slightly affected the flavour of the ham and did not affect its keeping qualities. In Norfolk, hams were sometimes smoked over fires of dried seaweed, which gave them a slightly acid flavour and a very firm texture. In some localities the hams were not smoked, but simply hung up in a muslin bag in a dry place. These were known as green hams. Green bacon, obtainable in shops today, is cured in the same way.

Cheese has been made in Britain from Roman times and possibly earlier. Cheshire cheese, still made and sold today, was mentioned in the Domesday Book. It is an excellent, slightly crumbly cheese, whether in its red or white form. A blue Cheshire used also to be made but is now almost unobtainable. Cheddar has always been the most popular of English cheeses and was the first cheese to be made to a standard recipe, so that the quality did not vary. Derby and Sage Derby are both very good, as are Lancashire (considered the best of all cheeses for toasting) and Leicester. Single and Double Gloucester are both very fine cheeses and not difficult to obtain. Stilton, perhaps the second most popular English cheese, was first made in Wymondham in Leicestershire in the eighteenth century.

The recipe for Wensleydale cheese was originally introduced by the Cistercians when they built Jervaulx Abbey at Wensleydale in North Yorkshire. The cheese was made at the Abbey farms until the dissolution of the monasteries in the sixteenth century and afterwards by local farmers.

Essex and Suffolk cheeses were considered hard and strong-tasting and at all periods held in ill-repute except for their cheapness.

Dorset Blue, or Blue Vinny, can hardly ever be found today. A very little is thought to be made near Dorchester, but the recipe has always been kept secret. The Slipcote cheeses, made at Wissenden, are today unobtainable, although the rather variable methods used to make them are described in more than one early book. They were small, soft and delicious cheeses, weighing about half a pound. They were placed between cabbage leaves and ripened for only about a week. When ripe, the skins loosened and could be slipped off. They did not travel well, but certain nineteenth-century gourmets considered them the best small cheeses to be found anywhere, the equal of Brie or Camembert.

A high proportion of the feasts and dishes described in this book are from the period of English history which began in the fourteenth and ended in the eighteenth century. During this time English culinary traditions were formed and different regions developed their own dishes. This was mainly because life in England until the end of this period was on the whole rural and therefore regional. Travel was slow and difficult and journeys were not lightly undertaken except by the natural traveller, such as Celia Fiennes, who spent most of her life riding over England for the pleasure of observing the countryside and its people. What the traveller had to expect is exemplified by the following extract from the diary of a certain Mr Young, who was travelling in the north of England in the last decade of the eighteenth century:

Rotherham (Crown). Very disagreeable and dirty. Hashed venison, potted mackerel, cold ham, cheese and melon. 1s.

Leeds (King's Arms). Cook dirty. Veal cutlets, tart and cheese. 8d. No beer.

Driffield (Nag's Head). Civil and cheap. Mutton steaks, ducks, tarts, cheese, mushrooms, capers, walnuts, gherkins, and other pickles. 2s.

Scarborough (New Inn). Cheap but dirty. Cold ham. Supper: chicken, lobster, anchovie, cheese. 1s 4d. (Coffee and tea, 6d).

Castle Howard (outside Carlisle). Excellent house, but dear – and a saucy landlady.

Stokesay-in-Cleveland. Civil but shabby.

Richmond. [Yorkshire] Brace of partridge, leesh of trout, cheese. 1s.

Greta Bridge. Middling.

Bowland. Civil but not cheap.

Newcastle. Extravagantly dear! Boiled fowl and oysters and one woodcock. 2s 6d.

Next day: roast fowl and one small haddock with 10 smelts on it. 2s 6d.

Glenwale. Boiled fowl, catchup sauce, roast potatoes. 8d.

Carlisle. Good. Broiled chicken with mushrooms, plover, plate of sturgeon, tart, mince pies and jellies. 1s 6d.

Penrith. Roast beef, apple pudding, potatoes, celery and potted trout. 1s.

Kendal. Civil and cheap. Brace of woodcock, veal cutlets. 1s.

Next day: boiled fowl and sauce, roast partridge, potted char, cold ham, tarts. Foreign sweetmeats. 8d., tea and coffee, 6d.

Both the quality of the dishes and the prices that were charged seem extraordinarily variable. It must be assumed that some of the inns were large post houses receiving several of the coaches which travelled north and south each day and that others were small and off the main roads.

With the coming of the steam train and the urbanization which began with the Industrial Revolution the natural divisions of the countryside began to change. Families who moved to an industrial town in search of better wages and improved circumstances continued to cook their local dishes. Many, however, were disappointed: work was hard to find and often poorly paid, and as a result many women went to work, or took in work at home, however little the money. Time as well as money, therefore, was short: food had to be bought cheaply and cooked quickly; sometimes it was as cheap to buy it cooked as to cook it. The feasts of the farm year no longer had meaning; only Christmas and Easter, the principal feasts of the Church, were celebrated and the country wife whose husband had moved to an urban job had to buy everything she cooked. In the early part of the nineteenth century there were many young women to whom this was an entirely unexpected change. Brought up in farm cottages, they had kept poultry, often including a goose for Christmas, and had grown vegetables and participated in the good food provided by the farmer and his wife when sowing was finished, at harvest and at Christmas. In the cities no one gave feasts for the workers to celebrate a factory order finished and the family earnings did not stretch far in the markets.

Thus, while the food of the countryside remained regional, the food of the cities, no matter where they were situated, was differentiated by income levels. *"Oysters and poverty"*, said Dickens through the mouth of Sam Weller, *"always seem to go together."* Certainly they were generally offered in the poorer streets, as were whelks and winkles, shrimps, hot pies and hot potatoes. Only hot chestnuts, sold at street corners, and muffins and crumpets carried on trays, the muffin man ringing a bell, were offered in rich and poor streets alike. Certain traditional foods developed in connection with different industries and recipes for some of these are given.

During the Regency and the Victorian era, the upper classes expected any great dinner to include several traditional English dishes, whether the head cook was English or French. These were not, however, likely to be regional, no matter where the dinner was being served. They were generally dishes served throughout the country, such as roasts, with their special sauces and accompaniments, great pies, poached or baked fish with shellfish, pheasants (their tail feathers stuck back in place) served with crumbs, bread sauce and red-currant jelly, or jugged hares with port added to the gravy.

The fashion of sending young gentlemen on the Grand Tour of Europe to put a final polish on their education gave them a taste for all things European, including food, and when they took over their estates, they imported French and sometimes Italian and Spanish chefs, but demanded that a proportion of English dishes be served. Carême in the late eighteenth century, Ude during the Regency and, later, Escoffier and Francatelli were all celebrities in London. The greatest of them all, Alexis Soyer, settled permanently in Victorian London. He appreciated the high quality of English meat, fish and vegetables, and realized that many of the regional dishes suited these excellent materials. As chef to the fashionable Reform Club, he had ample opportunity to serve English food in the grand manner to the greatest gourmets in the land.

Although the "subtlety" which had formed the centrepiece of every feast from medieval to Stuart times was long gone, "complimentary" dishes were considered proper on great occasions and were preferred if they were witty. Soyer was a master indeed at producing such inventions. Turkey à la Nelson was made in the shape of the *Victory*, the turkey trussed to form the hull of the ship with the poop made in pastry, and, attached to the breast, braised fillets of chicken, arranged like the sides of a ship, the whole sailing on waved mashed potato, with small ducks, made from chicken legs, placed around the ship and a sail made from thin slices of glazed tongue.

While Soyer and other great cooks were producing superb food for the upper classes all over the country, middle-class cooking reached its lowest point and earned the bad reputation which, for the most part, it deserved. This sad decline in standards was partly brought about by the success of the merchant classes, who built themselves fine houses and accumulated furniture and silver. Living in some luxury, therefore, their wives became too grand to cook in their own kitchens, but were not knowledgeable enough to instruct their cooks, nor quite rich enough to engage cooks of real talent and experience. Indeed, at this period, there were not enough trained cooks available.

Lazy, ill-directed cooks or overworked general servants produced the blanketing white sauce, the overcooked and half-drained cabbage and the greyish, boiled potatoes which visiting foreigners ridiculed. This situation continued until after World War II, when it became almost impossible to obtain anyone who would or could cook, or, indeed, any other household staff. The middle-class lady returned to her kitchen and in many instances found cooking the most rewarding of all household jobs. Traditional recipes, particularly those peculiar to the area in which she lived, were sought out and cooked with passionate care.

Some recipes have, of course, moved out of their original areas because in the past a bride generally moved to the home of her husband, and naturally often brought special recipes with her. Again, families move from one part of the country to another, often two or three times in the parents' lifetime. My own mother's family was Cornish and I have myself produced many traditional Cornish dishes in Essex and, nowadays, in Gloucestershire, and each of my three daughters, all good cooks, and my granddaughters, budding cooks, make one or another of those same dishes in other parts of the country. I hope this book may help people to find out where their recipes really come from and that all English readers of this book will make some of the dishes of their region, or of the region from which they come, if they do not already do so, and that they will serve them to their guests from abroad.

We have great advantages over those cooks of earlier centuries who made the traditional dishes of the localities in which they lived. We have running hot and cold water, clean, controlled heat in our ovens and electric beaters, mixers and blenders which whip up our egg whites, our cream, our batters or our cake mixtures in half a minute.

It is impossible to know for certain whether our fresh foods have more or less flavour than those of prepackaging days: we fear that they have less, but we cannot be certain. We can only buy the best available quality that we can afford.

We are lucky in that freezing means that many birds, fish and vegetables are available to us all the year round.

We are lucky in that we can prepare and keep dishes in the refrigerator for a day or two before serving and for a month or two if we put them in the deep-freeze.

We are only unlucky in that most of us, caught in our rat race, have less time to devote to careful shopping and cooking and must usually clear up for ourselves. Even then, many of us have dishwashers which will clean all but the largest pans.

All the recipes given in this book have been chosen to fit in with our contemporary way of life. Some are very quick and easy to make and require few ingredients; others are more elaborate, and may take two or three hours, not necessarily consecutively, to prepare. In fact, they are intended to be made in leisure time, assuming that the preparation is a pleasure as well as the eating. Some recipes are frankly extravagant and some are economical. If ingredients are unobtainable, substitutes are given but the originals are mentioned.

In this book all metric equivalents are approximate (weights and volume measures have been rounded up or down, for convenience). Tablespoons and teaspoons are standard measures; amounts given are for level spoonfuls where not otherwise stated. Oven temperature conversions are those recommended by the Association of Manufacturers of Domestic Electrical Appliances and the Metrication Board.

Let us now proceed on a culinary journey around England.

The Provinces of England

The map on the opposite page shows England divided into areas of culinary interest and not into any official geographic divisions. The photographs that follow illustrate a selection of dishes and ingredients that are traditionally associated with those areas.

East Anglia and the Eastern Counties

In an area where wide, rich farmlands give way to low-lying fens and marshes and a sweeping coastline, the traditional dishes are inevitably full of variety. Further contrast is provided by the vast difference in the amount of money that used to be available for food in the poor farmworker's cottage and at the wealthy colleges in Cambridge. Rich and poor alike, however, produced all sorts of delectable dishes. In the background, left to right, *Vinegar Cake, Asparagus Baskets, Huntingdon Stuffed Pears.* In the foreground, left to right, *Crème Brûlée, Baked Flounder, Mousse of Salmon, Shrimps in Cream with Lettuce.*

The North

The new middle classes who emerged at the time of the Industrial Revolution were largely responsible for lost culinary traditions in many parts of England. But the northerner, despite his new-found prosperity, was very sure of his priorities: however large his house, however many servants in his pay, he still wanted the good simple food he was used to eating. Typical dishes that might have been offered to him for his dinner or high tea were: back, left to right, *Yorkshire Teacakes, Lancashire Hot Pot, Green Pork with Green Dumplings, Lancashire Cheese Scones.* Front, *Leek Pie, and Shepherd's Pie.*

The Midlands

Satisfying, hearty dishes have always been popular in the wide belt of central England known as the Midlands. They were served with plenty of cider or ale at the sheep-shearing festivals in the Cotswolds; they lifted the spirits of the tired workers who returned home from a hard day's grind in the factories; and they were devoured with gusto by the hunting folk who worked up a ravenous appetite galloping after the hounds. In the background, *Bedfordshire Clangers.* At the back of the table, *Shropshire Pie, Whipped Syllabub.* Front, left to right, *Bakewell Tart, Braised Pheasant, Banbury Cakes, Ham Stuffed with Apricots, Melton Mowbray Pie.*

23

The West Country

The Celts who refused to submit to Roman and Saxon invaders were slowly pushed back to the south-west tip of England and finally settled in Cornwall (the rest fled to Wales). Their traditional dishes, added to over the years, were rarely found further afield than other parts of the West Country and even today clotted cream, thickly spread on home-made scones, and the yellow-tinted saffron cakes are the delight of holidaymakers from all over the world. The recipes from the other counties in the region typify the sort of dishes eaten in the lush farmlands of England. Left to right, *Devonshire Splits, Wiltshire Lardy Cake, Cornish Pasties, Forced Cabbage, Ham Mousse, Damask Cream.* In the foreground, *Brawn, and Clotted Cream.*

The South and South East

A wide variety of influences can be seen in the dishes of this region. Kent, famous for its fruit and hops, was invaded in early times by Romans, Jutes and Saxons who settled there, bringing with them their culinary traditions. In Sussex, centuries later, the Prince Regent's inventive chefs at the Royal Pavilion, Brighton, introduced all sorts of elaborate dishes to the south coast; while in the seaports, sailors' wives and cooks at the inns strove to re-create the dishes that were eaten on board ship, or tasted on foreign shores and demanded by the men when they came home on leave. Dishes that would have been cooked in this part of England include, on the seat, left to right, *Stuffed Herrings, Wild Duck with Orange, Goose Braised with Plums, Cherries Hot.* In the foreground, *Creamed Codlin Tarts, Manchet Bread, Sussex Pond Pudding.*

The Home Counties

The nobleman of the past who
had an estate in any of the
counties surrounding London
could appear regularly at court
but also, because it was not too
arduous a journey, return home
often to see his family and
entertain his friends. The
monarchs also saw the
advantage of a house that was
deep in the countryside yet
close to the capital and all
through the centuries built
palaces in the area. A tradition
of grand food served in the
great houses is reflected in the
Home Counties dishes that
have been passed down to us.
Back row, left to right,
*Spinach Tart, Christmas
Spiced Beef.* Centre, *Green
Peas in Cream.* Front, *Chicken
as Lizards, Country Toffee
Pudding, Young Chickens
with Peaches.*

London

Throughout the centuries no town or city in England has been able to offer the discerning gourmet a more tempting selection of dishes than he could find in London. Ships brought exotic ingredients from all corners of the Empire and home-grown produce from all over the country was brought for sale at the markets. Highly skilled chefs, employed by the rich, transformed these ingredients into fantastic dishes as good to eat as they were to look at. The less wealthy ate at the taverns and chop-houses where the dishes were less sensational but much acclaimed. Back row, *Macaroni Cheese, Cabinet Pudding.* Centre, *The Cavalier's Broil, Water Souchet.* Front, *Stewed Carp with Forcemeat Balls, Greenwich Whitebait.*

All Over England

Pastries and suet crusts, stocks, sauces and gravies have been made in much the same manner all over England from the Middle Ages to the present day, just as meat, game and poultry were roasted in the same manner wherever they were being prepared.

The making of stocks and the preparation of gravies today is much less extravagant and much less complicated than it was from the fifteenth to the eighteenth centuries when prime cuts of meat were boiled to rags for the resulting broth: others were half-cooked and their juice pressed out or, in some cases, pressed raw. The solids, deprived of juice and flavour, went to scullions and dogs.

There is no doubt that the first sauces ever eaten in England were made by Roman cooks and served to their masters and the British princes who had accepted their domination. Once the idea of a sauce had been accepted and experienced as a complement to roast or boiled meats, bringing out their flavour, cleansing or tantalizing the palate before the next mouthful, the British never looked back from this culinary discovery.

The nineteenth-century middle-class habit of smothering vegetables, boiled chicken and veal with a tasteless blanket of glutinous white sauce has given English cooking the reputation of having no good sauces, but this is quite untrue. Only in middle-class kitchens, where the cook was overworked and undertaught and the mistress uninterested, was there ever a lack of good, varied, well-flavoured sauces and gravies. The cooks of the great houses and in the farms and cottages have always made chutneys and ketchups, red-currant jelly, gooseberry sauce for mackerel, mustard sauce for herring and well-flavoured gravies whenever there was meat or bird.

Pastry, too, was first introduced into England by the Romans. They used a paste of flour and oil to wrap large birds or joints of meat in order to seal in the juices. They also served small birds, sweetbreads and kidneys in very thin, rich pastry coverings, one for each person. They do not seem to have developed the large pie which was so important in English medieval cookery.

Today, many people feel that pastry making is difficult and are resigned to the fact that their pastry does not always turn out well. They buy frozen short or puff pastry, both of which are excellent, and forget that there are other types, which can transform a pie, whether sweet or savoury, from an everyday dish into a luxurious one, taking very little extra time or effort.

East Anglia

and the Eastern Counties: Norfolk, Suffolk, Cambridgeshire, Essex, Lincolnshire

East Anglia and the eastern counties stretch from Greater London, whose suburbs cover the south and east of Essex, to The Wash on the north-west coast of Norfolk. The area also includes Suffolk, Cambridgeshire and the fen district of Lincolnshire. There are special points of interest about the regional cooking of each of these counties, but this part of England as a whole has a character and tradition of its own, quite unlike that of the west or even of the south-east, although Kent is only separated from Essex by the Thames Estuary.

It is, in general, a low-lying region with vast tracts of marsh and fen. In earlier centuries great forests covered hundreds of thousands of acres and, indeed, small areas of magnificent forest trees remain, the largest being Epping Forest, now carefully preserved. Epping Forest originally formed part of Waltham Forest, which once covered most of Essex and of which more than 5,000 acres were bought by the Corporation of the City of London and opened to the public in 1882.

After the Norman Conquest and until the nineteenth century the forests were royal preserves with their own courts of justice and special laws and officers to enforce them. The officers were much hated by farmers and villagers who, in Saxon times, had been allowed free hunting. The woodland supported vast herds of red deer, roe deer and fallow deer, all the property of the king. Poaching was fearfully punished, but free venison was irresistible and many a deer found its way into village kitchens. Certain precautions generally had to be taken: the deer had to be skinned and cut up in a secluded glade some distance from the hunter's isolated cottage or the small village where he lived. The hide and horns had to be roughly cleaned and hidden until the venison had been distributed and eaten. After that, who could prove that a deer had been killed by the man who was making horn spoons and knife handles from antlers on a winter's evening? And who could tell how a woman working on a deerskin jerkin had obtained the hide? Sometimes the forest lawmen would drag the villagers to the courts despite lack of proof, but sometimes they were lenient.

The venison had to be shared out so that no jealous neighbour would tattle and, if the lawmen were known to be about, the meat was cut into small pieces and stewed with pot-herbs and wild garlic to disguise the smell. The sheriff's men were entitled to enter a cottage to examine what was cooking. Every man claimed to be having hare or rabbit or one of his own geese for supper, and it was maintained that Essex women could make a hare not only taste like venison but smell like it, too. Small chunks of venison and deer's liver stuck on sticks and toasted in front of the fire were generally claimed to be hare, which they resembled in colour.

The forest also supported wild boar until the seventeenth century, when they became extinct, and herds of half-wild pigs feeding on the thick layers of beech mast and acorns, which were thought to give the pork a sweet, nutty taste. In general, every poor man was free to drive his pigs into the forest to feed, but from time to time payment for grazing rights was demanded and, as in the case of deer hunting, was bitterly resented.

Over the centuries royalty, on progress to or from London through the eastern counties, travelled slowly across the green fields outside the city, which gave place to deep forest and rolling farmlands. The monarch's routes were arranged to provide stops at the great houses of nobles who deserved and could afford the honour of a royal visit. In 1561 Queen Elizabeth I stayed at Wanstead, Loughton Hall and Pyrgo before reaching Ingatestone Hall in Essex, the home of her Secretary of State, Sir William Petre. Petre had bought the manor of Gynge Abbess in 1539 from the nuns of the famous nunnery of Our Lady and St Etheldreda of Barking, and had built a new house, *"very fair, large and stately, made of brick and embattled"*, on the site of the ancient convent building known as Abbess Hall. Fortunately, not only a large part of Sir William's great house but also his household accounts have been preserved and we can see the detailed expenditure on food alone for the Queen's visit. She was to spend two nights at Ingatestone Hall in July and early in the month Sir William rode down from London. With him went Mr Wilcocks the cook, the same cook who had prepared a great wedding feast at the hall almost ten years earlier for Catherine Tyrell, Petre's stepdaughter. With Mr Wilcocks went spices, colourings, *"turnsole"*, which gave a violet colour to jellies, and *"grains"*, which produced a bright red-gold leaf for decorating jellies and the *"subtleties"* which were modelled in marchpane bread (marzipan) and formed the centrepiece for the high table.

Other luxury foods for the occasion, sent from London to Mr Wilcocks's order, included a barrel of samphire, a small barrel of olives, a small barrel of capers, 200 oranges and 12 pounds of prunes.

Meanwhile, during these two weeks, servants were sent to the fens for wildfowl, and tenants and friends sent a stag, caponets (young capons), two pigs, old apples, two lambs, fish and dozens of oysters. Quails and egrets and many pigeons were brought to the kitchens. Four heron-shrewes (young herons), considered especially good eating, were brought from Kent on the Gravesend ferry. A salmon, a turkey cock and a dozen peachicks (young peafowl) were also sent to the house. Saffron came direct from Saffron Walden near Cambridge, where the fields were blue with the crocus whose stamens yielded the spice, highly prized both for its delicate flavour and for the golden colour it imparted to foods into which it was mixed.

Much of the food, however, came from the Ingatestone estate, which naturally had its own bakery (turning out some 20,000 loaves a year of three different qualities), orchards, vegetable and herb gardens and fish ponds. There was also a great dovecote from which large numbers of squabs and pigeons were taken (more than 1,000 between Easter and

Michaelmas), a poultry yard with special cages for keeping live partridges and quails after they had been snared, a rabbit warren and a fine range of dairy outbuildings.

Queen Elizabeth arrived at about noon on Saturday, 19 July. Saturdays were fish days when only one main meal could be served, with no meat, game or poultry. For a royal visit on a "fysshe day" only a sturgeon, a fish reserved for royalty in England, was adequate and Sir William Petre sent for one from London. We do not know how it was dressed, but it was probably salted, since salting improves sturgeon, which is very firm and close-textured. If the sturgeon was fresh it was generally cut up and marinated in vinegar and herbs, the pieces sometimes being put together again, after boiling, in the original form of the whole fish and much decorated with shrimps and whelks, olives and orange and lemon peel.

The sturgeon, the porpoise and the whale were the "fysshe of Kings", and appeared at most royal feasts until the end of the sixteenth century. Samphire, highly considered by the Romans, may well have been served with the sturgeon on this occasion, probably pickled in vinegar. It would have been growing on the coast not far from Ingatestone, but in this case samphire pickled in London was preferred. Today samphire can rarely be bought, although it can still be found and picked in certain seaside areas. It is a succulent plant, growing in the sands and dunes of estuaries and salt marshes. The name comes from the French *herbe de St Pierre* and when cooked the consistency is not unlike that of wild asparagus. When Shakespeare referred to *"one that gathers samphire, dreadful trade"*, he was writing about a different plant called rock samphire, which grows on cliffs, but his remarks were equally relevant since the gatherer of the marsh variety was in danger of being caught by the swiftly incoming tide.

In total, the entertainment of his Queen and her retinue for two or three days cost Sir William Petre about £136 for food and drink. This sounds reasonable to us, but in fact was the equivalent of more than five thousand pounds today. Mr Wilcocks, the cook, was given 20 shillings over and above his normal wages for working for seven days in the Ingatestone kitchens. Five assistant cooks were employed for several days and *"3 scalders, 8s. 2 turnbroaches* [spit roasters] *2s. and a woman washing the vessels, 8d."*

Inland Essex, near the borders of Suffolk and Cambridgeshire, is still as rural as any part of England. Open, arable countryside, wide and rolling, it has many farms and manor houses, where in the fourteenth and fifteenth centuries the serving men and wenches would have supped on the infamous Essex cheese, known for its vast size, its hardness and its strong, burning flavour.

John Skelton, a fifteenth-century poet and satirist, wrote:

> *A cantle of Essex cheese*
> *Was well a foot thick*
> *Full of maggots quick:*
> *It was huge and great*
> *And mighty Strong meat*
> *For the devil to eat*
> *It was tart and punicate.*

Essex cheeses were usually made from whole or skimmed ewe's milk, and if you were a serving man you ate your hard, *"tart and punicate"* cheese or you had nothing but your coarse, dark bread. Suffolk cheeses were much the same and in 1661 Pepys's wife was *"vexed at her people for grumbling to eat Suffolk cheese"*.

Going east, to the coast, we come to a region of wild marsh and moorland, little changed for centuries. Here, the sea erodes the low cliffs and at Dunwich seven churches are now under water; their bells are said to peal when storms strike the coast. Certainly, medieval coins and sea-worn timbers with the remains of carving are occasionally washed up on the beach. From Dunwich and the nearby little towns of Warberswick and Southwold come splendid shrimps and flounder and traditional ways of cooking them.

A little farther south, on the estuary of the Colne, Colchester – the Roman city of Camulodunum – has always been famous for its superb oysters. It is recorded that Dame Alice de Bryene of Acton Hall in Suffolk sent a groom of the kitchen with two horses on every Lenten Sunday of the year 1413 to Colchester to buy half a bushel of oysters, an eighth of a bushel of mussels and 300 whelks. The whelks cost nine pence and the groom was paid 13 pence. Whelks ranked high among shellfish; four thousand were cooked as a garnish for salted sturgeon and offered to the most distinguished guests at a feast for the enthronement of the Archbishop of Canterbury in 1504.

A further interesting point arises in connection with this Suffolk lady. It was permissible to serve eggs on fast days but not during Lent and no eggs were bought by Dame Alice from Ash Wednesday until Easter Sunday, although she frequently ordered eggs at other seasons. On Easter Sunday, however, she ordered some 200 and these (probably boiled and served with a green sauce) were served as a traditional dish for the Easter feast at which guests were present. Thus the origin of the Easter egg goes back at least to medieval times in England.

Farther north, the ancient town of Thetford stands in the remains of Thetford Forest, once a great royal hunting domain. Nearby, below the ruins of a Cluniac priory, archaeologists excavating the original Anglo-Danish settlement came on the remains of a peacock which had been cooked and eaten. This was of great interest because the Romans had introduced peafowl into Britain, and after they left, in the fifth century, the birds died out but are recorded as being reintroduced in Saxon times. This peacock is the earliest ever found in England and, from other remains found with it, must have adorned a Saxon feast, along with many more commonplace birds and beasts.

Norfolk, lying directly north of Suffolk and east of Cambridgeshire, has a great arc of sea coast from just south of Yarmouth to The Wash. It is east of any direct route from northern to southern England, and much of the countryside has remained largely undisturbed through the ages. There are great areas of sand dunes, marsh and the vast salt-water Broads, but, inland, it is fertile enough. Norwich, the county seat, is a city rich in tradition; indeed, until the eighteenth century the Sheriff of Norwich held 30 acres of land in fee for 24 herring pasties made from the first fish of the season and tendered to the king in London. This fee was taken seriously, the pasties duly being made, delivered and eaten at the appropriate state banquet. In 1629 the

Secretary of State complained to the sheriff about *"the poor quality of the fish and that the pies were short weight"*. Each pie should have contained five herrings with spices. Indeed, fish pies were often very elaborate, and it is likely that the Norwich pies were expected to contain more than the herrings and the spice, and that the absence of expensive ingredients was resented. A very grand fish pie consisted of a fine pastry coffin filled with boiled salmon, cod and haddock and *"brayed with spices"*. Dried figs, raisins, apples and pears were chopped, cooked in wine and sugar and added, and the top was "planted" with stoned prunes and quartered dates.

From near Norwich, we have the splendid diary of James Woodforde, who was the parson of Weston Longeville from 1776 until 1803. Squire Custance and his wife, who lived at Weston House, were his close friends who, with his niece Nancy, formed a group which dined at each other's houses in rotation. They called these occasions "Rotation Day Dinners".

This is the menu for the "Rotation Day Dinner" served on 1 January, 1782, which was recorded by Parson Woodforde in his diary:

> *Boiled Leg of Mutton w capers, Boiled Calf's head, Boiled Pig's Face, Roast Turkey, Currant Pudding, Mince Pies.*

King's Lynn, on the other side of the county, was once a wealthy port where sumptuous feasts were held by prosperous merchants. To the north of King's Lynn lies Sandringham House, which was acquired by Edward VII in 1861 (when he was Prince of Wales) and has remained in the possession of the royal family. This local prosperity has helped to preserve long-standing country and coastal ways of life, and many traditional Norfolk dishes, which have their direct origin in the Middle Ages, are still made today, having been preserved in the records and recipe books of the great houses. Norfolk dumplings, soups, various ways of cooking game and poultry, and several excellent fish and shellfish dishes are among the recipes given on the following pages.

The wide farmlands of Suffolk, which have always grown good wheat, oats and barley, encouraged gracious living and excellent cooking. The splendid house of Heveningham Hall, built with restrained elegance in 1788 for Sir Robert Taylour by the fashionable architect James Wyatt, exemplifies the prosperity of the great Suffolk landowner. This house is open to visitors and the extent of the kitchens can be seen. In the long, narrow yard which opens from the stableyard is the game larder, a tall cage on a brick base where large quantities of game could be hung on hooks in the open air but out of reach of cats and dogs. Very few examples of this type of game larder are known; it was more usual to hang game in a cool cellar or outbuilding. Today we eat our game comparatively fresh, but the Georgian and the Victorian gentleman insisted on his game being "high", particularly in the case of partridges and grouse.

Heveningham's superb park and gardens were laid out by Capability Brown, the eighteenth-century garden designer, and a fine orangery was designed by Wyatt. The entertaining was generally formal and extremely elegant, as such a setting required, but dishes traditional in Suffolk were included in the elaborate menus.

The fen country lies north and south of The Wash, in Lincolnshire,

Cambridgeshire and Norfolk. It is about 70 miles in length and at some points 35 miles wide. All this flat, low-lying area is a great silted-up bay of the North Sea. The Wash is the only unsilted part remaining.

A first attempt to drain the land was made by the Romans, who also built causeways so that travellers could cross without taking to boats. Much of the fen country was heavily forested and provided excellent royal hunting for the Normans and early Plantagenets, but neglect of canals and causeways from the fifth century on meant that the land became waterlogged, and further inundations of the sea killed the trees and produced a wilderness of reeds and watery swamp over which hung heavy mist at morning and evening. Here and there were islands of firmer and higher ground, and on many of these monasteries were built and townships grew up around them. A religious settlement was founded on the Isle of Ely in the seventh century, but was destroyed by the Danes. The present great Norman cathedral, brightly lit on winter nights, seems to float high above the misty countryside. In spite of the busy modern town around it today, it is not difficult to imagine earlier times when that great ship of light told the traveller crossing the misty fens that he was on the right road, and would soon reach the warmth and comfort of the monks' hospitality or, in later centuries, of an inn.

It is not difficult, either, to visualize the monks patiently working on the fertile slopes of their hill above the Great Ouse and on the fields they had drained below on the fen. All fenland is very fertile when reclaimed because it is full of humus from earlier forests, and the monks were able to fatten stock quickly and to grow excellent crops of wheat, oats and barley. On the sunny slopes below the cathedral, where the soil was less rich, they planted vineyards which became famous all over England. Indeed, the Normans called Ely the *Isle des Vignes*, although the Venerable Bede in the seventh century, attributed the name to the vast quantities of eels found in the nearby Great Ouse and the streams and canals round about.

The true breed of fenmen were almost a separate race. In Saxon times they were called Gyrvii and went about the marshes and shallow lakes of their countryside on stilts, except in hard winters when they changed the stilts for skates or bones and could traverse their icy domain with great ease at high speed. In the eighteenth century they were known in surrounding areas as "slodgers" because of their wet and muddy way of life. From earliest times they had built huts of reeds daubed with mud, on small islands of firm, rising ground in the marshy water; even when more substantial houses were built, barns and sheds were still made of reeds and mud. Villages were few: each family lived on their own island. The fenmen made coracles of bundled reeds as well as boats and punts of wood, and fished both for food and for market. They took vast quantities of eels and, in the spring, the elvers (baby eels) which swarmed everywhere, tiny and black, could be cooked to a kind of jelly thought to be extremely nourishing and wholesome. The rivers teemed with pike and perch, tench and bream, dace, rud and roach. Waterbirds of every kind, wild ducks and geese, herons, cranes and moorhens, abounded and all over the fens vast flocks of domestic geese were reared and driven to London to be sold at Michaelmas as "green geese" – unfattened geese that had grazed all the year on pasture.

The traditional dishes of the fenmen were naturally concerned mainly with the cooking of birds and fish, and those of the poor stilt-walker would have been simple, half-raw and half-burnt from being held on sticks before a reluctant fire or soggy from boiling in an iron pot. The fen country, however, was a kind of wild reservoir of waterbirds and fish for the whole of East Anglia and the eastern counties and for the London market, and from monasteries and convents, too rich for their own good, mention of more elaborate dishes comes down to us. From towns and from noble houses descriptions of feasts and their preparation are recorded, particularly from Cambridge, which, as a great university city, has its own customs and traditions in culinary as in many other matters.

Each college at Cambridge in the course of a year has several feasts of varying sizes and grandeur, and at most of them, even today, certain dishes are served which have been known for generations as specialities of the college concerned. King's College, for example, founded by Henry VI, makes a superlative crème brûlée with hot-house muscat grapes, peeled and pitted, in a layer at the bottom of the dish. The recipe for this and for a trifle known as The Dean's Trifle, which comes from Trinity College, are given. I have also given a recipe for a mousse of salmon to be served with gulls' eggs (although it is very good without them) which came from Peterhouse in the high days of their great chef, Cooper, who, in the 1920s and early 1930s, considered it his duty to educate the undergraduates of Peterhouse in gastronomy as well as to please the dons and the fellows. Peterhouse, the first college to be built at the university, was founded in 1284, and has always been richly endowed. Undergraduates, ordering food for dinner parties from the kitchens to be served in their rooms, had to pay only minimal prices for the most elegant and luxurious dishes, while Mr Cooper, suavely advising, guided their tastes from schoolboy gluttony to a sophisticated appreciation of the best in English and French cooking. From Cambridge town, as opposed to gown, came recipes for special small, flat, rich cakes known as Florentines and for Chelsea buns in the manner of Cambridge.

Huntingdon, some 20 miles from Cambridge, is situated on the Roman highway of Ermine Street, later the Great North Road, at the centre of a rich agricultural district. The traditional dishes are those of the rich farmlands of England, where wheat flourished and cattle thrived and fattened easily. In his *Five Hundreth Points of Good Husbandry*, 1557, the Essex poet and farmer Thomas Tusser says:

> *Wife, sometime this weeke if that all things go cleare,*
> *An ende of wheat sowing we make for this yeare,*
> *Remember you therefore though I do it not*
> *The Seede Cake, the Paties and Furmenty pot.*

The sowers, in fact, were entitled by tradition to expect a good meal, provided by the farmer. Meat is not mentioned, and perhaps was not served, the meal being a form of the traditional "cakes and ale". The harvest supper, a more definitive celebration, always specified some form of beef, ham, poultry and, usually, pies.

The seed cake traditionally given to the sowers was made with caraway seeds in a rich Madeira type of cake mixture; it has almost disappeared today because very few people any longer like the taste of caraway seeds. Furmenty, or frumenty, a kind of rich, sweetened wheat porridge, is also almost unknown today, although it is pleasant enough. The patties made on the farms for such occasions were very often filled with a cheese mixture and there is a traditional recipe from the area of Huntingdon and Cambridge, which produces cheese patties, light and yet filling, which are of a particular excellence.

The whole area surrounding Cambridge and including Ely, St Ives and Huntingdon was the home ground of Oliver Cromwell, who attended (as did Pepys) Huntingdon Grammar School. The Cromwell family owned Hinchingbroke House, which had been built, before Oliver Cromwell's time, on the site of a Benedictine nunnery and to which half the gatehouse of the splendid nearby Ramsey Abbey was transferred after the dissolution of the monasteries. In this house Cromwell's wife, Elizabeth Bourchier, daughter of a London merchant, lived with her husband and entertained for him. In 1664, four years after the Restoration of the Monarchy, a Royalist, scornful and inimical, published a small book called *The Court and Kitchen of Elizabeth, commonly called Joan Cromwell the wife of the late Usurper, truly described and represented.* It was intended to pour scorn on her parsimony and the poor table she kept. However, the book mentions several very excellent dishes served at her table: Dutch puddings, Scotch collops of veal, marrow puddings, boiled woodcock (traditional in East Anglia) and warden pies, which were made with warden pears, flavoured with rosewater and containing "raisins of the sun", almonds, orange peel, sugar and butter. The author claims that when the Protector and his family were in London, 112 pounds of beef were cooked every morning and all scraps collected and given to the poor. This seems to have been considered a skinflint amount of meat for a man in his position, forced to entertain all who came to his house, to provide, and the collection of the scraps appeared to the uncaring Royalist writer to be even more despicable. Today, 112 pounds seems a vast quantity of beef and the charity admirable.

In the eighteenth century the county of Huntingdonshire became famous for Stilton cheese, although this cheese, considered by many an eighteenth- and nineteenth-century gourmet to be the best in the world, was in fact made originally in Leicestershire. One such gourmet, Lord Ernle, gives the following explanation: *"Mrs Paulet of Wymondham in the Melton district of Leicestershire is said to have been the first maker of Stilton cheeses* [although at this time the cheeses did not bear that name]. *She supplied them to Cooper* [profession of barrel-maker, not his Christian name] *Thornhill who kept the Bell Inn at Stilton, Huntingdonshire, on the Great North Road from London to Edinburgh and they became famous among his customers and throughout England."* The manufacture of Stilton cheeses thus became an industry of the district of Stilton in Huntingdonshire instead of Wymondham in Leicestershire. Mrs Paulet, their originator, was a very old lady in 1780. Stilton was originally the only cheese made with double cream, that is from the cream of the evening's milk skimmed next morning and added to that morning's whole milk. Today it is often factory-made with whole milk and no added cream and is therefore more chalky than a true Stilton should be.

On the whole, East Anglia, wherever the forests were cleared and the marshes drained, has always provided some of the richest farmland in England and its tradition of food suggests this, wherever we have dishes which come from its great houses, its manors and its wealthy farms. There is, of course, a black side to this picture of rural prosperity. The farmer was prosperous, his family ate well, even his servants and the farmhands who ate in his kitchen had plenty. But the cottager, who had only a strip of garden and a share in common grazing rights, and who worked for the same farmer by day, might have little to put on his table. Suffolk was a poor county in the eighteenth century. Its children, some put to work as young as four years old as bird-scarers for pennies their parents were glad to get, were almost always rather hungry, and always longing for the sweet taste of pudding or cake, which they rarely got.

A very old Suffolk farm labourer was recently quoted as saying that the children of his village, when he was a child, would go anywhere and do anything for cake, no matter how boring or daunting the occasion. Quality was not in question: cake was cake and you never got it at home.

And what cake it was that was sometimes given to children! From an anonymous manuscript recipe book of 1887 comes this list of ingredients for a "*Plain Cake for School Children*:

> *One stone flour 10s.*
> *One stone currants 11s.*
> *Quarter stone sugar 2s. 7½d.*
> *Eggs and spice only to be added*
> *Made at home, and price of baking 1s. 6d.*
>   *Total cost: £1 5s. 1½d."*

Sufficient for 90 children to have three good-sized pieces each, the total weight would have been about 34 pounds. This particular recipe is attributed to a Mrs Bozle. It was certainly a very plain cake indeed and not one we would recommend making today, unlike the tried, tested and carefully handed down recipes which follow.

Huntingdon Stuffed Pears

Serves 4

2 large, ripe pears
¼ lb (120 g) Stilton cheese
2 tablespoons (30 g) butter, fairly soft
1 tablespoon double cream
3 tablespoons (30 g) finely chopped walnuts, plus 4 half-kernels
4 crisp lettuce leaves
Freshly ground black pepper
Juice of ½ lemon

This is a very good starting dish at dinner. The Stilton cheese must be firm but not at all hard.

Use a blender, or a bowl and a wooden spoon, to cream together the cheese, butter, cream and black pepper. Mix in the chopped walnuts. Set aside but do not chill.

Peel, halve and core the pears, hollowing out the centre of each half so that it will hold about 2 teaspoons of the Stilton mixture. Place the lettuce leaves on small plates and put a half-pear on each leaf. Fill the centres with the Stilton mixture and put a half-walnut on each. Squeeze lemon juice over the uncovered parts of the pears to prevent them turning brown. Serve as soon as possible, although half an hour or so in the refrigerator will not harm the pears.

Asparagus Baskets

1½ lb (¾ kg) puff pastry
64 green asparagus spears
1½ sticks (180 g) butter and a
  little more
Lemon juice
Salt and pepper

This dish was described by a lady whose mother had worked at Heveningham in Suffolk. I made it from her description and this is the recipe. It makes an interesting first course for an early-summer dinner party, and should be followed by a plain roast, preferably lamb. Frozen puff pastry, which is very good, can be used instead of home-made.

Eight individual soufflé dishes will be needed.
  Roll out the pastry about ⅛ inch (0.25 cm) thick. Leave to rest in a cool place. Tie the asparagus into bundles of 8 spears for each mould, then cut through the stems of each bundle so that only about 3 inches (8 cm) of the stems are left. Next, give one more quick roll to the pastry and cut out circles large enough to press down over the inverted soufflé dishes. Butter the inverted dishes before pressing the pastry over them. Put into a hot oven, 450°F (230°C, Gas Mark 8), and immediately put the asparagus bundles upright in boiling salted water in a large saucepan. Cover the pan and poach gently.
  After about 15 minutes the pastry should be done and should lift off the moulds. Reverse the little baskets. If the bottoms (previously the tops) have puffed up unevenly so that they cannot stand flat, quickly trim off a layer or two with a sharp knife. Place the baskets on a baking tray and put back into the oven for 5 minutes to crisp the insides.
  Lift out the asparagus, which should be tender, drain well and keep warm. Melt 6 oz (180 g) of the butter, adding lemon juice, freshly ground black pepper and salt if required.
  Take the pastry baskets out of the oven and arrange on a large, flat dish. Cut the strings on each bundle of asparagus as you lower it, heads upwards, into its basket. Spoon melted butter over each, keeping the butter within the basket. The finished baskets can be kept hot for 5 minutes or so in a low oven without coming to harm.

Samphire

2 lb (1 kg) samphire
1 stick (120 g) butter, melted

This way of cooking samphire is traditional in King's Lynn, once a rich and busy port, now a quiet seaside market town, with a long tradition of good food well served.
  Samphire, which is in season in high summer, used to be brought into the town for sale in the market and from house to house. It is picked in the salt marshes around The Wash and must be very well rinsed to rid it of all sand.

Plunge the samphire, roots upwards, in boiling, unsalted water. Boil for 7 minutes. Drain and serve on a large flat dish with a small dish of melted butter for each person. To eat, pull sprigs from the roots with the fingers, dip in butter and strip the flesh from the thin stems with the teeth.

Vegetable Pie

1½ lb (¾ kg) mixed vegetables:
  carrots, turnips, 1 large onion,
  peas, broad beans, butter or
  haricot beans, florettes of
  cauliflower and a few
  mushrooms
½ teaspoon grated nutmeg
Salt and freshly ground black
  pepper
⅝ cup (1.5 dl) good, well-
  seasoned brown gravy or well-
  seasoned white sauce about as
  thick as single cream
A little butter

Potato crust:

1½ cups (180g) self-raising flour
½ stick (60 g) butter
⅜ cup (180 g) cold, cooked
  mashed potatoes
¾ cup (90 g) grated Cheddar
  cheese
2 tablespoons milk
Salt
Beaten egg, if liked

A very good meatless pie which was served as a substantial main dish on many Suffolk farms. This recipe was included in a notebook from Wickham Market near Bury St Edmunds.

Chop and cook the vegetables, frying the onion and mushrooms. Grease a large pie dish. Put in the vegetables, sprinkle with the nutmeg, salt and pepper and stir to mix. Pour in the gravy or white sauce.

To make the crust, add a pinch of salt to the flour and rub in the butter. Lightly mix in the mashed potatoes and then the cheese. Add the milk and work together with your hand, then knead a little to a smooth dough.

Roll the dough out on a floured board to about 1 to 1½ inches (2.5 to 3.5 cm) thick. Moisten the edge of the pie dish with a little milk or water, press the dough lid well over the whole dish and trim edges to fit neatly. Brush over with beaten egg, if liked. Bake at 350°F (180°C, Gas Mark 4) for 40 minutes.

Mousse of Salmon

1 lb (½ kg) cooked salmon,
  skinned, boned and flaked
1¼ cups (3 dl) double cream
Juice of ½ lemon
Salt and pepper
Pinch of chopped tarragon,
  fresh or dried
Pinch of nutmeg
4 egg whites, stiffly beaten
1¼ cups (3 dl) mayonnaise,
  home-made for preference

The garnish:

24 stoned green olives
12 to 16 sprigs of watercress or
  a lettuce heart cut into 8
  pieces

Served at Peterhouse, Cambridge, in the 1920s, this mousse is very good as a first course at dinner or as a cold luncheon dish. In the original recipe the mousse was surrounded by 24 mottled, dark-green gulls' eggs, three for each serving, lying close and neatly around it on pale green lettuce. But gulls' eggs are rarely obtainable and very expensive and the mousse is excellent in its own right.

Pound the fish with a wooden spoon in a large bowl. Stir in the cream, lemon juice, seasoning, tarragon and nutmeg. Fold in the egg whites a little at a time. Fill a lightly buttered mould or pudding bowl three-quarters full and cover closely with foil. Stand it in a baking tin of almost boiling water and place in a moderate oven, 350°F (180°C, Gas Mark 4), for 30 minutes.

Turn the mousse out while still just warm and then chill for at least 1 hour.

Decorate with the olives and serve surrounded by the sprigs of watercress or lettuce, and with the mayonnaise.

Baked Flounder

2 flounder or small plaice
1 tablespoon each finely
  chopped parsley, chives and
  tarragon
2 tablespoons (30 g) butter
$\frac{1}{4}$ cup white wine
$\frac{3}{8}$ cup (60 g) fresh fine white
  breadcrumbs
Pinch of nutmeg
Salt and pepper

This recipe from the Suffolk coast dates from 1750.

Mix the chopped herbs, nutmeg and seasoning together. Butter a flat fireproof dish thickly, sprinkle in the herbs and seasoning, shaking the dish so that the whole of the inside is coated. Lay the fish on this green bed. Pour the wine over and sprinkle with salt and pepper. Melt half the remaining butter and pour over the fish. Cover quite thickly with the breadcrumbs. Dot with the remaining butter and bake at 450°F (230°C, Gas Mark 8) for 10 to 15 minutes. The dish should be put near the top of the oven so that the crumbs brown. If they appear dry, when half-cooked add extra dabs of butter.

Long Cod or Golden Ling

6 cod steaks, each about 1 inch
  (2.5 cm) thick
$\frac{1}{2}$ lb (240 g) fish trimmings
$\frac{1}{4}$ teaspoon saffron
3 large onions, very finely
  chopped
$\frac{1}{2}$ stick (60 g) butter
2 tablespoons cooking oil
$1\frac{1}{3}$ cups (120 g) fine oatmeal
1 lb ($\frac{1}{2}$ kg) carrots, peeled and
  diced
1 tablespoon dried mixed herbs
  or fresh parsley, thyme, chives
  and tarragon very finely
  chopped
Salt and pepper

Salted ling was the great standby of medieval and Tudor households on days when meat was not allowed. It is a large fish, longer from head to tail than the species we call cod, but comes from the same family.

The Babees Book (a late-fifteenth-century manuscript by an unknown author) says: "Ling perhaps looks for great extolling being counted beefe of the sea; and standing every fish day at my Lord Mayor's table; yet it is nothing but long cod. When it is salted it is called Ling . . . the longer it lyeth in the brine, the better it is; waxing in the end as yellow as a gold noble."

The following is a nineteenth-century recipe which comes straight from several medieval descriptions of dishes of salted ling, but which uses fresh fish rubbed with salt. Cod replaces ling, as they are indistinguishable and the name ling is rarely, if ever, used today. The sauce should be bright gold, slightly thickened by the oatmeal and sweetened by the carrots. It is a distinguished fish dish, very good with rice or boiled potatoes.

Boil the fish trimmings and the saffron in $3\frac{3}{4}$ cups (9 dl) of salted water for 30 minutes.

Meanwhile, rub the cod steaks with salt and pepper. Sprinkle a little of the onion on each cut side and press it into the fish. Dip all sides of each cod steak in the oatmeal. Fry the fish in a mixture of 1 tablespoon of the butter and the cooking oil until golden brown.

Lift the fish steaks on to a shallow fireproof dish. Fry the remaining onions and the carrots in the rest of the butter until a light golden colour. Spoon the onions and carrots between and over the cod steaks, add the herbs and season well. Strain the golden fish stock and pour it over the fish. It should almost cover the steaks. Cover the dish closely with foil and bake in the oven at 350°F (180°C, Gas Mark 4) for 35 minutes.

Uncover the dish and bake for a further 10 minutes for the top to dry and crisp a little.

Nombles of Fish

2½ lb (1 to 1¼ kg) cod, hake or
  haddock
5 cups (1.2 litres) court
  bouillon, made with the skin
  and trimmings of the fish, 1
  onion, 1 carrot, 2 celery sticks,
  1 teaspoon dried tarragon, all
  boiled together in water for 30
  minutes
1¾ cups (240 g) white
  breadcrumbs
1¼ cups (3 dl) milk
½ teaspoon ground cloves
½ teaspoon ground ginger or 2
  tablespoons finely chopped
  fresh root ginger
Salt and pepper
1 cup white wine
2 teaspoons wine vinegar
1 round of hot toast per person
Butter

The term "nombles" comes from "umbles", which
meant the offal or insides of any animal. It came to
mean almost any kind of thickened mince or rissole
made with meat or fish. The following recipe, only
slightly adapted to suit modern tastes and available
ingredients, is from *A Noble Boke of Cookry for a
pprynce Houssolde*, a manuscript from Holkham
dating from about 1480.

Stew the fish very gently in the strained court
bouillon for 30 minutes. Lift it out, remove all the
skin and bones and flake the flesh back into half the
broth.
  Make a panada by boiling the breadcrumbs in the
milk until very thick. Stir the panada into the pan
with the fish and broth. Add the cloves, ginger, salt,
pepper, wine and vinegar. The result should be about
as thick as scrambled egg. Add more broth if the
mixture is too solid. Serve on thickly buttered hot
toast.

Shrimps in Cream with Lettuce

1 lb (½ kg) cooked and shelled
  or defrosted shrimps or
  prawns
2 large lettuce hearts,
  preferably Cos
½ stick (60 g) butter
⅝ cup (1.5 dl) double cream
1 teaspoon onion juice, made
  by peeling, quartering and
  crushing an onion
½ teaspoon salt
Pepper
4 slices bread, each slice cut in
  4 triangles, lightly browned
  in butter and kept warm

This recipe, from a small manuscript collection,
comes from Southwold on the Suffolk coast. The dish
was traditionally served at summer dinner parties, or
on other special occasions, at a large house not far
from the town.

With a very sharp knife cut the lettuce into shreds
about ¼ inch (0.5cm) wide
  Put the butter in a saucepan and melt over medium
heat. It must not colour. Put in the lettuce and turn
in the butter until it is all coated. Reduce the heat to
simmering point and add the salt and a little pepper.
Cover and simmer for 4 minutes. Add the cream and
onion juice and stir well. Add the shrimps or prawns,
stir lightly and heat for 3 minutes more. Pile on a
dish with the croûtons arranged around the edge.

A Hen on her Nest

1 boiling fowl, 5 to 6 lb (2½ to
  3 kg)
½ lb (240 g) carrots
4 medium onions
1 teaspoon ground mace
1 teaspoon ground ginger
Parsley and thyme
1¼ sticks (150 g) butter
3 lb (1½ kg) potatoes, peeled
1⅞ cups (4.5 dl) milk
½ cup (60 g) flour
⅝ cup (1.5 dl) double cream
8 eggs
Salt and pepper

This nineteenth-century Norfolk recipe was
originally a way of cooking an old hen so that she
would be tender, and also so that she would provide
a good meal for a farmer's large family.

Boil the chicken with the carrots, onions, mace,
ginger, herbs and seasoning in just enough water to
cover for 2 hours. Lift out the bird and put it in a
roasting tin; spread it with ½ stick (60 g) of the
butter, which will melt at once on the hot bird. Put
it in the oven for 10 minutes at 400°F (200°C, Gas
Mark 6) so that it browns lightly.
  While the chicken is cooking, boil the potatoes and
mash them with ⅝ cup (1.5 dl) of the milk and
2 tablespoons (30g) of the butter.

Make a roux with the remaining butter and the flour and stir in $2\frac{1}{2}$ cups (6 dl) of the stock in which the chicken was cooked and the rest of the milk. Allow to simmer for 2 to 3 minutes, then pour in the cream and season well.

Keep the sauce hot while you hard boil and shell the eggs and arrange the potato in a border on a large flat dish (this is the nest). Put the eggs in the middle and pour half the sauce over them. Sit the browned hen on her eggs and bring to table. Serve the rest of the sauce separately.

Norfolk Pottage

1 chicken, about $2\frac{1}{2}$ lb ($1\frac{1}{4}$ kg)
2 lb (1 kg) good stewing steak, cut in thin slices, all fat and gristle removed
$\frac{1}{2}$ lb (240 g) veal fillet, cut in thin slices
2 bacon slices, finely chopped
1 veal sweetbread, washed, skinned and sliced (optional)
3 lamb kidneys or $\frac{3}{4}$ lb (360 g) ox kidney, skinned, cored and sliced
2 onions, cut in rings
1 lb ($\frac{1}{2}$ kg) carrots, scraped and diced
2 blades of mace
A little thyme, dried or fresh
$1\frac{1}{2}$ lemons
$\frac{3}{4}$ lb (360 g) mushrooms, sliced
6 large artichoke hearts, cut in quarters
1 lb ($\frac{1}{2}$ kg) shelled peas
2 lb (1 kg) new potatoes, scrubbed
7 tablespoons (105 g) butter
$\frac{1}{2}$ cup (60 g) flour
Salt and pepper

A very good dinner-party dish complete with all its vegetables, this pottage comes from an anonymous cookery book which dates from the seventeenth and eighteenth centuries. The recipe, intended for a feast day, would serve about 40 people. It calls for a whole leg of beef, a large piece of veal, half a pound of bacon, four ox palates, four sweetbreads, two dozen cockscombs, several fowls, 24 pints of water and various herbs and spices.

Translated into reasonable quantities and replacing the palates and cockscombs with kidneys, it remains a most excellent, strong and subtly flavoured stew, with an inimitable, rich, thick gravy. It is often served with dumplings.

You will require 2 large, heavy saucepans. In the bottom of each put half the onion rings and half the carrots. In 1 saucepan place the whole chicken and just cover with water, adding 1 teaspoon of salt, $\frac{1}{2}$ teaspoon of pepper, 1 blade of mace, a little thyme and the juice of half a lemon. In the second pan put all the other meats in layers, cover with water and repeat the seasoning. Stew very gently, closely covered, for $1\frac{1}{2}$ hours, adding, after 1 hour, half the mushrooms to each saucepan.

Meanwhile, prepare and cook the remaining vegetables: fry the artichoke hearts in 3 tablespoons (45 g) of the butter for 3 minutes on each side. Boil the peas and potatoes separately. Drain all the vegetables and keep hot until the meat is dished up.

Remove both the saucepans from the heat. Lift out the chicken and take all the flesh from the bones, keeping the pieces as large as possible. Lift out all the meat from the other saucepan and arrange with the chicken on a very large flat dish. Keep hot while you thicken the gravy.

Combine the stocks from the two saucepans. Make a roux in another saucepan with the remaining butter and the flour. Stir in a little of the stock and bring to the boil. Gradually add more stock until you have about 5 cups (1.2 litres) of gravy the consistency of thin cream. Check the seasoning, adding the juice of half a lemon and some freshly ground black pepper. Pour the gravy over the meats on the dish and serve at once with the potatoes, peas and artichokes arranged as a border.

Michaelmas Goose

1 goose, 8 to 11 lb (4 to 5 kg)
Seasoned flour
¾ stick (90 g) butter, for
  roasting
Apple sauce
Raisins
Lemon juice

The stuffing:

1 small onion, finely chopped
⅜ cup finely chopped sage
1 cup (120 g) fresh white
  breadcrumbs
The goose liver, poached in
  salted water for 20 minutes
  and chopped finely
1 egg
Salt and pepper

The tenant farmers and cottagers on large estates generally brought a present when they came to pay their rents on quarter-days. At the September quarter, geese were at their best. A "green goose" had grazed on pasture all summer and a "stubble goose" had been fattened additionally by grazing in the harvested wheat or barley fields.

Gervase Markham, in 1676, said that a green goose should have a sauce of sorrel and sugar mixed with a few scalded bilberries and should be served on strips of toast. But a stubble goose could have various sauces of apple, onions or barberries. (Barberries are the rather hard, sharp berries of the berberis and were used frequently until the eighteenth century.)

A Michaelmas goose was much less fat than a Christmas goose and did not need pricking. A goose as sold today requires pricking no matter when it is bought.

First make the stuffing by mixing all the ingredients together.

Stuff and truss the goose. Lightly rub the bird with seasoned flour, dot with butter and place in a greased roasting tin. Put in a 400°F (200°C, Gas Mark 6) oven for 30 minutes. Remove the bird from the oven and with a skewer lightly prick along the thighs and the sides of the breast. Do not prick the flesh but only the skin.

Put the bird back in the oven and reduce the heat to 350°F (180°C, Gas Mark 4). After 30 minutes remove the bird again, baste it, then pour away three-quarters of the fat accumulated in the pan. Prick the goose again and return to the oven for 1 hour if the bird weighs 8 to 9 pounds (4 kg), or for 1½ hours if it is 9 to 11 pounds (5 kg). If the breast is becoming too brown, cover it lightly with foil.

Serve with the apple sauce into which about 20 raisins and some lemon juice have been stirred.

Roast Goose with Prune Stuffing

1 goose, 8 to 11 lb (4 to 5 kg)

Prune stuffing:

1 lb (½ kg) prunes
2 cups (30 g) parsley, finely
  chopped
1½ tablespoons (8 g) sage, finely
  chopped
1½ tablespoons (8 g) thyme,
  finely chopped
1 medium onion, finely chopped
¾ cup (120 g) fresh fine white
  breadcrumbs
1 egg yolk, well beaten
Salt and pepper

Soak the prunes in boiling water for 20 minutes. Drain and cut away all the flesh from the stones and chop it into small pieces. Mix all the ingredients together and stuff the breast of the goose. Sew the edges securely so that the stuffing cannot ooze out. Cook the goose as in the previous recipe.

Roast Goose, Venison or Young Swan

1 young goose, 8 to 10 lb (4 to 5 kg) or about 6 lb (3 kg) haunch of venison
½ stick (60 g) softened butter if using goose; 1½ sticks (180 g) softened butter if using venison
1 lb (½ kg) flour

The stuffing:

3 to 4 shallots or 2 medium onions
2 lb (1 kg) best minced steak
Salt and pepper

The sauce:

1 cup port
1 tablespoon red-currant jelly
2½ cups (6 dl) good brown stock
Salt and freshly ground black pepper
Lemon juice, if required

This is the recipe used by Francatelli, chef to Queen Victoria from about 1846 to 1853, for cooking a cygnet. High-ranking among French chefs, he worked for English royalty and nobility for years. He appreciated traditional cooking and the quality of English ingredients, and he contrived to give Queen Victoria some of the traditional dishes she preferred (such as marrow on toast for tea in winter at Balmoral) while making state banquets suitably splendid. Cygnets from Norwich were occasionally served when she was in residence at Sandringham in Norfolk.

Francatelli always ordered Norwich cygnets, which he considered the best because they were specially fed. The cygnet, still in its untidy grey feathers, was not sent to table sewn into its plumage as were full-grown swans, but it made much better eating than a mature bird. Swans and cygnets, however, were almost invariably stuffed with rump steak, which was held by many to be the best part of the dish.

On 28 January, 1780, Parson Woodforde recorded in his diary that, when dining at Ringland, near Norwich, after a christening, a swan was served. He says: *"I never eat a bit of swan before, and I think it good eating with sweet sauce. The swan was killed 3 weeks before it was eat and yet not the least bad taste of it."*

We no longer eat cygnets and only a few swans are eaten each year at city banquets, but Francatelli's recipe is given here because it is an excellent way to cook a goose or part of a boned haunch of venison.

First make the stuffing. Chop the shallots or onions very finely and mix into the minced steak with plenty of seasoning. Stuff this mixture into the breast of the goose and sew up the flap of skin neatly. If there is any spare stuffing insert it through the vent of the bird, pushing it well forward with your hand. Spread the outside of the bird with half the butter. If venison is being cooked, stuff the hollow where the bone has been removed and cut 2 horizontal slashes, one on each side, and fill with the stuffing.

Mix the flour with 1¼ cups (3 dl) of cold water to make a firm paste. Roll this out so that it is large enough for the bird or the venison to be placed in the centre and the paste folded up and over to encase it completely. Dampen any edges that must be joined so that they stick together firmly.

Place the encased bird or meat on a large piece of foil and wrap it up completely. Roast at 350°F (180°C, Gas Mark 4) for 3 hours. Take off the foil and crust and discard. Sprinkle the bird or meat with flour and then spread with the remaining butter. Put it back uncovered into a hot oven, 450°F (230°C, Gas Mark 8), to brown for about 10 minutes.

Meanwhile make the sauce. In a medium-sized saucepan, briskly boil the port for 3 minutes and then stir in the red-currant jelly. When the jelly has melted, add the brown stock and bring again to the boil. Add salt and pepper. Check the seasoning carefully and add a little lemon juice if the sauce seems too sweet.

Wild Duck

1 duck
2 oranges
Seasoned flour
3 tablespoons (45 g) butter
1 teaspoon arrowroot or
  cornflour
$\frac{5}{8}$ cup (1$\frac{1}{2}$ dl) brown stock
Salt and pepper

Mallard or teal are usually considered the best.

Grate the skin of 1$\frac{1}{2}$ oranges and squeeze and strain all the juice. Rub the skin of the bird with seasoned flour, sprinkle with a little orange zest and put half a squeezed orange skin in the bird's vent. Place in a roasting tin in which the butter has been melted. Spoon a little butter over the bird. Put in a hot oven, 450°F (230°C, Gas Mark 8), and roast for 20 to 25 minutes.

Meanwhile, mix the arrowroot or cornflour with a little orange juice. Mix the remaining orange juice with the well-seasoned brown stock and bring to the boil. Pour a little on to the arrowroot mixture, stirring hard, then pour back into the stock, stirring all the time. Add the remaining zest and stir again. The sauce should be clear and thin and taste strongly of orange. It sets off the wild duck to perfection, as our ancestors well knew.

Roast Venison

3 to 4 lb (1$\frac{1}{2}$ to 2 kg) saddle or
  haunch of venison
1$\frac{1}{2}$ sticks (180 g) butter or $\frac{3}{4}$
  cup cooking fat
$\frac{1}{4}$ cup (30 g) flour
1$\frac{1}{4}$ cups (3 dl) stock

The marinade:

2$\frac{1}{2}$ cups (6 dl) red wine
1 carrot, peeled and sliced
1 onion, sliced
1 thyme sprig
1 bay leaf
2 tablespoons wine vinegar
3 tablespoons olive oil
1 garlic clove
2 teaspoons brown sugar
1 teaspoon salt
1 teaspoon freshly ground
  black pepper

Venison was preferred above all other meat as a feast-day roast. It is inclined to be dry, as meat from wild animals has less fat than meat from domestic animals, so it is best if it is marinated before roasting.

Mix together in a saucepan all the ingredients for the marinade and boil for 20 minutes. Leave to get cold. Lay the venison in the marinade and keep in a cool larder for 24 hours. From time to time turn the meat and spoon the marinade over it.

Remove the meat from the marinade and roast it in a fairly hot oven, 400°F (200°C, Gas Mark 6), allowing 15 minutes to the pound ($\frac{1}{2}$ kg). Baste frequently with the butter or cooking fat.

When the meat is cooked, remove it from the pan and keep hot. Pour off all but 3 tablespoons of the fat from the pan. Put the pan over heat and work in the flour. Gradually stir in the stock and the marinade, pouring it through a strainer. Stir well, check the seasoning and allow to simmer for 5 minutes. Serve the sauce separately.

Venison Baked in a Crust

3 to 5 lb (1$\frac{1}{2}$ to 2$\frac{1}{2}$ kg) haunch of
  venison
1 lb ($\frac{1}{2}$ kg) flour, plus a little
  more
$\frac{1}{2}$ stick (60 g) butter, softened
Salt and pepper
Thick brown gravy
Red-currant jelly

This is a Victorian recipe, which made use of the big iron ranges which transformed the Victorian kitchens and which banished for ever meat roasted on the spit in front of the fire.

Mix the flour with 1$\frac{1}{4}$ cups (3 dl) of water to make a stiff paste. Turn it on to a floured board, knead it a little and roll out to about $\frac{1}{2}$ inch (1 cm) thickness.

Rub the venison with salt and pepper and spread the softened butter over it. Lay the joint on the paste, lift up the edges and seal securely. Place in a roasting tin in a hot oven, 450°F (230°C, Gas Mark 8), for 15 minutes. Then reduce the heat to 325°F (170°C, Gas Mark 3) and cook for a further 2 hours.

Meanwhile, make the gravy. Break the crust from the venison and discard, carefully adding any liquid to the gravy. Season the gravy rather highly. Place the joint on a dish and serve at once with the gravy and red-currant jelly.

Suffolk Ham Toasts

Serves 6

½ to ¾ lb (240 to 360 g) lean, home-cooked ham or gammon, minced
2 tablespoons double cream
1 stick (120 g) butter
12 eggs
A little milk
Freshly ground black pepper
6 slices fresh white toast, from which the crusts have been removed

Suffolk hams were sweet-cured, preferably using honey, and then smoked. One or two Suffolk farms still cure their own hams by this method, and it is said to be possible to buy locally cured ham in Bury St Edmunds and to order a whole Suffolk ham in London. They are exceedingly good and quite different from the better-known York hams. Several very good recipes using smoked ham come from Suffolk. The following is an excellent lunch or supper dish, or a very good starting course for dinner. The eggs will not wait and it is best if those who are to eat the dish are already seated when the eggs are being scrambled.

If there is no cooked ham to be used up, buy a small joint of gammon and boil it with a spoonful of brown sugar and two or three cloves. Carve the best part in slices and reserve for another occasion. Mince the rest of the gammon.

Put the cream in a small saucepan and add the ham and a pinch of black pepper. Stir well together while the ham becomes quite hot. Cover and keep hot.

Make the toast and arrange the slices, lightly buttered, on a serving dish. Spread the ham mixture over each. Keep hot in the oven while you beat the eggs with milk and a little pepper. Melt the remaining butter, stir the egg mixture into it and continue to stir over gentle heat. The scrambled egg should be still almost liquid when you take the ham toasts from the oven and spoon it over each. Serve at once.

Sausages and Ham with Red Cabbage

Serves 4

3 lb (1½ kg) red cabbage, very finely chopped
¼ lb (120 g) gammon slices, cut in 1 inch (2.5 cm) strips
2 tablespoons (30 g) butter
1¼ cups (3 dl) good stock
1 teaspoon lemon juice
2 teaspoons castor sugar
1 lb (½ kg) pork sausages
1 teaspoon salt
¼ teaspoon white pepper

A Suffolk recipe which dates from 1823. Crusty brown bread (preferably home-made) and butter go well with this supper dish.

Put the cabbage in a casserole with the gammon, butter, stock, lemon juice, seasoning and sugar and bring to the boil. Then simmer gently, closely covered, for 3 hours in a slow oven, 300°F (160°C, Gas Mark 2).

Remove the casserole from the oven. Stir the cabbage well and check the seasoning. Most of the stock should have been absorbed. Before the cabbage is ready, fry the sausages. Heap the cabbage on a dish, stand the sausages against it and serve.

Breast of Lamb with Celery

Boned breast of lamb, about
  4 lb (2 kg)
6 thick slices of streaky bacon
4 onions, sliced
4 carrots, peeled and sliced
Thyme
Parsley
Mace
1½ quarts (1¼ litres) good
  brown stock
2 heads celery, stripped of
  outside stalks, cleaned and
  cut in 2 inch (5 cm) lengths
  with hard strings removed
Salt and pepper
Red-currant jelly
Lemon juice

John Simpson, the Marquis of Buckingham's cook, left this recipe in his notes for various dishes. Made at Gosfield Hall, Essex, in about 1805, it is extremely good and requires only creamed or plain boiled potatoes as an accompaniment.

Cover the bottom of a large, heavy saucepan with 4 of the bacon rashers, each cut across into 3 pieces. Put half the onions and carrots on this and then lay the lamb on top. Cover with the rest of the onions and carrots and add thyme, parsley and mace to taste. Put the remaining bacon over the top. Add the stock. Cover and simmer for 2 hours. At the end of 1 hour bring a saucepan of salted water to the boil and put in the celery. Boil the celery for 35 minutes or until tender. Drain well, put on the serving dish you will use for the lamb and keep hot.

Remove the lamb from the saucepan and wipe off excess grease with kitchen paper. Put the lamb into a very hot oven, 450°F (230°C, Gas Mark 8), near the top, for 10 minutes to crisp and brown.

Using a ladle, take 2½ cups (6 dl) of the stock from underneath the top layer of grease. Boil this fiercely in a small saucepan to reduce it by a quarter. Add 1 teaspoon red-currant jelly and a squeeze of lemon juice. Check the seasoning. Remove the lamb from the oven and place it on the celery. Pour the gravy around the lamb.

Do not serve the carrots, onions, bacon or remaining stock; allow these to cool overnight and when convenient take off the fat, put the vegetables and stock through a blender and use as a basis for soup.

Raised Mutton Pies

¾ lb (360 g) lean raw lamb from
  the fillet end of a leg, very
  finely chopped (not minced)
⅝ cup (1.5 dl) claret, boiled to
  reduce it a little
⅝ cup (1.5 dl) good brown stock
1 medium onion, very finely
  chopped
½ lb (240 g) mushrooms, finely
  chopped
1 teaspoon dried thyme
Salt and pepper
1 lb (½ kg) raised pie pastry or
  rough puff pastry
1 well-beaten egg
1 tablespoon finely chopped
  parsley

As made by John Simpson, head cook to the Marquis of Buckingham, who had a great estate at Gosfield Hall, near Braintree in Essex. In January 1805, a large flat dish of these little pies was served as a side dish at a large dinner. If the pies are to be served as a main dish, creamed potatoes and peas set them off very well.

Stir the reduced claret into the stock, add the meat, onion, mushrooms, thyme and seasoning and simmer very gently for 20 minutes. Pour off the gravy and allow it and the meat mixture to get quite cold.

Meanwhile, either mould 12 small pie cases from the raised pie pastry or roll out the rough puff pastry, cut out 12 large circles and line 12 small soufflé dishes. Cut and reserve 12 circles for lids.

Remove the grease from the top of the cold gravy. Fill the pies and put a spoonful of gravy into each. Keep the remaining gravy hot. Put the lids on the pies and make a small hole in the centre of each. Brush over with the egg and bake in a moderate to hot oven, 375° to 400°F (190° to 200°C, Gas Mark 5 to 6) for 20 minutes or until the pastry is crisp and golden brown.

When the pies are cooked, enlarge the holes in the lids a little with a skewer and carefully pour in a little extra gravy. Alternatively, cut the lids off with a very sharp knife, fill up the pies with gravy and replace the lids.

Sprinkle each pie with a little parsley and serve.

Norfolk Boiled Beef and Dumplings

Serves 8

4 lb (2 kg) fresh or slightly salted silverside of beef (the butcher will generally salt it for you if asked a few days before you need it. If fresh beef is used the recipe requires 2 teaspoons of salt)
1½ lb (¾ kg) carrots, scraped and sliced
1½ lb (¾ kg) turnips, peeled and cubed, if liked
6 celery sticks, cut in 1 inch (2.5 cm) lengths
12 black peppercorns
Parsley, sage and thyme tied in a bunch

The dumplings:

2 cups (240 g) self-raising flour
¾ cup (90 g) shredded suet
1 teaspoon salt
⅝ cup (1.5 dl) milk and water, mixed

This dish dates back to the Middle Ages, when it would have been known as a "Running Pottage" as the plentiful broth was clear and unthickened. Dumplings were always cooked in the broth and served with the meat and vegetables. Potatoes were boiled and served separately to prevent them making the broth cloudy.

Put the vegetables in a very large saucepan or fish kettle and cover with water. Add the peppercorns, salt (if fresh beef is used) and the bunch of herbs. Bring to the boil and then put in the beef—the water should cover the meat. Cover the pan and allow to simmer gently for 1½ hours.

Meanwhile, make the dumplings. Mix the flour, suet and salt in a bowl and stir in the liquid gradually. Shake some flour on to a flat surface and knead the dough for 30 seconds. Divide the dough and roll into small balls about 1 inch (2.5 cm) across.

After the beef has simmered for 1½ hours, drop in the dumplings and simmer for a further 20 to 30 minutes.

Norfolk Pudding

Serves 6 to 8

3 cups (360 g) self-raising flour
¾ cup (180 g) shredded suet
½ teaspoon salt

On 23 October, 1781, Parson Woodforde, at his home in Weston, Norfolk, wrote in his diary: "*We had for dinner a Fowl boiled, and a Tongue, a piece of rost Beef and a plain Norfolk Pudding.*" This is the traditional recipe, as it is made today. In the eighteenth century, the pudding would have been made with plain flour and tied in a floured cloth before being boiled. It would have been rather solid and heavy. As Parson Woodforde says that it was "plain", it would not have had currants or "raisins of the sun" in it, although these were often added to suet puddings at this time. Traditionally, butter and soft brown sugar would have been offered with it.

Mix the flour, suet and salt and add cold water, a spoonful at a time, stirring until you have a stiff paste; knead and work it a little. Put the dough into a greased bowl and closely cover with foil, placing a saucer or small plate on top of it. Stand the bowl in a large saucepan. Pour in boiling water to come half-way up the sides of the bowl. Steam in this way for 2½ hours, pouring in more boiling water from time to time when necessary. Never let the water go off the boil. Turn the pudding out and serve immediately.

The Dean's Trifle

8 oblong sponge cakes (bought
  in a packet)
Raspberry jam
Apricot jam
$\frac{1}{4}$ lb (120 g) ratafia biscuits or
  macaroons
$1\frac{1}{4}$ cups (3 dl) sherry
$2\frac{1}{2}$ cups (6 dl) double cream
4 tablespoons (60 g) castor
sugar
$\frac{1}{2}$ cup brandy
angelica
$\frac{3}{4}$ cup (120 g) glacé cherries
$\frac{3}{4}$ cup (120 g) crystallized
  pineapple

The Dean of Trinity College, Cambridge, in the late nineteenth century preferred this to any other trifle and insisted that it should appear on the High Table at all college feasts.

Cut the sponge cakes in half lengthways. Lightly spread 8 halves with raspberry jam and 8 with apricot jam. Arrange them in a very large glass or china bowl, jam sides upwards and piled two or three deep. Crumble the ratafias or macaroons and put them with the sponge cakes. Pour over the sherry and leave to soak for at least 20 minutes.

Whip the cream, sugar and brandy as for a solid syllabub. Pile over the wine and cake mixture and decorate with angelica, cherries and pineapple. Chill for at least 1 hour before serving.

The Prior's Sweet Omelette

4 eggs, separated
1 orange
2 tablespoons double cream
1 tablespoon clear honey
1 tablespoon (15 g) butter

Jocelyn de Brakeland wrote a chronicle of his abbey from 1173 to 1232. He says that the abbot always had four sorts of dishes on his table. He himself lived simply. He preferred sweet dishes made with milk and honey to rich meat pottages. His visitors, however, were served with venison from the abbey's own park and fish from its fishponds; both park and ponds were extensive and well-stocked.

This recipe, which comes from an early cookery book, clearly originated in a monastery and is exactly the sort of dish the Abbot of Brakeland preferred.

Cut the orange in half and cut one half into quarters. Grate the zest from the half orange and set it aside on a saucer. Squeeze the juice from the half orange and set aside.

Whip the cream until it stands, but is not at all solid. Fold in the honey and the orange juice and put in a refrigerator for a few minutes until required.

Beat the egg yolks well and the whites so that they just hold a peak. Make the butter very hot in an omelette pan. Fold the egg whites into the yolks and pour into the pan. No sugar or salt should be added. Turn the edge inwards from the sides of the pan as the omelette cooks. In 2 minutes it will be almost set, except in the centre. Immediately spoon the cream and honey mixture a little off centre, and fold one half of the omelette over it. Lift it quickly but carefully on to a hot dish. Sprinkle the orange zest over it and put a quarter of orange at each end.

Serve immediately and very quickly, simply dividing the omelette in two, with an orange quarter for each person to squeeze over it. It is essential to start eating it before all the cream and honey melts and runs out.

Crème Brûlée

$2\frac{1}{2}$ *cups (6 dl) double cream*
8 well-beaten egg yolks
$\frac{5}{8}$ *to 1 cup (120 to 180 g)*
demerara sugar
1 lb ($\frac{1}{2}$ kg) muscat grapes

As traditionally made in the kitchens of King's College, Cambridge. The muscat grapes add a delicious and delicate flavour and texture but the cream is also excellent without them.

Blanch, peel and pit the grapes and lay them in a wide, shallow, fireproof serving dish.

Bring the cream just to boiling point and keep it boiling for exactly 1 minute (this timing is important). Then pour it slowly, stirring constantly, on to the well-beaten egg yolks. Beat for 1 minute and return to the heat, stirring over simmering water (or held above very low direct heat) until it thickens well – never allow it to boil again. On no account add sugar – the whole point of the dish is that the cream is unsweetened. Pour the cream over the grapes. Chill well, preferably overnight.

Cover the cold cream with a $\frac{1}{4}$ inch (0.5 cm) layer of demerara sugar. Put it under a preheated grill, not too close to the heat. Watch it and move it further from the heat if the sugar begins to burn and darken. As soon as all the sugar has melted together, remove the dish and chill it again before serving. It should be possible just to tap the crust with a spoon to crack it.

Suffolk Cakes

1 stick (120 g) butter
4 eggs
1 cup (240 g) castor sugar
Grated zest of $\frac{1}{2}$ lemon
1 cup (120 g) self-raising flour

This recipe was collected before 1860 by Mrs Anstey.

Warm the butter so that it is just liquid but not at all coloured, and leave to cool a little while you beat the whites and yolks of the eggs separately. The beaten whites should just hold a peak. Fold in the yolks, sugar and grated lemon zest, beat in the butter and stir in the flour. Beat well and turn into well-greased bun tins or patty pans. Bake at 400°F (200°C, Gas Mark 6) for 10 to 15 minutes.

Vinegar Cake

2 sticks (240 g) butter
1 lb ($\frac{1}{2}$ kg) self-raising flour
1 cup (240 g) sugar
$1\frac{1}{3}$ cups (240 g) raisins
$1\frac{1}{3}$ cups (240 g) sultanas
$\frac{1}{2}$ cup (1.2 dl) milk
2 tablespoons vinegar
1 teaspoon bicarbonate of soda
mixed with 1 tablespoon milk

A Norfolk farmhouse recipe for a good, plain fruit cake that will keep for a week or so, the flavour improving all the time. The recipe requires no eggs.

Rub the butter into the flour to give a crumb-like consistency. Mix in the sugar and dried fruit.

Put the milk into a large jug or bowl and add the vinegar. Pour the bicarbonate of soda and milk mixture all at once into the milk and vinegar. It will froth and may overflow so should be held over the cake bowl. Stir the liquid into the cake mixture, beat well and put into a well-greased 9 inch (23 cm) cake tin. Bake at 350°F (180°C, Gas Mark 4) for 30 minutes and then reduce the heat to 300°F (160°C, Gas Mark 2) and bake for a further $1\frac{1}{4}$ hours. Lightly cover the top with foil if it is becoming too dark.

The North

Northumberland, Cumbria, Durham, Yorkshire, Humberside, Lancashire, Greater Manchester, Merseyside

Across the width of northern England, from Wallsend on the Tyne Estuary on the north-east coast to Bowness on the Solway Firth on the north-west coast, runs Hadrian's Wall, that great wall built by the Romans in the reign of the Emperor Hadrian to defend the part of the British Isles they had conquered. They never retreated south of the Wall but they never succeeded in holding any of the country north of it, either. It cuts across the two most northerly counties of England, Northumberland and Cumbria, running well south of the Scottish border. There was fighting on the Wall itself and on both sides of it from the second century AD, when it was built, until long after the union of England and Scotland. Only after the Stuart dynasty ended was there official peace, and even then murderous family feuds and a little cattle-rustling and sheep-stealing were expected in the area.

For centuries now, most of the Wall has appeared as a tall bank of green turf, with outcrops marking the mile-castles where small garrisons from the legion detailed to hold the Wall were stationed, sending out sentries on patrol half a mile in either direction. Every four miles there was a large fort, which held about 600 men. Sometimes one legion was seconded to the Wall, sometimes another, but all of them, from captain to simple legionary, hated it. It was wet and cold: they were under frequent attack from the small, dark, deadly Pictish bowmen to the north and from time to time by insurgent tribesmen from the south. Their rations were often short. The *pabulum*, the basic rations to which every legionary was entitled, often did not arrive on time. Although the hunting and fishing in that wild country traversed by the Wall were fine, they were also dangerous. A Roman soldier who went out after deer, grouse or hare was very likely to be the target of a little man with a bow. The best food in that cold, wet, comfortless place, where few if any crops were grown by anyone, was a kind of porridge made of any available cereal sent up as rations and cooked in the broth in which meat, bird or even salmon or trout was boiling. The officers in the fort might eat recognizable Roman dishes, but porridge with meat in it was what the legionaries lived on. It suited the climate and warmed and reassured a man from inside.

It was really a way of preparing hot and filling food which allowed endless variations of cost and elaboration. Even in its simplest and cheapest forms, the flavour could be varied by the use of different herbs or the addition of such vegetables as onions, leeks or kale.

"*Pottage*", said Andrew Boorde in his *Dyetry of Helth*, 1542, "*is not so much used in all Christendom as it is used in England.*" Pottage became, in fact, a staple food from Roman times until the eighteenth century throughout England, but particularly in the North. It could be plain, poor and dull; it could be simple and very good, or it could be extremely elaborate and expensive. The direct connection with Roman cookery is shown by the fact that, in the Middle Ages, the cooks of the great houses, when preparing several kinds of pottage for a feast, made up a wheat starch, very similar to the cornflour we use today, which was known as *amidon*. The name and the recipe were almost exactly the same as the *amulum*, which was described by Cato as being in use in Rome for thickening sauces in the first century AD.

Immediately north and south of the Wall the name pottage was softened to porridge and the simple dish of oatmeal boiled in salted water became the staple diet of all but the rich. Porridge to a Scotsman was as much a necessity as pasta to an Italian, and even today many people think of it as the Scottish national dish.

The typical pottage, however, was made with boiled meat of some kind, usually mutton in the Cumberland dales. When the meat was partly cooked, oatmeal, barley-meal or maslin (a mixture of wheat and rye) was added with salt, pepper or ginger, if available, herbs, onions or leeks, a little vinegar or verjuice and some honey or sugar. The pot had to be stirred constantly when the pottage began to thicken and when it was done it made, with the addition of a hunk of bread and a mug of ale, a complete meal, hot and sustaining.

As early as the thirteenth century, rice was imported into England and was considered an exotic delicacy. It was much in demand in noble houses as it was, of course, an excellent thickener for more refined types of pottage and very much used in the meatless Lenten meals.

Peas were considered excellent for pottages. Green and white peas were slightly more expensive than the large grey field peas, which were eaten by the poor peasant and fed to cattle. Pease porridge or pottage was a staple dish almost everywhere in Tudor and Stuart times, and in certain early French cookery books recipes for it are referred to as pottage in the English manner. Lentils, peas and beans were dried for poor man's pottage, which could then be made with a piece of bacon from the pig which almost all cottagers kept. If there was no bacon left the peas were cooked in stock or water, flavoured with herbs and thickened with flour or breadcrumbs or sometimes oatmeal. Such a pottage could be made as thick as a pudding and gave us the old rhyme:

Pease pudding hot,
Pease pudding cold,
Pease pudding in the pot
Nine days old.

A bitter comment on the sameness of the poor man's diet. In Northumberland today, pease pudding is served with roast pork and sometimes with goose.

Bean pottage became less popular after the Middle Ages, but recipes went with the first colonists to North America and the traditional Boston baked beans is one of the resulting dishes, as, indeed, are the canned baked beans beloved of most children on both sides of the Atlantic..

Cabbage and worts were often used in pottages, which were thickened with bread or oatmeal. An early recipe for a cabbage pottage says, "*Thick it with grated bread, but for a lord it shall be thickened with yolks of eggs beaten.*"

The early vegetable pottages cooked in broth or water, without meat, were called porrays. This name comes from the Latin *porrum*, a leek, leeks being the favourite of all pottage vegetables, but it was used for all thick green pottages, perhaps because the word is close to the Norman-French purée. The most usual porray is called Joutes in early manuscripts. The *Liber Cure Cocorum*, a fifteenth-century rhyming book from Lancashire, lists many wild and cultivated green plants, including the young leaves of the plum tree, in a recipe for Joutes.

In the nineteenth century the word pottage was replaced by the dread word stew. School stews and landladies' stews, particularly in wartime, have left us with memories so frightful that we prefer the word casserole. In fact, a sixteenth-century recipe from a great house for a pottage of partridges, an eighteenth-century recipe for a partridge "ragoo", a nineteenth-century partridge stew and a twentieth-century recipe for casserole of partridges would vary very little. The sixteenth-century pottage would probably be rather thick, the gravy being thickened with breadcrumbs, dried peas and possibly beaten eggs; the other three, if properly made, would be indistinguishable from each other, varying only in the herbs used, and the addition of leeks, cabbage (traditional with stewed partridges) or other vegetables.

Pottage is a good word, denoting a well-designed and comforting type of dish, with plenty of scope for a fine sauce enhancing the flavour of meat or fish of first quality. Among the recipes for traditional dishes from the north of England which follow, several with long pedigrees will be found. They have been chosen to show the wide variations in ingredients and the simplicity of the poor man's pottage compared with the rich sauce and spices of feast-day pottages in great houses. Other regions of England, of course, had their own recipes, some much the same, some rather different. Some of the latter will be given among the recipes traditional in the Midlands, Kent and the West, but all are very close to Roman cooking and it is in northern England that pottages have been most appreciated.

In the fifteenth century, housewives and cooks began to boil vegetables separately from meat or cereal and to drain them, cook them a few minutes with plenty of butter and then serve them, much as we do today, except that the quantity of butter was very large. Before the nineteenth century, when butter was used at all it was always used generously, indeed, in our terms, overgenerously. Many large pies containing some four pounds of meat and vegetables were finished off by adding a pound of butter under the crust. A pound of boiled and drained cabbage might have a quarter-pound of butter added to it. The vegetables, once separated from the meat, became important in their own right and some interesting ways of cooking them resulted.

Food in the north of England throughout the Tudor period remained curiously barbaric. The dishes which graced a noble feast tended to be elaborate in the extreme, with so many spices added to each that no individual flavour could have been detected. At the same time, the strict sumptuary laws of both Church and State carried heavy fines and embarrassing penalties, so that even the richest in the land were forced to eat more fish and less meat than they would have chosen. Indeed, so much did people dislike being forced to eat fish, either because they genuinely missed meat or simply because they disliked all restrictions and enjoyed finding ways round them, that they still trapped and ate beaver in the North Country as late as the early sixteenth century. A very early cookery book suggests beaver's tail with peas or frumenty and adds, "*Sweet is that fish which is not fish at all.*" Pliny had written in his *Natural History*: "*The beaver has a fish's tail, while the rest of its conformation resembles an otter's.*" Pliny was the accepted authority and only the tail was considered proper to eat on fish days. "*There have been those of them whose tails have weighed four pounds. The manner of their dressing is first roasting and afterwards seething in an open pot so that the evil vapour may go away – it is certain that the tail and forefeet taste very sweet. . . .*"

Even when it was not a question of a feast, but a simple breakfast to be served in the private chambers of the master of the household, the food seems to us today to be distastefully rough and strong tasting. This is the provision laid down in the early sixteenth century in the *Northumberland Household Book* for breakfast during Lent for the fifth Earl of Northumberland, Henry Algernon Percy:

> *A loaf of bread cut in trenchers* [these would have been made of second-grade bread cut about one inch thick and the fish would have been arranged on them as on plates; they might or might not have been partly eaten]*; 2 manchets* [smaller loaves of fine white bread]*; 2 pieces of salt fish; 6 baconed herring; 4 white herring or a dish of sprats; a quart of beer; a quart of wine.*

The children still in the nursery had a dish of butter, which was thought good for children, but was not particularly liked by adults except in cooking. The method of preparing the fish is not described, of course, as the list comes from household accounts and not from a recipe book, but ingredients such as rosewater, butter or spices would have been listed, so it is likely that the fifth Earl and his gentlemen of the bedchamber did indeed breakfast on plainly boiled salt fish.

On the big country estates simple food was fairly plentiful for all but the poorest peasants. The writer Philip Kinder of Derbyshire wrote in the mid-seventeenth century:

> *For diet, the gentrie, after the southern mode, have two state meals a day, with a bitt in ye buttery to a morning draught; but your peasants exceed the Greeks, who had four meales a day – for the moorlanders add three more; ye bitt in ye morning; ye anders meate and ye yenders meate and soe make up seaven and for certain ye greate housekeeper doth allow his people, especially in summertime, so many comenessations.*
> *The common inhabitants doe prefer oates for delight and strength above any other grains. . . .*

The preference expressed in the last statement is doubtful; wheaten bread, as white as possible, had been considered superior to all others since Roman times, but in Derbyshire and the North generally oats and barley were spring sown, and grew better than wheat in the harsh climate and, in many places, poor soil. Oatcakes, which were baked on flat iron griddles or bakestones, and required no kind of oven, were the usual bread of all but the well-to-do.

On the big farms, the year was marked by the feasts, which it was traditional for the farmer and his wife to provide. When sowing was finished, many farmers provided a traditional tea for their workers. When the harvest was safely in, there was a harvest supper, which included beef – either roast or stewed in ale. The cynical said that the latter gave the farmer a chance to use up a tough old cow. Christmas was celebrated for twelve days. The farm worker was usually given a bird or a joint to cook at home and was also entertained in the farm kitchen at New Year. Some farmers provided a feast at Michaelmas, when, by tradition, tenant farmers and cottagers came to pay their rents, often bringing one of their own geese, a piglet or other produce to soften their landlords' hearts so that their rents would not be raised for the year to come.

The north-east coast had been a stronghold of the Church since the seventh century, when St Cuthbert made the island of Lindisfarne (or Holy Island) his retreat. He was buried there, in that beautiful, lonely place, which is joined to the mainland only at low water by a great expanse of shimmering sand.

St Aidan was invited in the early years of the seventh century to come to Northumberland to preach to its inhabitants, many of whom were unconverted, or only nominally converted to Christianity. St Aiden chose Lindisfarne as the site of his church and monastery. The monks prospered until the end of the eighth century, when the Danes burnt the settlement, killing many monks. Those who remained patiently rebuilt the church and monastery and lived there for almost another hundred years, until a further Viking invasion seemed inevitable and they escaped to the mainland. They took with them the body of St Cuthbert and many holy relics. The church and monastery were indeed destroyed and the monks settled at Chester-le-Street and then at Durham, where eventually the cathedral was founded. The monks flourished, as they had flourished before. They brewed beer, as was a tradition in early monasteries of almost all orders, and the beer of Lindisfarne and, later, of Durham was strong and well-flavoured with herbs from the monastery gardens. The monks also grew herbs for medicines and salves, and vegetables for the table.

The island of Lindisfarne remained uninhabited but for rabbits until 1082, when the prior of the Durham monastery re-established there a cell of monks with whom the Durham monks kept in close touch. One or two records mention simple food, a kind of oat soup, some special breads, a green pottage, rabbit pasties and a fish stew. Several recipes from Alnwick and Durham probably originated with the monks.

In the middle of the sixteenth century a formidable castle was built just to the east of the island's only village. Until the nineteenth century, one side of the island was barren and sandy and supported enormous numbers of rabbits, which were not only an immediate source of food but were sold on the mainland, as were excellent oysters, prawns, shrimps and flat fish. The south side of the island is extremely fertile, and from early times vegetables were grown there and sold on the mainland.

The coast going north to the Scottish border at Berwick was wild, with treacherous sands and the inhabitants fought hard for better living conditions and education from earliest times. The Venerable Bede, on whom we rely for much of what we know of early English history, secular and religious, was brought up in Jarrow, lived, preached and wrote there all his life and was buried in Durham Cathedral. He visited outlying farms and taught many boys their letters as well as their religion. The monks of Monkwearmouth Priory understood and taught glass-making and Sunderland became famous for its glass, which brought the whole town prosperity.

All children know that *"Little Jack Horner Sat in the corner, Eating a Christmas Pie,"* and that *"He put in his thumb And pulled out a plum, And said What a good boy am I!"* It is not well known, however, that the pie came from Yorkshire, where the abbey of Glastonbury owned estates. Jack Horner (not so little) was steward to the abbot of Glastonbury (in fact the last abbot before the dissolution) and was sent by his master to take the pie to Henry VIII in London. Horner had his doubts about the pie, not as a culinary masterpiece, but as to whether it was edible at all. He put in his thumb and the plum he pulled out and kept was the deed of one of twelve manors in Somerset. The other eleven rolls he delivered to the King, but the Horner family owned the manor of Mells for many years after this date. The King accepted the manors, but the bribe did not save the monasterial lands either in Somerset or in Yorkshire.

On all the northern coasts, cockles were gathered and taken or sent in sacks to the nearest market towns or to great houses in the neighbourhood. The sacks were sold by weight and after the establishment of the railways were sent to Preston, Manchester and down to London, where they were an East End delicacy. It seems that 3,162 tons were despatched from Flookburgh in 1890, the price being a little over two pounds a ton. The cockles were often collected by a husband and wife working together, using a horse and small cart, which they drove out into the shallow water of sandy bays at low tide. In 1898 the extreme winter cold, with lumps of ice floating in the almost frozen sea, killed many cockles and the trade seems never to have completely revived. Oysters, after disease struck the beds, became extremely expensive; cockles have never become expensive but are much less often offered for sale and many of the recipes for cooking them have fallen out of use. Until the late nineteenth century, the cockle was to England almost what the clam is to America today.

Cockling accidents were many and tragic: the tide might come in fast and a cockler be late in turning his horse landwards; a woman lagging behind the cart could be swept away; the heavy sacks might be thrown out to lighten the load of a terrified horse struggling in mud and sand and water. But cockling was also considered partly a pleasure, as was the much safer work of collecting shrimps – those from Morecombe Bay in Lancashire were particularly famous. The shrimps were netted in very shallow water, taken home by the women, cooked, shelled, packed tightly into small jars with a seasoning of black pepper and mace and covered with clarified butter. They could then be kept for several weeks. This became a cottage industry in the early nineteenth century, the women being provided with pots and delivering them, filled, to a centre from which they were sent to London and other cities. Later, a factory was built and potted shrimps prepared by the original method became available all over the country. Today, the pots are frozen and can be kept for months.

With the coming of the railways the fuller exploitation of coal brought great wealth to northern landowners and to the new class of prosperous industrialists, among them, of course, the Duke of Northumberland, one of the greatest landowners in the North. Heavy industry and, in particular, steel and iron brought peasants in from the land to found the great northern cities. The Industrial Revolution saw the beginnings of England's great china industry, in the area known as the potteries, and, above all, of the cotton industry. All these industries affected the general culture of the North and the Midlands and with it the traditional cooking, which was adapted to shift work, to "snaps" taken down the mines, to a good high tea for a hungry man, and to special holiday dishes, which helped to mark and to celebrate the fact that today Dad was above ground, clean and in no danger. All such dishes had to be cheap to make. Miners, potters, steel or cotton workers were neither highly paid nor protected from unemployment until the present century. We find the same comment, on the preference of the hard-working poor for oatcakes, made by Sir Humphry Davy in 1819 about the Derbyshire miners, as was made earlier by Philip Kinder about their ancestors who worked on the farms, and we cannot fail to have the same doubts about it.

In spite of unprotected poverty, however, ingenuity and careful cooking and buying produced a tradition of good simple food, some of which is very much to our taste today as I hope the recipes which follow will show. Two special forms of pasty evolved over the years for the miner's "snap", the meal eaten down in the pit in mid-shift. The first, from Lancashire, is called Lancashire Foot and the second, which is found in most mining districts in the North, is called Collier's Foot. Both are a form of pasty. The short pastry is rolled into a narrow oblong and then rolled again from the middle outwards, away from the cook, so that the narrow end or heel is thicker and the whole is shaped like the sole of a foot. The thick heel end is piled with the filling, the thin toe is folded over the pile and then the pastry is sealed at the edges. Meat with potato, or hard-boiled eggs and cheese, and onions were the usual fillings. For Collier's Foot, the filling was generally sliced onion, sprinkled with salt, sliced cheese sprinkled with pepper and a rasher of bacon sprinkled with dry mustard. Sometimes a spoonful of ale or broth was added and sometimes a few slices of apple.

The foot fitted neatly into the oval-shaped tins which were specially made for miners to take down the pit. Such tins were attached to their belts, having no corners to catch or stick into a man who was crawling along a narrow tunnel.

Potters sometimes encased chops, rabbits or whole birds, most often pigeons, in the clay they were using, placing them in the kiln with the pots they were officially baking. They could not, of course, be eaten until the kiln was opened, but the food cooked totally enclosed in this way was so good that pots and casserole dishes began to be made with specially close-fitting lids. It was possible to cook an unplucked bird in this way, because the feathers would come off with the clay as it was broken away. This, of course, was the traditional way in which gipsies cooked hedgehogs. Even today in and around the pottery districts there are many traditional dishes where birds or joints of meat are completely wrapped in a huff paste made of flour, water and salt with a little butter rubbed into the flour. The paste, unlike the second form of huff paste described below, is not intended to be eaten, but when it is broken away it is often found to have taken up the fat and the flavour of the meat and to be delicious, and is served as a separate dish.

In the iron foundries and the shipyards, food was cooked on or around the great furnaces. Large scrubbed potatoes were brought to work and one hearth or another became the accepted cooking place. A sheep's kidney or a lump of cheese might have been inserted inside the scooped-out potato before a man left home. Onions were sometimes roasted and eaten hot with salt and bread.

Most of the colliers and many of the workers in heavy industry were on shift work, and the food they took to work was eaten either in the middle of the day or the middle of the night. A main meal at home, in effect either tea or breakfast, was necessary. It had to include a hot, substantial, savoury dish, unless money was so short that only tea and bread or potatoes could be produced.

Where a man and several children had to be fed, let alone the housewife herself, a hot meat pie could sometimes be afforded and could be made to go round by the use of huff paste, which has nowadays almost entirely disappeared. The huff for this kind of dish could be made simply of flour, salt and water, with a little suet rubbed into the flour.

The meat and any vegetables for the pie were placed in the dish and closely covered with the huff paste. When the meat was considered to be about three-quarters cooked, the huff paste was lifted off, cut in squares and put into the gravy. Another layer, which would require less cooking time, was added. This might be chopped bacon and some chopped cabbage or tomatoes and a few sliced sausages. A pastry lid was then put on in the usual way and the pie baked for another half hour. When the pie was served the man of the house was given most of the meat and bacon, and the wife and children ate the huff paste with gravy and vegetables. Everyone was given a piece of the crisp top crust.

Too often, however, tea was bread and jam and not very much of that. The poor families in the industrial cities, even at the beginning of the twentieth century, mostly bought their sugar and cheese by the ounce and their meat, bacon and fish by the pennyworth. Since the eighteenth century the working classes had become as devoted to tea as they had always been to beer, but they bought it by the screw – a pinch of tea in a screw of paper – or, at the most, by the ounce, and boiled the leaves several times over. There is a record of one family who bought tea 72 times in seven weeks.

In contrast, the landowners on whose estates coal was discovered became very rich almost overnight. Coal, after all, is the same black gold as oil, and so there arose a tradition of elaborate and elegant dishes from new landowners in the Midlands and the North as well as from those who had been defending their castles and tending their estates since the Middle Ages. Elegant but vast were the Victorian dinner parties given at their great mansions.

The new urban middle class had also spread and developed by the middle of the nineteenth century. It was made up of the merchants, shopkeepers, professional men and factory managers who prospered as such cities as Manchester, Liverpool, Sheffield and the towns of the Black Country developed. Large numbers of agricultural labourers who came to the mines, the potteries or the foundries might well wish themselves back on the land again, but others thrived amazingly and so did many of those who were already engaged in trade.

This new middle class, as has been pointed out earlier, did much to destroy the tradition of good English cooking, but this was less the case in the north of England than anywhere else in the country. The north-countryman might find himself the possessor of a solid house with a mahogany dining table, a red and blue Turkey carpet, a cook in the kitchen instead of his wife (and this was one of the roots of the trouble) and a servant to clean and wait at table, but he was not going to give up his midday dinner, for which he would come home from factory, mill or warehouse, and his accustomed high tea.

The Yorkshire high tea of the nineteenth century, too solid, too heavy for today's tastes, provides us with excellent recipes for traditional breads and tea cakes, scones, plain cakes and puddings, and savoury cheese and egg dishes. A really good high tea for six people would probably have been served on the dining-room table at some time between five and six-thirty and would have been expected to include some form of hot dish such as eggs and bacon, fish pie, smoked haddock or fried fish; either hot scones, hot buttered toast, hot tea cakes, Sally Lunns, muffins or crumpets; thin white and brown bread and butter; a large fruit cake; an iced cake; and a cold sweet such as jelly, blancmange or trifle. A plate of sandwiches might have replaced the bread and butter and, in summer, potted meat, potted game, shrimps, sardines or cold ham and perhaps a salad might have replaced the hot dish. A lot of strong tea would have been drunk.

Today, a Yorkshire high tea is not quite so lavish or so overwhelming, but it usually leaves no appetite for the sandwiches that may be offered with a "night cap" at about ten o'clock.

Yorkshire high tea on the scale described seems grotesque to us today, but it is nothing compared with the Game Dinner for 50 persons proposed by Mrs Beeton in 1861, and given here to show the standards expected in the prosperous north of England in the second half of the nineteenth century.

First course:
Hare Soup. Soup à la Reine. Purée of Grouse. Pheasant Soup.

Second course:
Larded pheasants. Leveret, stuffed and larded. Grouse. Larded Partridges. Hot raised pie of mixed game. Cold pheasant pie with truffles.

Entrées:
Fillets of hare. Partridges with cabbage. Curried rabbit. Fillet of pheasant and truffles. Game pudding. Lark pudding.

Third course:
Pintails. Quails. Teal. Woodcock. Snipe. Widgeon. Ortolans. Golden plover. Wild duck.

Sweets and removes:
Nesselrode pudding. Dantzic Jelly. Charlotte Russe. Plum pudding.
Maids of Honour. Gâteau Génoise Glacé. Compôte of Apples.
Apricot Tart. Vol au vent of Pears.

After all this there was an elaborate dessert of fresh and dried fruits, nuts and ice-creams.

Taken separately, many of the dishes are superlative and well within our powers. In most households, however, mushrooms (always available today as they were not in early times) must be substituted for truffles and some of the dishes cannot therefore have their original exquisite flavour, although they will still be outstanding. Recipes for these and for many other fine, traditional dishes of the north of England follow.

Oxtail Soup

Serves 4

1 oxtail, cut into joints
$\frac{3}{4}$ stick (90 g) butter
2 onions, sliced
2 turnips, peeled and diced
2 carrots, peeled and diced
3 sticks celery, cut into $\frac{1}{2}$ inch
 (1 cm) pieces
4 to 5 cloves
$\frac{1}{2}$ teaspoon grated nutmeg
Juice of $\frac{1}{2}$ lemon
2 tablespoons flour
$\frac{5}{8}$ cup (1.5 dl) sherry, if
 liked
Salt and pepper

Melt half the butter in a frying-pan and fry the oxtail. As the pieces brown, lift them out and put them in a large saucepan. Fry the vegetables in the same butter and add them to the meat. Add the cloves, nutmeg, salt and pepper. Fill up with water (you will need about 2 quarts/1.8 litres), add the lemon juice and bring to the boil. Skim the froth, then cover closely and simmer for 4 hours.

When the oxtail is cooked, melt the remaining butter in another saucepan and stir in the flour. Allow the roux to brown slightly but do not let it burn. Stir the boiling broth from the oxtail into the roux a little at a time, pouring it through a strainer.

Lift out the meat and separate the meat from the bones. Discard the bones and put the meat back into the pan. Pour the thickened stock back on to the meat and vegetables and add the sherry, if used. Serve the soup very hot.

Cream of Barley Soup

Serves 4

$3\frac{1}{2}$ tablespoons (60 g) pearl
 barley
2 tablespoons (30 g) butter
1 small onion, cut in pieces
1 small carrot, cut in pieces
1 stick celery, cut in pieces
1 quart (9 dl) chicken stock
 (stock cube will do, but home-
 made is better)
$\frac{1}{2}$ teaspoon grated nutmeg
2 egg yolks
$\frac{5}{8}$ cup (1.5 dl) single cream
Salt and pepper
Chopped parsley
3 slices bread, cut in $\frac{1}{2}$ inch
 (1 cm) squares and fried

A soup deriving directly from the early pottages served at several Northumbrian and Cumbrian farmhouses. This recipe comes from Carlisle, in the neighbourhood of Hadrian's Wall.

Wash the barley, put it into cold water and bring to the boil. Drain and set aside.

Melt the butter in a heavy saucepan and lightly fry the vegetables. Add the barley and the stock and stir. Simmer, covered, for 2 hours, stirring occasionally. Strain the soup. Season with nutmeg, salt and pepper and thicken by stirring in the beaten egg yolks and the cream. Do not allow the soup to boil again.

Sprinkle the top of the soup with the parsley and serve the little squares of hot fried bread separately.

Leek Pie

1 lb ($\frac{1}{2}$ kg) leeks, cleaned and
  cut into 1 inch (2.5 cm) pieces
$\frac{3}{4}$ lb (360 g) short pastry
$\frac{1}{2}$ lb (240 g) home-cooked ham or
  fried gammon slices, cut into $\frac{1}{2}$
  inch (1 cm) pieces
3 eggs
$\frac{5}{8}$ cup (1.5 dl) milk
White pepper

A recipe traditional all over the north-west of
England. The leeks should set in a creamy custard,
delicious with the crisp pastry.

Plunge the leeks into boiling salted water and
simmer for 5 minutes. Drain and allow to cool for
10 minutes.
  Line a flan tin with the pastry rolled out to about
$\frac{1}{8}$ inch (0.25 cm) thick. Roll out and reserve a thinner
circle for the lid.
  Cover the bottom of the flan with the ham or
gammon pieces. Beat the eggs (reserve a little for
glazing the pastry). Gradually beat in the milk and a
pinch of white pepper. Do not add salt as the ham
will salt the whole dish. Pour the mixture over the
ham and lay the cooled leeks in it. Put on the pastry
lid and seal carefully. Brush over with the reserved
egg and bake at 350°F (180°C, Gas Mark 4) for
30 minutes. If the pastry becomes too brown, cover
lightly with foil.

Fried Scallops with Bacon

12 scallops
$\frac{3}{4}$ cup (120 g) fresh fine white
  breadcrumbs
2 eggs
Fat for deep frying
8 slices lean bacon
Chopped parsley
Freshly ground black pepper

A traditional dish for high tea on the Yorkshire
coast, it is best served accompanied by thin slices of
brown bread and butter.

Have the scallops removed from the shells and
separate the coral from the white. Dip each portion
of both first in breadcrumbs, then in beaten egg
seasoned with a little pepper, and then in
breadcrumbs again. Fry the scallops in a basket in
very hot fat, about 400°F (200°C), for 3 to 4 minutes.
  Fry the bacon separately in a frying-pan. Drain the
scallops and serve at once sprinkled with the parsley
and accompanied by the crisply fried bacon.

Northumbrian Pickled Salmon

2 lb (1 kg) middle cut of salmon
1 teaspoon salt
$\frac{5}{8}$ cup (1.5 dl) dry white wine
6 cloves
12 peppercorns
$\frac{1}{2}$ teaspoon mace
$\frac{1}{2}$ teaspoon ground ginger or
  1 teaspoon chopped fresh root
  ginger
1 tablespoon currants
1 tablespoon finely chopped
  parsley

A very old feast-day recipe. The salmon is served hot
and is pickled to give it flavour, not to preserve it;
today we would call it marinated.
  The marinade was probably served as a sauce
originally, but may be a little too sharp for some
tastes today. Hollandaise sauce may be preferred.

Put the salmon in a saucepan with enough cold
water just to cover the fish. Add the salt and bring
gently to the boil. Skim off any froth and simmer,
covered, for 30 minutes.
  Lift out the salmon, drain it well and put it into a
deep dish. Put the water in which the salmon was
cooked into a bowl and while it is still hot mix in all
the other ingredients except the parsley.
  When the salmon is cool, stir the marinade and
pour it over the fish. Leave it for a day or overnight,
spooning the liquid over the fish from time to time.

Thirty minutes before the salmon is to be served, heat it very gently in the marinade and simmer for 15 minutes until it is heated through. Lift the fish on to a hot dish, sprinkle with the parsley and spoon the currants over it for decoration and flavour.

Skate with Two Sauces

Serves 4

2 lb (1 kg) skate, trimmed and
  trimmings reserved
1 onion, quartered
1 carrot, cut in two
Bunch of parsley, thyme and
  tarragon (if available)
Salt

Mustard sauce:

2 teaspoons dry English
  mustard
$\frac{1}{4}$ teaspoon turmeric
$\frac{3}{4}$ stick (90 g) softened butter

Anchovy sauce:

4 anchovy fillets
$\frac{3}{4}$ stick (90 g) softened butter
$\frac{1}{2}$ teaspoon anchovy essence
Pinch of white pepper
Squeeze of lemon juice

This recipe is given in a Yorkshire manuscript of the eighteenth century. Mrs Glasse in *The Art of Cookery Made Plain and Easy* (1747) gives much the same recipe, which she calls "*To crimp skate*". The dish is interesting because variations of the two sauces, which are really seasoned and flavoured butters, are described both by Apicius and in several medieval manuscripts. The sauces should be served in two small bowls or dishes for each guest, as was the custom in medieval times. Cod, turbot or halibut fillets are all very good served in this way.

Cut the fish into strips about 1 inch (2.5 cm) wide and 4 to 6 inches (10 to 15 cm) in length.
  Boil the vegetables, herbs, salt and fish trimmings in 5 cups (1.2 litres) of water for 30 minutes. Strain and reserve the liquor, discarding the fish trimmings, vegetables and herbs. Bring the liquor to the boil again and carefully lower the pieces of fish into it. Simmer gently for 5 minutes and lift out with a perforated fish slice. Serve immediately with the sauces. '

To make the mustard sauce, work the mustard and turmeric into the butter and beat to a soft paste.

To make the anchovy sauce, pound and mash the anchovy fillets and then beat them into the butter with all the other ingredients.

Puffs of Chicken

Serves 4

4 chicken breasts, skinned
1 lb ($\frac{1}{2}$ kg) puff pastry
2 teaspoons rosemary
1 teaspoon freshly ground
  black pepper
1 teaspoon salt
Juice of $\frac{1}{2}$ lemon
2 tablespoons dry white wine
Beaten egg, for glazing

A nineteenth-century dish from a great Northumbrian house. These puffs should be served with a border of small heaps of three different vegetables: diced carrots, peas, french beans, sweetcorn or asparagus tips, for example.

Only the fleshy part (the "supreme") should be used from each chicken breast. Cut this free of the bones; the trimmings can be used for stock.
  Roll out the pastry and allow to rest for 10 minutes. Mix the rosemary, pepper and salt and rub over each supreme on both sides.
  Cut the pastry into 4 large squares. Lay a chicken supreme in the centre of each square. Pour a little lemon juice and wine over each. Fold the pastry to form a neat envelope and seal by pinching the moistened edges together. Brush over with the egg and bake in a hot oven, 425°F (220°C, Gas Mark 7), for 35 minutes. If the pastry is becoming too brown, cover lightly with foil and reduce the heat a little.

Country Captain

6 chicken quarters, 4 wing and
  2 leg, the meat cut uncooked
  from the bone into small
  strips
4 large onions, finely sliced
¾ stick (90 g) butter
1 tablespoon flour
½ teaspoon turmeric
½ teaspoon coriander
½ teaspoon chilli powder
Salt and pepper

After his retirement to the country near Liverpool in the early nineteenth century, a certain captain, who had made many voyages under sail to India and China, would sometimes make a superb chicken dish with his own hands for visiting friends. His name has not come down to us, but his recipe has.

The dish is worth the 10 minutes' stirring, as the flavour and consistency are unique. A chicken gravy can be served separately if it is considered too dry.

Serve with plain boiled rice and green peas.

Fry one-third of the onions in a little of the butter in a very large, heavy pan until lightly browned, then scatter them on to a baking tray and put them into a medium oven, 350°F (180°C, Gas Mark 4), to crisp, being careful to avoid burning them.

Put 2 tablespoons (30 g) of the remaining butter into the pan in which the onions were cooked. Stir in the flour and all the spices and seasoning and make very hot. Put in the chicken pieces and the remaining onion. Stir constantly over low heat, adding more butter from time to time until the chicken and onions are slightly browned and quite tender (about 10 minutes).

Pile the chicken on to a dish and sprinkle the crisp onion over the top.

Hindle Wakes

1 large boiling fowl, about 5 lb
  (2½ kg)
⅝ cup (1.5 dl) wine vinegar
2 tablespoons brown sugar
1 lemon, quartered
Few sprigs of parsley

The stuffing:

1 lb (½ kg) large prunes, soaked
  and stoned
1¾ cups (240 g) fresh fine white
  breadcrumbs
½ cup (60 g) blanched almonds,
  roughly chopped
1 tablespoon finely chopped
  parsley, marjoram, thyme and
  chives, mixed
½ cup (60 g) shredded suet
⅝ cup (1.5 dl) red wine
Salt and pepper

The sauce:

¼ cup (30 g) cornflour
1¼ cups (3 dl) chicken stock,
  cooled and skimmed
Grated zest and juice of
  2 lemons
2 eggs
Salt and pepper

Hen de la Wake or Hen of the Wake – the hen to be eaten during the Fair. This recipe, collected near Wigan in about 1900, is a version of a medieval dish. It is a true feast-day dish, as good to eat as it is colourful to look at with its white meat, black stuffing and yellow and green trimmings. The dish was made the day before the Fair and left ready at home for the returning revellers.

Halve and reserve 6 prunes for decoration. Mix all the other ingredients for the stuffing together and stuff the fowl, both breast and cavity. Sew up the breast flap; draw together and sew the skin at the vent. Place the chicken in a large saucepan of water to which the wine vinegar and brown sugar have been added. Simmer for 3 hours, then allow the chicken to get cold in the stock.

To prepare the sauce, mix the cornflour with the stock. Stir in the grated zest of 1 lemon, the juice of 2 lemons and seasoning. Bring to the boil for 2 minutes. Set aside to cool slightly.

Beat the eggs and stir them into the sauce. Return the sauce to a low heat and beat until thick and creamy. On no account allow the sauce to boil again. Leave to get quite cold.

To serve, put the chicken on a platter, pour the sauce over the top and decorate with the remaining grated lemon zest, lemon quarters, the reserved prunes and sprigs of parsley.

Ham and Egg Pie

1 lb (½ kg) short pastry
¾ lb (360 g) cooked ham or
  gammon, preferably home
  cooked, cut in lean slices
12 eggs plus 1 extra egg yolk
  for gilding the pastry, if liked
Salt and freshly ground black
  pepper

A good, substantial cold luncheon or picnic dish. Ham and Egg Pie is excellent served with a dressed salad of lettuce and tomatoes.

Line a pie dish with the pastry rolled out to about ⅛ inch (0.25 cm) thick. Reserve a piece for the lid.
  Lay one-third of the ham slices on the bottom. Break 6 eggs, one at a time, into a cup and slide each on to the ham, avoiding breaking any yolks. Lightly season the eggs and cover gently with half the remaining ham, being careful not to break the yolks beneath. Slide the remaining eggs on top, season again and cover with the last of the ham. Put on the pastry lid. Brush over with the egg yolk, if liked. Bake in a moderate oven, 350°F (180°C, Gas Mark 4), for 30 minutes.

Mutton Pot Pie

2 lb (1 kg) fillet end of leg of
  lamb
2 lamb's kidneys, skinned,
  cored and cut in quarters
½ lb (240 g) haricot or butter
  beans, soaked overnight
3 slices streaky bacon, finely
  chopped
2 tablespoons (30 g) butter
2 medium onions, peeled and
  sliced
½ lb (240 g) carrots, peeled and
  diced
½ lb (240 g) turnips or parsnips,
  peeled and diced
5 cups (1.2 litres) any good stock
  (may be made up with stock
  cubes)
1 lb (½ kg) suet crust
½ teaspoon thyme
Salt and pepper
Flour

An early Cumbrian recipe still made in many places in the north of England. It is really a form of pottage.
  A large heavy saucepan with straight sides and a lid is required. When serving, it is necessary to cut out one section of crust in order to lift off the remainder. It is intended to be served straight on to plates, but the crust can be lifted and cut into portions and the meat and vegetables poured on to a dish.

Drain the beans and put them in a saucepan with fresh water. Add a little salt, simmer for 1 hour and drain.
  Meanwhile, bone the lamb and cut in ½ inch (1 cm) cubes. Roll the cubes and the kidneys in seasoned flour. Fry the bacon in the butter in a saucepan. When it begins to crisp, put in the lamb and kidneys and shake well. Roll the onions, carrots and other root vegetables in seasoned flour, add them to the pan and continue frying for 5 minutes with the lid on, shaking well from time to time.
  Remove the pan from the heat and pour in the stock, which should almost cover the meat and vegetables. Add the beans and the thyme and season rather highly. Bring to the boil and allow to simmer while you roll out the suet crust to about 1¼ inches (3 cm) thick and exactly the size of the pan. Mark out the circle to be cut with the pan lid. Roll any crust that is left into very small dumplings, flour them well and drop them in the pan, pushing them down into the stock. Put on the suet crust, which should rest on the meat and vegetables and should not come quite to the top of the pan, so that it has room to rise when the lid has been replaced, and continue simmering.
  After 1 hour the pot pie should be ready. When the lid is lifted the crust will be well risen, fluffy, and flavoured by the stew.

Mutton Pies

1 lb (½ kg) short pastry
*1 lb (½ kg) mutton or lamb from
 the fillet end of the leg, cut
 into very small dice*
2 onions, very finely chopped
*3 tablespoons finely chopped
 parsley*
*1¼ cups (3 dl) good brown
 gravy, with 1 tablespoon
 mushroom ketchup added*
1 egg yolk
Salt and pepper

A Cumbrian recipe which is much the same as that used for the mutton pies that were a favourite dish of King George V.

Roll out the pastry ⅛ inch (0.25 cm) thick and line individual soufflé dishes or deep patty pans with it. Reserve enough pastry to cut a lid for each.

Mix the onions and 2 tablespoons of the parsley into the meat, season well and fill each little pie. Pour a little gravy into each, put on the lids and crimp the edges together. Brush the pastry with the beaten egg yolk. Make a small hole or slit in the top of each pie.

Stand the pies on a baking tray and bake at 400°F (200°C, Gas Mark 6) for 20 minutes, then reduce the heat to 300°F (160°C, Gas Mark 2) and bake for a further 40 minutes. If the pastry seems to be browning too much, cover with foil.

Lift the pies from their dishes, sprinkle with the remaining chopped parsley and serve.

Lancashire Hot Pot

*8 lamb chops from the best end
 of neck*
¾ stick (90 g) butter
*A bunch of herbs including
 parsley, thyme, a sprig of sage
 and a bay leaf*
8 medium onions, chopped
*8 carrots, peeled and sliced in
 rounds*
*2 lb (1 kg) potatoes, peeled and
 thickly sliced*
⅜ cup (45 g) flour
2 teaspoons brown sugar
Salt and pepper

One of the best-known traditional dishes of northern England, Lancashire Hot Pot has been made all over the country since the nineteenth century, although sometimes it bears little relation to the original dish. It has always been made with chops from the best end of the neck of mutton or lamb. If beef or pork is used it is not a Lancashire Hot Pot, no matter what the cook or menu may state.

The recipe that follows is very good. An oyster for each person was sometimes put under the potato layer, or sometimes, in their season, mushrooms. You will require a large, deep casserole with a lid (a hot pot) for this dish.

Brown the chops on both sides in about two-thirds of the butter. Put the remaining butter in the bottom of the casserole in a lump, with the bunch of herbs resting on it. Stand the browned chops on their heads – that is, thick ends downwards – on the butter and herbs. The ends of the bones should stand just below the top of the pot. Brown the onions and carrots in the butter remaining in the frying-pan and pack among the chops.

Stir the flour into the fat remaining in the frying-pan to make a roux. Stir in 3¾ cups (9 dl) of water and bring to the boil. Season well, add the sugar and pour into the casserole – the liquid should come almost to the top of the chop bones.

Arrange the potato slices over the bone ends and resting on the other vegetables. The slices should overlap like roof slates. Sprinkle with a little salt and pepper. Cover the casserole and put it in a medium oven, 350°F (180°C, Gas Mark 4), for 2 hrs. Raise the oven setting to 400°F (200°C, Gas Mark 6) and take the lid off the casserole for 15 minutes, so that the potatoes may brown.

Rum Roast

*3 lb (1½ kg) best end neck of
 lamb, left in one piece but
 well chined by the butcher*
*2 tablespoons (30 g) butter or
 cooking fat*
*2 lb (1 kg) onions, peeled and
 cut in rings*
*6 sheep's kidneys, skinned,
 cored and cut in halves*
⅝ cup (1.5 dl) rum or brandy
⅝ cup (1.5 dl) stock or water
Flour
*Salt and freshly ground black
 pepper*

This was a dish for the sailor's return: it was served
in several seaport inns in the nineteenth century and
recipes are given in more than one cookery book. It
makes a good dinner party dish. The rum can well be
replaced by brandy. Traditionally potatoes baked in
their jackets were served with this rich dish.

Rub the skin side of the lamb with seasoned flour.
Put the butter or cooking fat into a large baking tin.
Set the joint in it and roast in a hot oven, 400°F
(200°C, Gas Mark 6), for 30 minutes.
 Remove the baking tin from the oven and put the
onions all round the meat, spooning fat over them.
Put the tin back in the oven to continue roasting for
a further 20 minutes.
 Take out of the oven again and turn and stir the
onions. Lift up the lamb and slip the kidneys under
the joint. Roast for 20 minutes more.
 Take out and place the lamb on a flat serving dish
with the onions, which should be soft and
transparent and just turning brown, all around it.
Put the kidneys on the onions. Pour half the rum or
brandy over the meat and keep hot while you make
the gravy.
 Pour off all but 1 tablespoon of fat and juices from
the baking tin. Stir in 2 teaspoons of flour. Stir in
the remaining rum or brandy and slowly add the
stock or water stirring until you have a smooth light
brown gravy. Season rather highly with salt and
black pepper and serve in a gravy boat.

Roast Lamb the Second Time

1 large leg cooked cold lamb
*2⅝ cups (¾ kg) mashed potato,
 highly seasoned and allowed
 to cool*
Seasoned flour
Salt and pepper
*Dripping from the first
 roasting, and butter or
 margarine if there is not
 enough dripping*
Gravy and mint sauce

This recipe came from a farm in the Yorkshire Dales.
It is still made in many North Country houses and
has been made in my originally Cornish family for
three generations. When a roast leg of lamb is
served, the family know that they will see it again
and that it will be even better than at its first
serving. At the original roasting, make extra gravy
and mint sauce.

It is best to roast the lamb for the first serving so
that it is still pink near the bone, and to carve it in
the correct way, so that the slices leave a large bite
out of the middle, exposing the bone at the bottom.
 For the second serving, rub salt and freshly ground
black pepper into the carved surface. Press all the
potato into the hollow and mould it a little over the
uncut surface, so that the leg appears complete.
 Dredge the leg with a little seasoned flour. Dot with
dripping (or with butter or margarine if there is not
enough dripping). Put at least 4 tablespoons of
dripping into a baking tin and place the lamb on top.
Bake at 400°F (200°C, Gas Mark 6), for 1 hour.
 To serve, lift off the beautifully browned potato and
carve the meat as usual. The lamb will be as moist
and have as much flavour as when it was first cooked
and the potato will be particularly delicious. Serve
with mint sauce and gravy.

Alnwick Pot Roast

$2\frac{1}{2}$ lb ($1\frac{1}{4}$ kg) haunch of venison
  or 3 lb ($1\frac{1}{2}$ kg) fillet end of a
  leg of lamb
2 onions, one stuck with
  6 cloves and the other finely
  chopped
2 tablespoons seasoned flour
$\frac{1}{2}$ stick (60 g) butter
$\frac{1}{2}$ lb (240 g) dried peas, soaked
  overnight
2 lb (1 kg) new potatoes or
  whole small peeled potatoes
Lemon juice
Salt

The marinade:

1 teaspoon celery salt
4 dried bay leaves, crushed
1 teaspoon dried rosemary
1 teaspoon dried thyme
12 black peppercorns
1 teaspoon salt
2 cups (4.5 dl) red wine
2 tablespoons honey

Alnwick Castle was the main seat of the Percy family, the Earls (and, later, Dukes) of Northumberland. The household accounts of two of their other castles are quoted earlier. Alnwick was a border fortress held by the Percys from 1309. This recipe for venison comes from an Alnwick manuscript and was almost certainly served at the castle. In the household book of the fifth Earl, written at Wresil, another of his castles, a count of all his deer in Northumberland, Yorkshire and Cumberland is recorded, the total being 5,571, and copies of warrants for their culling for his own table are also recorded.

In this recipe the venison is marinated overnight in honey and wine with herbs. In an early version it is suggested that mead can be used instead of honey and wine, if preferred, in which case just replace the wine, water and honey in the recipe with $1\frac{1}{4}$ cups (3 dl) mead, and $\frac{5}{8}$ cup (1.5 dl) each of wine, vinegar and water. The dish is thickened, like many early pottages, with dried peas. In later versions, potatoes are added during the cooking. This dish is extremely good made with lamb if this is preferred to venison. Serve with red-currant, rowan or crab-apple jelly.

Mix all the ingredients for the marinade together with $1\frac{1}{4}$ cups (3 dl) of water and bring to the boil in a large saucepan. Put the meat in a mixing bowl, pour the hot marinade over, add the onion stuck with cloves and leave all night.

Next day, lift out the meat, reserving the marinade. Dry the meat with kitchen paper and rub it all over with the seasoned flour. Fry the meat in the butter until slightly browned on all sides. Put the joint in a deep casserole and add the peas, the whole onion with cloves and the chopped onion. Pour in the marinade. Cover closely, bring to the boil, then simmer in a low oven, 300°F (160°C, Gas Mark 2), for $1\frac{1}{2}$ hours.

Check the seasoning and if the gravy is too sweet, add salt and a little lemon juice. Drop in the potatoes and cook for a further 30 minutes or until the meat is tender, the peas almost mushy and the potatoes cooked.

Lift the meat on to a large flat dish. Put the potatoes around it and some of the peas in gravy. Discard the whole onion and serve the remaining peas and gravy in a sauceboat with a ladle.

Shepherd's Pie

1½ lb (¾ kg) cooked lamb or
mutton, trimmed of all fat
and gristle
1½ lb (¾ kg) potatoes, peeled and
cut in halves
½ stick (60 g) butter plus a little
extra
¼ cup (30 g) flour
⅝ cup (1.5 dl) milk plus a little
extra
1¼ cups (3 dl) good onion-
flavoured meat stock
Salt and pepper

This recipe comes originally from the sheep farms of
Cumbria where, as in other sheep farming areas,
rather tough mutton had to be made palatable. The
shepherd's wife chopped the cold, cooked mutton and
beat it in a mortar. With a thickened stock and
potato on top, it was delicious and very filling. It
became a standard dish, made much easier with the
advent of the mincer.

Shepherd's Pie may be prepared the day before and
given its final cooking 30 minutes before serving. It
freezes well.

Mince the meat. Boil the potatoes until tender. Melt
3 tablespoons (45 g) of the butter in a saucepan and
stir in the flour. Add the milk and meat stock slowly,
stirring all the time. When the sauce is smooth,
fairly thick and just on the boil, stir in the minced
meat. Stir over very low heat for 3 minutes. Season
to taste and pour into a shallow, buttered ovenproof
dish and leave to get cold.

Meanwhile, mash the potatoes. Season with salt and
pepper, stir in the rest of the butter and a little milk
and whisk until smooth.

When the meat is cold, spread the potato at least
1 inch (2.5 cm) thick over the top and mark like a
ploughed field with a fork. Dot with a little butter
and cook in a 350°F (180°C, Gas Mark 4) oven for
40 minutes, by which time the top should be golden
brown.

Hot Pork Pie

6 pork loin chops
½ stick (60 g) butter
2 large onions, finely sliced
¾ lb (360 g) cooking apples,
peeled, cored and cut into 1
inch (2.5 cm) slices
1¼ cups (3 dl) dry white wine
½ lb (240 g) short pastry
Beaten egg, for gilding the
pastry
½ teaspoon ground nutmeg
Salt and pepper

An eighteenth-century recipe from Chester. This pie
is very different from most of those we make today. It
is exceptionally good, but it must be served as
follows: cut a triangle from the crust and lay it
upside down on the uncut part. Cut another triangle
and lay it right way up on one side of the first plate.
Lift out a chop and place beside the pastry. Take out
2 good tablespoons of apple, onion and gravy and put
over the chop, avoiding the pastry. Creamed potatoes
and peas or cabbage are good with this dish.

Trim all fat from the chops and rub a little salt,
pepper and nutmeg into each. Butter a pie dish and
lay 3 of the chops overlapping in the bottom. Put the
onions over them and the apples over the onions.
Lay the remaining pork chops on top, dot with dabs
of the remaining butter and pour in the wine.

Roll out the crust to at least ⅛ inch (0.25 cm) thick.
Cut a strip to go round the rim of the dish, and press
the covering crust well over it so that the edges are
completely sealed. Brush over with the beaten egg
and cut two 1-inch (2.5 cm) slits in the centre.

Bake in the centre of a hot oven, 400°F (200°C, Gas
Mark 6), for 30 minutes. Then reduce the
temperature to 300°F (160°C, Gas Mark 2) and bake
for a further 40 minutes. If the pastry is becoming
too brown, lay a piece of foil lightly over it.

Pot Pie

1½ lb (¾ kg) lean pork, from top
of hand or leg
2 pig's kidneys
4 slices streaky bacon
1 lb (½ kg) suet crust
2 tablespoons seasoned flour
½ lb (240 g) mushrooms, sliced
(these were only added when
in season)
2 cups (4.5 dl) stock (stock cube
will do)
Butter
Salt and pepper

This recipe is from Durham. It is really a steamed meat pudding but is always known locally as "Pot Pie", although it is entirely different from Mutton Pot Pie (see page 69). It was a dish for the day after a pig had been killed.

Remove all skin and fat from the pork and cut the meat into ½ inch (1 cm) cubes. Skin and core the kidneys and cut in the same way. Cut each bacon slice into 6 pieces.

Grease a pudding bowl with butter and line with the suet crust about ¼ inch (0.5 cm) thick, reserving a piece for the lid.

Mix all the meats together and roll them in the seasoned flour. Put the meat into the pudding bowl, add the mushrooms and fill up almost to the top of the meat with the stock. Dampen the edge of the pastry, cover with the lid and press firmly to seal. Cover the top with foil, turning it in over the edge of the bowl. Put a plate or saucer on top of the foil and stand the bowl in a large saucepan. Add water to come halfway up the sides of the bowl.

Bring the water to the boil, cover the pan and steam for 3 hours, adding a little more boiling water from time to time.

Green Pork

4 to 5 lb (2 to 2½ kg) top leg of
pork, scored for crackling
1 tablespoon seasoned flour
1½ sticks (180 g) butter or ¾ cup
dripping
Potatoes for roasting
12 to 16 green dumplings (see
page 75)
Peas, cabbage or spinach
Gravy
Gooseberry or apple sauce

The forcemeat:

2 cups (240 g) fine white fresh
breadcrumbs
1 cup (120 g) shredded suet
1 tablespoon finely chopped
fresh sage (dried will do but
it does not help the colour)
1 teaspoon dried oregano
4 tablespoons finely chopped
fresh parsley
Salt and pepper
1 egg
A little milk, if required

This is a farmhouse recipe from Derbyshire. Mrs S. Cullins kept a kind of recipe commonplace book in the early nineteenth century. No date is given, but the handwriting dates it. She says that her mother used sometimes to give them "a green dinner" consisting of a leg of pork with green stuffing, green dumplings, peas, cabbage, spinach and roast potatoes sprinkled with parsley. There was also "a red dinner" but she does not describe it. It seems likely that it would have been boiled salt beef with carrots and red cabbage cooked separately. This is interesting because the particular pleasure in the colour of food goes back to medieval times.

Slash the pork in 4 of the scores which the butcher has made for crackling, to a depth of 2 to 3 inches (5 to 8 cm). Additionally, cut just beneath the skin through the thin layer of fat on top of the meat to lift a flap about 3 inches (8 cm) long on top of the joint.

Make the forcemeat by mixing the breadcrumbs, suet, sage, oregano, half the parsley, ½ teaspoon of salt and a good pinch of black pepper. Break the egg into the mixture and stir and beat well. If the mixture is too dry to amalgamate, add a little milk.

Pull the cuts in the meat well open and stuff as much forcemeat as possible inside. Spread all the remaining forcemeat in the opening and between meat and skin.

Rub the whole joint with the seasoned flour. Put the meat in a baking tin with the butter or dripping and plenty of potatoes. Put the baking tin in a hot oven,

400°F (200°C, Gas Mark 6). After 1 hour baste the meat and potatoes. If the crackling is becoming dark, reduce the heat to 350°F (180°C, Gas Mark 4). Bake for 1 more hour.

Meanwhile, prepare and cook the dumplings and the peas, cabbage or spinach.

Remove the joint to a large dish and surround with the dumplings. Put the potatoes in a separate dish and sprinkle thickly with the remaining parsley. Put the peas, cabbage or spinach in another dish. Serve with a good gravy and the gooseberry or apple sauce.

Green Dumplings

Makes 12 dumplings

$\frac{3}{4}$ cup (90 g) shredded suet
1 cup (120 g) flour
2 tablespoons very finely chopped parsley
1 tablespoon finely chopped thyme, sage, marjoram, chives and tarragon (not mint)
$\frac{1}{4}$ lb (120 g) cooked spinach (or thawed frozen spinach)
$\frac{1}{2}$ teaspoon salt
$\frac{1}{4}$ teaspoon freshly ground black pepper

These small, round dumplings were boiled, served in a pottage or with a joint or poultry on North Country farms and cottages.

Stir the suet into the flour with the herbs, salt and pepper. Press about 6 tablespoons of juice from the cooked spinach (or pour off the water from frozen spinach and then press it well). Stir the green liquid into the flour mixture to make a stiff dough and knead it a little. Divide the dough to make walnut-sized balls. Set aside in a cool place.

Ten minutes before the dumplings are to be eaten, have about 5 cups (1.2 litres) of salted water boiling in a large saucepan. Drop the dumplings in and boil briskly (but not so hard that they will break up). Do not let the water go off the boil. Lift the little green balls out with a perforated spoon.

Veal and Oysters

Serves 4

4 pieces veal fillet, each 3 inches (8 cm) long, 2½ inches (6 cm) wide and ½ inch (1 cm) thick
12 oysters, clams or finely sliced mushrooms
1 egg, well beaten
1 teaspoon ground mace
$\frac{1}{4}$ cup (60 g) fresh fine white breadcrumbs
Butter or fat for frying
4 lemon slices
1¼ cups (3 dl) good brown gravy, into which 1 teaspoon of red-currant jelly has been stirred
Salt and pepper

The batter:

1 cup (120 g) self-raising flour
Pinch of salt
1 egg
2 tablespoons (30 g) butter, melted
$\frac{5}{8}$ cup (1.5 dl) milk

A Dickensian dish for which there are many recipes. This one comes from North Yorkshire. Fresh oysters are difficult to obtain and very expensive, but tinned oysters or clams are cheaper and excellent. Finely sliced mushrooms make a very good and easy variation, although the flavour is, of course, quite different.

First make the batter. Mix the flour and salt in a large bowl. Add the egg and beat the mixture until smooth. Beat in the butter and continue to beat while slowly adding the milk. Beat until quite smooth and covered with air bubbles.

Score each veal fillet across twice with a sharp knife and push the oysters, clams or mushrooms into the slits. Brush the meat all over with the egg and season with mace, salt and pepper. Sprinkle with the breadcrumbs and press them down a little on to the meat.

Dip the fillets carefully in the batter and fry gently for about 5 minutes on each side so that the veal is cooked through inside the batter, which should be golden brown. Garnish each veal fillet with a slice of lemon and serve the gravy separately.

Spiced Beef

Skirt of beef, about 8 lb (4 kg)
1 lb (½ kg) salt
2 teaspoons black pepper
1 teaspoon ground cloves
2 teaspoons ground mace
1 teaspoon dried thyme
1 teaspoon cayenne pepper
1 teaspoon paprika
2 lb (1 kg) carrots, scraped and
  sliced
2 lb (1 kg) onions, peeled and
  quartered
1 head celery, cut in 2 inch
  (5 cm) lengths
1½ lb (¾ kg) leeks, cut into
  2 inch (5 cm) lengths
Dumplings (see page 53) or ½ lb
  (240 g) gherkins

Although this recipe comes from Yorkshire, beef was cooked in this manner all over England from the Middle Ages onwards. In earlier centuries the beef would have been put into brine to preserve it through the winter, so extra salting would not have been required.

Buy the beef two or three days before the dish is to be served. It is essential to have a very large cooking pot with a lid and a large meat dish for serving.

The beef may be served hot or cold; if it is to be served hot, dumplings and vegetables cooked in the stock should be served with it. If it is to be served cold, it should be glazed with its own reduced stock and garnished with gherkins.

Ask your butcher to bone and trim the beef and to give you the bones and trimmings. Lay the beef out flat, skin side down. Rub in most of the salt, then sprinkle a snow of the remaining salt over the meat and lay it with the bones and trimmings in a dish. Leave in a cool place overnight.

The next day, drain off all the liquid and wipe the meat, removing all the salt that has not penetrated. Mix together all the herbs and spices and rub them into the meat, particularly into the slashes where the bones were removed. Roll the meat up tightly and tie with string in 3 or 4 places.

Put the reserved bones and trimmings into a very large, heavy pan. Place the beef on top, pour in cold, unsalted water to cover and bring to the boil slowly. Remove the scum, cover the pan and simmer gently for 1½ hours.

To cook the dumplings: if there is room, they can be put into the stock at the time the leeks are added and removed before the meat is lifted out, to avoid breaking them. They should be arranged on the vegetables around the meat. If the pan is not big enough to hold them, they can be steamed separately.

Remove and discard the bones and trimmings. Add all the vegetables except the leeks. Bring to the boil again and simmer for another 1½ hours. Add the leeks and cook for a further 25 minutes.

To serve hot, lift out the meat on to a very large flat dish. Lift out the vegetables with a perforated spoon and put them around the meat. Keep hot in the oven while you strain, taste and season the clear golden stock. Pour a little of the stock over the meat and serve some separately. Any stock that is left over will make an excellent basis for a soup.

If the beef is to be served cold, remove it from the pan and drain well. Lay it on a board or large dish, place another board over it and put weights on top. Leave the meat to get completely cold.

Meanwhile, strain the stock, return half of it to a clean pan and boil briskly until it reduces to a strong glaze; there should be about 2½ cups (6 dl) of stock left. When the beef is quite cold, remove the string, decorate with sliced gherkins and pour the glaze very gently over, so that the decoration is not disturbed.

Beef in a Fine Sauce

*4 lb (2 kg) good-quality stewing
  steak*
*24 small, whole onions or
  shallots*
*1 quart (9 dl) good beef or
  chicken stock*
1 cup red wine
2 tablespoons wine vinegar
1 teaspoon ground cinnamon
½ teaspoon ground cloves
*1 teaspoon freshly ground
  black pepper*
½ teaspoon turmeric
1 teaspoon salt
3 tablespoons (45 g) butter
⅜ cup (45 g) flour

"Brawn en Peverade" was the medieval name for this fairly grand pottage. Brawn at that time meant simply "meat". This pottage is delicious and distinctive; a feast-day dish which has been made in northern England since the twelfth century. The slight sharpness of the sauce was much liked in medieval cookery. It is traditionally served with "sippets" of fried bread and peas, green or dried.

Trim the steak and cut into rather thin pieces about 2 inches (5 cm) square. Lay the meat in a shallow casserole and put the onions on top. Mix all the ingredients except the butter and flour and pour over the beef. Bring to the boil, cover the casserole and put in a moderate oven, 350°F (180°C, Gas Mark 4), for 2 hours.

Remove the casserole from the oven and check that the meat is tender. Pour off all the liquor into a bowl. In a separate saucepan make a roux with the butter and flour. Gradually pour on the cooking liquor, stirring all the time. Allow the sauce to boil gently for 2 to 3 minutes. The sauce should be smooth and thick, tasting rich and spicy and slightly sharp. Pour the sauce over the meat and onions and serve.

Spiced Steaks Dressed with Eggs

*6 rump or fillet steaks, trimmed
  of all fat*
1 stick (120 g) butter
*6 hard-boiled eggs, finely
  chopped*
*2 tablespoons very finely
  chopped parsley*
*3 medium onions, very finely
  chopped and lightly fried in
  butter*
½ teaspoon ground ginger
1 teaspoon turmeric
½ tablespoon flour
⅝ cup (1.5 dl) good stock
3 tablespoons red wine
Salt and pepper

A very good and pretty dish from an eighteenth-century Lancashire notebook.

Lay the steaks on a large flat dish. Melt half the butter and pour it over the steaks, turning them so that both sides are coated. Mix together half the hard-boiled eggs and parsley and all the onions, ginger, turmeric, and salt and pepper to taste. Sprinkle half this mixture thickly over the steaks and press it on to them. Turn the steaks over and repeat with the remaining mixture.

Fry the steaks in the remaining butter, made very hot, for 6 minutes on each side. Remove the steaks carefully to a serving dish and keep hot while you make the sauce.

Stir the flour into the pan juices and add any butter, onion, parsley and spices from the dish in which the steaks were dressed. Stir for 1 minute and then slowly pour in the stock and wine. Bring to the boil, check the seasoning and pour the sauce around (but not over) the steaks.

Scatter the remaining egg and parsley over the steaks and serve immediately.

Raspberry Jelly

3 lb (1½ kg) raspberries, to give
2½ cups (6 dl) juice
1¼ lb (¾ kg) granulated sugar

This jelly, which can be used as soon as it is cold but which will keep for six months, was used in many sweets, but the following Delight of Raspberries is the most unusual. Both recipes come from a Cheshire manuscript of 1600.

Extract the juice from the raspberries, using a juice extractor, blender or sieve, and strain to remove the pips. Stir in the sugar and when it has dissolved bring to the boil. Boil briskly for 7 minutes. Pour while hot into heated pots, jars or small soufflé dishes from which it can be easily turned out. When cold, the jelly will be firmly set. The jars must be sealed while hot unless the jelly is to be used within 3 or 4 days.

Delight of Raspberries

2½ cups (6 dl) milk
⅜ cup (45 g) cornflour
¼ cup (30 g) castor sugar
1¼ cups (3 dl) double cream plus
⅝ cup (1.5 dl) whipped cream
1 to 2 pots raspberry jelly (see
recipe above)
1 oz (30 g) angelica

Mix the cornflour with a little cold milk. Add the sugar to the rest of the milk and bring to the boil. Pour half the boiling milk on to the cornflour paste, stirring well, then pour it back into the pan with the remaining milk. Boil for 3 minutes, holding the pan above the heat to avoid the mixture sticking. Allow the mixture to cool for 10 minutes and then stir in the double cream, beating well. Leave till quite cool and almost set.

Meanwhile, turn out 1 or 2 pots of raspberry jelly and cut in thin slices. Lay 1 slice in the bottom of each individual cocotte dish and 4 half-slices up the sides. Spoon in the blancmange and chill for at least 1 hour, or overnight if more convenient.

Turn out the Delight on to a large flat serving dish. Decorate each sparkling red jelly with a blob of whipped cream and lay thin strips of angelica between the little moulds.

Yorkshire Bilberry Pie

½ lb (240 g) short pastry
4 cups (9 dl) bilberries
¾ cup (180 g) castor sugar
2 large apples, cored, sugared
and baked until soft
1 egg

Bilberries can be picked on the Yorkshire moors and this recipe, which dates from 1867, comes from Haworth, famous as the home of the Brontës.

Roll out two-thirds of the pastry ⅛ inch (0.25 cm) thick and line a round 10 inch (25 cm) flan tin. Roll another thinner circle from the remaining pastry and set aside for the lid.

Mix the bilberries with the sugar and the apple pulp, scraped from skins. Fill the pie and put on the lid, sealing the edges with the beaten egg. Brush over with the rest of the egg. Bake in a hot oven, 450°F (230°C, Gas Mark 8), for 20 minutes, then reduce the heat to 350°F (180°C, Gas Mark 4) and cook for a further 15 minutes. If the pastry is brown enough, put the pie lower in the oven and lay a sheet of foil lightly over it.

Yorkshire Hot Wine Pudding

2 cups (4.5 dl) medium-dry
  sherry
Pinch of cinnamon
Juice of $\frac{1}{2}$ orange
1 teaspoon grated orange rind
$\frac{1}{4}$ lb (120 g) Casino fingers or
  any sponge biscuits, finely
  crumbled or grated
4 eggs
1 teaspoon castor sugar
Pinch of salt
$\frac{3}{8}$ cup (30 g) currants
2 tablespoons (30 g) butter,
  melted and just warm
Double cream, whipped

An early nineteenth-century recipe, very light but hot and alcoholic; much liked by gentlemen to end a good dinner after a day's hunting. It can be made in one large fireproof bowl or in several small soufflé dishes.

Heat the sherry to just below boiling point with the cinnamon, orange juice and rind. Add the sponge biscuits and set aside.
  Beat the eggs with the sugar, salt, currants and butter. Stir well into the sherry mixture and pour into the well-greased bowl or dishes. Cover lightly with foil and stand in a baking tin containing about 1 inch (2.5 cm) of water. Bake in a moderate oven, 350°F (180°C, Gas Mark 4), for 15 minutes, if in small dishes, or for 30 minutes if you are using one large dish. The pudding should set and rise and will probably push up the foil. Serve immediately, with whipped cream.

Yorkshire Teacakes

1 lb ($\frac{1}{2}$ kg) strong flour
$\frac{1}{2}$ stick (60 g) butter
Two $\frac{1}{4}$ oz packets (15 g) dried
  yeast
$\frac{5}{8}$ cup (1.5 dl) warm milk
1 well-beaten egg
1 teaspoon salt
2 teaspoons sugar

Judging by early recipes, these teacakes are very like the manchet loaves of the Middle Ages. One teacake about five inches (13 cm) across is always served to each person.

Warm a large mixing bowl. Rub the butter into the flour. Mix the yeast with the warm milk. Make a well in the flour mixture and pour the yeast and milk into it. Brush a little flour from the sides of the bowl over the pool of yeast. Cover the bowl with a tea towel and leave to stand in a warm place; that is, before a fire, in an airing cupboard or in the warming drawer of the cooker for 40 minutes or until the yeast has bubbled through the flour.
  Add the egg, salt and sugar to the flour and yeast mixture. Stir and knead until you have a dough that will leave the bowl clean. Pat the dough into a ball and leave it in the bowl. Cut a cross in the top. Cover the bowl and leave the dough to rise again for 30 minutes. It should double its size. Punch the dough down and knead lightly. Divide the dough into 8 pieces and make these into round, flat cakes. Put them on baking trays, cover with cloths and leave to rise for a further 10 minutes.
  Bake at 350°F (180°C, Gas Mark 4) for 20 minutes. Insert a skewer into the teacakes and if any dough sticks to it, return to the oven for a further 10 minutes.
  Serve hot, split and generously buttered.

Carrot Cake

½ cup (120 g) soft brown sugar
1 stick (120 g) butter or ½ cup
  margarine
5 tablespoons (60 g) raisins
½ lb (240 g) peeled and grated
  carrots
½ teaspoon grated nutmeg
1 teaspoon ground cinnamon
⅓ cup (60 g) finely chopped
  walnuts
2 cups (240 g) self-raising flour
1 teaspoon salt

For several centuries carrot cake has been traditionally served for high tea. It is really a kind of bread, since there are no eggs in it, and can be made in a round cake tin or an oblong loaf tin. The cake should be cut across in thick slices like bread, each slice well buttered. It is delicious hot or cold, and the carrots not only sweeten the dough but keep it moist and give it a rich colour.

Mix together in a saucepan the sugar, butter or margarine, raisins, carrots and spices with 2 tablespoons water. Boil fast for 3 minutes, stirring. Cool until only just warm. Mix the salt and walnuts into the flour and stir into the mixture in the pan. Mix thoroughly to a thick batter; if it seems at all dry, stir in a very little extra water. Put the batter into a well-greased tin and bake in a moderate oven, 350°F (180°C, Gas Mark 4), for 1 hour.
  Allow the cake to cool for 10 minutes before turning it out on to a rack.

Eccles Cakes

1 lb (½ kg) short pastry
⅔ cup (120 g) currants
¼ cup (30 g) finely chopped
  mixed candied peel
¼ cup (60 g) castor sugar
2 tablespoons (30 g) butter
¼ teaspoon grated nutmeg
¼ teaspoon ground allspice

These cakes have been made for the Eccles Wake for hundreds of years. It is said that their first commercial success came when Mrs Raffald, who was to the eighteenth century what Mrs Beeton was to the nineteenth century, gave her own secret recipe to a favourite servant girl as a wedding present. The girl went to live in the town of Eccles and made and sold the cakes so successfully that she made a fortune for herself and her husband.

Put the currants, peel, sugar, butter, nutmeg and allspice into a saucepan and heat gently until the ingredients can be stirred together. Turn the mixture into a bowl and set aside to cool.
  Roll out the pastry to about ¼ inch (0.5 cm) thick and cut into 4 inch (10 cm) rounds. Put 1 tablespoon of filling on each round, gather up the edges and pinch well together. Turn each cake over and press (without rolling) with the rolling pin to flatten; make a small slit in the top crust.
  Place the cakes on a baking sheet and bake in the oven at 400°F (200°C, Gas Mark 6) for 10 to 15 minutes. Sprinkle lightly with castor sugar and cool on a rack.

Boil-in-the-pan Fruit Cake

⅔ cup (120 g) sultanas
⅔ cup (120 g) currants
⅔ cup (120 g) raisins
1 stick (120 g) butter
½ cup (120 g) castor sugar
1½ cups (3 dl) milk
2 eggs, well beaten
2½ cups (30 g) self-raising flour

This way of making a cake was more usual in the nineteenth century than it is today. It has the advantage of making a rather plain mixture seem richer and lighter in texture than if the same ingredients are mixed by creaming or rubbing the fat into the flour.

Line a 7 inch (18 cm) cake tin with buttered greaseproof paper.
  Put the dried fruit, butter, sugar and milk into a saucepan and bring to the boil. Stir gently and simmer for 20 minutes. Remove from the heat and, when cool, stir in the beaten eggs. Sprinkle a little flour on the mixture and stir in. Repeat until all the flour is used. Put the mixture into the cake tin and bake at 350°F (180°C, Gas Mark 4) for 1 hour. Cover the top lightly with foil to prevent over-browning and move the cake to a lower shelf for a further 30 minutes.

Pepper Cake

1½ sticks (180 g) butter or ¾ cup margarine
3 cups (360 g) self-raising flour
½ cup (120 g) soft brown sugar
1 teaspoon ground cloves
1 teaspoon ground ginger
½ teaspoon freshly ground black pepper
3 eggs, well beaten
2 tablespoons brandy
1 cup (360 g) black treacle
¾ cup (120 g) chopped mixed candied peel (use raisins if preferred)

Traditionally served in farmhouses at Christmas, this rich, solid cake was made specially to be given to visitors and carol singers, as well as to the family.

Grease a 9 inch (23 cm) cake tin and line it with greaseproof paper, standing 1 inch (2.5 cm) above the top of the tin.
  Rub the butter into the flour until it has a breadcrumb consistency. Mix in the sugar and all the spices. Beat in the eggs and brandy. Then add the treacle and peel, beating well. The mixture should be dark and fairly slack.
  Pour the mixture into the cake tin and bake at 350°F (180°C, Gas Mark 4) for 1 hour. Test with a skewer. If it does not come out clean, bake for a further 10 minutes.

Lancashire Cheese Scones

1 cup (120 g) Lancashire cheese (Cheddar will do), finely grated
2 cups (240 g) self-raising flour
1 teaspoon salt
¼ teaspoon dry mustard
½ stick (60 g) butter
⅝ cup (1.5 dl) milk

Mix the flour with the salt and mustard. Rub in the butter until the texture resembles breadcrumbs. Mix in the cheese, then stir in enough milk to form a soft dough.
  Roll out the dough ½ inch (1 cm) thick and cut in triangles. Put the scones on a greased tray and bake in a hot oven, 425°F (220°C, Gas Mark 7), for 10 to 15 minutes.

Yorkshire Cheese Muffins

1 egg
⅝ cup (1.5 dl) milk
1 cup (120 g) grated cheese
3 cups (360 g) self-raising flour
¼ teaspoon salt

These are not true muffins, since they are not raised with yeast, but they come under the dictionary definition of muffin, which is, *"a light, flat cake, usually eaten hot with butter"*. They are always known as cheese muffins in the Yorkshire Dales and are sometimes eaten with apple jelly, which goes well with the cheese.

Beat the egg and add the milk and salt. Stir the grated cheese into the flour, make a well in the middle, pour some of the liquid into it and stir. Continue adding the egg and milk (reserve a little for gilding), beating well, until you have a firm, soft dough.
Roll out the dough on a floured board to 1 inch (2.5 cm) thickness and cut into rounds about 2½ to 3 inches (6–8 cm) in diameter. Brush with the reserved egg and milk, put on a floured baking sheet and bake at 400°F (200°C, Gas Mark 6) for 10 minutes. Serve hot, split and well buttered.

Lancashire Spreads

½ lb (240 g) Lancashire cheese (Cheddar will do), finely grated (makes 2 cups)
1 small onion, very finely chopped and lightly fried
4 slices streaky bacon, finely chopped and lightly fried
4 fairly thick slices of white bread, crusts removed
2 tablespoons (30 g) softened butter
Pepper

Spread toasts were a popular Elizabethan dish. The spread was originally served directly on to trenchers, which were made of rather coarse bread and were sometimes eaten and sometimes treated only as plates. In great houses, fine white manchet bread was toasted for the spread and the whole placed on a trencher or a platter.
The earliest spreads were made of chopped veal kidney or sweetbreads mixed with egg yolks, spices, sugar and rosewater. Towards the end of the seventeenth century, savoury toasts were preferred and scrambled or poached eggs, ham, bacon and anchovies were all served, as were various forms of cheese toasts. This one is peculiar to Lancashire.

Work the onion, bacon and pepper into the cheese with the blade of a knife, until they have blended into a paste. If Cheddar cheese is used, a little butter must be added to help the blending. Ten minutes before the toasts are to be served, toast the bread on one side only. Lightly spread the untoasted side with the butter and then with the prepared spread. Place under the grill but not too close to the heat, which should be turned low. Grill for 5 minutes. Serve at once.

The Midlands

Cheshire, Derbyshire, Nottinghamshire, Staffordshire, Salop (Shropshire), Oxfordshire, Gloucestershire, Leicestershire, Warwickshire, Hereford and Worcester, Northamptonshire, Bedfordshire

The Midlands, as the name makes clear, stretch across the middle of England, well to the north of Greater London, taking in Oxfordshire and Gloucestershire to the south and including Leicestershire and West Midlands to the north. Wales separates the Midlands from the sea to the west and East Anglia and Lincolnshire fill the same role to the east. Once described as *"the wide girdle of England in which she carries her industrial wealth"*, the Midlands were the very heart and centre of the Industrial Revolution.

Birmingham became, and remains, the greatest Midlands' manufacturing centre. The city, once in Warwickshire, has now been made into the small county of West Midlands, although in fact its suburbs extend into Staffordshire and Worcestershire.

Metal-working of all kinds has always flourished, from steel and heavy machinery through fine silver and plate to pins and needles. Cotton goods, cheap jewellery, beads and all kinds of knives, scissors and working tools were manufactured both for the English and the export trade. From the beginning of the nineteenth century the city grew and the surrounding countryside and nearby cities shared in the prosperity. In Coventry the motor and motor cycle industries were established and coal was easily available from mines in the north-east of the county.

Transport between Birmingham and London has never been a problem. Merchants and traders, agents and buyers made the journey by coach in the eighteenth century; in the nineteenth century express trains took them to their destination even faster. Today an Inter-city train gets to London in an hour and on the motorway you can get there in two hours.

With so much industry, it is surprising how much of the lovely Warwickshire countryside, with its pastures, orchards and market gardens, remains unspoilt, and how many of its traditions are still followed. Entirely rural in its setting on the river, Stratford-upon-Avon, Shakespeare's birthplace, is one of the most famous small towns in the world and around it lies rich green countryside.

The town of Warwick, in whose streets Shakespeare walked, contains much that has hardly changed since he did so. Lord Leycester Hospital, over by the west gate of the town, was founded by the Earl of Leicester in 1571, when Shakespeare was seven. It was built to house 12 *"poor and impotent"* persons, and is now lived in by disabled ex-servicemen and their wives. The link with Shakespeare, who must many a time have passed the hospital and walked through the gates, is very strong.

Warwick Castle, standing on a great rock above the river, was built for defence by the first Earl of Warwick, who was given his title by William II. The young Shakespeare, a poor commoner, son of a glove-maker, would not have been welcome there, but today all are welcome who can pay the entrance fee, no matter what their estate.

The long range of the Cotswold Hills runs south-west from Warwickshire into Worcestershire, Oxfordshire, Gloucestershire and down into Wiltshire and Somerset in the West Country.

On these limestone hills, sheep have always flourished. The early Cotswold breed of sheep is very large, with long crinkled fleeces, long ears and forelocks over their eyes. The original breed is now preserved only at the Cotswold Farm Park, since many farmers over the years have developed crosses with other breeds, in some cases for better meat, in others for higher fertility. The early sheep were known, with affection and admiration for their hardiness and the wealth they brought, as Cotswold Lions. They were, and remain, the largest sheep in England.

These great sheep, or little long-haired lions, made vast fortunes for merchants and factors in the wool trade. In the Middle Ages enormous quantities of wool were exported, and although sales declined after the taxes imposed in the fourteenth century, the manufacture of cloth increased and weaving became an important cottage industry, particularly in Gloucestershire.

During the Middle Ages many good men, whether they were noble or common, who had made money and continued to make it, repaid their good fortune by building great houses for their families, guildhalls for their towns and churches and monasteries to the greater glory of God. There were great monasteries at Tewkesbury, where the Abbey was founded in the twelfth century, at Evesham, Winchcombe, Hailes and Gloucester. Prinknash Abbey was built for the abbots of Gloucester, but was taken over by the Benedictines some 50 years ago and remains a monastery of this order.

A little to the north of Gloucester is the village of Prestbury, which goes back to Saxon times and began to prosper in the Middle Ages, when it was granted a market every Tuesday and a three-day fair every year. The manor belonged to the Bishop of Hereford, and Prestbury was under Church patronage. The greatest occasion in its history occurred in 1289, when Bishop Swinfield came with a large retinue for his inauguration. He arrived on Tuesday 21 December and fasted on a fish diet until the day of his inauguration and the feast which followed it. The feast seems to have been attended by about 100 distinguished guests, and as many as 200 less distinguished people. The latter would have been seated at the tables at the lower end of the hall and would have been offered plainer food and a more restricted choice of dishes.

The supplies bought in for the feast are recorded as follows: two whole oxen and three separate quarters; two calves; four pigs; two does; 80 head of poultry; a dozen partridges (no doubt all that could be obtained and certainly reserved for the bishop's high table); an unstated number of geese and other birds, large quantities of several qualities of bread and several large whole cheeses. Spices, herbs, pickled walnuts, milk of almonds, sugar and rosewater, artichoke bottoms, "raisins of the sun", currants, butter, cream, breadcrumbs for thickening and pastry for pies and tarts would have been used with all this meat to produce such dishes as pottages, Chickens Endored, Frumenty with Venison, Mawmeny, Leche Royal, Viand Royal, Mortrewe, Pommes dorres, Brawn with Mustard, Leche Lumbard, several large pies, and the elegant "subtlety", which was the centrepiece of each of the usual three courses of a feast.

At this feast, wines and liqueurs were served which had been made by the brethren of the various local abbeys and monasteries. The recipes, exclusive to each abbey, included honey, herbs, flowers and berries, which were added to wines made by the monks from grapes grown in their own vineyards, or sometimes to wine made from dandelions, elderberries or cowslips.

Shearing feasts on the Cotswold farms were as important as harvest festivals, although this was not the case in other parts of the country. Shearing took place in May and June and the traditional dishes of the shearing feast were boiled poultry, served with the first green peas if they were ready, salads, mutton, hams and roast pork, with boiled puddings and sometimes great pies.

North Leach, in Gloucestershire, now only a small Cotswold town admired by visitors but less extravagantly so than Burford or Broadway, was the very centre of trade for wool merchants in the fifteenth century and was very prosperous indeed, as can be seen today in the handsome church and the fine brasses within it, which mark the graves of these wealthy townsmen. An early recipe for a very fine pie of mutton, apples, raisins and spices is recorded as being made in North Leach, but in the eighteenth century it was the men of Burford who had a reputation throughout the Cotswolds for "eating more and paying less" than the people of any other town. This was, in part, because Wychwood Forest stretched almost to their doors and was well stocked with deer, which many considered their right to poach if they were willing to risk the penalties imposed under the game laws. For some reason Burford farm labourers were peculiarly successful and were said to eat as much venison in a week as a London alderman might taste in a year. It was thought that if a royal licence was issued, permitting everyone to hunt freely in the forest on every Whit Sunday, the people of Burford would perhaps be grateful and kill fewer illicit deer. All able-bodied men made full use of this privilege and every family ate venison, pheasants and other birds for a week or more after Whitsun. This week of good eating was generally followed by a few days on the usual meatless diet of the ill-paid labourer, but, for the men of Burford, a few days of this were enough. As darkness fell, faces were blackened with soot and before daylight a deer or two had been skinned, jointed and well hidden. A man shared with his neighbours and so no one gave him away. Life in Burford was back to what it had been before Whit Sunday.

Just to the west of the Cotswold Hills the River Severn rises in Wales and flows out through its estuary into the Bristol Channel, passing through Gloucestershire and Worcestershire, widening below Gloucester until, as it flows by Berkeley, Purton and Sharpness, it is a mile-wide expanse of tidal water broken by sandbanks, shimmering across the flat land on the east, shadowed by hills and forest on the west bank. The lovely and ancient village names are repeated in the sandbanks of the river: Framilode and Framilode Sands, Frampton-on-Severn and Frampton Sands, Lydney and Lydney Sands, Shepperdine and Oldbury and their sands.

The river swarmed with waterbirds, and migrating geese arrived just when the salmon season was over. There were many heronries along the banks and these birds were often sold at Berkeley. Young herons (called heronshewes) were highly esteemed by the gentry and were often served at royal feasts. Wild duck, cormorants and gulls were all caught by those who also fished in the Severn. The birds were skilfully plucked or skinned, seethed in a pot or roasted on a spit. Sinewy and often tasting of fish, they cannot have been good eating, but at least they were a free gift from the river.

Salmon were caught and eaten in the Forest of Dean as they were on the other side of the Severn. They were caught in long-nets and in the wide, shallow lave-nets and with rod and line, and poached with spears. Every cottager and farmer's wife along the river could cook a piece of salmon or a whole fish so that it emerged just as it should be: gently baked, or boiled with thyme and parsley, or cut in slices and fried. Many a fisherman preferred to cook his own fish, and many still do so. Certain connoisseurs preferred the cheek pieces, or "oysters", behind the fish's eye and ate them separately on a piece of hot buttered toast.

The Severn provided an enormous variety of fish in earlier times. In the seventeenth century a certain John Smythe of Nibley compiled a list of the fish caught near Berkeley:

> Sturgeon, porpoise, thornpole [I cannot identify this], a 22-foot Jubertas [young whale], herrings, hogge, seal, swordfish, salmon, wheat trout or fuen, turbot, lamprey, lampern [probably the same as lamprey], shad tweat [the twaite shad, a small bony fish, which comes from the sea to spawn], wray [ray], flounder, sand flooke [which resembles sole], hake, an haddock, a rancote [I cannot identify this], sea tad, a plaice, millet, also mullet, ling, dabbe, yearling, horncake [I cannot identify this], lumfish, a gurnard both red and grey, a whiting, a little crab, the conger, the dorrey [dorey], the huswife, the herring, the sprat, the pilchard, the prawn, the shrimp, the eel, a barue, a cod, a card, an eel part, a mackarall, the sunfish, the fauzan or great fat eel, elvers supposed by some to be the young eel, the base [bass], the sea bream, the halibut.

It is interesting that in the seventeenth century there was some doubt as to whether elvers were baby eels. Such doubt probably arose from the fact that when the elvers hatch they seem to swarm in millions, while larger eels, although frequently caught, are not found in great numbers. Elvers have always been netted in the Severn and are taken in great quantities, particularly just below Gloucester. They can survive for a long time in tanks of river water and used to be taken by barge to other parts of England. Today they are not eaten in this area except by a few of those who live by the river, but there is an export trade to Spain for restocking rivers, and to Japan.

Sturgeon, seal (always counted as a fish until the eighteenth century), thornpole and porpoise were royal fish, for which all over England the lord of the manor (in this case Lord Berkeley) had to pay an agreed sum. John Smythe writes: "*The lord makes no retribution for Whales.*" And when a young whale some 22 feet long was taken to Berkeley Castle on a long dray, pulled by 35 yoke of oxen, those who had brought it from the river received nothing but its meat and the oil, which was considered good medicine for many diseases.

Lord Berkeley owned all the fishing in his manor, but the fisherman also had certain rights. "*The tide floweth,*" said John Smythe, "*three hours and ebbeth 9 hours in each twenty four and of these tides one tide every week is known as the lord's tide and the next tide is called the Parson's tide, for his tithe fish.*" On these days the lord and parson were entitled to all the fish that was caught, although it was not impossible to hide a salmon or two under water and to collect them after dark.

There was also a very ancient custom at Berkeley whereby, at certain seasons, any stranger might fish with a lave-net or a rod and take any fish except the previously mentioned royal fish, shad, fully grown salmon or lampreys.

The stranger's catch was known as "galeable fish" and the lord of the manor had the right to half the value of all of it. The lord, or his agents (known as galors), could either take the fish and pay half the price to the fisherman or refuse the fish and demand half their value instead. The fisherman, however, could avoid the "gale" by running with his fish above the high-tide mark before the galor could "*come, cry or call to him*". If he succeeded, he stuffed grass into each fish's mouth to show that they were free. There were 18 miles of shore belonging to the manor of Berkeley and it was difficult for the keepers to patrol all of it closely; "gale", however, was only allowed at low tide, so it was a long run above the tide mark carrying a netful of fish.

Young whales, 20 to 30 feet long, have appeared from time to time in the Severn, and in the 1880s a great, fully grown whale appeared which gave its name to Whale Wharf, near Littleton. Several sharks, one more than six feet long, have been taken and porpoises were caught quite frequently from the Middle Ages to the eighteenth century. The porpoise was highly considered at Lenten feasts, as its mammalian flesh, like that of the whale, is more like meat than true fish.

The Severn lamprey, once the luxury of English royal tables, is scarcer than in times past. A few fishermen who live by the river still catch and eat them, but they are not bought by fishmongers or served in hotels. Some consider that parts of them are poisonous. Yet Henry I, Henry II and John were all greedy for this strange sucker-fish. Henry III had lampreys sent every year from the Severn to wherever he was holding court. He commanded them at Canterbury, ordering the high sheriff of Gloucester "*to bake for him all the lampreys he can get and send them him by his cook. And that when he shall be nearer Severn, then to send them unbaked so long as they may come sweet, for him and his queen to eat.*"

From medieval times the city of Gloucester was required to send a pie of lampreys every year as part of its dues to the Crown. The fame of these pies reached the ear of Catherine the Great of Russia and she demanded that Severn lampreys should be sent to her. Cooked and sealed with butter into a great pie, the lampreys were dispatched, but it is not recorded whether Catherine preferred them to her native sturgeon and its caviare.

Sturgeon are also caught in the Severn from time to time. Certainly two or three were taken as late as 1942; one of these was ten feet long and weighed 240 pounds. Henry III had made a grant of all sturgeons taken in Berkeley manor to its lord, and a man bringing one to the castle received a bow and arrow or, in later times, a sovereign. The flesh is supposed to taste of the finest chicken and sole combined.

The lords of Berkeley Castle, many times visited by royalty through the centuries, sometimes suffered unexpectedly on these great occasions. When Queen Elizabeth I was on a visit, she killed 27 stags in the park in one day's hunting – far too many for the good of the herd – and she made matters worse by remarking that Lord Berkeley did not have his oaks looked after properly. There is still a herd of both fallow and red deer in the deer park of the castle.

About ten miles from Berkeley is the small town of Thornbury, some miles inland from the Severn, from which it is separated by flat, fertile farmlands, which until the eighteenth century were marshes subject to frequent flooding. The people who lived there suffered from peculiarly violent agues, or in modern terms malaria. Thick on the marshes grew wild asparagus, which was sold in the Bristol markets.

Thornbury Castle was begun early in the sixteenth century by the third Duke of Buckingham, who was executed for high treason in 1521. At his death the castle was unfinished. It was derelict for years until, in 1824, it was bought by Henry Howard and put into some kind of order. It was the home of the Howard family until 1966, when it was sold to Mr Kenneth Bell, who runs a first-class restaurant in the Great Hall and is, at the time of writing, converting the derelict north wing to provide hotel accommodation. The area around Thornbury has, for centuries, produced fine cider and very good cheese. Mr Bell has planted vineyards around the castle which call to mind that grapes were grown and wine made as a matter of course in England in the Middle Ages, when the climate was warmer.

It is of particular interest that the castle provides distinguished hospitality today, because records exist of a very great feast held there on Christmas Day, 1507, in the old manor house and castle, by Edward, Duke of Buckingham. Three hundred guests were invited for dinner and supper. The weather was extremely cold and vast fires were kept burning in the Great Hall and the Old Hall of the manor house, the Great Chamber and the Duchess's Great Chamber in the castle as well as in many subsidiary rooms.

The Duke and some of the guests, invited a few days early, had hunted all the previous week. Quantities of fish had been brought in by Severn fishermen. Four hundred eggs were purchased, apart from those provided by the castle poultry yards. The accounts show that one carcass and seven rounds of beef were bought, as well as nine sheep, four pigs, one and a half calves, four swans, four geese, five sucking pigs, one peacock and a few mallards, teal, widgeon, woodcock and snipe. All the venison, a further large quantity of meat and many more birds would have come from Buckingham's own estates and are, therefore, not mentioned as expenditure. The amount of bread baked was 491 loaves, with three quartern loaves (loaves made from a quarter of a stone of flour) and two manchets (finest wheat bread) in addition. Rhenish and Gascony wine was provided and rum is mentioned. These would almost certainly have been brought up the Severn on barges and then transported on drays or pack-horses to the castle. Whether duty was paid on all this liquor or whether some of it was contraband, with or without the Duke's knowledge, is not, of course, recorded. For the rest there was malmsey wine, ale and cider.

The guests included bailiffs, clerks and some of the tenants of the manor farms, as well as the Duke's chancellor and treasurer, his sister, the Lady Anne, the Abbot of Keynsham and others classed in the records as gentry. Robust entertainment was provided throughout the day, to suit all tastes. That there was bear baiting is certain as it is noted that the bear was provided with two loaves of bread on this day. There was singing and other music, and one or possibly several plays were performed. There were special services in the private chapel, conducted by the Abbot of Keynsham, and it is likely that there was jousting in a field near the castle which is still known as the Tiltfield.

Leaving Berkeley, Thornbury and the Severn, and going north-east, the other great river of the Midlands is the Avon. Along its banks as it flows through Worcestershire, stretches the Vale of Evesham and Evesham town, which is the centre of the fruit-growing district of Worcestershire. Nearby Pershore is famous for plums; Worcester itself is famous for Worcester Pearmains, a sweet, red, early-ripening dessert apple. Evesham in spring is surrounded first with greenish-white plum blossom and snow-white pear blossom and later with acre upon acre of pink apple blossom. The air smells of honey and flowers, and bees buzz everywhere. If modern industry is not, in reality, very far away, it is veiled by the haze of blossoming trees and does not alter the ancient peace of the countryside. The town grew up around the great abbey, founded in the eighth century by the Bishop of Worcester but destroyed after the dissolution of the monasteries, since the estates were sold by the Crown and the abbey rented to local masons as a stone quarry. Only the bell tower, which had been completed just a few years earlier, remains. It is said to be the last important building erected by monks before the dissolution. The bells rang out every three hours from 9 am to 9 pm, and at each peal the monks went to pray. It was unkindly said that they invariably followed their prayers with a meal, which meant that dedicated men of God ate five times in the day, while ordinary citizens contented themselves with three or, at the most, four meals. Whatever the truth about the monks, several interesting traditional dishes from Evesham are recorded and are given in these pages.

Fox-hunting, too, has given England may rather specialized traditional dishes, and that part of the Midlands known as "the shires" is its heart and home. "The shires" are Leicestershire, Rutland (now part of Leicestershire) and Northamptonshire and these are the territories of some of the greatest hunts.

Stag-hunting had almost died out in England by the eighteenth century and now only occurs in Scotland and on Exmoor. It had been the sport of kings and nobles since time immemorial but its place was taken by fox-hunting. The Beaufort and the Berkeley, whose territories lie outside the shires, are long-established hunts, with fine packs of hounds and many followers. The main shires hunts are the Belvoir, originating from Belvoir Castle in Rutland (the seat of the Dukes of Rutland), the Cottesmore, the Quorn, the Fernie and the Pytchley. *"The*

English country gentleman galloping after a fox – the unspeakable in full pursuit of the uneatable," is Oscar Wilde's superbly witty comment on fox-hunting in *A Woman of No Importance.* The fox *is* uneatable, unlike the deer, yet all these hunts and many others all over the country have left a tradition of special dishes. Hunting has always been democratic in the sense that anyone who could ride a horse and who had one available and could pay a subscription could follow the hunt. Princes and princesses, dukes and duchesses, lords and ladies, parsons, farmers and villagers all ride together. As a result, the tradition of hunting food varies from the elaborate to the very simple. The dishes include Quorn Roll; Melton Mowbray Pie; several savouries to round off dinner for a hungry man who had ridden hard all day and had eaten only sandwiches for lunch; solid Huntsman's Cake for tea by the fire or to wedge in the sandwich box for lunch; a nineteenth-century recipe for salmon kedgeree as a filling dish for breakfast before hunting with the Berkeley. In a Leicestershire cookery manuscript cinnamon toast is suggested for tea for ladies returning from hunting, *"while gentlemen may prefer anchovy or beef marrow toast".* These hunting dishes are all from the shires.

Oxfordshire, however, is known primarily for one of the greatest and earliest seats of learning in the world, situated in the lovely city of Oxford itself, close by the ancient royal domain of Woodstock and the Duke of Marlborough's great palace of Blenheim. Oxford, until the beginning of the twentieth century, was the university, and the university was the City of Oxford. As in Cambridge, there was town and gown, often at physical odds with each other, but there was little or no industry nearer than Witney, where blankets of pure wool, famous throughout the country, were – and still are – made.

Every Oxford college has its great hall, with long refectory tables, and its kitchens, which nowadays provide the same food, plain and usually plentiful, for undergraduates and for dons at the high table. On guest nights or for college feasts, special menus are arranged by the college bursar and the college chef, and private luncheons and dinners are also cooked in the kitchens and served in the master's lodge or in the rooms of anyone who orders them. Most colleges have two or three traditional dishes, which are usually suggested by the chef.

Industry has encircled Oxford today, and the *"city of dreaming spires"* is an island surrounded by housing estates, factories and motorways. Happily, the town retains its integrity; its river, the Isis, still flows between green banks. It is also fortunate that the industrial belt does not stretch very far. The small town of Woodstock, eight miles north of Oxford, stands unspoilt, divided by its river into Old and New Woodstock, although New Woodstock contains the Norman church of St Mary Magdalene. The wide street turns a little and leads to one of the great wrought-iron gates of Blenheim Park.

Woodstock manor, a royal domain, was recorded as heavily forested in the Domesday Book. Henry I kept a menagerie there and it was traditionally the place where Henry II in the twelfth century courted "Fair Rosamund", Rosa Mundi, the Rose of the World. She was the daughter of Walter de Clifford, and it is likely that she was educated at Godstow Nunnery, where the King saw her and fell devastatingly in love with her. He is supposed to have built a bower for her at

Woodstock, and a well in the park is known as Rosamund's Well. All sorts of legends grew up around this romantic love, including a version of the fairy tale of the Sleeping Beauty. Gradually Woodstock Forest was reduced, as were so many of the forests of England, but the manor house at Woodstock remained a favourite royal residence until it was destroyed in the Civil War. After the decisive victory of Blenheim the estate was given in perpetuity to the Duke of Marlborough. Sir John Vanbrugh was engaged as architect and Capability Brown laid out the grounds, with avenues planted to represent the plan of the battle.

The great house was formal in design, as required by Sarah, Duchess of Marlborough. Dinners were lavish and dishes elaborate. Sarah had for years lived very close to Queen Anne (they were Mrs Morley and Mrs Freeman to each other in private) and Queen Anne was interested in food. Her chef, Patrick Lamb, who in 1710 wrote *Royal Cookery or The Complete Court Cook*, had been head cook to Charles II, James II, William III as well as Queen Anne and many of his palace dishes were ordered by the peremptory Duchess at Blenheim, where some, at least, became traditional. Patrick Lamb believed that English raw materials were the best in the world and that the tradition of English cooking was as good as or better than that of France. He pleased all his royal employers and, at second-hand, the Marlboroughs. Great houses in eighteenth-century Oxfordshire took a lead from Blenheim and some of Lamb's recipes were adopted far afield. A few are given in these pages.

In Bedfordshire, a county of fine crops and certain areas of sheep-farming, industry has taken over the cities of Bedford and Luton and vast dormitory areas encircle them. But farther out, towards Ampthill and Woburn, areas of beautiful countryside remain.

In the eighteenth-century mansion of Luton Hoo, begun by the architect Robert Adam in 1767, the great kitchens speak of high living. Woburn Abbey, seat of the Dukes of Bedford, stands stately on the border between Bedfordshire and Buckinghamshire. Outside its formal gardens lie 3,000 acres of parkland, some of it forested, part of it devoted to a fine, free-ranging zoo. Woburn is on a vast scale, but only a few miles away lies Aynhoe, with its much smaller but extremely elegant mansion. Here, in the dining-room, the table is set with a gold dinner service, and in the attendant village every cottager was encouraged to plant an apricot tree beside his front door, and, as the trees flourished, Aynhoe became known as the Golden Village.

Bedfordshire dishes in the fifteenth and sixteenth centuries were influenced by Catherine of Aragon, who held two manors in the county and introduced lace-making, which became an extensive cottage industry. There is an early recipe for Bedfordshire Florentines, which may have appeared on her table, but the best-known recipe from this county is Bedfordshire Clangers.

Little has been said about the manufacturing cities of the Midlands and this is because traditional food disappears far more quickly in large towns than in the countryside. In all English cities, at all income levels, there are a few women who cook with care and pride dishes learnt from parents and grandparents; a few men who demand "what mother used to make" and, in the last years only, one or two restaurants that search out and offer local dishes; but it is in the villages, manor houses and on farms that traditional food has kept its local individuality.

Summer Soup

1 lettuce, outer leaves removed,
  well washed and cut into $\frac{1}{2}$
  inch (1 cm) strips
$\frac{1}{4}$ lb (120 g) spinach, chopped
1 cucumber, peeled and cut into
  $\frac{1}{2}$ inch (1 cm) cubes
8 shallots or 2 medium onions
  or 12 spring onions, chopped
$\frac{1}{2}$ lb (240 g) potatoes, peeled and
  cut in $\frac{1}{2}$ inch (1 cm) cubes
5 cups (1.2 litres) chicken stock
12 parsley sprigs
2 bay leaves
6 thyme sprigs
3 lemon thyme sprigs
$\frac{1}{2}$ teaspoon salt
$\frac{1}{2}$ teaspoon pepper
$1\frac{1}{4}$ cups (3 dl) double cream
1 tablespoon finely chopped
  mint and parsley mixed

The pastry triangles:

$\frac{1}{2}$ lb (240 g) short pastry
$\frac{2}{3}$ cup (60 g) grated Cheddar
  cheese
$\frac{1}{4}$ teaspoon cayenne pepper
1 egg yolk, beaten

This soup comes from a farm near the great house of Luton Hoo. It is written out in an early nineteenth-century collection of recipes which came from a cook at the great house. The soup depends on all the vegetables and herbs being fresh from the garden. It should be served chilled, with very hot triangles of cheese pastry.

Put all the vegetables into a saucepan with the stock. Tie the herbs in a bunch and add to the pan with the salt and pepper. Bring to the boil and simmer, covered, for 30 minutes. Remove the herbs and allow the soup to get cold; when cold stir in all but a tablespoon of the cream. Put the soup in the refrigerator to chill for at least 1 hour before serving.

Meanwhile, roll out the pastry, sprinkle with the cheese and the cayenne pepper, fold over and roll out to about $\frac{1}{4}$ inch (0.5 cm) thick. Cut the pastry into neat triangles, brush over with the beaten egg yolk and bake at 400°F (200°C, Gas Mark 6) for about 10 minutes.

Ladle the chilled soup into 4 bowls. Put a teaspoon of cream on top of each and sprinkle with the chopped mint and parsley. Serve with the hot pastry triangles.

Game Soup

$2\frac{1}{2}$ lb ($1\frac{1}{4}$ kg) venison with some
  bone or 1 partridge, 1 pigeon
  and 1 wild duck, or 1 game
  bird and 1 fresh rabbit
2 large onions, stuck with
  8 cloves
3 carrots, scraped and sliced
2 small turnips, peeled and
  quartered
1 head celery, trimmed, washed
  and cut in 1 inch (2.5 cm)
  lengths
6 mushrooms
4 parsley sprigs and
  1 tablespoon finely chopped
  parsley
4 rosemary sprigs
4 thyme sprigs
$\frac{1}{2}$ teaspoon ground ginger
$\frac{1}{2}$ teaspoon freshly ground
  black pepper
$1\frac{1}{2}$ teaspoons salt
3 quarts (2.8 litres) stock
3 oz (90 g) gammon, cut in
  strips
Butter
$\frac{1}{2}$ cup (1.2 dl) medium sherry or
  4 tablespoons cooking brandy

This is a huntsman's soup that is more like a pottage or stew than a soup, and makes a complete and excellent meal requiring nothing but bread, red wine or ale, and some cheese and fruit to follow. It is best to make the soup the day before or early in the morning of the day it is wanted, as it must have time to get cold before skimming. Small dumplings or squares of fried bread can be added, if liked.

Cut all the best part of the venison into very small slices or carve all the best meat from the birds or the rabbit and reserve.

Put the bone or carcasses into a very large saucepan or casserole, on a bed of the prepared vegetables. Place the herbs (but not the finely chopped parsley) on top. Mix the spices and seasonings into the stock and pour it into the pan. Bring to the boil, skim and then simmer, covered, for 3 hours. At the end of this time, strain the stock and allow it to become quite cold.

Remove all the fat from the top of the stock and check seasoning. One and a quarter hours before the soup is required, fry all the meat lightly in a little butter and add to the stock with the sherry or brandy. Bring the soup to the boil and simmer for 1 hour.

When serving, see that each plateful contains some of the meat and is garnished with a sprinkling of chopped parsley.

Huntsman's Omelette

¾ cup (120 g) fresh fine white
  breadcrumbs
Salt and pepper
Nutmeg
⅜ cup (0.9 dl) double cream
2 shallots, finely chopped
2 oz (60 g) mushrooms, sliced
1 stick (120 g) butter
1 chicken liver or 2 oz (60 g)
  lamb's or pig's liver, finely
  chopped
2 lamb's kidneys or 1 pig's
  kidney, skinned, cored and
  finely chopped
8 eggs

This recipe from Gloucester dates back to the Middle Ages, but is still made as a lunch or supper dish today. It is an egg dish rather than an omelette, and very good indeed. In earlier times, it was finished under a salamander, a flat sheet of iron with a handle, heated almost red hot in the fire and held over any dish which required last minute browning. The omelette is best served with a salad and thin slices of brown bread and butter.

Put the breadcrumbs into a bowl and mix in a pinch of salt, and a sprinkling of pepper and nutmeg. Pour in the cream, stir and leave for 30 minutes for the crumbs to swell and absorb it.
  Meanwhile fry the shallots and mushrooms gently in about half of the butter, turning them until they are just beginning to soften. Push them to the side of the pan and fry the liver and kidney, turning all the time, for 2 minutes. Then mix the mushrooms and shallots with the meat and put into a small dish to keep warm.
  Heat the grill. Beat the eggs well with 1 teaspoon of salt, then beat in the cream and breadcrumb mixture. Melt most of the remaining butter in a large frying-pan. As soon as it begins to foam, pour in the egg mixture and fry for 2 minutes, working the sides into the middle with a palette knife or spatula. After 2 minutes put the meat mixture into the still unset centre. Dot the meat with the remaining butter and hold the pan under the grill for 30 seconds. Some of the egg will puff up around the meat. Serve immediately.

Strong Ale and Cheese

6 oz (180 g) Double Gloucester
  cheese, cut in thin slices
1½ tablespoons (30 g) prepared
  mustard (Tewkesbury or
  Urchfont mustards are very
  good for this dish)
1¼ cups (3 dl) strong ale
4 large slices of freshly toasted
  white bread, crusts removed

Double Gloucester cheese was made from the milk of the Old Gloucester breed of cows. They were known in the Middle Ages and had hardly changed by the eighteenth century, when the Duke of Beaufort, Master of the Beaufort Hunt, ordered his tenant farmers to confine themselves to this breed because they had lost all fear of hounds and barely raised their heads when the pack swept through the fields.
  Today, excellent Double Gloucester is made commercially and this recipe is quite different if made with any other cheese. Drink ale or red wine with this dish and, if possible, serve a bowl of fresh watercress, without dressing.

Put the cheese into a small, shallow, fireproof dish so that the slices are about ½ inch (1 cm) deep. Spread the mustard over the top. Pour in the ale, which should just cover the cheese. Bake at 450°F (230°C, Gas Mark 8) for 15 minutes. Remove the dish from the oven and pour and spoon the cheese mixture on to the slices of toast. Serve at once.

Worcester Potted Lampreys

4 lampreys or mackerel
1 teaspoon ground mace
1 teaspoon dried tarragon
½ teaspoon turmeric
2 bay leaves
6 cloves
2½ teaspoons white pepper
2 teaspoons salt
1 cup (120 g) shredded beef suet
2 sticks (240 g) butter, clarified

The Severn lampreys were caught as far upstream as Worcester, and also at Gloucester and Berkeley. Gloucester was famous for lamprey pies (in which part of their dues to the Crown were paid) and Worcester for potted lampreys. This recipe is given mainly for interest although it is still possible to ask Severn fishermen for lampreys and to get a few of these fish, which were once passionately sought after and are now completely out of favour. Mackerel potted in this way are excellent, too, as their flesh, like that of the lamprey, contains a lot of oil. They will keep for ten days in the refrigerator or for several weeks in a deep-freeze.

Clean the fish and remove their heads (also tails and fins if mackerel are being used). Leave on the skins, but in the case of the lampreys have the cartilage and the string on each side removed. Allow to drain for several hours.
  Mix the herbs, spices and salt and rub the fish all over with them, then place the fish in a stone jar or heavy casserole, curling them round the sides of the pot, which should hold them with only about 1 inch (2.5 cm) to spare on top.
  Sprinkle any herbs, spices and salt which have not adhered to the fish, into the pot.
  Melt the suet and add the clarified butter, stirring gently. When hot pour over the fish. The fat should fill up all the spaces between the fish and cover them by ½ inch (1 cm). When cold, put into the refrigerator.
  When the fish are to be used, remove and discard some of the butter. Lift out the fish with the remaining butter and fry very gently on both sides, for about 10 minutes or until cooked through.

Salmon Kedgeree

½ lb (240 g) cooked fresh salmon, skin and bones removed and the flesh finely flaked
5 tablespoons (75 g) butter
4 cups (½ kg) cooked long-grain rice, which has been slightly salted in cooking
2 hard-boiled eggs, finely chopped
1 tablespoon finely chopped parsley
1 teaspoon salt
½ teaspoon freshly ground black pepper

A very filling breakfast dish for a man who will be taking violent exercise all day in the open air. A typical eighteenth-century hunting gentleman probably followed it with kidneys and bacon and slices of cold ham and beef. The salmon would have been left over from the day before. It is very good for lunch or supper.

Heat the butter in a large saucepan until just melted and stir in the rice, which can be hot or cold. Stir well for a moment, then add the salmon and the eggs and stir very gently so that the eggs are evenly distributed, but not too much broken up. Add the parsley, salt and pepper. Stir again, turn into a fireproof dish, cover and put into a 350°F (180°C, Gas Mark 4) oven for 25 minutes if the rice was cold, or for 5 minutes if the rice has just been cooked.

Salmon Pie

2½ lb (1¼ kg) salmon, cut in
  slices, each slice ½ inch (1 cm)
  thick (ask for bones and
  trimmings)
¾ lb (360 g) short pastry
¼ lb (120 g) prawns, shelled
¾ stick (90 g) butter
⅝ cup (1.5 dl) dry white wine
1 tablespoon finely chopped
  parsley
1 teaspoon finely chopped
  tarragon
Salt and pepper
1 teaspoon ground mace
1½ lb (¾ kg) new potatoes,
  scraped and boiled until just
  tender, then cut in thin slices
1 egg yolk, beaten

The court bouillon:

Trimmings and bones from the
  salmon
2 carrots, scraped and cut in
  half lengthways
2 or 3 shallots or 1 small
  onion, cut in quarters
⅝ cup (1.5 dl) dry white wine
4 sprigs parsley and 2 sprigs
  tarragon, tied together
1 teaspoon salt
12 black peppercorns

So many salmon were taken from the Severn in some
seasons that local fishermen's families and guests
who came for the fishing tired of eating it simply
cooked and required more interesting ways of
serving this great fish.

First make the court bouillon. Put all the ingredients
into a saucepan and add 5 cups (1.2 litres) of water.
Bring to the boil and skim. Boil, covered, for 40
minutes. Strain and allow to cool.

Poach the salmon in the court bouillon for 12
minutes. When cooked remove the fish and allow to
cool. Reserve the court bouillon.

Roll out the pastry and leave to rest.

When the salmon is almost cold, remove all the
skin. Line a large pie dish with the pastry,
dampening the edge of the dish and pressing the
pastry on to it. Lay the slices of salmon in the dish
with the prawns.

Melt about two-thirds of the butter and stir it into
the white wine, with the herbs, seasoning and mace.
Stir in ⅝ cup (1.5 dl) of the court bouillon and pour
all this over the salmon, which should not be
completely covered. Put the sliced new potatoes on
top, to cover the fish. Melt the remaining butter and
brush the potatoes with it. Brush the pastry edge
over with the beaten egg yolk. Bake at 400°F (200°C,
Gas Mark 6) for 30 minutes.

Haddock and Bacon Pot Pie

1 lb (½ kg) smoked haddock
  fillets, poached (if frozen, pull
  off skin before they thaw)
4 slices back bacon
¾ lb (360 g) tomatoes, blanched,
  peeled and quartered
3 tablespoons (45 g) butter
½ cup (90 g) fresh fine white
  breadcrumbs
½ teaspoon freshly ground
  black pepper

This Shropshire recipe is so good as a supper dish,
with a glass of red wine and some cheese and fruit to
follow, that once made it will be asked for again.

Cut the rind from the bacon. Cut the slices into ½
inch (1 cm) squares. Lightly fry them and set aside.

Flake the haddock, removing all the skin and any
bones. Mix in the pepper. Grease a baking dish with
one-third of the butter. Lay in the fish. Put the
tomatoes over it and the bacon over the tomatoes.
Sprinkle the breadcrumbs all over and dot with the
remaining butter. Cook at 350°F (180°C, Gas Mark 4)
for 20 minutes. Raise the heat a little for the last 10
minutes if the breadcrumbs are not well browned, or
finish under the grill.

Broiled Carp

3 to 4 lb (1½ to 2 kg) carp
Dried thyme
Ground nutmeg
Salt
Flour
Black pepper
2½ sticks (300 g) butter
4 gammon slices, each ¼ inch
  (0.5 cm) thick
⅝ cup (1.5 dl) claret
6 fresh oysters or 1 small tin
1¼ cups (3 dl) chicken or veal
  stock (stock cube will do)
3 hard-boiled eggs
¼ lb (120 g) frozen prawns,
  cooked and shelled
Lemon juice

From the Middle Ages until the nineteenth century almost all great houses had their "stews", or fish ponds, and carp was one of the largest and most popular of the fish bred in them. Most well-to-do households, therefore, ate a fairly elaborately served carp four or five times a year. Today, most good fish shops will get a carp of two to eight pounds (1 to 4 kg) if given two or three days' notice, and will scale and clean it.

The recipe that follows is headed *"To Broyle a Carp"* and comes from Mrs Anne Blencowe's cookbook, 1694. Lady Blencowe was the daughter of a distinguished Whig mathematician and cryptographer, John Wallis. She married Sir John Blencowe, who was an MP and a judge, when she was nineteen and lived in Northamptonshire. Most of her recipes, although often cryptic, are very good.

". . . scarbanada it on bothe sides, wash it over with butter and season ye scarbanada with time, Nutmeg and salt. Then put it on your Gridiron and boyle it sloly over charcoals. Keep it basting. You may broyle some Collops of Gammon with it. Sett upp on ye coals in a stewing dish a quarter of a pint of Claret a little Oyster Licker, Minced Oysters and hard eggs with a hanful of prans. When your Carp are Broyled dish them up and Garnish them with fryed Collops of Gammon and pour on your licker being thickened with a ladelful of Brown Butter."

Cut six 2-inch (5 cm) slits transversely on both sides of the fish, through the skin but not too deep, from below the head to 2 inches (5 cm) from the tail (carbonados). Rub thyme, nutmeg and salt into these. Rub a little flour all over the fish, with further salt and black pepper.

Lay the carp in a baking tin in which you have melted 2 sticks (240 g) of the butter. Spoon the butter well over the fish. Place the tin in a 400°F (200°C, Gas Mark 6) oven and bake for 30 minutes, basting frequently. If the fish is not well basted, the flesh becomes woolly.

While the fish is cooking, prepare the gammon. Cut rind and fat from the slices and cut each into four. When the fish has cooked for 30 minutes, remove from the oven and lay the gammon in the butter around the carp. Cover the carp only with foil and return to the oven for 10 to 15 minutes, turning the gammon pieces once. Test with a skewer through one of the carbonados to see if the fish is done.

Meanwhile make the sauce. Make a roux with the remaining butter and ⅜ cup (45 g) of flour. Stir in the claret and the liquor from the oysters, fresh or tinned, and then add the chicken stock; the sauce must have the consistency of thin cream. Add the hard-boiled eggs, finely chopped, the oysters, chopped (rather than minced), and the prawns, halved. Stir lightly and season with salt and plenty of black pepper, and a squeeze of lemon juice to taste.

Dish up the carp as Mrs Blencowe suggests.

Oxford John

2 lb (1 kg) fillet end of a leg of
lamb
2 tablespoons seasoned flour
½ stick (60 g) butter
3 shallots or a medium onion,
chopped
2 teaspoons finely chopped
parsley
2 teaspoons finely chopped
thyme
1¼ cups (3 dl) good brown
gravy slightly thickened
4 slices white bread, cut in ½
inch (1 cm) squares and fried
crisp in butter
Salt and pepper

An early college recipe for mutton collops. The dish,
which is very good and quite unlike stewed lamb or
mutton, is also good made with venison. Serve with
red-currant or rowan jelly.

Cut the lamb into very thin, small slices (collops),
discarding all bone, fat and sinew. Lightly rub the
collops with seasoned flour. Fry gently in the butter,
adding the shallots and herbs as the meat begins to
cook. After 2 minutes turn the collops and then turn
again after 2 minutes more. After 6 minutes, the
collops will be done; pour the gravy into the pan and
stir well. As soon as the gravy is hot, dish up on to a
serving platter, sprinkle the fried bread squares over
the top and serve at once. The meat will become
tough if kept hot.

Bedfordshire Clangers

1 lb (½ kg) good stewing steak
or lean pork, all skin and fat
removed and cut into ½ inch
(1 cm) dice
¼ lb (120 g) ox kidney or 1 pig's
kidney, skinned, cored and
cut into ¼ inch (0.5 cm) dice
1 large onion, very finely
chopped
1 lb (½ kg) suet crust
½ cup (90 g) seedless raisins
2 large cooking apples, peeled,
cored and cut into ½ inch
(1 cm) dice
Salt and pepper
Milk
Flour
Butter

This is an early recipe. The origin of the name,
always in the plural although one large roll was
generally made, seems to be obscure. There are some
odd names in Bedfordshire, some of which came from
the lacemakers who were probably brought there by
Catherine of Aragon.
 Clangers would warm, fill and sustain a farm
worker on a cold winter's day. They could be made
very cheaply using scrag-end of mutton or ends of
bacon and omitting the raisins which gave the dish
its special character. Or, in a more prosperous
family, Clangers could be made with good steak or
pork and some of the appropriate kidney. The fruit in
the crust is as good with the meat as red-currant
jelly with mutton. The roll looks like a plum duff and
when it is cut the meat is a surprise. A good brown
gravy may be served separately.

Season all the meat with plenty of salt and pepper
and mix with the onion.
 Roll out the suet crust to about ¼ inch (0.5 cm) thick
in a long oblong shape and divide it in two. On one
piece sprinkle the raisins and lay the apple dice on
top of them. Put the second piece of suet crust over,
so that the apple and raisins are sandwiched,
sprinkle with a little flour and gently roll out so that
the fruit is well embedded in the crust.
 Spread the seasoned meat and onion all over the
suet crust except for about 1 inch (2.5 cm) at the ends
and sides. Damp these edges with a little milk and
roll up tightly, sealing all the meat inside. Press the
ends well together. A few raisins should show
through the crust.
 Enclose the roll in buttered foil and then tie it in a
cloth, which has been dusted with flour on the
inside. Boil in water in a fish kettle or large
saucepan for 3½ hours. Do not let the water go off the
boil and replenish with more boiling water, when
necessary. Lift out the Clanger, unwrap it and put on
a flat dish in a moderate oven for 10 minutes to dry.

Quorn Roll

1 lb (½ kg) suet crust
12 slices streaky bacon, rind
  removed and cut across in ½
  inch (1 cm) strips
2 onions, finely chopped
2 teaspoons finely chopped
  thyme
2 teaspoons finely chopped
  parsley
¼ teaspoon white pepper
1 tablespoon Golden Syrup
Butter

This very filling but delicious suet roll used to be made for those stable and kennel lads who lived in. The Golden Syrup makes a delicious moist gravy with the onions and bacon.

Roll out the suet crust about ¾ inch (2 cm) thick. Cover with the bacon strips to within about 1 inch (2.5 cm) of the edge. Sprinkle the onions all over, then the herbs and the pepper. Lastly drop the Golden Syrup all down the middle in a long line. Roll it up tightly, like a Swiss roll, and seal the ends together. Carefully lift the roll on to a sheet of buttered foil and roll this round it, but not very tightly, as it must be allowed to swell. Flour a pudding cloth on both sides, lay the roll on it and wrap it round not too tightly, tying the ends with string.

Bring a large saucepan or fish kettle of water to the boil and drop in the roll. Cover the pan and boil steadily for 2 hours, filling up with more boiling water, if necessary.

To dish up, lift out the roll, with two spatulas or fish slices, on to a serving dish. Undo and roll off the cloth and the foil and pull them from under the roll. Set in a medium oven, 350°F (180°C, Gas Mark 4), on the serving dish for 5 minutes, so that the outside dries slightly.

Cut in thick slices to serve.

Sweet Devil

1½ lb (¾ kg) gammon joint
½ lb (240 g) fresh black cherries,
  pitted, or 3 peaches or 6
  apricots, stoned and sliced
6 tablespoons (90 g) castor
  sugar
¼ teaspoon cayenne pepper
½ teaspoon paprika
½ teaspoon turmeric
½ teaspoon mace
¼ teaspoon white pepper
1 teaspoon lemon juice
3 tablespoons sweet red wine
½ stick (60 g) butter
4 tablespoons (60 g) fresh fine
  white breadcrumbs
4 slices white bread, crusts
  removed and each slice cut
  across in 2 triangles

An Oxfordshire recipe from the early nineteenth century. This is a dish that a single gentleman might offer to friends, with trout to precede it, a cold pudding or cheese and fruit to follow and a bottle of good port at the end of the meal. A rather rough, dry red wine is the best drink to serve with the dish, as it is too spicy for a really good burgundy or claret, and the sweetness of the dish makes an ordinary wine taste extraordinary.

Boil the gammon joint for about 1 hour or until it is cooked through.

While the gammon is boiling, arrange the fruit in an ovenproof dish and sprinkle with a third of the sugar. Put the dish in a low oven, 325°F (170°C, Gas Mark 3), for 10 minutes. Remove the dish from the oven and set aside.

Drain the gammon and cut it in 4 thick slices as neatly as possible.

Mix the remaining sugar, all the spices, the lemon juice and the wine in a frying-pan and stir well. Boil for 2 to 3 minutes, working in half the butter. As soon as it has thickened a little, put in the gammon slices. Turn them after 2 minutes and cook for a further 3 or 4 minutes. Using a fish slice, lift out the gammon on to a flat dish.

Spoon the fruit all around the gammon, with as little juice as possible. Pour the remaining juice into the frying-pan and stir well until boiling. Check to see if the sauce requires any more cayenne or other spices and add salt if the gammon has not made it salty enough. The sauce should be sweet, as hot as liked, have a reddish colour and the consistency of thin cream. Pour it all over the gammon slices and the fruit. Sprinkle the gammon with the breadcrumbs (avoiding the fruit as much as possible) and brown under a grill or in the top of a very hot oven.

Meanwhile, lightly fry the bread triangles on both sides in the remaining butter. Serve the Sweet Devil at once with the fried bread triangles standing around the edge of the dish.

Ham Stuffed with Apricots

Serves 8 to 10

4 to 6 lb (2 to 3 kg) uncooked sweet-cured ham or gammon
1 lb ($\frac{1}{2}$ kg) plain flour
$\frac{1}{2}$ lb (240 g) fresh apricots, not too ripe
1 cup (120 g) fresh white breadcrumbs
4 tablespoons Golden Syrup or treacle
Demerara sugar
10 to 20 cloves
$\frac{3}{8}$ cup (90 g) blanched almonds, fried to a pale golden colour

This recipe probably comes from Oxfordshire where the famous Moor Park strain of apricots was developed. It is a very good cold luncheon dish.

Cut the bone out of the ham. Mix the flour with enough water to make a stiff dough – this is the crust in which the ham will be baked.

Cut the apricots away from their stones and put them into a saucepan with 2 tablespoons of water. Cook for 4 minutes to release the juice a little. Remove the pan from the heat and stir in the breadcrumbs. Work the mixture together and press it into the hole in the ham from where the bone was removed. Tie round the ham with string to keep it firm. Spread the ham with the syrup or treacle, sprinkle over a little sugar and stick with the cloves.

Roll out the crust and lay the ham on it. Pull the sides of the crust over the ham and mould together so that the ham is sealed in.

Put the ham on a baking tray and bake at 400°F (200°C, Gas Mark 6) for 1$\frac{1}{2}$ hours. Remove the ham from the oven and when it is cool enough to handle remove and discard the crust. Stick the almonds on top of the ham between the cloves. The apricot stones may be cracked and their kernels used (although not, of course, fried) instead of almonds if preferred.

Mutton Chops with Chestnuts

Serves 4 to 6

8 mutton or lamb loin chops
1 tablespoon seasoned flour
$\frac{1}{2}$ stick (60 g) butter
2 large onions, finely sliced
20 chestnuts, peeled and boiled until just soft
2$\frac{1}{2}$ cups (6 dl) good stock
$\frac{5}{8}$ cup (1.5 dl) red wine
$\frac{1}{4}$ teaspoon ground mace
1 teaspoon dried thyme
$\frac{1}{2}$ teaspoon salt
$\frac{1}{2}$ teaspoon black pepper

A Warwickshire recipe, very good on a cold winter's night. Plain boiled potatoes are best with this dish and a winter salad served separately.

Trim almost all the fat from the chops. Dip the chops in seasoned flour and fry them gently in the butter for 2 to 3 minutes on each side. Put them in a casserole.

Lightly fry the onions in the same pan. When the onions are just becoming transparent, scatter them over the chops. Add the chestnuts to the casserole. Mix the stock, wine, mace, thyme, salt and pepper. Pour the liquid over the chops, cover the casserole and simmer gently either on top of the stove or in a low oven, 300°F (160°C, Gas Mark 2), for 2 hours.

Pork and Apple Pie

$1\frac{1}{2}$ lb ($\frac{3}{4}$ kg) lean pork cut into $\frac{1}{2}$
inch (1 cm) pieces
1 lb ($\frac{1}{2}$ kg) cooking apples,
peeled and cut into $\frac{1}{2}$ inch
(1 cm) cubes
2 tablespoons (30 g) castor
sugar
1 medium onion, finely chopped
$1\frac{1}{4}$ cups (3 dl) good stock
Salt and pepper

Potato crust:

3 sticks (360 g) butter
2 cups (240 g) self-raising flour
$1\frac{1}{2}$ lb ($\frac{3}{4}$ kg) potatoes, mashed
1 teaspoon salt
A little milk
Egg for gilding, optional

Serve with green peas or green salad in individual
dishes.

In a deep pie dish place a layer of half the pork,
sprinkle with salt and pepper, cover with a layer of
half the apple and sprinkle with half the sugar and
all the onion. Repeat the layers in reverse so that the
top layer is pork. Pour in the stock.
Now make the crust. In a large mixing bowl rub the
butter into the flour. Mix in the potato and the salt.
Turn the pastry out and knead well. Roll out the
pastry $1\frac{1}{2}$ inches (3.5 cm) thick and cover the pie.
Brush with milk. A potato crust should not have slits
cut in the centre, nor a raised decoration, but the
edges can be marked with a fork and the crust can
be gilded with egg if liked.
Bake in a slow oven, 300°F (160°C, Gas Mark 2), for
$1\frac{1}{2}$ hours. The crust should be a rich golden brown.

Melton Mowbray Pie

2 lb (1 kg) pork, from leg or
shoulder
Pork or veal bones
2 onions
2 sage leaves, 1 finely chopped
1 bay leaf
Marjoram
Thyme
Salt and pepper
2 tablespoons (30 g) butter
A little milk

The crust:

1 lb ($\frac{1}{2}$ kg) flour
Salt
$\frac{1}{2}$ lb (240 g) lard or half lard
and half butter
$\frac{5}{8}$ cup (1.5 dl) milk and water
mixed
1 egg, well beaten

This raised pork pie is a speciality of Melton
Mowbray and is the most famous of all English pies.
In the shires, hunting folk sometimes took a slice of
it instead of sandwiches to eat when they were out
with the hounds. Others had it for high tea when
they got home. Every cook and housewife had her
own special recipe. The earliest recorded recipe dates
from the fourteenth century and had raisins and
currants in the pork filling. Special tins for raised
pies may be purchased. They have hinged sides,
which are often embossed, leaving the pastry
patterned, and are easy to use. The results are
handsome, but the original Melton Mowbray pies
were raised by hand, as described below.

First put the bones to boil in 1 quart (9 dl) of water
with the onions, the whole sage leaf, the bay leaf, a
sprig or two of marjoram, some sprigs of thyme, salt
and pepper. Boil for 2 hours, to reduce the stock to
little more than $2\frac{1}{2}$ cups (6 dl) of liquid, then cool and
skim off all fat. Taste the stock and check seasoning.
It should have begun to jell as it cools.
While the stock is boiling, prepare the filling. Cut
the pork in dice approximately $\frac{1}{4}$ inch (0.5 cm) square
(kitchen scissors are easier to use than a knife) but
do *not* mince. Fat may be included, but not skin or
gristle. Mix together the pork, 1 teaspoon of salt, $\frac{1}{2}$
teaspoon of pepper and the finely chopped sage leaf.
Prepare the crust by sifting together the flour and $\frac{1}{2}$
teaspoon of salt. Rub 4 tablespoons (60 g) of the fat
into the mixture with the fingertips. Put the rest of
the fat on to boil with the milk and water. Make a
well in the flour and when the liquid is boiling, pour
it in and stir with a wooden spoon. Knead well and
let the pastry stand for 10 minutes.
The raising of the pie may be done in several ways,
but this is probably the easiest. Take a round
casserole or cake tin the size of the pie you want to

make. It must have straight sides and be of sufficient height. Roll out the pastry into a large, roughly circular piece about $\frac{1}{2}$ to $\frac{3}{4}$ inch (1 to 2 cm) thick. Stand the round pot or cake tin, open end up, in the middle of the pastry and work it up to cover the sides of the pot. Turn the pastry-covered pot on its side and roll it a few times to smooth the outside and loosen the pot. Gently work the pot out; the pie case should remain standing.

Fill the pie case at once by packing the pork mixture closely down into it to within $\frac{1}{4}$ inch (0.5 cm) of the top. Put in 2 tablespoons of cold water and dot the top of the meat with the butter. Trim the top of the pie with a sharp knife, roll out the trimmings, and cut out a lid that is larger than the top of the pie case. Dampen the top edges of the pie case with a little milk, press on the lid and firmly crimp the edges all round to make a raised ridge. The top of the pie can be left plain with 2 or 3 slits or a round hole neatly cut in the middle, or it may be decorated with leaves and a rose.

If you want to raise the pie without using a pot, cut a round for the bottom which is $\frac{1}{2}$ inch (1 cm) bigger in diameter than you think you require. Roll your paste into long thin snakes, as children do with plasticine or as a potter does with clay for certain pots. Coil the snakes round the edges of the bottom, one on another, until you have walls of the required height. Then carefully work them as smooth as possible outside and in with your fingers, always working the paste upwards. Fill the pie and put on the lid as described above.

Brush the pie all over with the beaten egg. Bake at 375°F (190°C, Gas Mark 5) for 20 minutes to set the pastry; then reduce the temperature to 325°F (170°C, Gas Mark 3). Put the pie lower in the oven, cover the top lightly with foil and bake for a further $1\frac{3}{4}$ hours.

Remove the pie from the oven about 10 minutes before the end of the cooking time, brush over with the remaining beaten egg and return to the oven.

Lastly, reheat the jellied stock. As soon as the pie comes out of the oven, slowly pour the stock through the hole in the top of the crust until it fills the pie.

Leave the pie to become quite cold before serving.

Partridge Casserole

Serves 4

1 brace partridges
4 onions, 2 left whole and 2 sliced into rings
2 slices streaky bacon
$\frac{3}{4}$ lb (360 g) carrots, sliced
3 slices (60 g) lean bacon, diced
1 teaspoon salt
Pepper
3 tablespoons chopped parsley
1 teaspoon thyme
1 large or 2 small Savoy cabbages
1 quart (9 dl) stock made from the giblets of the birds

This recipe comes from an eighteenth-century book. Very probably the head of the household would have demanded a whole bird to himself. A large thick slice of home-made bread would have been put on his platter, the partridge placed on it and a good helping of the cabbage, carrots and gravy added.

Put a whole, peeled onion inside each bird. Truss the birds and lay a slice of bacon over each. Put them into a casserole on a bed of the carrots, onions and diced bacon. Sprinkle with seasoning and herbs.

Parboil the cabbage for 3 minutes, drain and cut in quarters. Pack the cabbage quarters around the partridges, pour over the stock and cook in the oven at 325°F (150°C, Gas Mark 3) for 2 hours.

A Shropshire Pie

$1\frac{1}{2}$ lb ($\frac{3}{4}$ kg) puff pastry
1 rabbit or chicken, about $2\frac{1}{2}$ lb
 ($1\frac{1}{4}$ kg), jointed
1 lb ($\frac{1}{2}$ kg) top leg of pork,
 skinned and diced
1 large tin artichoke hearts (or
 6 fresh)
$1\frac{1}{4}$ cups (3 dl) red wine
1 egg yolk
Nutmeg
Salt and pepper

The forcemeat balls:

2 slices streaky bacon
1 tablespoon chopped fresh
 parsley, thyme and a little
 sage
$\frac{1}{4}$ lb (120 g) mushrooms, finely
 chopped and lightly fried
1 cup (120 g) fresh white
 breadcrumbs
1 egg yolk
Nutmeg
Pepper
A little milk

A good rabbit pie was much enjoyed by our ancestors and appeared on the grandest tables in the land. Rabbits are eaten less often today but this eighteenth-century recipe given by Mrs Glasse is also very good made with chicken.

These quantities will make two pies, one to be served hot and one cold a day or two later.

Line 2 pie dishes with the thinly rolled puff pastry, reserving enough for the lids. Put the rabbit or chicken joints in the dish and season with salt and pepper and a sprinkling of nutmeg. Season the diced pork and lay on top of the rabbit or chicken. Cut the artichoke hearts into quarters and place them on top.

Make the forcemeat by chopping the bacon finely, adding the herbs, mushrooms and breadcrumbs and mixing well. Season with a pinch of pepper and nutmeg. Mix with egg yolk and form into 10 or 12 very small balls. A little milk can be added if the mixture is too dry to roll. Dot the little balls about on the pie filling. Mix the wine with an equal quantity of water and pour in so that the meat is almost covered.

Roll out the reserved pastry to make the lids and cover, sealing tightly where the edges meet by brushing the lower edge with egg yolk. Cut a small slit in the centre of the lids. Roll out any remaining fragments of pastry and cut out 3 or 5 leaves and a rose for the centre. Paint over with the remaining egg yolk and bake in the oven at 400°F (200°C, Gas Mark 5) for 40 minutes. Then reduce the heat to 350°F (180°C, Gas Mark 4) for a further 40 minutes. Lightly cover the pastry with foil if it is browning too much.

Birds Encased

6 young pigeons, cleaned and
 trussed, or 12 plump quails,
 prepared
$1\frac{1}{2}$ lb ($\frac{3}{4}$ kg) puff pastry
1 stick (120 g) butter
1 egg, well beaten
Salt and pepper

For the pigeons:

$\frac{1}{4}$ lb (120 g) mushrooms, sliced
$\frac{5}{8}$ cup (1.5 dl) well-seasoned,
 thickened brown gravy with a
 tablespoon of red wine or
 sherry in it
1 teaspoon finely chopped
 thyme

For the quails:

24 white grapes, peeled and
 pitted
2 tablespoons dry white wine

This dish was referred to in a sixteenth-century description of a London feast and there is also a seventeenth-century recipe from the Cotswolds. The birds used were plovers, wheatears, young pigeons or young partridges. Today, young pigeons or quails are usually obtainable.

Serve with whole french beans or young peas, and with half a blanched tomato, topped with a black olive, between each pastry-encased bird.

Roll out the pastry to about $\frac{1}{8}$ inch (0.25 cm) thick (in two sections if more convenient) and leave to rest in a cool place.

Fry the pigeons or the quails in the butter on all sides. Allow the birds to cool a little. If using pigeons, lightly fry the mushrooms in the same pan.

Roll the pastry out again to a little less than $\frac{1}{8}$ inch (0.25 cm) thick. Place one of the birds on the pastry and cut a rough circle around it, leaving enough to be raised over the bird so that it will be in a little sealed bag of pastry. Remove the bird and cut the remaining pastry according to this pattern.

Place a bird in the centre of each piece of pastry.

Put 2 grapes with each quail, sprinkle with a little salt and pepper and moisten with the wine. For pigeons, put a few mushroom slices with each, sprinkle with the thyme, salt and pepper and put a spoonful of gravy over each.

Pull up the pastry and pinch well together at the top. Brush over with the beaten egg.

Bake the pigeons at 450°F (230°C, Gas Mark 8) near the top of the oven for 10 minutes. Then move the birds to a lower part of the oven. Place a sheet of foil lightly over them, reduce the heat to 350°F (180°C, Gas Mark 4) and bake for a further 35 minutes.

Bake the quails in the same way, but give them only a further 10 minutes at the lower temperature.

Lift the encased birds very carefully on to a flat serving dish and serve immediately.

Salmi of Duck

Serves 4

2 wild or domestic ducks, roasted for 30 minutes only and allowed to cool
1 medium onion, finely chopped
3 tablespoons (45 g) butter
1 tablespoon flour
1 teaspoon dried thyme
1 teaspoon dried parsley
2 bay leaves
$\frac{1}{4}$ teaspoon grated nutmeg
Grated rind of 1 orange and 1 orange cut in quarters
2 teaspoons red-currant jelly
$\frac{5}{8}$ cup (1.5 dl) red wine
1 tablespoon brandy
$\frac{1}{4}$ lb (120 g) mushrooms, sliced and sautéed in butter
2 teaspoons lemon juice
Salt and pepper
4 triangular pieces of crustless bread fried crisp in butter

A dish often ordered by Victorian and Edwardian gentlemen at their clubs or for a stag dinner at home. This recipe comes from Balliol College, Oxford, and was sometimes ordered by academic gentlemen for private dinners, which were prepared in the college kitchens and sent up with due ceremony to their rooms. The birds are roasted very rare a short time before they are wanted, and then put into a sauce, in which they are gently heated. This is rather an exacting recipe but well worth the trouble and equally good, although quite different, with pheasant or partridge.

Carve all the meat from the ducks, the breast in long slices, the rest as you can get it away from the bone. Set aside in the refrigerator.

Put the bones in a saucepan, just cover with salted water and boil for at least 1½ hours. Strain off the stock.

Fry the onion in the butter until just transparent and golden. Stir in the flour, cook for a minute and gradually stir in the stock. Add the herbs, the nutmeg and the grated orange peel and stir in the red-currant jelly. Season with salt and pepper and simmer for 30 minutes, uncovered, stirring occasionally, until the sauce is as thick as double cream.

Pour and rub the sauce through a strainer into another saucepan, add the wine, brandy and the mushrooms and simmer for 5 or 6 minutes. Add the lemon juice. Check the seasoning and put in the duck. Leave on or near the lowest possible heat for another 15 minutes so that the duck pieces are heated through, but do not boil. Pour the duck and sauce into a serving dish, stick the fried bread around the edge with one corner in the sauce, and put an orange quarter near each.

Braised Pheasant

1 brace old pheasants
2 large onions, cut in rings
½ stick (60 g) butter
4 slices streaky bacon, cut into
  ½ inch (1 cm) pieces
1 tablespoon seasoned flour
2 teaspoons red-currant jelly
2½ cups (6 dl) good brown stock
⅝ cup (1.5 dl) red wine
1 teaspoon Worcestershire
  sauce
2 teaspoons cornflour
½ cup (90 g) shelled walnuts,
  roughly chopped
Salt and pepper

This is a Victorian recipe from Oxfordshire. A brace of old birds was sometimes cooked like this for an informal autumn dinner and served with rice and the first brussels sprouts of the season.

In a frying-pan fry the onions in the butter, then put them into a large casserole. Fry the bacon in the same pan and put on top of the onions. Set aside the pan with the fat in it.

Rub the birds all over with the seasoned flour and place them side by side, breast upwards, on top of the bacon. Melt the red-currant jelly in a saucepan and stir in the stock, the wine and the Worcestershire sauce. Pour the mixture over the pheasants, cover the casserole and cook in the oven at 350°F (180°C, Gas Mark 4) for 2 hours.

Lift the pheasants out on to a flat serving dish and keep hot. Bring the liquid in the casserole to the boil again. Stir 1 tablespoon of cold water into the cornflour, then spoon a little of the boiling stock into it, stirring hard. Tip the dissolved cornflour into the casserole, stirring all the time. Boil for 2 minutes. Check seasoning. This sauce should have the consistency of thin cream and a rich taste. Pour it over the birds and put back into the oven.

Quickly make the frying-pan hot again, pour away all the excess fat and fry the walnuts for 30 seconds, shaking the pan all the time. Take the dish out of the oven, sprinkle the walnuts over the pheasants and serve immediately.

Jellied Game

2 old pheasants, or 3 old
  partridges, legs removed
  below the thigh and wings at
  the pinions
1 teaspoon cayenne pepper
1 teaspoon salt
1 teaspoon freshly ground
  black pepper
2 sticks (240 g) butter
1¼ cups (3 dl) dry red wine,
  boiled until it is reduced by
  half
1 quart (9 dl) chicken or beef
  stock (stock cubes will do)
Marjoram, thyme and parsley,
  tied together in a bunch
20 black olives, stoned
½ lb (240 g) mushrooms, sliced
2 tablespoons finely chopped
  parsley
Juice of ½ lemon
Six ¼ oz packets (45 g) gelatine
  melted in a little warm water

A Cotswold recipe for cooking elderly game birds so that they have all the tenderness and flavour of young birds.

Mix the cayenne, salt and black pepper into the butter. Rub the birds thickly all over, inside and out, with the butter and push any remaining butter inside them. Put the birds, breasts downwards, into a deep pie dish which just holds them side by side.

Mix the reduced wine with the stock and pour over the birds so that they are just covered and put in the bunch of herbs. Cover the pie dish and cook in a 350°F (180°C, Gas Mark 4) oven for 2½ hours.

Remove the dish from the oven. Skim off some of the butter, which will have risen to the top, and drop in the olives and the mushrooms. Put the dish back into the oven for a further 30 minutes.

Remove the pie dish from the oven again and pour off the gravy into a bowl, disturbing the birds, mushrooms and olives as little as possible. Discard the herbs and stir in half the parsley, the lemon juice and then the gelatine into the hot gravy. Pour the gravy back over the birds and allow them to get quite cold. When cold chill for at least 1 hour. Scrape off all the butter, which will have set over the top, and turn the jellied birds out on to a flat serving dish. Sprinkle the top with the remaining parsley.

Venison Roll

1 lb (½ kg) venison, minced or
finely chopped
½ lb (240 g) streaky bacon,
minced or finely chopped
¾ cup (120 g) fresh
breadcrumbs
1 medium onion, very finely
chopped
2 tablespoons finely chopped
parsley
1 teaspoon chopped thyme
1 egg, well beaten
Salt and pepper
Seasoned flour
Red-currant jelly
Gravy

This recipe comes from a Warwickshire estate. It is also very good made with lamb instead of venison. It would have been tied in a pudding cloth and boiled in the days before cooking foil, but the oven cooking is an improvement.

Mix all the ingredients, except 1 tablespoon of the parsley, the flour, jelly and gravy, together, stirring the egg in last. Work the mixture into a long roll and then turn in seasoned flour. Wrap the roll very tightly in foil and lay in an oval casserole with water to cover. Bring just to the boil on top of the stove and then simmer in the oven at 300°F (160°C, Gas Mark 2) for 2 hours.

Ten minutes before serving, carefully lift out and unwrap the roll and lay on a flat dish. Sprinkle lightly with a little salt and pepper and put back in the oven to dry off and brown the outside a little. Sprinkle with the remaining parsley and serve with red-currant jelly and a good brown gravy.

Jugged Hare

1 hare, cleaned and jointed
1⅓ cups (120 g) fine oatmeal
Salt and white pepper
Butter
1 medium onion, peeled and
stuck with cloves
1 large cooking apple, cored,
peeled and cut in slices
1 small lemon cut into pieces
½ lb (240 g) mushrooms, sliced
Thyme, parsley, marjoram and
3 bay leaves, tied in a bunch
or a bouquet garni
½ cup (1.2 dl) red wine
2½ cups (6 dl) beef stock (stock
cube will do)
12 forcemeat balls (see
page 210)
Red-currant jelly
12 pieces of toast

As ancient a recipe as any still served in England. A tall fireproof jar or casserole is required, large enough to hold the hare joints and some liquid. A large earthenware crock can be used. It must stand in a saucepan of boiling water deep enough to take the foil-covered container under its own lid.

Season the oatmeal with ½ teaspoon salt and ½ teaspoon pepper and rub it over the joints of the hare. Fry the joints lightly on all sides in a little butter.

Put the head, neck and ribs (which will not be served, as there is little meat on them, but which will enrich the gravy) in the bottom of the container. Sprinkle with oatmeal. Then pack in the fried joints, and then the onion, apple, lemon, mushrooms and herbs. Sprinkle again with oatmeal and a little more salt and pepper. Mix the wine and stock and pour in to fill up the container. Cover closely with a double thickness of foil and stand in a large saucepan of boiling water. Cover the saucepan and keep boiling for 3 hours. Towards the end of the cooking time fry the forcemeat balls in a little butter.

Remove the hare joints to a serving dish and strain the gravy, discarding the head, neck and ribs of the hare.

Stir the gravy and check its seasoning. It should be dark and rich and slightly thickened by the oatmeal. Pour the gravy all over the hare. Arrange the forcemeat balls around the edge of the dish and serve very hot with red-currant jelly and 2 pieces of dry toast for each person.

Mixed Fruit Stirabout

1 lb (½ kg) fruit (gooseberries,
  currants, raspberries,
  blackberries, diced rhubarb or
  any mixture)
4 tablespoons (60 g) castor
  sugar
½ stick (60 g) very soft butter
1 cup (120 g) flour
½ teaspoon salt
Scant 2 cups (4.5 dl) milk

This is another of the hot, filling puddings made by
farmers' wives, using fruit from the garden or
hedgerow as it came into season. It was traditionally
served with sugar and thick cream.

Cream together the sugar and butter. Sift the flour
and salt together and add to the creamed mixture.
Stir in milk until the mixture has the consistency of
a thick batter. Add the fruit, mixing carefully in
order not to break it up. Pour into a greased
fireproof dish or baking tin and bake at 350°F (180°C,
Gas Mark 4) for 30 minutes.

Whipped Syllabub

Juice and finely grated peel of
  2 lemons
½ cup (120 g) castor sugar
2 tablespoons brandy
2 tablespoons sherry
2 cups (4.5 dl) double cream

A seventeenth-century recipe, which comes from
Oxford, although this kind of syllabub was
fashionable all over the country, and was sometimes
used on a trifle instead of cream. It is very rich and a
small glassful is all that anyone requires. Serve with
almonds biscuits or sponge fingers.

Allow the lemon peel to infuse in the lemon juice for
2 or 3 hours before you make the syllabub. Strain the
juice on to the sugar, stir in the brandy and sherry,
and mix well. Put the cream into a bowl and very
slowly add the liquid, beating all the time. When the
cream is just thick enough to hold a peak, pile it into
glasses and leave in the refrigerator for at least 6
hours or overnight so that the flavour may reach its
full intensity.

Pershore Plums

1½ lb (¾ kg) red plums
  (Victorias are very good)
1½ lb (¾ kg) yellow plums (true
  greengages or Coe's Golden
  Drops are good)
1 tablespoon (15 g) butter
½ teaspoon grated nutmeg
½ teaspoon ground cinnamon
¾ cup (180 g) castor sugar
¼ cup (60 g) blanched almonds
¾ cup (90 g) shelled walnuts
1¼ cups (3 dl) double cream,
  whipped just to hold a peak

This eighteenth-century recipe from a manor house
in the Pershore district is referred to as a special
summer treat. It is a celestial late summer dish, but
the plums must be freestone varieties and ripe but
firm.

Halve the plums lengthways and remove the stones.
Butter a very large, shallow dish (a baking tray lined
with foil can be used but earthenware or oven
glassware is better).
  Lay out the plum halves in close rows, cut sides
upwards, red at one end and yellow at the other.
Take pinches of nutmeg and cinnamon and sprinkle
a very little on each half, and then sprinkle thickly
with two-thirds of the sugar. Put in a moderate oven,
325°F (170°C, Gas Mark 3), and bake uncovered for
35 minutes.
  Take the dish out and drop an almond or a walnut
into each plum half, sprinkle with the remaining
sugar and return to the oven for a further 5 minutes.
  Remove the dish from the oven, cool and then put
in the refrigerator for at least 1 hour. Put a good
spoonful of whipped cream on each plum and serve.

Tipsy Cake

1¼ sticks (150 g) butter
⅞ cup (210 g) castor sugar
2 eggs
1 cup (120 g) flour
A little milk to mix
¼ cup (60 g) blanched almonds
1¼ cups (3 dl) red wine
4 tablespoons brandy
1¼ cups (3 dl) double cream,
  whipped to just hold a peak

An eighteenth-century recipe from Oxford. Tipsy Cakes were served at ball suppers everywhere but this particular cake was traditional at Clarendon Club suppers in Oxford. The cake should be baked on the morning of the day on which it is to be served.

Cream 1 stick (120 g) of the butter and ½ cup (120 g) of the sugar. Beat in the eggs and then the flour, add 2 tablespoons of milk and beat very well again. Turn the mixture into a well-greased 8 inch (20 cm) cake tin and bake at 400°F (200°C, Gas Mark 6) for 35 minutes. Cover lightly with foil if the cake is browning too much. Allow the cake to cool a little in the tin before turning it out. When cold, cut the cake into 1 inch (2.5 cm) cubes and pile them into a glass bowl.

Fry the almonds in the remaining butter until they are a pale fawn colour. Scatter a little of the sugar into the pan and shake the almonds in it for a minute. Turn the almonds out on to kitchen paper, with any loose sugar, to drain and cool. When cold, chop them coarsely leaving some in halves. The loose sugar can be left in small lumps.

Mix the wine, brandy and the remaining sugar and pour over the cake. Leave to chill until it is almost time to serve. The cake should have taken up all the liquid. Pile the whipped cream over the top and scatter with the almonds and sugar.

Orange Tart

½ lb (240 g) short pastry
4 oranges
1 lemon
⅞ cup (210 g) castor sugar
6 eggs, separated

This recipe, found in an Oxford manuscript, dates from about 1780. The tart was supposed to have been a favourite of George III's queen, Charlotte of Mecklenburg. It is not included in Patrick Lamb's book, but is very much the kind of dish which he suggests for the third course of a royal dinner. It may well have been served at Blenheim. The original recipe produces a tart about 14 inches in diameter, which would have served about 20 people. For a large dinner at this time, there would probably have been four tarts with different fillings, preferably of different colours, one at each corner of the table.

Roll out the pastry and line a 9 inch (23 cm) tart tin with it.

Finely grate the peel and squeeze the juice from the oranges and the lemon into a bowl. Stir in ¾ cup (180 g) of the sugar and the well-beaten egg yolks, beat well and pour into the pastry-lined tin. Bake at 300°F (160°C, Gas Mark 2) for 45 minutes, or until the mixture has set.

Meanwhile, beat the egg whites with the remaining sugar until they hold a peak. Take out the tart, pile this meringue quickly on top and return to the oven for 10 minutes. The meringue should be crisp and lightly browned on the outside but soft inside. Serve immediately.

Oldbury Tarts

2 lb (1 kg) gooseberries
2 lb (1 kg) flour
2 sticks (240 g) butter
1 cup (240 g) lard
1¼ cups (120 g) demerara sugar

These little gooseberry tarts are famous all over Gloucestershire. Many local people maintain that the edges stand up better if the tarts are made the day before they are baked.

Top, tail and wipe the gooseberries. Put the flour into a bowl and make a well in the middle. Cut the butter and lard in small chunks and put into the well. Pour ⅝ cup (1.5 dl) boiling water quickly over the fat, stir with a knife until it has melted and then pull the flour down into it, continuing to stir with the knife blade until the mixture forms a softish paste. Break off a small piece of the paste and roll out, on a floured pastry board, to about the size of a saucer. Repeat this process but this time roll out the pastry to about the size of the top of a cup. Continue in this way until all the pastry has been used up.
  Turn up the edges of the larger pieces of pastry about 1 inch (2.5 cm) all round and cover the bottom of each with gooseberries. On to each put 2 teaspoons of demerara sugar and then a smaller piece of pastry, sealing it to the inner side of the tart, not over the top. Pinch the standing-up edge all round to flute it. Bake at 400°F (200°C, Gas Mark 6) for 20 minutes.

Bakewell Tart 1

½ lb (240 g) puff pastry
⅜ cup (90 g) strawberry or
  apricot jam
4 egg yolks and 3 egg whites
⅔ cup (90 g) fresh fine white
  breadcrumbs
¾ cup (90 g) ground almonds
⅜ cup (90 g) sugar
¾ stick (90 g) butter, just melted
Pinch of salt

An early nineteenth-century recipe from the town of Bakewell in the Peak District of Derbyshire.

Roll out the pastry ⅛ inch (0.25 cm) thick. Allow it to rest for about 20 minutes, then roll it out again and line a 9 inch (23 cm) flan tin. Lightly spread the bottom with the jam.
  Beat the egg yolks. Add the breadcrumbs, ground almonds, sugar and butter and beat well. In another bowl beat the egg whites with the salt until they just hold a peak. Fold the egg whites into the egg-yolk mixture until they are well amalgamated. Pour the mixture on to the jam and spread evenly over the whole surface. Bake immediately in a hot oven, 425°F (220°C, Gas Mark 7), for 30 minutes or until the filling is firm and lightly browned.

Bakewell Tart 2

½ lb (240 g) puff pastry
⅜ cup (90 g) strawberry or
  apricot jam
¾ stick (90 g) butter
⅜ cup (90 g) sugar
4 egg yolks and 3 egg whites
¾ cup (90 g) plain flour
¾ cup (90 g) ground almonds
Pinch of salt

In this later recipe, the breadcrumbs are replaced by flour.

Line a flan tin and spread the pastry with jam as for the previous recipe.
  Cream the butter and sugar; stir in the egg yolks, the flour and the ground almonds. Beat the egg whites with the salt until stiff and fold them into the mixture. Pour on to the jam and bake as in the other recipe.

Baked Blackberry Roll

½ lb (240 g) self-raising flour
½ teaspoon salt
½ stick (60 g) butter, plus a little
  extra
⅝ cup (1.5 dl) milk
1 lb (½ kg) ripe blackberries
2 heaping tablespoons (30 g)
  brown sugar
½ teaspoon cinnamon

This is a very old recipe. The hedgerows of Warwickshire are full of blackberries and the farmers' wives have always been quick to send the children out to pick them. Warwickshire was Shakespeare's county. A poor boy from a large family, he would certainly have been sent blackberry picking.

Sift the flour and salt together and rub in the half stick (60 g) of butter. Stir in enough milk to make a soft dough, but be careful not to make it sticky. Knead the dough just enough to make a round smooth ball and then pat it flat to ½ inch (1 cm) thick oblong. Sprinkle the blackberries on it, together with the sugar and cinnamon. Roll up into a roly-poly shape, seal the ends and put it, with the join downwards, on a greased baking sheet. Brush with a little melted butter and bake in a hot oven, 400°F (200°C, Gas Mark 6), for 25 to 30 minutes or until firm and golden brown.

Banbury Cakes

1 lb (½ kg) puff or flaky pastry
1½ sticks (180 g) butter, softened
2 tablespoons honey
1½ cups (240 g) candied lemon
  and orange peel, or replace
  with sultanas if preferred
1⅓ cups (240 g) currants
1 teaspoon grated nutmeg
1 teaspoon ground allspice
1 teaspoon cinnamon
1 egg white
¼ cup (60 g) castor sugar

Very good indeed, if served hot.

Roll out the pastry to about ⅛ inch (0.25 cm) thick and cut into 4 inch (10 cm) squares.
  Beat the butter and honey together and stir in the fruit and spices. Put a spoonful of this filling in the centre of each pastry square, gather the corners to the centre and pinch firmly together. Cut 2 tiny slits in the top and brush each cake over with the egg white. Sprinkle thickly with sugar, arrange on a well-greased baking tin and bake at 400°F (200°C, Gas Mark 6) for 10 to 12 minutes.

Cider Cake

1 stick (120 g) butter
½ cup (120 g) castor sugar
3 eggs, well beaten
2 cups (240 g) self-raising flour
⅓ cup (60 g) coarsely chopped
  walnuts
¼ teaspoon grated nutmeg
⅝ cup (1.5 dl) dry cider

Cider cake is traditional in Oxfordshire, Herefordshire, Worcestershire and Gloucestershire. There are several recipes, mostly from the nineteenth century, but they vary very little. This one produces a very good, moist cake with a distinctive flavour. It is delicious topped with whipped cream and served as a sweet.

Cream the butter and sugar. Add the eggs and then half the flour, mixed with the walnuts and the nutmeg, and beat well. Beat the cider so that it froths and mix it in. As soon as it has amalgamated with the other ingredients, stir in the remaining flour and beat again. Pour the mixture into a greased shallow tin, 8 to 9 inches (20 to 23 cm) in diameter and bake in the middle of a 400°F (200°C, Gas Mark 6) oven for 50 minutes.
  Allow the cake to cool for 5 minutes before turning it out of the tin.

Huntsman's Cake

1 stick (120 g) butter
½ cup (120 g) castor sugar
4 eggs, separated
2 cups (240 g) self-raising flour
1 cup (120 g) ground almonds
½ teaspoon salt
⅔ cup (120 g) currants
¾ cup (120 g) candied mixed
 peel
⅜ cup (60 g) glacé cherries
½ cup (60 g) shredded almonds
1 cup (2.4 dl) sherry
1 teaspoon sodium bicarbonate
1 tablespoon vinegar

This is one of the best of all fruit cakes. It used to be made in the Cotswolds for the traditional after-hunting tea at which boiled eggs, bread and butter, and hot scones, crumpets or muffins were also served.

Cream the butter and sugar. Add the egg yolks one at a time, beating well in. Add the flour, ground almonds, salt, currants, peel, cherries and almonds gradually, then pour in half the sherry. Fold in the stiffly beaten egg whites, and finally the sodium bicarbonate dissolved in the vinegar. Put the cake mixture into a greased and papered tin and cover with a piece of greaseproof paper. Place in a hot oven, 425°F (220°C, Gas Mark 7). After 10 minutes lower the heat to 325°F (170°C, Gas Mark 3) and bake for 2 hours.
  When cooked and still very hot, pour over the remaining sherry, by spoonfuls, and leave the cake in the tin, covered with a cloth, until it is quite cold.

Leicestershire Market Day Savoury

6 pork chops
2 pig's kidneys
2 lb (1 kg) potatoes
1 lb (½ kg) onions
1 lb (½ kg) tomatoes, blanched,
 peeled and quartered
1 small apple
1 teaspoon dried sage
2 cups (4.5 dl) stock
Salt and pepper

This dish would be left cooking for hours, while the farmer's wife went to market. It requires a minimum of two hours but its flavour is improved by longer cooking.

Peel and slice the potatoes and onions. Skin, core and slice the kidneys. Put the chops in a casserole, then add a layer of potato slices and a layer of onion slices. Next, add the sliced kidneys followed by the tomatoes and then another layer of onion and potato. Sprinkle this layer with the peeled, chopped apple, the sage and salt and pepper. Pour in the stock. Cover the casserole with a tight-fitting lid or with foil and put in a slow oven 300°F (160°C, Gas Mark 2) for 2 to 4 hours.

An Oxford Savoury

1 small tin anchovy fillets
8 flat mushrooms, each about
 1½ inches (3.5 cm) across,
 stalks removed
½ stick (60 g) butter
4 slices white bread, cut in
 circles about 3 inches (8 cm) in
 diameter
1 teaspoon prepared English
 mustard
2 tablespoons whipped cream,
 slightly chilled

Recorded in about 1870, this savoury was served at the high table or sometimes in the master's lodge at Balliol College. It is a pleasure to drink a good claret with this dish.

Drain the anchovies and cut the little fillets into very small pieces, using scissors. Set aside. Lightly fry the mushrooms in half the butter.
  Toast the bread. Spread each piece with the rest of the butter and then with a very little mustard. Sprinkle some of the chopped anchovy fillets on each piece of toast. Place 2 mushrooms slightly overlapping on each toast and just before carrying the dish to table, put 1 teaspoon of chilled whipped cream in the centre of each hot toast.

The West Country

Somerset, Devon, Cornwall, Dorset, Wiltshire, Avon

During the 30 years from about 1820 to 1850 the easiest, fastest and safest way to reach the west of England from London was by mail coach or any other crack coach, such as the Exeter Defiance, which made the run. Only a very wealthy and distinguished man would take his own coach or carriage such a distance, unless he had time in hand and could break the journey and rest his horses by staying with friends or family *en route*.

It was not a safe or easy journey and the fast and famous mail coaches were more liable to accidents than those whose owners prided themselves less on keeping to their schedules. The roads of England were made by the Romans and had been neglected for 1,500 years. Towards the end of the eighteenth century efforts were made all over the country to improve them, but towns and villages were reluctant to give much labour and even the levies raised by the introduction of toll gates did not entirely solve the problem. With the increase of trade early in the nineteenth century, communications had to be improved. Not only coaches but wagon-loads of goods had to be able to pass from Manchester (known as Cottonopolis) to London or from London to Southampton. The gentry wanted to go to fashionable Bath and 22 coaches made the run daily. Among them was the Comet, which can still be seen in Dodington Carriage Museum, near Chipping Sodbury, Avon. This was a crack coach, which travelled to Bath via Marlborough and then on to Bristol.

There was a great deal of fear and uncertainty among all travellers. Some had fears of drunken coachmen and a runaway team. Many winter travellers particularly dreaded the snow; others were terrified of the high winds, which could sometimes overturn a laden coach, and yet others feared the horror of floods. Indeed, some coaches ran in the summer only.

Some accidents, however, could not be foreseen. The Exeter Mail, which raced daily to Devonport, took the same route over Salisbury Plain and past Stonehenge as the Quicksilver. Before daylight on the morning of 20 October, 1816, the coach was a few miles outside Salisbury when the coachman became aware that the large animal, which he thought was a calf and which had kept pace for several miles with the horses, was alarming them so much that they were almost out of control. When he reached a small inn known as Winterslow Hut, not one of his normal stops, he pulled up and immediately a lioness sprang at his offside leader, a bay horse called Pomegranate. The driver had pulled out his blunderbuss when some men appeared out of the darkness with a mastiff. They were chasing the lioness, which had escaped from a travelling menagerie. They set the mastiff on the lioness, which left the horse and tore the dog to pieces before she was captured with nets. The horse was badly mauled, but survived and was shown in the menagerie, apparently on easy terms with the lioness and the mastiff. The dog must have been a substitute, as the incident is vouched for as being accurately described. The Post Office owns a painting of the scene with the lioness attacking Pomegranate, and also an original poster of Ballard's Grand Collection of Wild Beasts including lioness, horse and mastiff.

After the incident the Exeter Mail went on to Salisbury with only one leader (an arrangement coachmen called "unicorn") where no doubt the passengers were even more thankful than usual for breakfast.

Meals, always hurried, might be bad, but they might be unexpectedly good. Certain inns were famous for local produce and travellers took York hams, Stilton cheese (sent to the Bell at Stilton from Leicestershire, where the original cheeses were made), Banbury cakes, Bath buns and Bath chaps, Shrewsbury cakes and Wiltshire hams and bacon (the last two obtained at the breakfast stop in Salisbury) on with them as presents, and often bought them again on the homeward run for their own families.

Most coach journeys, of course, offered nothing worse than dust, exhaustion, boredom and the discomfort of sitting at such close quarters – a fine young lady going to visit relatives might feel quite faint from the emanation of her unwashed neighbour. The Beehive Line, which was established to make travel more comfortable, refused to carry fish or fishmongers and provided reading lights for passengers.

To reach Exeter, the traveller had to pass through the western counties of Wiltshire, Dorset, Somerset and Devonshire, crossing Salisbury Plain, wild and bleak and mostly uninhabited, where the mist could descend in a moment so that the horses had to slow down to a walking pace and gentlemen riding inside kept their pistols in their hands. Highway robbery does not seem to have occurred very frequently on the western run, but it was always a risk.

Nevertheless, things were better than they were for the traveller in the seventeenth and eighteenth centuries who had to contend with appalling road conditions. In 1698 Celia Fiennes, daughter of the second son of the first Viscount Saye and Sele, made a journey which she calls in her journal "*My great journey to Newcastle and to Cornwall*". It was a great journey indeed and all made on horseback. Starting from London, she rode north and west into Derbyshire, back through Cheshire into Wales, north again to Lancashire and the Lake District and along the border to Newcastle, through Durham and Manchester across to Shrewsbury, and then through Worcester, Gloucester, Bristol, Wells and Taunton to Exeter, Plymouth and Land's End. Celia Fiennes was 36 when she made this journey, travelling alone but for her servants. She was a lady of aristocratic birth and of very strong puritan persuasions. She was one of the earliest of the eccentric English ladies who devoted their lives to travel, although, unlike Lady Mary Wortley Montague, Mary Kingsley and, in our own times, Freya Stark, she confined her journeys to the British Isles.

At St Austell, in south Cornwall, she discovered an inn with *"a pretty good dining room and chamber within it, and very neat country women; my landlady brought me one of the West Country tarts this was the first I met with, though I had asked for them in many places in Somerset and Devonshire, its an apple pye with a custard all on the top, its the most acceptable entertainment that could be made me; they scald their cream and milk in most parts of those countys and so its a sort clouted cream as we call it, with a little sugar, and so put on the top of the apple pie. I was very much pleased with my supper. . . ."* Other traditional specialities of St Austell are skinless sausages and hogs' pudding, but these do not seem to have been offered to her, although both are excellent.

Each small Cornish port had its fishing fleet, as it had since the Middle Ages and as most of the ports, now larger, do today. In the eighteenth century the diet of the poor in Cornwall consisted mainly of fish, in particular pilchards and mackerel, eaten fresh when the catch came in or salted down in barrels and jars. They also relied on potatoes, barley bread and a kind of grain known in Cornish as *pillez*, now no longer cultivated. The families of the poorest tinners (tin miners) hardly ever ate wheaten bread and rarely ate meat. In the extreme west of Cornwall, inland from Land's End and the Lizard, large herds of goats were farmed and sold in the markets between Michaelmas and Christmas. This meat was very cheap and was considered by travellers to be not unlike venison.

When fish was scarce, as it was in 1784 in the fishing town of Fowey, the fishermen and their families lived almost entirely on limpets, whole families spending six or eight hours a day scraping them off the rocks, eating some raw as they were collected and taking a sackful home to boil for a hot meal at night. Wild foods played a quite considerable part in the diet of tinners and smallholders alike. Children too young to be sent underground or even to work on the surface, were sent to collect each plant or fruit as it came into season. The mild climate and the fertile valleys just inshore behind the beaches, produced much that added iron, vitamins and variety. Dandelion leaves, watercress, nettle tops, carline thistles, mushrooms and all the fruits of the hedges – crab-apples, hips and haws, blackberries, wild raspberries and strawberries – were there for the picking for those whose parents and grandparents had taught them where to look.

It is recorded that at a dame school in south Cornwall, the fees were one penny a week. Every Friday the old dame would remind the children that they must bring something on Monday. It need not be a penny. She would take a candle, a corner of a pasty, some berries or something for a salad, but they must pay or go home. Most of them paid with a piece of the Sunday pasty. For Sundays, holidays and feast days, pasties were always made if wheat flour was available; sometimes they were even made with a crust of barley and rye flour. Pasties with a filling of potato and onion (if there was no meat, fish or bacon available), heavy cakes, stamp cakes and saffron bread were all made whenever they could be afforded for any feast or celebration.

The gentry and the merchants, who invested in the mines, naturally lived very differently from the tinners and other poor labourers, and fared very well. They were known as adventurers because they were venturing their money in a mine which might or might not be rich in tin or copper. Each mine had a count house, usually a substantial and handsome stone building standing a short distance from some of the main shafts, and the mine captain's house was attached or nearby. The clerks who worked in the main room of the count house, which was usually some 40 feet long, stood at their tall desks entering the quantities of ore brought up, the amount of coal used and the wages due. On Accounting Day, which might be once a month or once a quarter, the desks were put away, long trestle tables were covered with white linen cloths, and a huge dinner, traditionally of roasts of beef, mutton and chicken giblets and star-gazing pies, conger eel pies, and, if possible, crab and lobster pies, was served to the shareholders by the wives of some of the clerks and the mine officials. Great quantities of porter and ale and smuggled brandy and rum were drunk.

Outside the count house door, piles of ore were displayed and if the mine was "cutting rich" a more simple feast was served to each shift of tinners as they "came up to grass". This was traditionally a whole roast ox with good bread and plenty of beer. If the mine was producing little, the tinners were not feasted on Accounting Day. However, despite the fact that they were always poor and, in bad years, on the brink of starvation, and despite the fact that their sons had to work underground from the age of 10 or 12 while their wives and daughters worked on the surface (known as the grass) breaking up the lumps of ore, they celebrated many holidays not known as such to Church or State in the rest of the country. The first day of May was the beginning of their year and many, but not all, celebrated Christmas Day twice, according to the new calendar and again 11 days later according to the old calendar. There was Paul's Tide on 14 January, the first Friday in March, Midsummer Day, Picrous Day, which fell on the second Thursday before Christmas, and several others. The mine captains and the adventurers were not unnaturally infuriated by these holidays, but the tinners insisted on them as their right and as there was more work in the mines than miners to do it, they could not be prevented. A tinner who was sacked had only to walk a few miles and apply for work at another mine. Often he had no need to move his home. The mine owners, therefore, contributed a shilling a man on each of the main holidays and the traditional, violent Cornish games were played; plenty of ale was drunk and often there was smuggled wine or brandy and spirits saved from a recent wreck.

There was one form of holiday which seems to have been peculiar to the Cornish and which was very important to the tinners. The dangerous Cornish coast from St Ives in the north, round Land's End and the Lizard to Fowey on the south coast, has at all times been the scene of hundreds of shipwrecks; vessels of all sizes and nationalities have come to grief there, some in dense fog, some driven ashore in sudden gales and some sailing off-course and on to the rocks. The Cornish, from the poorest to the landed gentry, considered that anything that was of the slightest value was theirs for the taking from a wrecked ship.

At the news that a ship was in trouble off nearby rocks, the tinners who were above ground would seize axes and hatchets and rush straight to the site and children would warn the underground shift, who would come up as quickly as possible. The mine would be deserted at some risk of water seepage as well as loss of time, and as many as 2,000 tinners would congregate on the rocks and the beach nearest to the ship. Everything that was washed ashore was theirs, to drink or eat or sell at market. Passengers and sailors alike, drowned or living, were stripped of their clothes and valuables, although once stripped, they might be taken to shelter.

It will be seen from the foregoing that Cornwall was indeed very different from any other part of England. One reason for this difference is that in Roman and Saxon times those of the Celtic inhabitants of Wessex who refused to submit to conquest were driven farther and farther west and perforce settled in Cornwall and Wales. Thus, many of the traditions of Cornwall are different from those of neighbouring Devonshire, and this applies to Cornish cookery. In the seventeenth and eighteenth centuries the wives of the more prosperous farmers, mine owners and tradesmen introduced scalded cream in quite large quantities into pies, particularly with lobster, crab or chicken. Scalded or "clouted" cream was the favourite of all Cornish children, served on fresh, home-made scones with honey or apple jelly and, at a later date, with treacle. Cream and treacle served on scones or on plain boiled rice was always known as "thunder and lightning". Many other dishes, more or less peculiar to Cornwall, are based on pastry which was usually a good but fairly solid short or rough puff crust. Farmers' and fishermen's wives made a flat cake of rough puff pastry with currants which was scored in one-inch squares and always known as heavy cake. They also made a kind of apple sandwich and small pastry cakes marked with the butter stamper and called stamp cakes. The Cornish use of saffron is interesting because it continues to the present day and is almost entirely confined to bread, cakes and buns. Nowhere else in England is it possible to walk into a baker's shop and buy cakes containing saffron over the counter as a matter of course. In medieval times, saffron was much used to colour dishes of lamb, chicken, rabbit, fish or rice, as it still is today in many Mediterranean and Middle Eastern dishes. In England, after the eighteenth century, its use became much less frequent and, as far as can be ascertained, it has never been used in baking outside Cornwall. Saffron imparts a subtle flavour to bread and cakes which not everyone can distinguish but which the true Cornishman misses if it is omitted. It also gives a good, clear yellow colour with a dark golden crust.

The River Tamar marks the boundary between Cornwall and Devon and flows into Plymouth Sound, as does the Plym farther east. Between them lies Plymouth, a fine city in lovely countryside and the great port of Tudor and Stuart times from which sailed some of the most famous of England's seafarers.

Drake sailed out of Plymouth in the *Golden Hind* in 1577 and in two years and nine months returned again having sailed round the world. Also out of Plymouth sailed Raleigh, Sir Humphrey Gilbert, Sir Richard Grenville, Hawkins and Frobisher.

Sir Humphrey Gilbert lived at Compton Castle near Paignton, where his descendants have lived ever since, although it is now the property of the National Trust. The castle has a particular interest for American visitors because Sir Humphrey took possession of Newfoundland in 1583 in the name of Queen Elizabeth I, and this was the first British colony.

Two hundred years after the founding of the colony the Maine Society of Daughters of American Colonists presented a memorial plaque, which is hung in the castle.

The castle's kitchens are large, and there is equipment from all periods; a huge hearth completely fills one end of the main kitchen with a bread oven at one side of it and cauldrons, spits and jacks ready, it seems, for use. Tubs and pans are arranged on the tiled floor and even today there is the contented feeling of a place where very good and plentiful food has been prepared through the centuries for a large household and its guests.

Plymouth was the last port at which the *Mayflower* called on her voyage across the Atlantic. She sailed from Southampton on 15 August and returned because the accompanying vessel was unseaworthy, then left again from Plymouth on 16 September. From Plymouth came the last fresh water, fruit, vegetables, carcass meat and meat on the hoof that the 100 or so Pilgrim Fathers she carried would taste until they made landfall on the American coast (at what became Provincetown).

Even on a voyage of two months, fresh and even tolerably good preserved foods were a problem. On all voyages until the late nineteenth century, cabin passengers and any others who could afford it, took as many extras as their purses and their ingenuity allowed. So did the ships' captains and their officers. The crews existed from port to port on standard rations.

A fascinating collection of notes and recipes for food to take on a long voyage was made by Dorothy Hartley, whose splendid book *Food in England* was written in 1954. She had been able, when a young woman, to question her elderly aunt, who had made several voyages to West Africa in the 1850s. This lady and her family had used a sixteenth-century recipe for preparing cooked birds for shipboard and found that ducks, salted for 24 hours, then roasted, drained, packed in a large pot, and covered with several pounds of melted and stewed butter, to which cloves, mace, nutmeg, bay leaves and bay salt had been added, kept perfectly for as many weeks as they could refrain from eating them.

The ladies of the family, who were experienced in sea travel, spent several days in the kitchen of their Welsh house, preparing for a voyage. They enjoyed the preparations and their own ingenuity, priding themselves on having some unexpected luxury to offer when the captain dined with them even towards the end of the voyage. They made a condensed cream, which kept very well in little pots; lemons were packed in boxes of sand; mustard and cress and watercress were grown in crocks in the cabins, providing the visual pleasure of green growing plants and the epicurean pleasure of fresh salad. They also made squares of condensed veal and chicken soup, according to a seventeenth-century recipe called "Veal Glue for Travellers". These they found particularly useful for those who were seasick. For the first good meal, these accomplished ladies boned a goose, stuffed a boned capon inside it, a chicken inside that, then a pigeon and finally a lark with a luck token inside it. The whole great solid bird was put in a thick pastry crust and slowly baked. After it had been allowed to get quite cold, two pounds of melted butter were poured into the space between crust and bird and a little saved to brush over the crust as thickly as possible. The pie was then wrapped in a clean cloth and packed in a box of straw and, being completely sealed with butter, would keep two or three weeks. The crust was not intended to be eaten, but it often was if it had not become mouldy or rancid. Eggs were preserved in crocks of water-glass, and hard-boiled eggs were pickled and taken in jars, along with other pickles and chutneys. Pens of laying hens were taken so that there were a few fresh eggs each day, until it was decided to eat the hens themselves.

Potted meats and potted game, potted shrimps and pickled herrings were also taken. A nineteenth-century recipe for pressed beef, from a different source, says: "*If you send it to sea, add bay-salt when you boil and put no green herbs and season high and put it in a pot and cover with melted beef suet.*" A 16-pound flank of beef is suggested for this recipe. Beef Cheese was a regular ship's store for captain and officers in the sixteenth and seventeenth centuries and it is suggested that it was taken on the *Mayflower.*

Lemon juice had been made a regular issue to all sailors in the Royal Navy in 1795 and this ended the terrible threat of scurvy. It was not compulsory in the merchant service for another hundred years (by which time limes were being used instead), and immigrant and slave ships often did not provide it except for their crews. Unless such passengers were already undernourished and short of vitamin C, the voyage had to exceed about two months for scurvy to be a real danger, and even when a sufferer was very far gone – gums swollen, joints haemorrhaging badly – two or three days on fresh food would bring an improvement. Captain Parry in *Voyages in the Arctic,* 1819, wrote: "*A number of men employed all day in picking scurvy-grass for purpose of boiling with our pea soup. The taste . . . somewhat resembled turnip tops . . . but whatever may be its anti-scorbutic qualities, it has little or nothing to recommend it to the palate.*" Scurvy-grass, also known as spoonwort, grows within the Arctic Circle as well as on the sea coasts and mountains throughout northern Europe. Sadly, the boiling would have removed much of its vitamin C content.

Parry also made his crew collect sorrel leaves, found in Iceland and Greenland in the summer. He says: "*Two afternoons in each week . . . occupied by all hands in collecting the leaves . . . to be served in lieu of lemon juice, pickles and dried herbs* [it was an advantage to be as saving as possible with the lemon juice in case they were caught in the ice], *a part of the leaves was served to the messes as puddings, salads, pickles, or boiled greens. . . . It is well known to be a never failing specific for scorbutic affections.*"

Seamen were fed from barrels of salt pork and sometimes salt beef, dried peas and beans, and the famous ship's biscuits, which were as hard and as thick as outsize dog biscuits. On Sundays there was usually plum duff for pudding. Smollet, the eighteenth-century novelist, describes in *Roderick Random* how seamen were fed: "*We heard the boatswain's pipe to dinner and immediately the boy . . . returned with a large wooden platter full of boiled peas . . . crying 'scaldings', all the way as he came. . . . Mr Morgan himself enriched the mess with a lump of salt butter . . . and a handful of onion shorn with some pounded pepper . . . they told me that on Wednesdays and Fridays the ship's company had no meat. . . .*"

All through the centuries Devonshire has been for the most part a well-fed county. Devonshire cream, Devonshire dumplings, Devonshire junket and Devonshire cider were bywords at the beginning of the twentieth century, denoting the rich but simple dishes which holiday-makers on farms and in seaside villages might expect.

The great tracts of Devonshire moorlands, Dartmoor and part of Exmoor, pastured many sheep and the wool trade brought part of her prosperity while moorland mutton was demanded by travellers to the West. In the seventeenth and eighteenth centuries, in the vast kitchen at Saltram House, on the Plympton side of Plymouth, mutton was spit-roasted and, on occasion, a whole side was braised in the local cider, in a large fish kettle, "*with many small onions, thyme and marjoram, nutmeg and mace, young peas if you have 'em, with a good bunch of mint*". I have given this recipe for a smaller piece of lamb.

Exeter, north-east of Plymouth, became in Saxon times a royal city and among the titles of succeeding queens was that of Lady Paramount of Exeter. For these honours Exonians were called on to pay heavy dues to the crown. The city prospered, however, because of the wool trade and the very fine qualities of serge, which was produced in the town itself and in local villages. The Worshipful Company of Weavers, Fullers and Shearmen of the City of Exeter became a famous guild, well known throughout the land and known in Exeter not only for its excellent supervision of the wool trade but for the banquets given in the great hall. Venison from the Exmoor herds, salmon from the Exe or from the Tavy, just over the border in Somerset, sea trout or peal, lobsters and fine crabs, moorland mutton and beef from the old-fashioned, tawny south Devon cows were cooked with spices and wine, cider and cream to make dishes as rich and elaborate as the guildsmen tasted when business took them to London. The citizens of Exeter, obstinately loyal, hardworking and talented at the organization of whatever business they undertook, understood also the good things of life and their hospitality was famous. The traveller who stopped at an Exeter inn rarely had any complaints.

North-east of Exeter, near Barnstaple and approaching the Somerset border, stands Arlington Court, built in 1822 on the site of the ancestral home of the Chichester family. Miss Rosalie Chichester, the last of her line, left a description of a luncheon picnic in the grounds in 1878. This was to be a grand occasion as the family had been on a long cruise on their yacht, the *Erminia*. Sir Bruce Chichester decided to sail round Land's End and up to Ilfracombe, where four carriages and a brake met the party at the pier. Guests in their own equipages joined them on the road and there were 30 or 40 carriages in procession by the time they reached the main gates of Arlington Court. Luncheon was to be at one o'clock and a cricket match was to follow it.

The picnic was laid out in a meadow overlooking the lake. Ice, in the late nineteenth century, came in large blocks, as ship's ballast, and was packed in straw and transported to the ice house of any mansion near the port of entry. Almost every mansion had an ice house dug out of a hillock in their park and it was often disguised by an ornamental building. In the ice house at Arlington Court, the cold food was chilled until it was required. Any hot food came down from the large, light kitchens packed in hay boxes. On this occasion there was a hot and a chilled game soup, local salmon with cucumber and peas in aspic, veal rolls, chicken in aspic, home-cooked ham, a cold baron of beef, lettuce and tomato salad, small hot potatoes from the gardens, strawberries and raspberries with clotted cream, Adelaide trifle and moulded ice puddings.

Low tables, with legs which unscrewed, were made by the estate carpenter especially for picnics. Folding wicker chairs, deck-chairs and tartan rugs were used. The food must have been delicious and the scene, since it was beautiful summer weather, brilliant.

The great abbey of Glastonbury, near Wells in Somerset, one of the richest monastic buildings in England, was destroyed by fire in 1184. Precious relics, much treasure and manuscripts, which might have unravelled many an historic tangle, were also destroyed. The rebuilding started immediately, however, and continued over the next 200 years. The succeeding abbots became very wealthy in their own right; too wealthy, indeed, for their own good, since most of the abbey's lands were confiscated at the time of the dissolution. In the fourteenth century the abbots of Glastonbury lived like princes and the abbot's kitchen remains intact to prove it. The rest of the abbot's house has disappeared, except for a beautiful vaulted porch. The site of the great hall can be traced and is very large, with the elaborate kitchen building adjoining. All visitors of standing, sometimes royal and often noble, would have been entertained by the abbot. A hundred years earlier their food would have been cooked in the monks' kitchen and brought over by the serving brethren, no doubt with a few extra dishes added in their honour, but all half-cold on arrival.

The fourteenth-century kitchen, built for Abbot Breynton, was a large stone building with fireplaces, bread ovens and chimneys in each corner. The flues were built behind the vaulted ceiling and led out through the high lantern roof, so that this kitchen, probably almost alone among medieval kitchens, was smokeless except when small birds, slices of meat or whole fish were roasted on the raised charcoal hearths. In this specially designed building a feast could be prepared by the lay brethren trained in cooking, only using ingredients from the abbey's own lands. Plenty of fine cattle and sheep grazed nearby and there was a stewpond where carp, roach and tench swam until they were netted.

Pike and other fish swam in the nearby lake and herons and mallards were plentiful on its shores. The brethren would have kept a poultry yard, with enclosures for pheasants and partridges as well as the usual hens, ducks, geese and occasional turkeys. There are known to have been fine orchards and no doubt a large kitchen and herb garden was carefully tended. Whether those who cooked for the abbot and his noble guests were allowed to eat the leavings from his table or had to return to the refectory to eat the much simpler food of the monks we do not know.

Bristol, situated at the head of the Bristol Channel where the Avon flows into the Severn Estuary, was the greatest trading port of the West Country and perhaps its richest city. It was considered part of Somerset until 1974, when it became officially the chief city of the new small county of Avon. The port was well placed for trade with Wales and Ireland and also for the long voyages to the West Indies.

In the seventeenth century, Bristol merchants underwrote voyages to the African slave coast, where the specially fitted vessels filled up with slaves, who were taken to Jamaica and sold to English plantation owners. The voyage was already showing profit, but the ships loaded up with sugar and came home again to Bristol, where their cargo, always in demand, was sold for even greater profit. Naturally, Bristol merchants became rich and built themselves mansions and terraces of fine houses as elegant as those in nearby Bath.

The ships were also engaged in the spice trade with the Levant and every spice imaginable went into the dishes of the table of a successful Bristolian. Pineapples were carefully brought by ships' captains especially for the wives of the ship-owners. Sometimes, bananas and mangoes, carefully wrapped, survived a quick passage; turtles were brought back alive in tanks which were kept on deck. Bristol food could be exotic indeed.

It is recorded that turtles and pineapples were sent on to London markets as, of course, was much of the sugar and many more homely West Country products, in particular good butter and Cheddar cheese.

Cheddar cheese was first made in the Somerset village of Cheddar on the edge of Sedgemoor, near the geological fault known as the Cheddar Gorge. It was the first English cheese to be made to a regular formula. The cheese became popular in the seventeenth century and was made in many parts of Somerset, Dorset and Devon. It was sent to the Bristol and London markets and taken as a ship's store from Bristol and Plymouth. It was the custom to take the milk from one milking from all the farms around the village and so make up a large batch of cheese. Celia Fiennes noted that this was also done in Cheshire.

By the seventeenth century, cheese fairs were held in many places, local cheeses being bought by pedlars for resale as well as by private customers. The Guild of Cheesemongers was started towards the end of the eighteenth century and representatives travelled through all the cheese-making counties, buying up large quantities of cheeses, which were sent by sea, river and canal to London. Dorset produced small quantities of the Blue Vinney cheese (no longer obtainable), which was highly thought of by many cheese fanciers throughout the nineteenth century. Neither Devon nor Wiltshire was known for any particular cheese, although plenty was made for home and local use and every good housewife had her own recipe for the traditional herb-flavoured cheeses. These were made in Roman times and were very popular in the Middle Ages, when curd cheese, to which mixed herbs or their strained juices were added, was known as "spermyse". Sage cheese, the green brightened with spinach juice, was made in Wiltshire, although today all sage cheese is attributed to Derby. Marigold petals were also worked into cheese to make a colour contrast with the sage.

South from Bristol and across the border into Dorset lies some of the most typically English countryside in the south-west. Much of the country is rich and gently undulating, patterned in spring and summer with crops of wheat and barley, roots and vetches, the commons alight with golden gorse, the crops neatly divided by dark green hedges.

It is not only part of Thomas Hardy's Wessex, it is the part of it in which he himself was born, brought up and to which he returned to write. His grandfather built the thatched cottage called Hatchlands in 1800 and it is said that as he quite frequently smuggled in brandy, he had the "squint" in the porch put in so that watch could be kept on the lane for excisemen.

The descriptions of the countryside in his novels are inimitable. This is the scene of the sheep-washing in *Far from the Madding Crowd*:

> *The river slid noiselessly as a shade, the swelling reeds and sedge forming a flexible palisade upon its moist bank. To the north of the mead were trees, the leaves of which were new, soft and moist, not yet having darkened under the summer sun and drought. . . . From the recess of this knot of foliage the loud notes of three cuckoos were resounding through the still air.*

This sensitive description contrasts with the robust account of the food for the sheep-shearing supper, which is given by one of the shepherds, Cainy Ball. Hardy makes very clear the desire for the sheer quantity and the richness of the suety puddings which would fill the bellies of countrymen who worked hard and were always hungry.

"We workfolk shall have some lordly junketing tonight," said Cainy Ball. . . . "This morning, I see 'em making the great puddens in the milking pail – lumps of fat [suet] *as big as yer thumb, Mister Oak: I've never seed such splendid large knobs of fat before in the days of my life – they never used to be bigger than a horse-bean. And there was a great black crock upon the brandise* [dialect word for a large trivet or pot-rest] *. . . but I don't know what was in within."*

"And there's two bushels of biffins [a kind of red-cheeked cooking apple] *for apple pies," said Maryann.*

"Well, I hope to do my duty by it all," said Joseph Poorgrass. . . . "Yes; victuals and drink is a cheerful thing. . . . Tis the gospel of the body, without which we perish, so to speak it."

The great manor of Cranborne Chase is now a wildlife sanctuary for the protection of animals and plants. Dorset abounded with wild flowers but these are being sadly reduced in numbers, even deep in the country, as hedges are cut and drainage increased to do away with the wet lands. The foundations of Cranborne Manor date back to the twelfth century. The house stood in thick forest and it is probable that it was enlarged by King John and used as a hunting lodge. He is recorded as having stayed in the house on 12 occasions and hunted in the forest more often. The estate, bounded by three rivers, covered 700,000 acres, and it remained a royal domain until the seventeenth century. In 1604, James I created Robert Cecil, his Secretary of State, Viscount Cranborne, and Cecil, finding Cranborne Manor almost a ruin, set about rebuilding it, leaving some parts of the medieval building standing, including the dungeons, where prisoners, mostly those arrested for poaching in the royal forest, had been lodged. These dungeons, the walls of which are four feet six inches thick, are now used as kitchens.

James I, who was devoted to hunting, visited Cranborne frequently after he had given it to Robert Cecil, and James II stayed there in 1683, two years before he came to the throne. Records show that he was there with his retinue for ten meals and that 1,000 eggs were bought in at a cost of £1 8s. 6d.

Several of the great houses of Dorset and Somerset have stood, altered but not entirely rebuilt, since the fifteenth century. Barrington Court in Somerset is one; Court House at East Quantoxhead, which belongs, village as well as manor house, to the Luttrell family, is another and Athelhampton in Dorset is a third.

Athelhampton came into the possession of the Martyn family in the fifteenth century. A licence was given by Henry VIII to enclose 160 acres as a small deer park and to build a battlemented house. Much of this house still stands. In 1595 Nicholas Martyn died, leaving four married daughters but no male heir. The house and the estate were divided in four, but gradually the family fell on hard times, and it was sold and sold many times again over the years.

Today, Athelhampton is beautifully kept and seems completely at peace, but its corners and corridors must have hissed with the whisper of plot and counter-plot. Its owners were involved in the Babington plot and the dissolution of the monasteries, as well as in the Civil War, the Restoration and the Monmouth rebellion. Through all these, the great grey house stood serene in its gardens, almost encircled by the gentle River Piddle. The crest of the Martyn family, carved in several parts of the house, was a chained ape, holding a mirror with the motto *"He who looks at Martyn's ape, Martyn's ape shall look at him."* Sir William Martyn had charge of the duties on wines throughout the West Country, responsible only to the Crown. The wine cellars, in which were stored confiscated casks as well as the family's wine, have recently been put in order. They combine with the kitchens to make it very clear that in this house through the centuries there was always food and drink, not only for those who lived there but for any traveller, whether he came in state or *"secretly alone"*, whether he came for pleasure or in trouble.

Barrington Court, near Ilminster, is one of the finest Tudor houses in England. Its records go back to the Conquest and it first belonged to the Daubeny family. The second Lord Daubeny built the house on the site of an earlier building. From the late seventeenth century it deteriorated until the 1920s, when it was bought by the Lyle family and restored as nearly as possible to its original dignity and beauty.

The original Tudor kitchen has been preserved. It is of immense size, taking up the whole south-west wing of the house. The main hearth occupies the whole of the south end. The lintel of the arched opening is formed of two blocks of Ham stone, each eight feet long, three feet high and one foot thick, supported on two piers, which form niches on each side of the main fire in which the boys who turned the spits would be protected from the great heat. There is no doubt that a whole ox could be roasted on this hearth. The original charcoal braziers, for roasting small birds and for grilling and frying, are still in position set into the window recess with a hole in the wall below them to provide the forced draught necessary to keep the charcoal red hot. The whole kitchen is carefully designed so that many hands could prepare the vast quantities of food needed for a great household and its guests.

By the stableyard stands a small barn with a row of double stalls down each side. These were called busstalls and each housed a cow and her calf. These calves were strictly for the house and were never weaned. They were not killed until almost full grown and the meat was known as buss-beef and was considered a great delicacy. The young animals would have eaten some hay and would have been turned out to pasture with their mothers in summer, but they would always have taken some milk and the resulting meat would have been light in colour, with a good deal of fat, probably at its best when roasted. This method of producing very tender beef has not been used for some 300 years and we have no idea what such meat was really like.

The high hills of Somerset, the Mendips and the Quantocks, have retained some of their wildness to this day. The long range of the Mendips has always provided look-out posts against the possibility of invasion. Beacon fires were built ready for lighting on Beacon Hill in the Mendips and at other points along their range, to call sixteenth-century countrymen and men from the Somerset and Devon towns to defend the coast against the expected Spanish landing. Two hundred years later the same beacons were manned in expectation of a French invasion, and in 1940 on those same hill tops watch was kept for German parachutists and a German invasion by sea.

Semi-wild cattle still roamed in the Quantocks in the seventeenth century, and in the Court House in the village of East Quantoxhead a plan of the parish dating from this time shows men herding them. The whole village of East Quantoxhead has belonged to the Luttrell family since the compiling of the Domesday Book, and the family house, close to the church, has been·little altered since 1629, when a new wing was built and other alterations made. Most of the original kitchens remain. The main fireplace is 12 feet wide and the smaller one, close to it, measures six feet. There is a cider house next to the kitchen and a cell where drunks were shut up for the night. There is also a set of strong oak staves, six feet long and tipped with a curved iron shoe. These are still occasionally used for "glatting". This strange form of hunt was traditional and very ancient. All available dogs were taken down to the foreshore at low tide and would pick up the scent of conger eels (which is strong) and nose and scratch at the boulders beneath which the eels lay. The men moved the boulders with the glatting irons and as the eels darted across the wet sand, the dogs sprang on them. The conger eel is often five or six feet in length with a fierce bite, and the dogs were thrashed by the writhing coils and often badly bitten. Conger-eel pie was considered a delicacy, as was smoked, fried and jellied eel, and eight fine congers would provide a good dish for 50 people, so the sport had practical value. In the Luttrell family house, the glatting of eels is shown in a seventeenth-century plaster overmantel relief.

The Court House also contained a special court for cock fighting, . situated in the centre of the building and overlooked by the windows of the ladies' withdrawing-room so that they could enjoy the spectacle in comfort. The house has been well loved and, except for the latter part of the seventeenth century, well looked after. The signs and traces of·a wilder, more primitive countryside, where conger hunts, cock fighting and deer hunting in the hills were frequent sports, and where the whole village was owned by the lord of the manor, are clearer in East Quantoxhead than anywhere else in the West Country.

Across the border in Wiltshire the feeling of the countryside seems to change. Wiltshire has the remains of three great forests and plenty of good pasturé in the valleys and flatlands along her rivers, but most of the county is rough grass, clothing the chalk of the Marlborough Downs and Salisbury Plain. The whole of this part of England was heavily populated throughout the Stone, Bronze and Iron ages. Every mile or two on the plain, archaeologists have found traces of huts and settlements from all these periods, and the great stone circles of Stonehenge and Avebury bring before our eyes the hundreds of tribesmen who brought the stones and erected them under the direction of their priest-kings. At Avebury the stones raised to pagan gods about 4,000 years ago stand close to cottages, a church, a welcoming pub and a lovely sixteenth-century manor house. In the little museum are the remains of the burial of a child, and under the foundations of more than one of the great stones are remains of human sacrifices. Yet the pub is cheerful and the church and manor house serene. The cottages are well kept, as Wiltshire cottages generally are; sleek Friesian cows rub against the stones and sheep graze beyond the earthworks of a fortified camp at the end of the village. Clearly, so much time has passed that the grief and terror of thousands of years ago have been washed away as a river smooths the pebbles of its bed.

Wiltshire has more than its share of such contrasts. Littlecote, which dates from the fifteenth century and belonged to the Darrell family, has obviously been well loved despite a troubled past.

Henry VIII stayed at Littlecote when he was courting Jane Seymour, who was related to the Darrells. Naturally this was a time for great feasting at Littlecote. Several outbuildings had to be used as subsidiary kitchens, although hundreds could be catered for in the main kitchen. Cooks were lent by other landowners and the countryside was scoured for birds and beasts and fishes of all kinds. Fortunately for cooks and scullions, who had been working night and day for weeks at Littlecote, the royal marriage took place at Wulf Hall, the home of Jane Seymour, but this was such a short distance away that many of them were sent over to help. No details of the occasion have been discovered, but doubtless it differed little from Henry's other five wedding feasts.

Littlecote passed to Lord Chief Justice Popham and the Popham family lived in the house for 600 years. Two hundred years after Henry's marriage, Colonel Alexander Popham raised his own regiment for the Parliamentary Cause. Arms and jerkins of buffalo hide, which would turn a sword thrust and which were worn under breast plates, are hung on the walls of the Great Hall. In another part of the house there is a Cromwellian chapel, as plain as the Puritans required, and one of a very few still in existence and untouched in the country.

These unusually violent contrasts seem to be peculiarly marked in the great Wiltshire houses. Wilton House, the home of the Herberts since Henry VIII gave the land to William Herbert after the dissolution of the monasteries, is almost palatial. The Earls of Pembroke, with the exception of the twelfth earl, were devoted to it, but the third and fifth earls ran through great fortunes and many of Wilton's earlier treasures had to be sold to pay their debts. In the sixteenth century, Sir Philip Sidney, brother-in-law to the earl, wrote his great pastoral poem *Arcadia* in the peace of Wilton's park.

Zeals House, very near the Dorset border, is built on the site of a moated fourteenth-century manor. In the Civil War it belonged to John Grove, a fanatical king's man. He joined in the rebellion against the Commonwealth in 1655 and was beheaded at Exeter Castle. The story goes that Charles II was hidden in the house by Grove's son. This is not authenticated, but there is a secret room in the roof, reached only by walking the length of the house on boards across the rafters. If these were removed there would appear to be no access to what would seem a small cupboard door.

The house has a fine seventeenth-century orangery, and a square sixteenth-century dovecote for 800 doves. There is a small lake for trout for the house and in earlier times there was a vinery and a melon house. In the kitchen quarters the original servants' hall remains. This long room was intended as a dining hall for the servants of guests, gamekeepers, gardeners and cottagers who came on business, as well as house servants. It had an immensely long table down which serving trolleys were pushed – a very unusual early nineteenth-century innovation. In 1859, a new block of domestic offices was connected to the old kitchens by covered passage. There is a fine dairy, a room for salting hams and bacon, a series of game larders and some extra servants' rooms.

The great White Horse, cut out of the skin of turf which covers the chalk of the Wiltshire Downs, and the great standing circle of Stonehenge itself, keep the far distant past before the eyes of those who live in Wiltshire. The cathedral town of Salisbury, the county town and the seat of assizes, reflects the chequered history of the county. At least one Salisbury inn flourishing today was the breakfast stop for coaches which had left London at eight o'clock on the previous evening and were on their way to Exeter. Some of the Bath coaches stopped at Marlborough, where the George Hotel, still elegant and comfortable, although, alas, not traditional in the food it serves, was the stage for fresh horses. Marlborough cattle market was famous in the West Country through the eighteenth and nineteenth centuries and continues to be well attended today. The Wiltshire border marks the end of the West Country if the traveller is progressing towards London, and seems, indeed, a long way from Cornwall.

Serves 8 to 10

Eighteenth-century Pea Soup

7½ cups (1.8 litres) old green
  peas (6 lb/3 kg in the pod)
3 celery sticks finely chopped
2 large Cos lettuces, any faded
  outside leaves discarded, and
  the rest washed and shredded
6 mint sprigs
1 stick (120 g) butter
2 cucumbers, peeled, seeded
  and cut into ¾ inch (2 cm)
  pieces
3 medium onions, peeled and
  sliced
½ cup (60 g) flour
2½ cups (6 dl) young green peas
  (2 lb/1 kg in the pod)
⅝ cup (1.5 dl) cream
Salt and pepper
Croûtons

The Shrewsbury family from whom this recipe comes claim to have made it at least once a year since 1770.

Bring about 3 quarts (2¾ litres) of water to the boil in a very large saucepan. Add the old peas, celery, half the lettuce, and the mint. Cover the pan and boil gently for about 20 minutes or until the peas are tender. Strain off the liquid into a large mixing bowl and put the vegetables through a mouli (vegetable mill) into it.

In another saucepan, melt the butter and cook the cucumber, onions and the remaining lettuce very gently until the onions are just softening. Purée these vegetables and add to the pea purée reserving some of the butter in the pan.

Pour the reserved butter into the large saucepan and stir in the flour to make a roux. Stir a little of the purée into the roux gradually adding the remainder. When the soup is smooth, add salt and pepper and bring to the boil. Add the young peas and cook gently for 30 minutes. Check the seasoning. Serve hot with a tablespoon of cream on top of each serving. Offer the croûtons separately.

125

Palestine Soup

3 lb (1½ kg) Jerusalem
 artichokes
Lemon juice
1 medium onion, cut in
 quarters
2 teaspoons salt
1 teaspoon white pepper
2½ cups (6 dl) milk
¾ stick (90 g) butter
¼ cup (30 g) flour
4 tablespoons double cream
1 tablespoon finely chopped
 parsley

This name was given to soup made from Jerusalem
artichokes for obvious reasons. In reality, however,
artichokes have nothing to do with Jerusalem. The
word was a corruption of the Italian *girasole*,
sunflower, and Jerusalem artichokes belong to the
sunflower family.

Palestine soup has been made in many parts of
England for centuries but this particular recipe
comes from Somerset. It is one of the best white
soups in the world.

Peel the artichokes; the irregular shape of the roots
means that there will be some waste but about 2½
pounds (1¼ kg) should be left. Drop each root as it is
peeled into cold water to which a squeeze of lemon
juice has been added. When all are done, put them in
a saucepan with the onion, salt and pepper and just
cover with cold water. Simmer gently until quite
soft – about 20 minutes. Add the milk and about one-
third of the butter and bring to the boil again. Allow
to cool slightly, then purée the artichokes and liquid,
using a blender or vegetable mill.

In the saucepan in which the artichokes were
cooked, melt the remaining butter and stir in the
flour. Cook for 1 minute and then slowly stir in the
artichoke purée, allowing it to come just to the boil.
The result should be a soup of the consistency of
thin cream. Stir in the cream, check the seasoning
and serve very hot, sprinkling each bowl with
chopped parsley.

Jugged Celery

2 lb (1 kg) cooking apples,
 peeled, cored and quartered
1 tablespoon brown sugar
2 slices of back bacon, 1 kept
 whole and the other finely
 chopped
2 heads of celery, washed and
 trimmed, with some of the
 strings removed
1 small onion, finely chopped
3 cloves
¼ teaspoon rosemary
¼ teaspoon pepper
¼ teaspoon salt

This is a very old Devonshire dish, which used to be
served with roast venison or hare. It is also excellent
with roast lamb or duck. The flavour of the celery
and apple and the tenderness of the celery are
outstanding.

You will need a straight-sided earthenware crock,
holding about 5 cups (1.2 litres) and measuring 4 or 5
inches (10 to 13 cm) in diameter. The celery is not so
good when cooked horizontally.

Stew the apples with the sugar and 1 tablespoon of
water in a saucepan for 20 minutes or until they
make a soft pulp, stirring from time to time.

Put the whole slice of bacon in the bottom of the
crock, and pour in the apple. Push the sticks of
celery into it so that they stand upright, close-packed
and with the apple coming almost to the top.
Sprinkle in the onion, cloves, rosemary, pepper and
salt. Cut the tops of the celery sticks even with the
top of the crock. Press these short bits among the
celery sticks and sprinkle the top with the chopped
bacon bits. Stand the crock in a saucepan with
boiling water coming halfway up the sides. Cover the
saucepan and simmer for 2 hours, replenishing the
water from time to time.

Pour the contents of the crock into a bowl and
serve.

Pye of Trout

4 trout, cleaned and scaled,
  heads and tails removed
$\frac{1}{4}$ lb (120g) mushrooms, thinly
  sliced
$\frac{1}{2}$ stick (60g) butter
2 slices streaky bacon, cut in $\frac{1}{4}$
  inch (0.5cm) strips
1 small tin artichoke hearts,
  drained and cut in halves
  (about 10 halves)
24 capers
4 bay leaves
2 sprigs each parsley and
  thyme, tied in a bunch with
  fennel and chives
$\frac{5}{8}$ cup (1.5dl) white wine
$\frac{1}{2}$ lb (240g) puff or flaky pastry
Salt and freshly ground black
  pepper

This recipe comes from Truro and is dated 1738. It is a grand and delicious pie, originally made in a "coffin" of raised pastry. The proportion of pastry to filling is more in accordance with today's tastes, however, if it is made in a pie dish. The original raised pie was probably very large containing 20 or more trout. In Cornwall trout were, and in some places still are, often caught only a short distance from the point where the incoming tide floods inland up the streams. Cornishmen think that this gives their trout a special firmness and extra flavour. However, so much sea fish, including the brown or sea trout, is eaten by Cornishmen that the freshwater trout, although plentiful, are a change and a delicacy. Serve with a salad of watercress and thinly sliced oranges.

Lightly sauté the mushrooms in half the butter and, when just beginning to soften, add the bacon strips and fry until they are transparent but not at all crisp.

Butter the pie dish. Lay half the artichoke hearts and half the mushrooms and bacon in the dish. Then put the trout on top, side by side, head to tail. Put the capers on the trout and sprinkle with salt and pepper. Lay on the rest of the artichokes, the bay leaves and the bunch of herbs. Sprinkle on a little more salt and pepper and finish with the remaining bacon and mushrooms. Cut the remaining butter into very small pieces and scatter them on top. Pour in the white wine and cover the dish closely with foil. Bake at 350°F (180°C, Gas Mark 4) for 30 minutes.

Remove the dish from the oven, take off the foil and allow to cool for at least 20 minutes. Then put on the crust in the usual way and bake at 450°F (230°C, Gas Mark 8) for 20 minutes or until puffed and golden brown. Serve very hot.

Baked Mackerel

4 medium mackerel, opened
  only enough to clean them,
  with heads and tails removed
$1\frac{1}{4}$ sticks (150g) butter
$\frac{5}{8}$ cup (1.5dl) white wine
2 teaspoons chilli vinegar
$\frac{1}{2}$ teaspoon cayenne pepper
1 teaspoon salt
$\frac{1}{2}$ teaspoon freshly ground
  black pepper
$\frac{1}{4}$ cup (30g) flour
$\frac{2}{3}$ cup (90g) fresh fine white
  breadcrumbs

The Cornish have cooked mackerel and pilchards in many different ways for the last five centuries.

This is a dish from a manor house in south Cornwall. Serve with green peas flavoured with mint. Pilchards, herring and whiting may be cooked in the same way.

Grease a shallow ovenproof dish lavishly with about one-third of the butter. Lay the mackerel in the dish head to tail, backs upwards. Mix the wine, vinegar, cayenne, salt and pepper and pour over the fish. Mash half the remaining butter with the flour and divide the mixture into 4 pieces. Press 1 piece on to each fish. Cover with buttered foil and bake at 350°F (180°C, Gas Mark 4) for 15 minutes.

Remove the dish from the oven, take off the foil and scatter the breadcrumbs all over. Dot with the remaining butter and bake near the top of the oven for a further 15 minutes when the crumbs should be golden brown.

Roast Sea Bream

Serves 4

1 large bream, about 2½ lb
(1¼ kg)
¾ cup (90 g) shredded suet
1 tablespoon finely chopped
parsley
¾ cup (120 g) fresh breadcrumbs
Salt
A little milk, to mix

This is a very old recipe from St Just in Cornwall.
Serve with parsley butter and boiled potatoes.

Have the bream cleaned and scaled. Stuff it with
about two-thirds of the suet, the parsley,
breadcrumbs and a little salt, well mixed with a little
milk. Put the fish in a baking dish, sprinkle with the
remaining suet and a little salt. Bake in the oven at
350°F (180°C, Gas Mark 4) for 35 minutes until
golden brown, basting from time to time.
  If the fish seems at all dry during cooking, baste
with more suet or a little butter. The suet, being
oilier than butter, makes the plain stuffing richer and
crisps the skin.

Mullet Pie

Serves 4

1 grey mullet, about 2 to 2½ lb
(1 kg) cleaned and cut in
cutlets
1 large bunch fresh parsley
with some of the root, well
washed
¼ teaspoon dried thyme
¼ teaspoon powdered ginger
1 teaspoon salt
½ teaspoon pepper
2 cups (4.5 dl) milk
¼ cup (30 g) flour
2 tablespoons (30 g) butter
3 tablespoons clotted cream (if
possible) or double cream
¾ lb (360 g) potato pastry (see
page 100)
1 egg, well beaten

An eighteenth-century recipe from a farmhouse near
Sennen Cove, one of the loveliest coves on the north
Cornish coast. Serve with peas and a green salad on
separate plates.

Put the fish cutlets into a saucepan with the herbs,
ginger, pepper, salt, milk and ⅝ cup (1.5 dl) of water.
Bring to the boil and simmer gently, covered, for 20
minutes. Lift out the fish (reserve the cooking liquid)
and remove all the skin and bones from each cutlet.
Keep the pieces as large as possible and lay them in
a pie dish.
  In a saucepan, make a roux with the flour and
butter. Strain the reserved cooking liquid and gently
stir it into the roux. Allow the sauce to boil for 2
minutes, stirring all the time, then remove the pan
from the heat and add the cream, stirring lightly, but
not amalgamating it entirely with the sauce. Check
the seasoning. Pour the sauce over the fish and allow
to cool for 10 minutes. Roll out the pastry. Press the
crust on to the pie dish. Gild with the egg. Bake at
400°F (200°C, Gas Mark 6) for 25 minutes.

Devonshire Buttered Shrimps

Serves 4

½ lb (240 g) frozen and
defrosted or fresh, shelled
cooked shrimps or prawns
⅝ cup (1.5 dl) white wine
½ stick (60 g) butter
4 eggs
¼ teaspoon grated nutmeg
¼ teaspoon salt
¼ teaspoon black pepper

A very early recipe. Serve in small individual dishes
as a starting course with hot, freshly made toast.

Bring the shrimps or prawns to the boil in the wine,
adding the nutmeg, salt and freshly ground black
pepper. Stew gently, uncovered, for 5 minutes.
  Meanwhile, melt the butter in another saucepan.
Stir in the eggs, holding the pan off the heat and
allowing them just to begin to thicken. As soon as
the prawns are ready, spoon them into the egg
mixture with the wine, stirring after each spoonful
and never resting the pan on the heat. Immediately
the mixture begins to thicken and becomes creamy,
pour into small dishes, serve and eat at once.

Cornish Crab Pie

2 large crabs
¼ teaspoon nutmeg
½ teaspoon cinnamon
¼ teaspoon ginger
2 tablespoons claret
½ stick (60 g) butter
2 to 3 artichoke hearts, boiled
(tinned will do)
3 hard-boiled eggs, finely
chopped
24 white grapes, pitted
½ lb (240 g) asparagus, boiled
until just tender, or 1 small
tin asparagus tips
Juice of 1 orange
Generous ⅜ cup (120 g) clotted
cream
¾ lb (360 g) puff pastry
1 egg yolk, beaten
Salt and freshly ground black
pepper

Once eaten, never forgotten. This is a nineteenth-century recipe of surpassing delicacy and richness. It is perhaps a dish to eat once in five years. The crabs are best if freshly caught. A lettuce salad on a separate plate is the only possible accompaniment.

Have the crabs dressed. Remove all the claw meat. Mix the rest of the meat with the nutmeg, cinnamon, ginger and claret. Set aside. Butter a pie dish, put in the artichoke hearts, and on them put the chopped eggs, then the spiced crabmeat, and then the grapes and asparagus tips. Sprinkle with salt and pepper and pour in the orange juice. Spread the cream on top and into the cream push all the meat from the crabs' claws.

Roll out the pastry, press the edges of the covering crust on to the pie dish to seal, decorate with a rose and gild with the egg yolk. Bake at 450°F (230°C, Gas Mark 8) for 25 minutes and serve immediately.

Truro Pasties

6 mackerel or pilchards,
gutted, or 12 skinless sausages
½ to 1 lb (¼ to ½ kg) puff pastry
or flaky pastry
1 tablespoon mild mustard,
such as Tewkesbury or
Urchfont, mixed with 1
tablespoon milk or cream
2 teaspoons dried tarragon or
chopped fresh tarragon
1 tablespoon finely chopped
parsley
2 teaspoons finely chopped
mint
1 beaten egg

A big weekly market used to be held in Truro, the county town of Cornwall. The market sold livestock, cereals, butter, cheese and cream, leather and cloth, china, glass, pots and pans and whatever fruit, vegetables, fish, cakes or other foods that the local inhabitants might bring in. There was always a stall that sold fish pasties, kept hot in a tin oven over a little fire, for everyone's dinner. These were made not individually but in a long strip, with the head and tail of each fish protruding from the pastry. The stallholder would cut off the number of fish required by a customer and put the rest back to keep hot. St Austell, north-east of Truro, was well known for similar pasties made with skinless sausages.

Roll out the pastry into 2 oblongs, each about 14 inches (36 cm) long and 8 inches (20 cm) wide. If pilchards or sausages are being used, make the oblongs half the width.

On one of the oblongs lay the fish ¼ to ½ inch (0.5 to 1 cm) apart, heads all pointing one way, leaving about 1 inch (2.5 cm) of pastry at each end. Spread the upper side of each fish with the mustard mixture and sprinkle with the herbs. Put the second piece of pastry over the top and press down between each fish and along the ends. The heads and tails will protrude on either side. If you prefer to remove the heads and tails, seal all the pastry edges.

If you are using sausages, lay them in pairs along the pastry strip and omit the tarragon. Leave the ends just protruding from the pastry to become deliciously crisp and brown.

Brush the pastry over with the beaten egg. Bake in the middle of the oven at 450°F (230°C, Gas Mark 8) for 30 minutes.

Cornish Pasties

The pastry:

1 lb ($\frac{1}{2}$ kg) flour
2 teaspoons salt
1 stick (120 g) butter
$\frac{1}{2}$ cup (120 g) lard
1 egg, well beaten

Filling 1:

$\frac{3}{4}$ lb (360 g) frying steak, cut in
$\frac{1}{4}$ inch (0.5 cm) dice, all skin
and fat discarded
$\frac{1}{2}$ lb (240 g) potatoes, peeled and
cut in $\frac{1}{2}$ inch (1 cm) dice
2 onions, peeled and very finely
chopped
A little stock
Salt and pepper

Filling 2:

$\frac{3}{4}$ lb (360 g) lamb, from the fillet
end of the leg cut in $\frac{1}{4}$ inch
(0.5 cm) dice, all skin and fat
discarded
$\frac{1}{2}$ lb (240 g) potatoes, peeled and
cut in $\frac{1}{2}$ inch (1 cm) dice
2 onions, peeled and very finely
chopped
1 medium turnip, peeled and
cut into $\frac{1}{4}$ inch (0.5 cm) pieces
A little stock
Salt and pepper

Filling 3:

4 slices lean bacon, cut in fine
strips
3 leeks, well washed and
chopped very fine
$\frac{3}{8}$ cup (60 g) fresh fine white
breadcrumbs, seasoned with
salt and black pepper
4 tablespoons milk
2 tablespoons clotted or double
cream
Salt and pepper

This is a nineteenth-century recipe from a farm near Talland, and makes the most excellent pasties. The pasty was the perfect meal for farmer or fisherman, and many Cornishmen have always been both. Many different raw materials, sweet and savoury, were made up as pasties according to what was available and whether meat could be afforded. On baking day, while the bread was proving, a pasty was made for each member of a family and marked with their initials on one corner. In this way, individual tastes could be allowed for: onion could be omitted for some; more meat could be given to the men than to the small children; some preferred bacon and potato to a beef and potato filling. The initials had another advantage. The pasty owner ate from the other end. Thus, if he was forced to lay his pasty down while he attended to some emergency, whether at sea or in the fields, he and his companions knew which was his pasty.

The pasties taken by the men to work were hot from the oven, whether freshly made or reheated, and were wrapped in a cloth before being put into a lunch tin. They were probably not very hot when eaten, but even cold, they are savoury and filling. Of course, when times were hard, they often contained only potato or breadcrumbs with cheese or onion or leek. Sometimes they were made with pilchards or mackerel from the last catch. Here, however, I shall give the three fillings most used when times were good. A pasty should never contain mince or meat which has already been cooked.

Mix the flour and salt together. Rub in the fat until the mixture has the texture of fine breadcrumbs. Mix with very cold water to form a stiff paste. Add the water gradually and use more if the crumbs are not all taken up, so that the dough leaves the bowl clean.

Roll out the pastry to about $\frac{1}{8}$ inch (0.25 cm) thick and cut 6 circles about 6 inches (15 cm) in diameter.

Mix all the ingredients for any one of the fillings in a bowl and season well. Put about 1$\frac{1}{2}$ tablespoons of the mixture in the centre of each pastry circle. Brush all round the edges of the pastry with egg and bring them together over the top of the filling, crimping them as you go, so that you have a kind of border all along the top of the pastry. Cut a small slit in the centre of the top just below the border and mark initials in one corner, being careful not to cut right through the pastry.

Bake at 350°F (180°C, Gas Mark 4) near the top of the oven for 20 minutes and then for a further 40 minutes lower in the oven. If the pasties seem to be getting too brown, lay a sheet of foil lightly over them.

Saltram House Lamb

$4\frac{1}{2}$ lb (2 kg) leg of lamb
2 tablespoons seasoned flour
1 tablespoon (15 g) butter
24 small onions, peeled and left
 whole
$\frac{5}{8}$ cup (1.5 dl) strong stock
5 cups (1.2 litres) dry, rough
 cider
1 teaspoon dried or 3 to
 4 sprigs fresh marjoram
1 teaspoon dried or 4 to
 5 sprigs fresh thyme
$\frac{1}{2}$ teaspoon ground nutmeg
$\frac{1}{2}$ teaspoon ground mace
$1\frac{1}{2}$ lb ($\frac{3}{4}$ kg) shelled peas
At least 12 sprigs fresh mint
Juice of $\frac{1}{2}$ lemon
Salt and pepper

A fairly large leg of lamb is best for this recipe, since mutton is now not easily obtainable. A joint weighing about $4\frac{1}{2}$ lb (2 kg) is enough for 4 to 6 people with enough left over to provide about 4 portions of cold lamb. Sometimes, instead of serving it cold, an elegant hash (in the proper sense of the word) was made as a side-dish for the next day. A recipe for this is given on page 132. Do not be tempted to serve potatoes with the Saltram Lamb. It is much better with thick slices of fresh, crusty white bread, home made, if possible.

Rub the lamb all over with seasoned flour. Grease the bottom of a fish kettle or large, oval casserole with butter and put in the onions. Set the lamb on a rack in the fish kettle or casserole. Mix the stock with the cider and stir in the herbs and spices. Pour half the liquid over the lamb and the onions – it should cover the bottom $\frac{1}{2}$ inch (1 cm) of the joint.

Put the kettle or casserole uncovered into a medium oven, 375°F (190°C, Gas Mark 5) for $1\frac{1}{2}$ hours. Remove from the oven and pour the peas round the joint, sticking the sprigs of mint among them. Bring the remaining liquid to the boil and pour it over. Return to the oven and cook for 20 minutes. Lift the joint on to a serving dish and keep hot. Test the peas and if not yet tender, cook, covered, for 10 minutes more.

Before serving, remove the sprigs of mint, add the lemon juice and check the seasoning. Spoon some of the peas and onions round the joint and serve the rest, with all the liquid, separately in a vegetable dish or tureen.

Mendip White Lamb

4 lamb steaks, each $\frac{1}{2}$ to $\frac{3}{4}$ inch
 (1 to 2 cm) thick, from the
 fillet end of the leg (these are
 not a usual cut today but the
 butcher may cut them if
 asked)
2 strips lemon peel
$\frac{1}{2}$ teaspoon garlic salt or 1
 garlic clove, crushed
A bouquet garni, made of 2
 sprigs rosemary, 3 or 4 of
 thyme and 3 or 4 of marjoram
$\frac{1}{2}$ teaspoon mace
$1\frac{1}{4}$ cups (3 dl) milk
2 tablespoons (30 g) butter
$\frac{1}{4}$ cup (30 g) flour
$\frac{3}{8}$ cup (0.9 dl) double cream
1 tablespoon finely chopped
 parsley
Salt
$\frac{1}{2}$ teaspoon white pepper

This is an unusual way of cooking lamb. The recipe appears in a manuscript from a manor house between Cheddar and Priddy and dates from the early eighteenth century. It is recommended as a good dish for a dinner for visiting friends. In this kind of household a pie, a roast of pork, a dish of chickens and one of peas might be set on the table with the lamb. A second course of one or two lighter savoury dishes and some jellies and a syllabub would follow.

Trim the lamb steaks of all skin and fat. Lay them overlapping in a casserole. Add the lemon peel, garlic salt or garlic, bouquet garni, mace, 1 teaspoon of salt (less if you are using garlic salt) and the white pepper. Add $\frac{5}{8}$ cup (1.5 dl) of cold water to the milk and pour over the lamb. Cook in the oven at 350°F (180°C, Gas Mark 4) for $1\frac{1}{4}$ hours.

Lift the steaks on to a flat dish and keep warm. Melt the butter in a saucepan, stir in the flour and slowly add the strained liquor in which the steaks cooked. Bring to the boil and stir in the cream. As soon as the sauce comes to the boil again, pour it over the lamb steaks, sprinkle with parsley and serve immediately.

Hash of Lamb in Cider

*1 lb ($\frac{1}{2}$ kg) cooked lamb, cut in $\frac{1}{2}$
inch (1 cm) dice, trimmed of
all fat*
$\frac{1}{2}$ stick (60 g) butter
*1 lb ($\frac{1}{2}$ kg) carrots, cut across in
very thin slices*
*2 large onions, cut in very thin
rings*
$\frac{1}{2}$ teaspoon dried rosemary
$\frac{1}{2}$ teaspoon dried thyme
$\frac{1}{2}$ teaspoon turmeric
$\frac{1}{4}$ teaspoon mace
$\frac{1}{4}$ teaspoon black pepper
1 teaspoon salt
1 tablespoon flour
*2$\frac{1}{2}$ cups (6 dl) good stock or use
a stock cube*
1$\frac{1}{4}$ cups (3 dl) dry, rough cider
*1 tablespoon finely chopped
parsley*

The cooking term "hash", which comes from the
French *hacher*, to chop, means sliced or diced meat
and vegetables. It was the name given to certain
esteemed dishes from the Middle Ages onwards but
fell into grave disrepute at the hands of many
appallingly bad nineteenth-century cooks.

A hash requires a very good sauce, preferably with
a little wine, ale or cider added and some fresh
vegetables cooked in it. This Devonshire recipe uses
cider but this can be replaced with wine or ale. The
sauce is fairly thick and the meat, lightly fried in
butter, is delicious. Triangular croûtons of fried
bread, stuck round the edges of the dish just before
serving, are a better accompaniment than potatoes.
Peas, green beans and spinach are all good with it.

Put half the butter into a large saucepan and fry the
carrots and the onions, turning constantly for 3 to 4
minutes. Sprinkle in the rosemary, thyme, spices,
pepper and salt. Stir in the flour and allow to cook
for 30 seconds. Mix the stock and cider in slowly,
stirring and turning the vegetables. Bring to the boil
and boil fairly briskly for 25 minutes, stirring often.
After 20 minutes melt the remaining butter in a
frying-pan and gently fry the small cubes of lamb for
about 3 to 4 minutes, turning and shaking them.

Check that the vegetables are tender and the sauce
well seasoned. Pour into a shallow, fireproof serving
dish and put the cubes of lamb on top of the sauce
and vegetables. Sprinkle with parsley and serve
immediately, or keep hot for not more than a few
minutes before sprinkling with parsley and serving.

Mutton and Turnip Pie

*2 lb (1 kg) lamb, from the fillet
end of the leg*
2 teaspoons curry powder
$\frac{1}{4}$ cup (30 g) flour
3 tablespoons (45 g) butter
2 lb (1 kg) small young turnips
*Juice and grated zest of 1
orange*
*2$\frac{1}{2}$ cups (6 dl) stock (stock cube
will do)*
$\frac{3}{4}$ lb (360 g) puff pastry
1 egg yolk, well beaten
Salt and pepper

This combination has always been favoured in
Cornwall, where mutton and turnips are also a
traditional filling for pasties.

This recipe, from a manor house in south Cornwall,
has two special additional flavours, mild curry and
orange. The flavours of orange and young turnips are
particularly good together.

Trim all the skin and fat from the lamb and cut the
meat into $\frac{1}{2}$ inch (1 cm) dice. Mix the curry powder,
salt and pepper with the flour and roll the lamb in it.
Fry the meat in the butter, stirring and shaking
occasionally, until lightly browned on all sides.

Peel the turnips and cut in $\frac{1}{2}$ inch (1 cm) pieces,
sprinkle with the orange zest and pour the juice over
them. Leave for 5 minutes. Put a layer of lamb in a
pie dish, then a layer of turnips and alternate until
all is used. Pour in the stock, cover with foil and
cook at 350°F (180°C, Gas Mark 4) for 1$\frac{1}{4}$ hours.

Remove the pie dish from the oven and allow to
cool to blood heat before putting on the crust.

Decorate with pastry leaves and a rose. Brush with
the beaten egg yolk. Bake at 450°F (230°C, Gas Mark
8) for 20 minutes or until the pastry is puffed up and
golden brown.

Forced (Stuffed) Cabbage

2 green cabbages, with plenty
of heart
4 hard-boiled eggs, chopped
$\frac{1}{2}$ lb (240 g) raw minced veal,
lamb or chicken
4 slices streaky bacon, very
finely chopped
$\frac{3}{8}$ cup (60 g) fresh fine white
breadcrumbs
$\frac{1}{4}$ cup (30 g) grated Parmesan
cheese
$2\frac{1}{2}$ cups (6 dl) strong and well-
seasoned stock (stock cubes
will do)
Salt and freshly ground black
pepper

This recipe, quoted by Florence White, came
originally from Mrs Martha Bradley who lived in
Bath and recorded it in 1749. She says, "This is a
very cheap and elegant dish, and the young cabbages
that are now, in June, just coming into season are the
fittest of all for it." Serve with plain boiled rice.

Cut out the hearts of both cabbages, keeping the
outer leaves attached to the stalk. Plunge the outer
leaves into boiling, salted water and scald for 4
minutes. Lift out and leave to drain on a rack.
  Chop the hearts of the cabbages very finely and put
into 1$\frac{1}{4}$ cups (3 dl) of boiling salted water. Boil for 10
minutes, then drain and mix with all the other
ingredients except the stock. Divide this forcemeat in
half, shape it into two balls and fit them inside the
scalded cabbages. Fold the leaves well over the
stuffing and tie up the cabbages tightly with string.
Lay the cabbages carefully in the stock in a shallow
casserole, cover closely with foil and cook in the
oven at 350°F (180°C, Gas Mark 4) for 1 hour.
  To serve, carefully cut the cabbages through with a
very sharp knife so that the forcemeat hearts are
exposed. Baste each with some of the stock they
cooked in and serve immediately, lifting each half on
to a plate and spooning some of the gravy over it.

Beef Cheese

3 lb (1$\frac{1}{2}$ kg) good minced beef
$\frac{3}{4}$ lb (360 g) minced gammon
$\frac{3}{4}$ cup (90 g) shredded beef suet
1 medium onion, very finely
chopped
$\frac{1}{4}$ teaspoon ground cloves
$\frac{1}{4}$ teaspoon ground mace
$\frac{1}{2}$ teaspoon dried thyme
$\frac{1}{4}$ teaspoon rosemary
$\frac{1}{2}$ teaspoon freshly ground
black pepper
1 teaspoon salt
4 tablespoons cooking brandy
$\frac{1}{2}$ clove garlic
6 slices streaky bacon, cut in
halves lengthways with rinds
removed

This is a particularly excellent meat loaf. The recipe
comes from Plymouth. It was standard store on
certain passenger ships and there is a tradition that
Beef Cheese was taken on the Mayflower to America.
It kept perfectly for months because the suet floated
to the top and covered the meat, which was thus
sealed. It was sealed again because a "huff" crust of
flour and water was put over the oblong tin in which
the beef was baked. It was essential to allow it to
cool in the oven by turning off the heat and leaving
it overnight. This meant that no bacteria could enter
the soft warm crust as the air in an oven which has
not been opened since it was heated is sterile.
  Today, the way to keep it is to freeze it, so the
quantity of suet is reduced and the huff paste (which
was thrown away when the Beef Cheese was served)
is omitted. Serve hot with tomato or mushroom sauce
or brown gravy, or cold.

Mix the beef, gammon and suet very well together.
Stir in the onion. Mix all the spices, herbs and
seasonings and then stir them into the meat. Pour in
the brandy and stir again.
  Take an oblong baking tin or fireproof dish of a size
to hold the meat mixture comfortably. Rub all over
the inside of the tin or dish with the garlic. Lay the
slices of bacon in a lattice over the bottom and
partly up the sides. Put in the meat mixture and
press it down well, smoothing the top. Cover closely
with foil and bake in the middle of the oven at 300°F
(160°C, Gas Mark 2) for 4 hours.

Brawn

4 lb (2 kg) pork belly
1 lb ($\frac{1}{2}$ kg) lean pork
1 pig's trotter
$\frac{1}{2}$ teaspoon sage
$\frac{1}{2}$ teaspoon thyme
1 teaspoon freshly ground
* black pepper*
1 teaspoon salt
2 hard-boiled eggs

Brawn was an essential cold dish at royal and noble feasts from the twelfth to the seventeenth centuries. After that it continued to be made at many farms and manor houses when a pig was killed, but it was served less often on grand occasions. In early manuscripts it is always referred to as *"A Shield of Brawn"*, but it is not clear whether this was because it was made in such quantity that only a shield was a large enough dish for it, or whether it was made rather flat and moulded to look like a shield. This is a very simple Wiltshire recipe which is very good as a summer lunch or supper dish. Mustard or a sauce made of mustard and cream is traditionally served with brawn and sets off the flavour. A potato salad and a green salad should also be served with it.

Put the pork, the trotter, herbs and seasoning into a large saucepan, pour in $7\frac{1}{2}$ cups (1.6 litres) of water and bring to the boil. Skim, then cover the pan and simmer very gently for 2 hours.

Lift the meat and the trotter on to a large dish. Allow to cool a little, then remove all skin, bones and gristle and return them to the stock. Reserve the meat. Boil the stock briskly, uncovered, until the liquid is reduced to about 1 quart (9 dl).

Meanwhile, peel and quarter the eggs and arrange them in the bottom of a bowl or mould. Cut all the reserved meat and about three-quarters of the meat fat in $\frac{1}{4}$ to $\frac{1}{2}$ inch (0.5 to 1 cm) dice and put on top of the eggs. The bowl should be almost full. As soon as the stock is reduced, strain it over the pork. Cover the mould and leave it in the refrigerator to set, preferably overnight.

Scrape away any fat that has set on the top. Pull the brawn gently away from the sides of the bowl with the hands and turn out. It should be very firm. To serve, cut in neat pieces.

Bath Chaps

1 pig's cheek (order from the
* butcher 2 or 3 days before it is*
* required)*
Generous $\frac{3}{4}$ cup (180 g)
* demerara sugar*
2 teaspoons (15 g) saltpetre
* (this can be omitted)*
$\frac{1}{4}$ cup (120 g) bay salt (coarse
* sea salt)*
1 lb ($\frac{1}{2}$ kg) salt
Dry breadcrumbs

Bath Chaps were originally home cured from the cheeks of Gloucester Old Spot pigs, which were the breed most often kept by cottagers and farmers in Gloucestershire and Somerset. These pigs had rather elongated jaws and the rolled cheeks made neat long shapes, rather like small boneless legs of lamb. They were a local speciality, much liked in Bath where they were served at late suppers. They have a good flavour but a lot of fat in proportion to lean. They can be bought ready for table in many good West Country butchers and it is hardly worth making them at home unless other parts of the pig are being salted, or you particularly like to make traditional dishes.

Serve cold with a good mild mustard, a green salad and plenty of hot, dry wholemeal toast.

Wash the cheek well in cold water. Spread and rub the sugar mixed with the saltpetre, if you are using it, well into all sides. Lay it in a large dish, mix the salts and smother the pig's cheek in the mixture. Keep for 10 days in a cool place or in the refrigerator, turning it every 2 days and spooning the salt over it.

At the end of this time drain the cheek, wash it in cold water and soak it in fresh cold water overnight. Drain it again, roll it lengthways and tie it tightly with string. It will need 6 to 7 ties. Put the pig's cheek in a pan of cold water, bring to the boil and skim. Cover and simmer gently for 2 hours. Drain, cut string and remove any skin. Cover the cheek thickly with crumbs, allow to get quite cold and serve at any time during the next 3 or 4 days.

Farmer's Loaf

Serves 4 to 6

2 gammon slices, about 3 to 4 oz (90 to 120 g) each
¾ stick (90 g) butter, softened but not melted
2 cups (½ kg) cottage cheese
2 teaspoons finely chopped parsley
½ teaspoon finely chopped thyme
½ teaspoon salt
½ teaspoon freshly ground black pepper
6 eggs

This is a Somerset recipe, made on the farms when milk and eggs were plentiful. It is unusual and delicious, whether served cold with a good mixed salad and mayonnaise, or hot with a hollandaise or tomato sauce.

Fry the gammon slices. Remove all the fat and rind, chop the gammon finely and allow to get quite cold.

Blend the butter and cheese in a blender or with a wooden spoon. Mix in the chopped gammon, the herbs and the seasoning. In a separate bowl, beat the eggs until they froth and then mix them, little by little, into the butter and cheese until the mixture is like a heavy cream.

Butter a 1 quart (9 dl) mould or pudding bowl and pour the mixture into it. Cover the mould with foil and then stand it in a baking tin containing about 1½ inches (3.5 cm) of hot water, and cook in the oven at 350°F (180°C, Gas Mark 4) for 1¼ hours. Test with a skewer to make sure it is set. It should turn out perfectly.

Ham Mousse

Serves 4 to 6

1 lb (½ kg) lean cooked ham, finely minced
2 eggs, separated
1¼ cups (3 dl) white sauce
⅝ cup (1.5 dl) sherry
Four ¼ oz packets (30g) powdered gelatine
Nutmeg
Salt and pepper

A very good lunch or supper dish. The recipe comes from Wiltshire and is known to date back to the early nineteenth century.

Blend the egg yolks with the cooled white sauce. Reheat gently without allowing to boil, as the mixture curdles easily. Season with a little salt, plenty of pepper and nutmeg, and stir in the sherry.

Dissolve the gelatine in a little hot water and stir into the sauce. Then add the minced ham. Remove the pan from the heat, stir well, and when cold, fold in the stiffly beaten egg whites. Pour the mixture into a mould. Cover the mould and put it in the refrigerator. Turn out when thoroughly chilled and set.

Ham and Egg Toasts

4 gammon slices
1¼ sticks (150 g) butter
4 large slices of bread, white or
  brown according to taste
8 eggs, well beaten and
  seasoned with salt and pepper
Prepared English mustard
½ cup (60 g) very finely grated
  Cheddar cheese
Sprigs of watercress or 1
  tablespoon finely chopped
  parsley

A nineteenth-century farmhouse supper dish from Devizes. The gammon slices would, of course, have been cut by the farmer's wife from a flitch of her own curing; the toast would have been made from her own bread and the eggs would have come from the poultry yard. The butter and cheese would have been home-made, too. Scrambled eggs, sometimes called buttered eggs, were served on toast from Elizabethan times, when what were called "spread toasts" first became popular as savouries. They derive directly from food served on a "trencher" of bread. The earliest spreads seem usually to have been made from chopped chicken or sweetbreads, sweetened with sugar, raisins, currants or honey, and flavoured with rosewater, orange-flower water or spices. The ingredients must all be prepared ahead, cooked and combined very quickly and eaten at once.

Fry the gammon slices lightly on both sides in a large pan using ½ stick (60 g) of the butter. They should be slightly brown on both sides and soft right through when pricked with a fork. Keep the gammon hot while you lightly toast the bread. Butter the toast and put a gammon slice on each piece. Keep hot in the oven.

Melt the remaining butter, and stir in the beaten eggs. Stir over very low heat, always moving the mixture from the bottom of the pan so that it does not stick. As the egg begins to thicken, set it aside for a minute. Take the toast and gammon from the oven, spread the gammon with a very little mustard and turn the gammon slices over, so that the mustard is between the toast and the gammon.

Quickly pile equal quantities of the scrambled egg on each gammon slice, sprinkle with cheese and then with the watercress or parsley. Serve and eat immediately.

Saddle of Hare Sauced with Cream

1 saddle of hare, prepared for
  roasting
2 tablespoons (30 g) butter
1 large onion, peeled and cut
  in rings
2 medium carrots, scraped and
  cut in rings
2 tablespoons seasoned flour
2 bay leaves
½ teaspoon dried rosemary
4 slices streaky bacon
⅝ cup (1½ dl) red wine
1 teaspoon lemon juice
⅝ cup (1½ dl) clotted or double
  cream
Salt and pepper

In early recipes roast hare was always basted with milk or cream as it turned on the spit. The milk was caught in a tray with the juices of the hare beneath the spit and just before the hare was served a knob of butter rolled in flour was well stirred in, and the resulting sauce poured over the hare. This Devonshire recipe was made with clotted cream, but is still very good (although slightly different) if made with fresh double cream. The hare should be carved in thin slices down its length and is best served with plain boiled rice and a green salad on separate plates for each person.

A sixteenth-century manuscript refers to a dish of hares prepared for a great feast for a bishop. Four roast saddles were placed in line down a huge pewter platter. Underneath each were four or five small birds, also spit-roasted. A roast chicken stuck out from one end and was decorated to look like a head and a roast pheasant with tail feathers stuck out from the other end. Over the resulting monster, a sauce of cream and wine was poured and the whole scattered with browned crumbs and finely sliced and browned almonds. The huge dish would have been carried in and shown to the bishop and those next to him and then taken away so that each saddle could be carved and a few slices served with a little bird, a slice of chicken or pheasant and some sauce for each diner.

Melt the butter in a baking tin and put in the onion and carrots. Rub the upperside of the saddle with seasoned flour and put the bay leaves on it. Sprinkle with rosemary and then cover with the bacon slices. Place the saddle on the vegetables, so that it is standing on its short ribs. Pour over the wine and lemon juice. Roast at 400°F (200°C, Gas Mark 6) for 45 minutes.

Remove the baking tin from the oven, take off the bacon and discard the bay leaves. Put the hare on a dish and the vegetables in a separate serving dish and keep hot. Pour off all the fat from the baking tin leaving the meat juices. Put the pan over heat and stir in the cream. Stir until it boils and thickens the juices. Add a little more salt and pepper, pour the sauce over the saddle and serve.

Rabbit Fried with Onions

Serves 4

2½ lb (1¼ kg) rabbit, jointed
2 eggs, well beaten
2 cups (240 g) fresh fine white breadcrumbs, seasoned with 1 teaspoon salt and ½ teaspoon white pepper
1 stick (120 g) butter
1 lb (½ kg) onions, cut into fine rings
2 tablespoons (15 g) flour
1¼ cups (3 dl) well-seasoned stock (a stock cube will do) in which 3 strips of lemon rind and the rabbit liver have been simmered for 20 minutes
1 teaspoon lemon juice
4 tablespoons double cream

Rabbit was highly esteemed and frequently eaten by rich and poor until our own times when it has lost favour. From the Middle Ages until the eighteenth century, domestic rabbits (known as coneys) were kept in enclosed warrens and often taken with nets and fattened in hutches for a week or two before being killed for table. The poor man trapped all the wild rabbits he dared to take and the farmer, wishing to protect his crops, enjoyed the sport of shooting them.

This Dorset recipe is intended for coneys. Serve with creamed potato, green beans, peas or spinach.

Plunge the rabbit joints into boiling salted water and boil for 5 minutes. Remove, drain well and allow to get cold. When cold, dip each joint in the beaten egg and then in the breadcrumbs.

Using 2 frying-pans, heat the butter; it should be just sizzling but must not be allowed to darken. Fry the onions gently in one pan, turning and stirring from time to time so that they cook evenly. In the other pan fry the rabbit joints very gently for about 12 minutes, turning them until browned all over.

Spoon the onions on to a flat serving dish and keep hot. Lay the rabbit joints on the onions as they brown. Stir the flour into the juices in the onion pan, adding a little more butter if necessary. Pour in the strained stock, stirring well. Discard the liver or chop it up and add it to the sauce if liked. Finally, add the lemon juice and the cream. Stir again, check the seasoning and serve in a gravy boat.

Casserole of Partridges with Cabbage

2 partridges, trussed
4 bacon slices
1 onion, peeled and cut in
  rings
1 carrot, sliced
2 tablespoons (30 g) butter
½ teaspoon dried thyme
½ teaspoon nutmeg
1 teaspoon salt
½ teaspoon freshly ground
  black pepper
2½ cups (6 dl) chicken stock
2 green summer cabbages,
  outer leaves discarded, finely
  chopped

Traditional in Somerset, where partridges used to be more plentiful than they are today. Old birds can be used and impart a delicious flavour to the cabbage. Serve with plain boiled potatoes and red-currant or crab-apple jelly.

Chop half the bacon slices and put them into a large casserole that has a lid. Fry the onion and carrot in the butter and put them on top of the bacon. Lay the partridges on this bed. Sprinkle with thyme, nutmeg, salt and pepper. Pour over the stock, cover the casserole closely and cook in a moderate oven, 350°F (180°C, Gas Mark 4), for 1½ hours. Remove the casserole from the oven, pack in the cabbage and return to the oven for 30 minutes.

**Makes about ½ pound
(240 g) cream**

Clotted Cream

2½ quarts (2.4 litres) milk
⅝ to 1¼ cups (1½ to 3 dl) single or
  double pasteurized cream
  (optional)

Clotted cream has always been made in Cornwall and Devonshire and is also known as "scalded cream". It takes 36 hours to make. Clotted cream is used in many Cornish and Devonshire pies and puddings, eaten with junket and fresh and stewed fruit, and on scones or Devonshire splits with treacle or jam. Since county boundaries are matters of convenience and not physical realities, clotted cream is, of course, made in Somerset and Dorset, near the Devonshire borders, but it will not be found in other parts of England. It keeps well and is often sold to visitors to the West Country to be posted in special tins as presents to friends and families.

Put the milk bottles in the refrigerator until early evening. Then pour the milk into a wide, shallow fireproof pan: a large skillet or a preserving pan would be suitable. If you want a large quantity of clotted cream, add the pasteurized cream at this point. There is no need to stir. Leave the milk overnight in the refrigerator or in any cool place.
  In the morning set the milk on a very low heat, being careful not to shake or disturb it when you move it. If the source of heat is gas or electricity, it is as well to put an asbestos mat under the pan. Let it stand on the heat for 8 to 10 hours. Remove the pan from the heat, again being careful not to disturb the milk and again, when cool, put it in the refrigerator or in a cool place overnight.
  In the morning skim off the cream with a wide-bladed palette knife or a slice. It should be yellow and wrinkled on top and quite thick.

Dorset Dumplings

½ lb (240 g) suet crust
1 stick (120 g) butter, softened
1 generous cup (240 g) demerara
　sugar
2 teaspoons ground ginger
⅝ cup (1.5 dl) rum
4 medium cooking apples,
　peeled and cored
4 cloves
Clotted or double cream

This is a traditional eighteenth-century recipe for apple dumplings as made in Dorset. The rum and butter makes them just a little better than any other apple dumplings.

Roll out the crust thinly into a large square and cut in 4 pieces. Mix together the butter, sugar, ginger and rum. Put one apple in the centre of each square of crust and fill up the core with the rum mixture. Stick a clove in each. If any mixture is left over, it should be melted just before the dumplings are served and poured over the outsides. Fold the crust over the apples, pressing and moulding the edges so that each apple is sealed in. Grease the perforated bottom of a steamer and set the apples on it. Steam over boiling water for 1½ hours. Remove the dumplings carefully to an ovenproof serving dish and put in a medium oven, 350°F (180°C, Gas Mark 4), for 5 minutes to dry the outsides. Serve with clotted or double cream.

Clifton Puffs

1 lb (½ kg) puff pastry made
　with 3 tablespoons (30 g)
　ground rice and ¾ cup (90 g)
　ground almonds added to the
　flour
1 medium apple, peeled, cored
　and finely chopped
⅔ cup (120 g) currants
⅔ cup (120 g) seedless raisins
¾ cup (120 g) candied peel or
　sultanas
2 cups (120 g) almonds,
　blanched and chopped
1 teaspoon grated nutmeg
4 tablespoons brandy or sweet
　sherry
Juice of ½ lemon
1 egg white
⅜ cup (90 g) plus 2 teaspoons
　castor sugar

Clifton is a part of Bristol, lying mostly above the Avon Gorge. Many fine merchants' houses were built there in the seventeenth and eighteenth centuries. A Clifton baker invented these puffs, which were always triangular in shape and always eaten hot. They were sold from his shop but were sometimes also taken in baskets and offered for sale to coach passengers bound to or from Cheltenham. The puffs are very good served with whipped or clotted cream for the sweet course at dinner.

If frozen puff pastry is used, mix the ground rice and almonds and sprinkle evenly over a pastry board. Roll the pastry over the mixture, fold it and roll once more, so that the rice and almonds are incorporated. They give the pastry a crisp consistency and an almond flavour.
　Make the filling by mixing all the remaining ingredients except for the egg white and 2 teaspoons of the sugar and stir well together. If possible, allow the mixture to stand for an hour or so, as this softens the fruit and improves the flavour.
　Roll out the pastry very thin and cut into 4 inch (10 cm) squares. Put a spoonful of filling on each square, brush the edges with egg white and fold over to form a triangle, pressing the edges well down. Brush each puff with the remaining egg white, sprinkle with the sugar and place on a greased baking tin. Bake at 450°F (230°C, Gas Mark 8) for 10 to 15 minutes. Serve hot.

Devonshire White Pot

4 egg yolks and 3 egg whites
2½ cups (6 dl) milk
1 tablespoon rosewater or
  orange-flower water, if
  available
¼ teaspoon grated nutmeg
4 tablespoons (60 g) castor
  sugar
1¼ cups (3 dl) clotted or double
  cream
1 bread roll, crust removed and
  centre cut in thin slices
2 tablespoons (30 g) butter

White Pots were made in the Middle Ages and were still called by this name in the late eighteenth century. After this the dish disappeared. Devonshire White Pot was considered a speciality because clotted cream was used.

The dish itself is something between a soufflé and a baked custard. It is quick and easy to make and very good. Some recipes include raisins but it is better made plain and served with an accompanying dish of stewed blackberries and apples, fresh raspberries or blanched and sliced peaches.

Beat the eggs well and add the milk a little at a time, still beating. Beat in the rosewater or orange-flower water, the nutmeg and sugar and finally the cream, beating very well if clotted cream is used.

Lay the thin slices of bread roll in a fireproof dish and pour the mixture over. The dish should be filled to within 1 inch (2.5 cm) of the top. Cut the butter into small pieces and place all over the top. Bake at 350°F (180°C, Gas Mark 4) for 35 minutes.

Damask Cream

2 cups (4.5 dl) double cream
Pinch of ground mace
Pinch of ground cinnamon
1½ tablespoons castor sugar
1¼ cups (3 dl) rosewater
1 generous teaspoon rennet
⅝ cup (1.5 dl) single cream
50 scented dark red rose petals

A junket from Bath.

Put the double cream in a heavy saucepan, add the mace and cinnamon and heat gently until just simmering. Stir in 1 tablespoon of the sugar and all but 2 tablespoons of the rosewater and finally the rennet. Turn the mixture into a wide, shallow bowl. Leave in a cool place for 2 hours or longer.

Just before serving pour over the single cream mixed with the 2 tablespoons of rosewater and sprinkle with the remaining sugar. Stand the bowl on a larger flat dish and surround with the rose petals. Serve a few petals with each helping so that the diner may smell roses as he eats.

Devonshire Junket

5 cups (1.2 litres) milk
1 tablespoon castor sugar
2 teaspoons rennet

Junkets were made all over England from the Middle Ages onwards and the basic dish was always much the same: milk is induced to curdle (form curds and whey) by the addition of rennet. Rennet was originally obtained from the pancreas of a calf, but the rennet of today is chemically manufactured. In Devonshire, junkets were particularly popular and Devonshire men considered them better than any others. They were always served with clotted cream and sometimes sprinkled with nutmeg or cinnamon. A tablespoon of brandy was stirred in with the rennet on grander occasions.

Bring the milk just to blood heat and stir in the sugar and then the rennet. Pour it into a large, deep bowl and put it in a cool place for 1 to 2 hours to set.

Orange-flower Cream

2 lemons
¾ cup (90 g) castor sugar
4 eggs
1 quart (9 dl) double cream
2 tablespoons orange-flower
  water (if unobtainable, use 1
  tablespoon curaçao)
Crystallized orange slices, for
  decoration

This cream is the true "*Banketting Stuffe*" to which Gervase Markham refers and for which England was famous in the eighteenth and nineteenth centuries. The recipe given here dates from about 1700 and derives from the dish referred to as "*Leche of Cream*" or sometimes "*White Leche*" in the Middle Ages. Leche meant slice, for the curd was cut into slices.

Grate all the zest from both lemons and put in a saucepan with 2 quarts (1.8 litres) of water. Add the sugar when the water becomes hot. When the sugar has dissolved, boil for 4 minutes. Remove the pan from the heat and set aside for 1 minute.

Beat the eggs into 2½ cups (6 dl) of the cream, then stir slowly into the hot syrup, always in one direction. Allow the mixture to stand undisturbed in a cool place for 2 hours. Use a perforated slice to lift the curd into a colander and leave it to drain and set. Discard the liquid whey. When the curd has set turn it out on to a china dish. Whip the remaining cream with the orange-flower water and put it all around the curd. Decorate with crystallized orange slices and serve very cold.

Port Wine Jelly

2½ cups (6 dl) port wine, of
  reasonable but not excellent
  quality
Eight ¼ oz packets (60 g)
  powdered gelatine, soaked in
  a little warm water
¾ cup (90 g) castor sugar
1¼ cups (3 dl) red wine (not
  expensive)
¼ teaspoon cinnamon
¼ teaspoon nutmeg
Juice of ½ lemon

This recipe comes from a manor house near Frome in Somerset and is dated 1878. It is still made every year during Christmas week, as it is a change from Christmas pudding or mince pies.

Reserve half the port and put the rest with all the other ingredients and ⅝ cup (1.5 dl) of water into a saucepan and stir until it comes almost but not quite to the boil. Add the reserved port and stir well. Pour through a strainer into a mould which has been rinsed with cold water. Leave in the refrigerator for at least 6 hours before unmoulding.

Queen's Custard

1⅞ cups (4.5 dl) single cream
4 egg yolks
2 tablespoons (30 g) castor
  sugar
1 tablespoon Cointreau or
  maraschino (if liked)
⅝ cup (1.5 dl) double cream
2 glacé cherries

The following two recipes are from eighteenth-century Bath. The Queen's Custard uses the yolks and the Lemon Pudding uses the whites of eggs.

Bring the single cream almost to the boil. Meanwhile beat the egg yolks with the sugar in a bowl. Pour the cream in a slow stream on to the eggs, stirring gently. Stand the bowl in a saucepan of simmering water and stir constantly until the custard thickens. Allow to cool for 30 minutes. Stir in the Cointreau or maraschino, if used, and pour into 4 little glass custard cups or small soufflé dishes and chill for at least 1 hour or longer, if convenient.

Before serving, whip the double cream, pile it on to each custard cup and put half a cherry on top.

Chilled Lemon Pudding

Strained juice of 4 lemons
2 tablespoons castor sugar
Six $\frac{1}{4}$ oz packets (45 g)
  powdered gelatine, dissolved
  in 4 tablespoons warm water
8 blanched almonds, halved,
  each half split in two
1 small piece angelica
12 to 16 boudoir sponge fingers
4 egg whites
$\frac{5}{8}$ cup (1.5 dl) double cream

Add enough water to the lemon juice to make 3 cups (7.5 dl). Bring just to the boil and stir in the sugar and the gelatine. Set aside to cool. When the jelly is just beginning to set, pour a small pool into the bottom of a charlotte mould or soufflé dish. On the layer of jelly arrange the almonds like daisies and cut a small piece of angelica to form the centre of each daisy. Arrange the boudoir fingers around the sides of the mould, their ends in the jelly. Trim the tops, if necessary.

Whip the egg whites to hold a peak and fold them into the remaining lemon jelly. Check the flavour and add more sugar, if liked. Pour the fluffy mixture into the mould and put into the refrigerator for at least 2 hours. Turn out carefully and surround with lightly whipped cream.

Devonshire Scones

2 cups (240 g) self-raising flour
$\frac{1}{2}$ teaspoon salt
$\frac{3}{4}$ stick (90 g) butter
$\frac{1}{2}$ tablespoon castor sugar
1 egg
2 tablespoons milk

Slightly richer than many recipes for scones, these are from north Devon and are particularly good eaten cold with clotted cream and strawberry jam.

Mix the salt into the flour and rub in the butter to a crumb-like consistency. Whisk the sugar, egg and milk together and stir into the flour mixture to make a soft dough. Roll out about $\frac{3}{4}$ inch (2 cm) thick. Cut in rounds with a 2 inch (5 cm) cutter or in triangles. Combine the dough trimmings and roll and cut them again. Bake in the centre of a hot oven, 400 to 425°F (200 to 220°C, Gas Mark 6 to 7), for 10 minutes.

Bath Buns

$1\frac{1}{2}$ cups (360 g) flour
4 egg yolks, well beaten with 3
  whites, remaining white
  reserved
1 oz (30 g) fresh yeast, dissolved
  in a little warm water
$\frac{1}{4}$ teaspoon vanilla essence
2 sticks (240 g) butter
$\frac{1}{2}$ cup (120 g) castor sugar
$\frac{2}{3}$ cup (120 g) sultanas
2 tablespoons (30 g) granulated
  sugar

The original eighteenth-century recipe contained caraway comfits instead of sultanas. These are now unobtainable and, in any case, the flavour of caraway seeds is disliked by many people today. This recipe also suggests flavouring with rosewater and sherry, but this gives the delicious, buttery rich buns a rather unexpected and slightly musty flavour.

Mix one-third of the flour with the beaten eggs, yeast and vanilla in a bowl. Cover and set in a warm place to rise for 30 minutes. Meanwhile, rub the butter into the remaining flour and work in the castor sugar, so that a stiff paste is formed.

When the yeast mixture has risen, work it into the butter paste, adding the sultanas as you do so.

Butter baking sheets and shake flour over them. Put tablespoonfuls of the bun mixture well apart on the baking sheets. Brush each bun over with the unbeaten white of egg and sprinkle with granulated sugar. Leave to prove for 30 to 40 minutes or until the buns have puffed up. Bake at 400°F (200°C, Gas Mark 6) for 20 minutes. The buns should be well spread, risen and a light golden brown.

Devonshire Splits

1 lb (½ kg) strong flour
2 tablespoons (30 g) castor
  sugar
⅝ cup (1.5 dl) lukewarm milk
1½ teaspoons dried yeast
1½ teaspoons salt
¾ stick (90 g) butter

Today, when a Cream Tea is offered, Devonshire Splits are often replaced by scones. Scones can be very good with clotted cream and jam but the true Cream Tea served to visitors in the first half of the twentieth century consisted of splits, cream and home-made jam. Children were sometimes given splits with cream and Golden Syrup, which were known as "thunder and lightning". Splits should contain very little sugar and plenty of salt and are good hot for breakfast or filled with ham or cheese for a picnic.

Mix 4 tablespoons of the flour with 1 teaspoon of the sugar in a large bowl. Mix the milk with 2 tablespoons of lukewarm water, stir in the yeast and when it has dissolved pour the mixture into the flour and sugar. Mix well, cover the bowl and leave in a warm place for 30 minutes or until frothy.

  Mix together the remaining flour, sugar and the salt. Heat the butter so that it is just soft and beginning to run. When the yeast has frothed the liquid, stir in the flour and then mix in the butter well. Work the mixture into a dough with your hands until it leaves the bowl clean. Turn on to a floured board and knead until you have a smooth dough – this usually takes 3 to 4 minutes. Cover and leave in a warm place to rise until the dough has doubled in bulk.

  Knead lightly again and divide into 14 pieces. Roll each piece into a ball and put them well apart on greased and floured baking tins. Cover again and leave to rise for 30 minutes. Bake in the centre of a hot oven, 425°F (220°C, Gas Mark 7), for 20 minutes.

Church Cakes

1 stick (120 g) butter or
  generous ⅜ cup clotted cream
  (the latter is preferred in the
  medieval recipe)
½ cup (120 g) castor sugar
¼ teaspoon ground cloves
¼ teaspoon ground mace
1 teaspoon saffron, soaked in 2
  tablespoons warm water
2 eggs plus 1 extra yolk
2 cups (240 g) self-raising flour

In the year 1478 cakes were made for a feast at St Ewen's Church, Bristol. The accounts show the ingredients:
  A bushel of meal for cakes,
  Item for saffron for the same cakes,
  Item for milk and cream,
  Item for eggs to the same.
  We are not given the recipe for these particular cakes but a recipe of about 1500 uses the same ingredients. Saffron at this time was used all over England in many dishes and saffron cake and bread were not confined to the Cornish, as they are today.

Cream the butter or cream with the sugar and dry spices. Strain in the saffron water. Beat in the eggs and finally the flour, a little at a time. When the mixture is well beaten place spoonfuls on a well-greased baking tin. Space well apart, as they will spread and rise during cooking. The original recipe says, *"the paste will be very short, therefore make them very little"*. A scant tablespoonful is about the right amount for each little cake. Bake at 400°F (200°C, Gas Mark 6) for 8 to 12 minutes.

Wastels y Farced

*1 french loaf, not too long or
stick-like*
½ cup (90 g) currants
*4 tablespoons (60 g) plus 2
teaspoons castor sugar*
¼ teaspoon grated nutmeg
¼ teaspoon cinnamon
¾ stick (90 g) butter, softened
2 egg yolks, well beaten

This is a fourteenth-century recipe from a Salisbury manuscript. It is of interest because it shows the demand for enriched breads, which were just beginning to be made.

Wrap the loaf in foil and put it in a 350°F (180°C, Gas Mark 4) oven for 20 minutes. Cut off and reserve the crust from along the top of the loaf and scoop out all the bread. Keep the shell hot while you break the bread into small pieces.

Put the breadcrumbs into a bowl. Stir in the currants, 4 tablespoons (60 g) of the sugar and the spices and work in the butter. Finally mix in the egg yolks. Stuff the mixture into the shell. Replace the top of the loaf; pressing it down well. Dissolve the 2 teaspoons of sugar in 1 tablespoon of water and brush the mixture over the bread. Bake for 20 minutes at the same temperature as before. If some of the filling is left over, bake in a separate little pile on the tin beside the loaf.

Serve very hot, cutting a thick slice for each person.

Wiltshire Lardy Cake

*1 lb (½ kg) white bread dough
ready for baking*
*¾ cup (180 g) lard, divided in 3
parts*
*⅜ cup (90 g) granulated sugar
into which is mixed 1
teaspoon mixed spice (if liked)*
*½ cup (90 g) currants or mixed
currants and sultanas*

This is a very old recipe made in many a farmhouse and cottage on the day the bread was baked. It was cooked in the bread oven with the last batch of loaves and served for tea or supper. Its smell of freshly baked dough is almost as good as its taste and consistency. It is well worth making on its own. The traditional baking-day supper was two boiled eggs apiece, with slices from a small crusty loaf specially made for the meal, followed by the lardy cake. Tea and/or cider were drunk with this meal.

Roll out the dough on a floured pastry board. Put dabs of one-third of the lard at about 1 inch (2.5 cm) intervals all over it, sprinkle lightly with one-third of the sugar and half the currants and fold both ends into the middle and then both sides into the middle. Turn to the right and roll out again. Repeat the larding, sprinkling and folding process. Roll out once more, lard again and sprinkle with sugar only. Fold as before and roll out about 1 inch (2.5 cm) thick. Put in a large, square, greased baking tin. Score across in squares with a sharp knife and bake at 400°F (200°C, Gas Mark 6) for 20 minutes. The cake is best served hot and eaten with plenty of butter. It can be reheated in a cool oven.

The South and South East

Sussex, Kent, Hampshire, Isle of Wight

The counties of Kent, Sussex and Hampshire, although parts of them today are near to being overwhelmed by Greater London and are regarded as Home Counties, may yet, in terms of their culinary traditions, be considered as making up the south-eastern and southern region of England.

Kent, since it ceased in the ninth century to be a separate kingdom, has been called the Garden of England. It is a green and fertile county, heavy woodland giving way to orchard and pasture and, on the lower parts of the Weald, to heavy clay where hops flourish. The hop-gardens spread out around the farmhouses and every farm has its tall, conical, brick oast. The hops, wired and netted, are trained on tall poles.

Hops are picked in late August and early September and the picking traditionally used to be the paid country holiday for London's Eastenders. They crowded the special hop-pickers' trains and spent a riotous two weeks, sleeping in barns or huts on some farms, or sleeping rough on others, singing and sometimes swearing, remembering half-forgotten and forbidden country lore such as the catching of rabbits and pheasants for the camp-fire pot or the stealing of a hen from a cottage yard. Thus for a fortnight each year cockney children saw the open country, the animals and another way of life from their own.

Year after year the same large families – sometimes four generations together – came back to the same farms. The hop-picking was carefully organized; the pickers were divided into "companies" reporting to a "bin-man" who checked their five- or six-bushel bags before they were emptied into the bin. Gypsies were also accepted as hop-pickers on many of the farms. They fought and flirted with the landowners, told their fortunes and picked their pockets. Sharp Romany wits were pitted against those of equally sharp cockneys.

Sadly, this tradition came to an end about 50 years ago. Today, hops are machine-stripped and only one or two farms still give work to hop-pickers from the City. Not everything has changed, however; a musky smell, intensified by the shimmering heat from the kilns still hangs over the hop-gardens, and it is still believed that the smell is soporific and that everyone who works with the hops sleeps heavily in September.

The Domesday Book mentions vineyards, fisheries and cheese-making in Kent. Cherries, for which the county is famous, and which used to flood the London markets in a good year, were introduced from Flanders and were first planted in Kent at the behest of Henry VIII. An eighteenth-century Kentish farmer, John Boys, produced a book called

A General View of the Agriculture of the County of Kent. In it he conveys his pure pleasure in the Kentish landscape, its blossom, fruits and crops and its fine beasts (he was passionately proud of his flock of Southdown sheep).

Fruit was grown all over Kent but did particularly well near Maidstone. The varieties of cider apples Boys recommended had splendid names – Sharp Russet, Golden Mundy, Risemary and Kernel-permain. Quince Apple, Loansmain and Golden Nob were for cooking and eating. The famous May-dukes cherries, introduced in the seventeenth century from Haarlem, and the slightly later ripening Flemish Couronnes, were sent to London markets but were also bought by pedlars to sell on Margate Sands. Morello cherries, sour when raw, went straight to Covent Garden, where they were sold for pies, tarts and jam-making.

All this rich country from the North Downs into the Weald has culinary traditions founded on fine wheat, meat and fruit cooked into rather elaborate dishes. This is probably partly because Roman influence came early to Kent, since Ramsgate (a contraction of Romansgate) was one of their chief ports of entry, and partly because in the fifth and sixth centuries, the Jutish and Saxon farmers who came to Kent were successful agriculturists and introduced their own traditions while adopting some of those of the country in which they had settled. There are many Kentish dishes in which fresh fruit is cooked, often with pastry, and served hot with some form of custard. Ducks were cooked with cherries as early as the eighteenth century and Michaelmas goose with late plums. Fish was extravagantly used by the wealthy. Whitstable oysters were considered among the finest in England and a nineteenth-century dish made from the head and shoulders of a very fresh cod, boiled partly masked with shrimp sauce, surrounded with a *"hundred oysters and as many prawns, with a great wreath of parsley around the edge of the platter and the claw meat of lobsters set in it like pieces of coral"*, featured at the dinners of the Lord Warden of the Cinque Ports. This dish was traditional at Ramsgate and is mentioned as being served at Canterbury. Dover soles are world famous and several ways of serving them originated on the Kentish coast.

The land, however, changes when the Weald gives way to Romney Marsh and Welland Marsh. Until the twentieth century the marshes were strange and lonely and a high proportion of their inhabitants wished to keep them so, since smuggling amounted to a way of life, and a prosperous one, for many who gave the appearance of being poor fishermen and farm labourers. Parsons, squires, monks and abbots, farmers and bailiffs on at least three great estates, supplemented their incomes and increased their comfort with wine and brandy, other spirits, tobacco, silks and lace. One pound of tea could be bought in France for the equivalent of seven pence and could be sold in London for five shillings.

There are great houses throughout Kent, all of which have played a part in retaining the traditional cookery of this part of England. Among them is Knole, the largest house in the whole of England. Built on a very early foundation, possibly on the site of a Roman villa (Roman foundations have been unearthed under the main larder), the estate was bought by Archbishop Bourchier in the fifteenth century, inherited eventually by Cranmer, who gave it to Henry VIII, and finally granted by Queen Elizabeth I to Thomas Sackville. Ever since, Knole has been the home of the Sackville family, who were granted the title Earl of Dorset in 1604 and then Duke of Dorset in 1720. The great rambling house covers four acres and has seven courtyards and more than 50 staircases. There are several long galleries, banqueting halls and ballrooms and more than 300 rooms. The main kitchen block and servants' quarters are vast, and smaller pantries and kitchens in other parts of the building were made for convenience in serving informal meals to guests, relatives or pensioners occupying outlying rooms. V. Sackville-West, who grew up at Knole, has written about the house and about the Sackville family with penetrating vision and affection.

In 1709, when Lionel Sackville, the seventh Earl and first Duke of Dorset, was appointed Lord Warden of the Cinque Ports and Lieutenant of Dover Castle, he gave a dinner at the castle. His salary, as Lord Warden, was £160 a year plus £50 as Lieutenant of the Castle. The dinner cost £76 16s. 9d., which was more than a third of his annual salary. Naturally the young Earl had private money, although no Sackville ever had more than was needed to keep Knole in some sort of repair.

The menu is typical of the early eighteenth century and shows marked changes from earlier feasts both in the naming of the dishes and in the arrangement of the meal.

First course:
5 soups, 12 dishes of fish, 1 Westphalia Ham and five fowls [the first mention of Westphalia ham I have been able to find], *8 dishes of pullets and oysters, with bacon, 10 Almond Puddings, 12 haunches of venison, roast, 6 dishes of roast pigs, 3 dishes of roast geese, 12 Venison pasties, 12 white Fragacies* [fricassées] *with Peetes* [pig's feet], *8 dishes of "ragged" veal* [veal stewed in the piece and then pulled by hand into small strips].

Second course:
14 dishes of ducks, turkes, and pigeons, 15 codlin tarts, creamed, 12 dishes of roast lobster, 12 dishes of umble pies [livers, kidneys, hearts, probably from deer], *10 dishes of fried fish, 8 dishes of Chickens and rabbits.*

Ryders:
5 dishes of dried sweetmeats, 12 dishes of jelly, 6 dishes of Selebub [syllabub] *cream, 13 dishes of fruit, 8 dishes of Almond Pies gilt, 12 dishes of Custard Florentines* [custards made with chopped cooked apples, currants and, probably, almonds], *8 dishes of lobster, 120 Intermediate plates of sorts* [all sorts of small cakes and custards].

Side table:
A large chine of beef stuck with flags and banners, 1 loaf of double refined sugar, Oil and Vinegar.

Penshurst Place, not far from Knole, stands discreetly near the meeting of the Medway with the River Eden. The village of Penshurst had been an early settlement in deep woodland. The manor was presented to Sir John Pulteney by Edward II and Sir John, a rich merchant, began the present house in 1340, building the Great Hall, which remains as the centre of the house today. Edward VI gave the house to Sir William Sidney and it was his son, Sir Henry, who decided to enlarge it while keeping the original structure. Sir Henry's son was Sir Philip, admired by all of his generation. A tree was planted at his birth in 1554 and Ben Jonson wrote of it as a *"taller tree, which of a nut was set At his great birth where all the Muses met"*.

Sir Philip Sidney was 32 when he was killed in battle. At court he was considered *"the perfection of man"* and *"the observed of all observers"*. He had packed his short life with full, hard living: writing, fighting, attending at court, building Penshurst, making love and above all making friends. Fulke Greville was at school with him and wrote his biography. He was himself a man of considerable achievements, but he chose as his epitaph *"Servant to Queen Elizabeth, Counsellor to King James, Frend to Sir Philip Sidney"*.

Jonson wrote of Penshurst:

> *The early cherry and the purple plum*
> *Fig, grape and quince, each in his time doth come,*
> *The blushing apricot and woolly peach*
> *Hang on the wall, that every child may reach.*

The park was full of game: *"the purpled pheasant with the speckled side"*, and *"the painted partridge waiting to be killed"*. Trout swam in the streams, and carp, perch and pike in the ponds. Swans and peacocks were living ornaments in the gardens and no less ornamental when gracing the table at a feast.

At Penshurst, the traditional dishes of Kent were served at the long oak tables in the fourteenth-century Great Hall, and the roasts of beef and venison were often *"ordered so great"* that even those at the lowest tables, accustomed to bread and cheese, could be served with meat.

In the suburb of Eltham, just to the south of London, lies the site of a medieval palace. Today the surrounding area is busy and shabby, with traffic pouring south to the coast and returning north to the city. It is difficult to imagine the pleasant green meadows, the clear streams and the narrow, dusty roads which once surrounded what became the grandest of the royal country houses. Two thousand courtiers dined there several times with Edward II at Christmas and an Emperor of Byzantium was amazed at the splendour of the buildings. Stag-hunting in the park, tournaments and jousts were all arranged at Eltham for the king, foreign envoys and other visitors.

The palace, in the early Middle Ages, had belonged to the Bishops of Durham and was used by these northern princes of the Church when they travelled to London to attend parliament or ecumenical councils. At the beginning of the fourteenth century, the Bishop decided that his possessions, secular and temporal, were so great that it would be wise to present Eltham Palace to Edward II in order to keep his favour.

Henry VIII stayed often at Eltham and spent a great deal of money on improvements. The kitchen quarters were enlarged and made more convenient and tunnels were dug under the moat to carry away kitchen refuse. The Palace of Greenwich, however, began to be preferred by the royal family. Henry VIII visited Eltham only to hunt in the park and Queen Elizabeth rarely went there. After the execution of Charles I, when Eltham was confiscated by Parliament, it was stripped of furniture and much of the building was reduced to ruins. The Great Hall with its magnificent hammer-beam roof was used as a barn, but it was restored in the 1930s and is now the home of The Institute of Military Education.

In 1525 Henry VIII approved a set of documents known as "The Eltham Ordinances", which set out in great detail a series of much-needed reforms and economies in the running of the royal household. The allowances of food for the different ranks of courtiers and servants were all laid down for each and every meal and the quantity of the different kinds of bread in particular was stipulated. A recipe for the finest white bread, called manchet, as made at Eltham in the sixteenth century, is given in these pages. There is no way of telling whether the finest wheat flour of that date was much coarser than ours today, although this is probable. Nor can we know if the wheat itself had a different flavour. But if we eat a loaf made according to the Eltham recipe, we are eating as nearly as possible the same bread that Henry and his queen and courtiers ate for their breakfasts in 1525. Lower down the social scale no allowance of manchet bread was made and only large loaves made of coarse wholemeal flour were provided.

East Kent includes the Isle of Thanet, which ceased to be a true island when the Wantsum Channel silted up. Most of this area, stretching west and south towards Canterbury, was a royal domain in early times and in the first centuries of Christianity the Saxon kings endowed several monastic foundations there. The towns of Minster and Monkton both began as abbeys. The farm lands were rich and the monasteries rented them to tenant farmers, retaining for prior and abbot the hunting and fishing rights and insisting on extra dues over and above the rents.

Monkton Court was the country house and hunting lodge of the prior of Monkton Abbey and part of an inventory of his rich furnishings remains. He had a pillow of white linen with a white silk tassel and a silk bed cover, embroidered with lions and clouds. In his kitchen there were pans and cauldrons to be used for his table alone and he had platters of pewter and of silver for festivals and wooden platters for fast days. The abbot of St Augustine's Abbey at Minster spent his rest periods at nearby Salmestone Grange, where he hunted, and interviewed his tenants when his clerks had collected their rents. When the abbot was not at Salmestone, only two monks were in residence, their duties being to keep the house in order and to repeat the daily offices in the private chapel.

Both these religious foundations seem to have been reasonably generous to the poor. Their records mention that loaves, fresh or salted herrings, and boiled dried peas were doled out to all who were hungry. In spite of this, the obvious wealth of the prior and the abbot enraged their tenants, who were almost at starvation point after several bad harvests. At the beginning of the fourteenth century, they advanced on Salmestone Grange and besieged the two monks in residence for a fortnight. The men of Minster and of Salmestone village did not want charity even from men of God, and believed that their farms would support them if they were not required to pay a tithe on every crop they grew, and every beast they slaughtered. They saw the abbot and his monks hunting over their land and on pain of death could not openly take a deer themselves when their families were starving.

This amazing siege got them very little. There were some small concessions and some fiercer punishments, but the Peasant's Revolt was yet to come and meanwhile, for farm labourers and tenant farmers, times were as hard as ever. It was the same all over the country. *"I have no penny,"* quoth Piers in William Langland's fourteenth-century poem *Piers Plowman:*

> *Only two cheeses*
> *A few curds and whey*
> *And an oat-cake*
> *And two loaves of beans and bran*
> *Baked for my infants . . .*
> *I have no salt bacon*
> *Nor no egg, by Christ,*
> *Collops for to make . . .*

This part of Kent was Dickens's countryside. He lived, as a child, at Chatham and died at his house, Garshill Place, just outside the town. His last writing was done in the chalet in the garden of this house.

Dickens spent some time at Broadstairs, where he finished *Nicholas Nickleby*, living two doors from the Albion Hotel, and in nearby Kingsgate he wrote *The Old Curiosity Shop*.

In *The Pickwick Papers* Mr Jingle says *"Kent, sir – everybody knows Kent – apples, cherries, hops and women."*

The Weald does not end at the border of Kent with Sussex but lies partly in East Sussex. The traditional dishes from this area are simple and of the same tradition as those of Kent. It is when we reach the south coast and arrive at Brighton that we may find a royal tradition of unsurpassed luxury which lasted from about 1800 to 1837. George IV, as Prince of Wales, came to stay at Brighton with his uncle, the Duke of Cumberland, in 1783. From that time Brighton was assured of its claim to be "England's premier maritime watering-place". The Prince of Wales liked the bracing coast, the farm lands and the South Downs behind the little town so much that he acquired some land near the sea, on which he built a curious red-brick house, consisting of a domed salon, a bedroom suite, a music room and separate kitchens and domestic offices, designed for him by the architect Henry Holland. It was known as The Pavilion and in it the Prince, with Mrs Fitzherbert, his mistress, entertained all the fashionable world, with no expense spared.

In 1800 the Prince acquired the whole estate on which Brighton Pavilion now stands. A small house was built by the river for Mrs Fitzherbert. The stables of the main house were designed in the Indian style of the Hall au Blé in Paris. Finally the Prince called in the architect Repton to advise him on extensions. Repton had been working on a mansion for a merchant of the East India Company and recommended that the Pavilion should be built entirely in Indian architectural style. "Prinney" pronounced his final drawings "perfect" and said he would not alter any detail, but in fact it was John Nash,

Repton's partner, who started the building and the style was a kind of general oriental rather than strictly Indian. At first the interior of the Pavilion was decorated largely in Chinese style, but by the time Prinney came to the throne he preferred French "First Empire" furnishings and the decoration was altered.

From the beginning, however, the Prince recognized the importance of the kitchens and considered that no chef could produce the dishes of genius which he required unless he had the latest inventions and the best possible equipment to help him.

The great kitchen was a show place, which visiting ladies begged to be allowed to see. The supporting pillars were made to look like palm trees. J. W. Croker described the equipment in his journal of 1818:

> *Such contrivances for roasting, boiling, baking, stewing, frying, steaming and heating; hot plates, hot closets, hot air and hot hearths, with all manner of cocks for hot water and cold water and warm water and steam and twenty saucepans, all ticketed and labelled, placed up to their necks in a vapour bath.*

The huge, hooded, open fire-place had spits and jacks which were turned by a wind-vane rotating in the chimney. Long, fixed tables accommodated each chef and his assistants and there was an immense steam table in the centre on which finished or almost finished dishes were kept hot under covers.

For some eight months Marie-Antoine Carême, among the greatest of all French chefs, moved from Carlton House to cook at Brighton, exploiting the beautiful kitchen to the full.

He waited each morning on the prince, and presented the inspired menus he proposed, explaining the particular benefits to health as well as pleasure of the different dishes in combination. For a banquet in 1817 he and his kitchen staff produced 116 dishes.

It is difficult, today, to imagine what a very grand dish made by Carême looked like. He was an artist, a natural architect and sculptor, using sugar and marzipan instead of plaster or clay. Each of his great dishes, particularly the sweets, was intended to be examined and admired before it was cut into and served. Apart from this the consistency and flavour of his sauces were said to be always a little more delicious than those of any other chef. In this book, however, it is not appropriate to describe any but the traditional English dishes Carême served in the eight months he was at the Royal Pavilion.

Firm-fleshed turbot, caught in the deep, cold waters of the English Channel, was cooked at Dover Castle, at Arundel and at manor houses in Kent, Sussex and Hampshire, just as Carême cooked Turbot à l'Anglais at the Pavilion, only his presentation was different. The great fish, probably some 30 inches in length, was gently seethed in an enormous copper kettle, specially made to the shape of the turbot. The head, considered a delicacy, was sometimes tied in place to protect it. The turbot was traditionally poached in water to which a little milk had been added, plenty of salt, lemon juice and a little white wine. It required exactly six minutes to the pound. The fish was dished up very carefully in order not to break the delicate skin, and the flesh had to be as firm as chicken, but more moist; if successful, the flavour was considered incomparable in fish. A very fine white sauce, flavoured with either tarragon or fennel, was served with the turbot and it was garnished with crayfish or prawns, scallops or oysters and parsley.

The method was traditional on the south coast. Carême's turbot was cooked similarly until it was ready for its sauce and its garnish. For these he used several lobsters from which a most delicate lobster sauce was made and served in silver sauce boats. The lobster coral was worked into an exquisite lobster butter. Carême piped a deep border of finest creamed potato around the edge of a vast, oval, silver platter. Up the sides of this border he placed medallions of lobster flesh, alternated with medallions of fine black truffles. At this point, the carefully drained fish was placed within the border by two assistant cooks. Tiny baskets of pastry, each containing a pale pink rose made from the lobster butter were placed all round the top of the potato border. The fish itself was sprinkled with a veil of finely chopped, lightly fried parsley. Such a dish would serve 20. Each person would be given a small slice of turbot, a tiny piece from the head, a slice of truffle, a piece of lobster and a tiny pastry basket of lobster butter, and they would help themselves to the delicate, creamy pink sauce. So delicate was the flavour of the lobster, and the contrasting slice of truffle, so light and crisp the little baskets with the richness of their lobster butter, and so stimulating the sauce that the flavour and consistency of the turbot was brought out, and in no way lost. "*A perfectly balanced dish*," said Carême, in one of the books which he considered the most important part of his life work.

Three other traditional dishes which Carême served at the Royal Pavilion were large eels, skinned, filleted, poached and served in elaborately decorated jellies; wild duck from Romney Marsh, spit-roasted with oranges; and small mutton pies, which continued as a tradition in the royal family until the reign of George V, who was very fond of them. In the preface to one of his books, Carême related that one morning at Brighton Pavilion, when he presented his menu for the day to the Prince, His Royal Highness said, "*Carême, you will kill me with food. I have a fancy for everything you put before me. The temptation is really too great.*" "*Your Highness,*" replied Carême, "*my great concern is to stimulate your appetite by the variety of my dishes. It is no concern of mine to curb it.*"

Carême was first and foremost a Frenchman, however, and he finally went back to France because he hated the English fogs and disliked London where "*all was sombre*" and he missed that "*most, most alluring French conversation*".

The Reverend Thomas Fuller, a parson of epicurean tastes, said in 1662 that there were three good things in Sussex: an Arundel grey mullet, a Chichester lobster and a Selsey cockle. Early in the twentieth century, Arthur Becket, in his book *Spirit of the Downs*, added to the list an Amberley trout, a Pulborough eel, a Rye herring and an Eastbourne wheatear. The latter, a member of the ortolan family, is protected today. In the 1930s, Admiral Chambers, another devotee of Sussex and a gourmet, suggested adding Southdown mutton (only lamb is obtainable today); a Patching truffle pie (alas, truffles are no longer to be found near Patching); figs from the fig gardens at Goring; grapes and tomatoes from Worthing glass-houses and mushrooms from the South Downs.

Hampshire spreads out from the great port of Southampton and the mouth of the Christchurch Avon. The Solent and Spithead separate the Isle of Wight from the mainland and are thought to mark the course of a river which in geological time, ran through land now long submerged. From Roman times, through the Middle Ages, there was a close link with France from the Isle of Wight and the Hampshire coast.

The Isle of Wight itself, with its mild climate, lovely beaches and woodlands filling the valleys below the chalk downs, has always been considered a favoured place. The Romans built at least two villas on the island, which they called Vectis; William the Conqueror deeded it to William Fitz-Osborn, but retained it for the Crown after his death. The Domesday Book records salt-works at four different townships, and several quarries, and that alum and fine sand for glass-making were dug out at Alum Bay. Wheat, oats and barley were grown and 29 mills were kept busy grinding corn for the island. On the site of an early British stronghold Carisbrooke Castle was built, probably by William Fitz-Osborn, and became the island's seat of government, always occupied by the governor or the warden who represented the Crown.

The culinary traditions of the island are simple and not very different from those of the south coast generally. A recipe for cinnamon doughnuts which were sold hot in the streets at Newport and Cowes in the eighteenth century, is given and a recipe for A Dish of Crisp Little Fish which comes from Newport.

Queen Victoria was often taken on visits to the Isle of Wight when she was a child. Later, when she had children of her own, she remembered the pleasure she had felt in its sheltered beaches and the lovely, quiet countryside. She felt that there was no place where the heir apparent and his siblings could spend time in natural play, under the eyes of their parents, tutors and nurses, but away from the formal presence of the court and its guests. At Buckingham Palace the Queen did not often have time between meetings and receptions in the state rooms to visit her children in their far-off, attic nurseries. At Windsor the nurseries were near her own apartments but there were no gardens set aside for the royal family. She disliked Brighton Pavilion, partly because of its slightly rakish grandeur and partly because the town had grown around it. "*Sea air*," she said, "*but no private beach.*" So in 1844 she requested the Prime Minister, Sir Robert Peel, to find her an estate on the Isle of Wight where the royal family could spend holiday periods in private. One year later she bought Osborne House from Lady Isabella Blatchford. Looking out on the Solent, Osborne had 1,000 acres of park and woodland and "*a charming beach quite to ourselves*".

At Osborne family luncheons often consisted of simple roasts, steamed or boiled fish, little pies, sausages, milk puddings, fruit jellies and blancmanges, baked apples or apple charlotte. These were all served plainly without much garnishing or decoration and enjoyed by the Queen and Prince Albert. The children had to eat what they were given whether they enjoyed it or not.

The port of Cowes, built on both banks of the River Medina, stands on the sites of two forts built by Henry VIII for coastal defence. Yacht races were held at Cowes as early as 1780, but 50 owners of large yachts established the Yacht Club there in 1812 and it became the Royal Yacht Club in 1820. From then until World War I, yachts of all sizes, classes and nationalities moored in the yacht basins during Cowes Week, and on the big British, American and French yachts fantastically elaborate luncheon and dinner parties were given. Wealthy yachtsmen brought their master cooks from London, Paris and New York, expecting them to use all their skills and ingenuity not only in cooking but in acquiring materials. Hampers and packages from London and Paris arrived on the steamers and were piled on the quayside. Farmers, fishermen and market gardeners arrived early with their produce. For very large parties, sweets and pastries were sent down from London ready made and, when galley space was inadequate, a kitchen might be hired at an inn. Cowes Week has brought a tradition of culinary luxury to the Isle of Wight, although there is no tradition of special dishes.

A few miles away at Southampton, in the areas immediately behind the docks, there is a tradition of special dishes never served in the polite world of yachting. Inky Pinky is a fine stew of beef and carrots, sometimes with dried peas added and always with a glass of ale stirred into the thickened gravy; onion soup is thickened with cubes of bread and half a glass of rum is poured into each bowlful; scaldings, which are dried peas cooked to a mush with butter stirred in, chopped raw onion added and a piece of fried salt pork laid on each plateful, were served both ashore and at sea.

Shrimps with watercress, winkles in vinegar, boiled whelks, cockle and potato pies were all traditional in Southampton. Fish Pot and Meat Pot were made by sailors' and dock workers' wives in the nineteenth century. A little dripping and a chopped onion were put into an earthenware casserole. Then mixed small fish, and pieces of damaged larger ones which were brought round for sale in baskets after the market on the quay was over, were salted well and added. A couple of pounds of damaged fish could be bought for a penny or two. The pot was tightly closed and put in the oven. When the Fish Pot was cooked, the skin and bones were removed and the fish and onion mixed into mashed potato. Meat, which was bought as scraps at the end of the day from the butcher's shop, was treated in much the same way. If available, half a glass of rum was poured over the portion given to the man of the house and he drank the rest of the glass. Strong tea was drunk with this dish and bread and butter or dripping served with it. Beef with Balls (Boiled Beef with Dumplings) was another dish demanded by sailors home from sea.

The naval ports of Portsmouth and Gosport had their traditional dishes also. Spotted Dick or Plum Duff, a boiled suet pudding with raisins, was served at sea on Sundays and seamen demanded it at home when they were on leave. Nineteenth-century ships' officers, from midshipmen to captains, were traditionally provided with roast beef, boiled or roast capons and boiled mutton with caper sauce by their loving relatives. For those without relatives in the neighbourhood, Southampton inns knew what to provide at a price. It is interesting that sailors in both the Royal Navy and Merchant Navy were known to want on shore several of the dishes which were fed to them at sea and about which they grumbled ceaselessly. They were filling, satisfying dishes and, made with fresh ingredients, they were as good on land as they were bad at sea. There must have been added pleasure in eating scaldings when the peas were good and there was plenty of fresh onion and a large piece of pork crisply fried, and remembering it on shipboard at the end of a voyage, made with half-cooked maggoty peas, half-rotten onion and an almost invisible piece of salt pork.

The New Forest clothed the land right down to Southampton Water in earlier times. It was a royal forest and William the Conqueror increased its bounds, and instituted severe laws for the protection of the huge herds of deer. Anyone who owned or rented land had to keep his beasts tied within their holdings for at least half the year. No fencing was permitted to keep the deer out of cultivated areas. No timber or undergrowth could be cut. Records show several forest commoners who were deported in chains for killing a single deer. Until the New Forest Act was passed as late as 1949, there was constant argument about commoners' rights in the forest and the removal of the deer from certain areas.

Beaulieu Abbey was a Cistercian foundation cut out of the forest and overlooking the Solent. It was given to the Order by King John in 1204, traditionally in reparation for the fact that some time earlier, at Lincoln, he had ordered his horsemen to run down some of the Cistercian brethren and had afterwards been warned in a dream that he should repent and attempt to expiate his crime.

The Cistercians at Beaulieu were famous for their hospitality to travellers. Many royal visits are recorded. King John and Henry III came to the Abbey and Edward I came several times. Henry VII visited it twice some 150 years later and Henry VIII spent a week there in the year of his accession. On most of these royal visits, the Abbey was partly used as a hunting lodge. Travellers of every rank who passed through the lonely forest thankfully sought its shelter and the good food always provided. Perhaps at times the Abbey was hard-pressed. In 1278 Abbot Dennis was fined 40 marks for *"breaching the Beaulieu Close and placing therein stakes and engines"* (sharpened stakes and traps for taking deer). A close was a small enclosed area planted with hazels to produce small timber.

Thomas Wriothesley, who bought the Abbey at the dissolution, demolished it and sold the materials, from which the house of the Governor of the Isle of Wight was built. (This house later became the club premises of the Royal Yacht Squadron.) The monks' dormitory and the refectory, which had seen such kind hospitality, remained standing.

In the seventeenth century the whole estate passed into the Montagu family, as the marriage portion of the daughter of the fourth Earl of Southampton. It passed out of the family in the nineteenth century, but Queen Victoria granted the owner the title of Baron Montagu of Beaulieu and it now belongs to the third Baron. The estate in the last three generations has been magnificently restored. The house is open to the public and the Montagu Motor Museum is famous. Lord and Lady Montagu have instituted a great deal of research into the history of the house and its surroundings and traditions, including traditional cooking.

Out of the New Forest, the coast and the river, came many ways of cooking standard dishes which today are interesting rather than useful and a few which are well worth making. Recipes are given for some of the latter. Among the former is an outlaw's dish called the Burning Branch, mentioned in a private letter which describes a peat or charcoal fire, six or more feet long, which burned in a trench. A long, thin green wand was fixed above it on crossed poles, just high enough not to catch fire. Threaded on the wand, gutted and skinned or plucked were small birds, squirrels, collops and umbles of venison, if available, pheasants and other large birds towards the middle, trout, perch, or grayling at one end, with any small sea fish or collops of large fishes. The birds and fish could be turned with a stick as they cooked and the smallest could be pulled off while the rest continued to roast.

Gypsies frequented the forest from the fifteenth century onwards and the names of well-known gypsy families are still common in and near the forest. In England the Welsh and New Forest gypsies were considered the most truly Romany, their customs and taboos strictly kept, their language always spoken among themselves and marriage with gorgios deplored. We hear of hedgehogs baked in clay in the time-honoured manner and pots on tripods in which young rabbits were boiled with wild garlic and roots and herbs. Above all, the gypsies lived on venison. The deer were quietly killed and secretly cooked. Sometimes one would be cut up, wrapped in part of its own hide and placed over a fire in a pit which would be covered with leaves. At other times the venison was put in a pot over a charcoal fire, the whole covered over with turves and green branches, so that there was no smell and only the smallest ribbon of smoke. A clever trick was to light a tiny fire on the concealing turves with a little pot of medicinal herbs bubbling in it and some women watching over it. No verderer would suspect the greater and hotter fire and pot concealed beneath. This was called "*cooking under the hill*".

Pigs were kept by all who had access to the common grazing of the forest. They fed on acorns and beech mast and their flesh was supposed to have a delicious nutty flavour. A fine New Forest dish was a leg of pork spit-roasted over a bed of beech-nut kernels. The tiny beech nuts would have taken hours to shell, but children, kitchens-boys and, at the monasteries, novices had no choice but to complete such a task if it was set. The pork dripped on to the bed of kernels and some of the nuts were spooned over the joint as it turned. When cooked, it was said to taste better than any other roast. An adapted recipe using other nuts is given and is outstandingly good, although it cannot have the same quality as the beech-mast-fed pork served with the beech-nut kernels.

Some 12 miles from Southampton, over land that was once all forest, is the cathedral city of Winchester, once the capital of Wessex and later, equally with London, the capital of all England.

Winchester was, from the time of Alfred, a seat of learning and an important ecclesiastical see, much visited by royalty throughout the Middle Ages. There was fine hunting in the forest all around it. The total number of red and fallow deer in 1670 amounted to about 8,000 and was probably greater still in earlier centuries. In 1403 a great feast was served to celebrate the marriage of King Henry IV with Joan of Navarre, who had arrived in Penzance some ten days earlier and had made the slow, difficult journey up the length of Cornwall and across Devon and Dorset to Winchester Castle. It is not clear how many days were allowed her for recovery before her marriage, but the royal feast must have lasted for several hours and required a good heart and a good appetite.

The banquet was probably held in the castle hall which still stands. There were six courses, three mainly of meat and three of fish. The meat included roast venison, made into hot puddings and served with frumenty. There were cygnets, capons, sucking pigs, rabbits, bitterns and partridges. There was galantine and brawn and the famous Viand Royal, which appeared twice, once made with veal and once with fish. The fish courses included porpoise with frumenty, roast lampreys and a lamprey pie, sturgeon, *"Troutez"* and *"Flounders fryid"*. *"Graspeys"* also formed part of the fish course. The word was applied usually to the royal fish, whale, sturgeon or porpoise, but sometimes included other excellent fish, as it probably did in this case since porpoise, and sturgeon are separately mentioned. Ten different birds were served, apart from "small byrdys". Unusually, no cranes, sea birds, geese or ducks were included and pigeons and young herons (frequently served at feasts) only appeared at the three-course supper. At this less formal meal, presumably for fewer guests, peas and strawberries appeared and this is very strange since the marriage was celebrated on 7 February. The peas are referred to as "pescods": were they dried peas? Were the strawberries a preserve or a conserve? The Harleian manuscripts give no answer to these questions. The Queen survived her wedding day and journeyed with the king, her husband, through the New Forest and through Windsor Forest to London where she was crowned exactly three weeks later.

At Winchester, a little more than 400 years after this royal marriage feast, Jane Austen died. She had lived most of her life in Hampshire, first at Steventon, then for four years in Southampton and for her last eight years at Chawton, near Alton. (She also lived in Bath for a few years.) The tidy, substantial Georgian house at Chawton may be visited. Here she wrote *Emma*, in which she described the evening spent by the hypochondriac Mr Woodhouse with the extremely elderly Mrs Bates. The contrast between the dishes served at the ball attended by the younger generation on the same evening and the spare and rather insipid food prepared for the timid Mr Woodhouse and his guests is ludicrous.

Miss Bates, having visited her mother and returned to the ball, explains to her niece:

> *". . . there was a little disappointment. The baked apples and biscuits, excellent in their way, you know; but there was a delicate fricassée of sweetbread and some asparagus brought in at first and good Mr Woodhouse, not thinking the asparagus quite boiled enough, sent it all out again. Now there is nothing that Grandmamma loves better than sweetbread and asparagus so she was rather disappointed. . . ."*

At the ball itself we are told that there was soup and Miss Bates enquires of her niece, *"Dear Jane, how shall we ever recollect half the dishes for Grandma?"* We are left to imagine the hams, the chickens in aspic, the salmon, the jellies and trifles, all this a little pale compared with the robust medieval feast held 400 years earlier but only a few miles away, and a little pedestrian compared with the dinner further away still at Brighton with which, on that same evening, Carême was almost certainly serving the Prince Regent.

Spinach with Cream and Eggs

2½ lb (1¼ kg) spinach, stalks
  removed
½ stick (60 g) butter
1 teaspoon salt
2 tablespoons (15 g) flour
1¼ cups (3 dl) single cream
1 onion
Pepper
Nutmeg
Juice of ½ lemon
4 hard-boiled eggs, cut in half
  longways

In 1759 William Verral of Lewes wrote of this recipe: "This being a very genteel dish it is a pity to leave it."

Put the spinach in a pan with ⅝ cup (1.5 dl) of water, 1 tablespoon (8 g) of butter, and half the salt. Bring briskly to the boil. Remove the pan from the heat, drain the spinach and press out all the juice. Chop the spinach very finely.
  Put the chopped spinach in a pan with the remaining butter, stir in the flour and the cream, the whole onion, the rest of the salt and a little pepper and nutmeg. Stir over low heat for 10 minutes. Remove the onion, stir in the lemon juice and serve, garnished with the hard-boiled eggs.

Broad Beans with Tarragon

1½ lb (¾ kg) young broad beans,
  shelled
¾ stick (90 g) butter
3 egg yolks
1¼ cups (3 dl) double cream
Juice of ½ lemon
1½ tablespoons finely chopped
  fresh tarragon
Salt and pepper

This is a traditional dish in Kent where broad beans are sown before Christmas and are sometimes ready for the table in April. The beans must be very young and freshly picked and the tarragon shoots young and tender. It is the first spring vegetable dish and is much looked forward to by those with sheltered gardens. It is no good with frozen beans. Serve in individual dishes as a starting course with brown bread and butter, or with grilled gammon as a main course.

Melt the butter in a heavy pan. Add the beans, cover closely and cook gently for about 15 minutes, stirring from time to time.
  In a bowl, beat the egg yolks into the cream. Stir in the lemon juice a little at a time and finally mix in the tarragon and the seasoning.
  Remove the pan from the heat and allow the beans to stand for 30 seconds. Pour the sauce over the beans and stir gently, holding the pan just above the heat. It must on no account boil. Serve immediately.

Buttered Hop Tops

1 lb (½ kg) hop shoots
Salt
½ stick (60 g) butter
Pepper

This recipe from Kent can only be made with the very young top shoots of the hops, picked to only four leaves down the stem before or during May.

Lay the shoots in a dish with enough cold water to cover them and add ¼ cup (60 g) of salt. Leave to soak for 2 hours. Drain the hops and drop into boiling water (again enough to cover them) and boil rapidly for 10 minutes, or until tender. Drain, chop up the hop shoots and return to the hot pan with pepper, salt and the butter. Serve at once, very hot.

A Grand Salad

6 artichoke hearts, or a tin of
  smaller ones, well drained
24 tiny new potatoes, boiled,
  allowed to get cold and each
  cut in half
1 Webb's lettuce heart, very
  finely shredded
1 tablespoon finely chopped
  parsley
1 teaspoon finely chopped
  tarragon
1 teaspoon finely chopped mint
1 teaspoon finely chopped
  thyme
$\frac{1}{4}$ lb (120 g) very young french
  beans, boiled and each cut in
  half
12 very young carrots, scraped,
  boiled and finely sliced
$\frac{5}{8}$ cup (1.5 dl) salad dressing
12 nasturtium flowers, if
  possible

From a notebook of Kentish recipes dated 1841, this outstanding salad is a perfect starting course for an early summer dinner. It was intended to be served on a large flat dish with a wreath of nasturtium flowers around it but is better served in individual dishes, with thin slices of brown bread and butter.

In each dish first put the artichokes, cut in halves or quarters according to size, and the potatoes, then a layer of chopped lettuce. Mix all the herbs together and sprinkle about half on the lettuce. Pile the french beans and carrots on this, pour over the dressing and sprinkle with the rest of the herbs. Finally, put two nasturtium flowers on each dish.

Salamagundy

1 Webb's lettuce, outer leaves
  removed, chopped very fine
6 hard-boiled eggs, yolks and
  whites chopped separately
6 oz (180 g) cold cooked
  chicken, finely chopped
6 oz (180 g) cold cooked tongue
  or ham or both, cut in
  matchstick strips
12 sprigs of parsley
6 small onions, or shallots,
  finely chopped
12 anchovy fillets, well drained
  and each cut in 4 pieces
2 cucumbers, peeled and diced
6 tomatoes, blanched and
  quartered, pips and juice
  removed, and the pieces cut
  through again
Salad dressing

A traditional salad dish for which there are recipes dating from as early as the fifteenth century from several parts of England. It was often served in London where the vegetables could be bought at Covent Garden. This recipe is from Hampshire. It was intended as a centrepiece on the supper table or for the second course of a dinner. It was always set out on a very large dish or platter with a small raised dish in the middle. Either a small plate was placed on an inverted bowl or a cakestand was used. Sometimes a larger bowl was inverted and covered with rings of ingredients with an ornament made of butter, or a sprig or two of parsley with two or three primroses, nasturtiums, violets or marigold buds (all considered edible) stuck in the top layer. The ingredients on the flat platter were either arranged in rings or in small saucers around the raised centre and the spaces in between were filled up with parsley. Any ingredients can be omitted, or others, such as beetroot, celery or cooked peas added, but seven or eight are needed. A Salamagundy is excellent for a summer lunch.

If using an inverted bowl, cover it first with chopped lettuce and then build rings of the other ingredients over it. Arrange all the ingredients separately on the large dish and decorate with the curled parsley, stuck in here and there. Make the outside ring of chopped lettuce. Arrange the anchovy fillets on the ring of chopped egg whites. Serve the salad dressing separately.

Grilled or Fried Dover Soles

1 sole about 1¼ lb (½ kg) or 2
  smaller ones
2 teaspoons seasoned flour
2 tablespoons (30 g) butter
2 teaspoons very finely chopped
  parsley with a single sprig of
  tarragon, if liked
1 lemon, cut in quarters
Salt and pepper

A Dover sole eaten on the day it is caught is one of
the greatest sea fish of the world. Most of the soles
from the south coast are sent to London and are
none the worse for a quick, short journey. The
Victorians, who appreciated Dover soles, thought of
dozens of ways of garnishing them and dressing them
up. They were served with lobster, prawns, green
grapes, mushrooms or artichoke hearts. They were
cooked in cream with truffles or in a fine cheese
sauce, with melted or black butter, with slices of
apple, or filleted and stuffed. All these dishes are
good and are not quite the same if made with a
slightly cheaper flat fish such as lemon sole or plaice,
but Dover sole, particularly if not too large, is best
of all cooked and served quite plainly.

Soles should be served with a quarter of a lemon, to
squeeze over them, and plenty of very thinly sliced
fresh bread and butter. They may be sprinkled with a
very little fresh parsley with which a single sprig of
tarragon is finely chopped. The fishmonger will clean
and skin the sole and this is necessary as the skin is
rough and prickly. The fish is better served whole
than filleted.

Rub the seasoned flour over both sides of the fish.
In a large, heavy frying-pan, heat the butter until it
is foaming. Put in the sole. If large, cook for 6
minutes on the first side and then carefully turn with
a slice and cook for 4 minutes on the second side. If
small, cook for 4 minutes on the first side and about
3 minutes on the second side.

Dish up quickly, sprinkle with the herbs, put
quarters of lemon at the sides of the dish, pour any
remaining butter over the fish and serve very hot.

Poached Dover Soles

1 sole, about 1¼ lb (½ kg) or 2
  smaller ones
⅝ cup (1.5 dl) dry white wine
Salt and pepper
Tiny pinch of mace
Tiny pinch of ground ginger
1 tablespoon (15 g) butter
2 tablespoons (15 g) flour
¼ cup (60 g) cream
2 teaspoons finely chopped
  parsley and tarragon,
  optional

The inclusion of a pinch of ginger brings out the
flavour of the sauce and the fish. It was frequently
used in fish dishes until the seventeenth century.
If preferred, the thickened sauce can be omitted and
the soles served with a little of the liquor in which
they cooked.

Ask the fishmonger for the skin and any trimmings
from the soles and boil them for 10 minutes in ⅝
cup (1.5 dl) of water. Strain the liquid into the wine
and add a little salt and pepper and the mace and
ginger. Lay the sole in a large, fireproof dish (2 soles
should be placed side by side). Pour the liquid over
them, cover closely and put in the oven at 350°F
(180°C, Gas Mark 4) for 20 minutes.

Remove the fish from the oven and keep warm on a
flat dish. Reserve the cooking liquid. Melt the butter
in a small saucepan. Add the flour, cook for 1
minute, stirring, and then pour in the reserved
cooking liquid. Stir while it boils for 1 minute and
then mix in the cream.

Pour the sauce over the fish, sprinkle with the
parsley and tarragon, if liked, and serve at once.

Stuffed Herrings

6 herrings, cleaned
4 tablespoons (60 g) white
* breadcrumbs*
2 cups (30 g) chopped parsley
¼ cup (30 g) chopped suet
½ teaspoon grated lemon rind
1 tablespoon milk
6 slices streaky bacon
⅓ cup (60 g) fine oatmeal
Butter
Salt and pepper

As cooked on the Rye Marshes.

Mix together the breadcrumbs, parsley, suet, lemon rind and milk and season with salt and pepper. Stuff the fish with the mixture and put them in a buttered pie dish on their backs. Cut each bacon slice in half, roll up and pack among the fish. Sprinkle with the oatmeal, then bake at 400°F (200°C, Gas Mark 6) for 25 minutes.

Red Mullet

6 red mullet
1 small tin anchovies, drained
* and very finely chopped*
2 medium onions, very finely
* sliced*
2 tablespoons (30 g) butter into
* which ¼ cup (30 g) flour has*
* been worked*
1¼ cups (3 dl) red wine
½ teaspoon nutmeg
½ teaspoon salt
½ teaspoon white pepper
2 sprigs each of thyme,
* tarragon, lemon thyme and*
* marjoram tied in a bunch or*
* use a bouquet garni*
2 teaspoons lemon juice
2 hard-boiled eggs, finely
* chopped*

The red mullet has always been prized by gourmets although curiously it has never become an expensive luxury. It is sometimes called the "woodcock of the sea" because it should not be cleaned but cooked whole, with its "trail", as a woodcock should be cooked. It is an extremely delicate fish, nearer to a fine perch than any other sea fish. In the 1850s the Duke of Portland, a notable gourmet, insisted that, taken straight from sea to table, it was the only fish worth eating and its liver an unsurpassed delicacy. He once paid a guinea for a four-pound (2 kg) fish – mullets are usually about a quarter to one pound (120 g to ½ kg) – because it would have such an enormous liver. The duke also considered that, at that period, Weymouth, in Dorset, was the best place for these fish. He therefore visited the small seaside town every summer. His custom was to have all the delectable livers served in a butter-boat so that an equal helping could be given to each guest, avoiding the possibility that someone might be disappointed to find that his mullet had a very small liver. All along the south coast in Hampshire and Sussex mullet are still plentiful. The traditional eighteenth-century recipe given here comes from Arundel Castle, which has belonged to the Dukes of Norfolk for 500 years. The vast castle stands above the river Arun, a few miles inland from the Sussex coast. A similar recipe was first recorded in the seventeenth century.

Lay the mullet in a large skillet or a fish kettle. Put the chopped anchovies and onions on the fish. Divide the flour and butter mixture into 4 little balls and put them at the ends and sides of the dish. Mix the wine with 2½ cups (6 dl) of water, stir in the nutmeg, salt and pepper and pour gently over the fish. Lay the bunch of herbs on top. Bring to the boil, cover the pan and simmer very gently for 15 minutes. Remove the herbs and add the lemon juice. Stir the liquid very gently without disturbing the fish, check the seasoning and simmer for a further 10 minutes.
  Lift the mullet on to a flat serving dish. Stir the sauce, which should have the consistency of thin cream. Do not strain the sauce but pour it over the mullet as it is. Garnish by sprinkling with the finely chopped hard-boiled egg.

Red Mullet with Parsley Butter

4 red mullet, livers removed
  and carefully kept
1½ sticks (180 g) butter
1 tablespoon finely chopped
  parsley
2 teaspoons lemon juice
¼ cup (30 g) seasoned flour
1 tablespoon dry white wine
Salt and freshly ground black
  pepper

This recipe comes from the Isle of Wight.

Soften, without melting, half of the butter, then beat in the parsley and the lemon juice, a pinch of salt (unless the butter is salty enough) and ¼ teaspoon black pepper. Beat well, divide into 4 pats and put aside until required. The parsley butter should not be chilled; it should remain soft but firm.

Heat 4 tablespoons (60 g) of the remaining butter in a frying-pan. Lightly rub each fish with seasoned flour and fry gently for about 4 minutes on each side. Test with a skewer to make sure they are cooked right through. Lift the fish on to a warmed serving dish and keep hot.

Melt the remaining butter in the pan and gently put in the livers. Fry for 30 seconds, turn them and pour the wine over them. Put the livers at one end of the dish of mullets and pour any remaining butter and wine in the pan over all the fish. Just as they are going to table, put a pat of parsley butter on each fish. Serve quickly so that the butter is just beginning to melt. The true gourmet eats the tiny liver first.

Carp or Pike Baked in Slices

2½ lb (1¼ kg) carp or pike
½ lb (240 g) veal or pork
  forcemeat (see page 210)
2 tablespoons seasoned flour
1 stick (120 g) butter
1 tablespoon finely chopped
  parsley
Juice of ½ lemon
Salt and pepper

An eighteenth-century recipe from Arundel in Sussex.

Cut the fish through crossways into 1½ inch (3.5 cm) slices. Cut out the backbone from each slice and fill the hole with some of the forcemeat. Rub each slice with seasoned flour. Lay the fish flat in a buttered fireproof dish. Cover with foil and bake at 400°F (200°C, Gas Mark 6) for 15 minutes or until cooked through.

Transfer the fish to a serving dish and keep hot while you make the sauce. Melt the remaining butter in a saucepan. Add the juices from the fireproof dish, the parsley, lemon juice and seasoning. Bring to the boil, stirring. Pour the sauce over the fish and serve.

Fish Curry from the Isle of Wight

2 lb (1 kg) fresh haddock
½ teaspoon turmeric
¼ teaspoon cayenne
¼ teaspoon nutmeg
¼ teaspoon ground ginger
¼ teaspoon white pepper
¼ teaspoon mace
½ teaspoon salt
2 tablespoons (30 g) butter
  (clarified is best)
¼ lb (120 g) cooked prawns
1 hard-boiled egg, finely
  chopped

This is like no recognized Indian curry but it was made on the island at least until a few years ago and was always referred to as Indian. It probably comes from a visiting maharajah, who would have had his food prepared by his own cook while visiting the Royal Yacht Squadron. Serve with rice, peeled, sliced and salted cucumber and a quartered orange.

Bring the haddock to the boil in just enough salted water to cover. Boil gently for 20 minutes. Drain and allow to cool a little, then remove all skin and bone and flake the flesh.

Mix all the spices and the salt together in a small bowl. Grease a frying-pan with a little of the clarified butter and when hot put in the spices and shake them in the pan for 30 seconds. Put in the remaining butter, shake again and stir in the haddock. Stir and shake for 2 minutes over low heat and then stir in the prawns and the chopped egg and heat again for 1 minute. The fish should be coated with the golden spices. Put it in a hot dish and serve immediately.

A Dish of Crisp Little Fish

Serves 4

4 small whiting or flounders
8 small herring
4 very small mackerel
$\frac{1}{4}$ lb (120 g) cooked shelled prawns or the flesh of $\frac{1}{2}$ shelled lobster
2$\frac{1}{2}$ cups light batter for coating
Oil
1 lemon, cut in 8 thin slices

This dish was often served to visitors to the Isle of Wight in the nineteenth century. It was accompanied by thin slices of brown bread and butter, watercress and English sauce (hollandaise) and never by chips or any form of potatoes. The fish should be mixed and traditionally includes a few prawns or pieces of lobster.

Clean the fish and remove the heads and tails. Pour the well-mixed batter into a shallow dish and lay all the fish in it, turning and rolling them gently until they are thinly coated all over. Do the same with the prawns or lobster but keep them separate.
  The fish can be deep or shallow fried as preferred, but oil must be used as butter does not give sufficient crispness. Put the fish in the oil only when it is really hot (about 400°F, 200°C) and fry them very crisp and brown. Add the prawns or lobster at one side of the pan and fry for 2 or 3 minutes only. Longer cooking makes them tough.
  Lift all the fish and shellfish on to a warmed flat dish and serve at once, garnished with slices of lemon.

Prawn and Mushroom Pies

Serves 6

1 lb ($\frac{1}{2}$ kg) short pastry or flaky pastry
$\frac{3}{4}$ lb (360 kg) mushrooms, sliced rather finely
$\frac{1}{2}$ stick (60 g) butter
$\frac{3}{4}$ lb (360 g) cooked prawns
$\frac{5}{8}$ cup (1.5 dl) double cream
Milk
1 egg, well beaten
Salt and pepper
1 tablespoon finely grated parsley

These were a speciality of Sussex. They were saucer pies baked in rather small saucers which had been chipped and so were no longer in use. Cauliflower or spinach are both good with these pies.

Sauté the mushrooms gently in some of the butter and allow to cool. Roll out the pastry to about $\frac{1}{8}$ inch (0.25 cm) thick and cut into 12 rounds. Grease 6 saucers with the remaining butter and line each with the pastry.
  Drain the prawns well and mix them with the mushrooms, adding salt and pepper to taste. Pile the mixture into each lined saucer and spoon cream over each pile until it is used up. Dampen the edges of the pastry with a little milk and put on the lids, pinching the edges well together all round. Brush over with beaten egg and cut into small slits in the centre of each.
  Bake at 400°F (200°C, Gas Mark 6) for 20 minutes or until golden brown and crisp. Remove the pies from the oven, slide carefully from their saucers on to a flat dish, sprinkle with a little parsley and serve.

Oyster Loaves

4 rather small crisp white rolls
Oil for deep frying
6 fresh oysters, or a tin of
  oysters
1 tablespoon (15 g) butter
2 tablespoons (15 g) flour
⅝ cup (1.5 dl) double cream
White pepper
Nutmeg
Salt
Cayenne pepper
4 sprigs of watercress

This recipe comes from Whitstable Bay, famous for its oysters. Oyster loaves were sometimes served as a breakfast dish and sometimes as a side-dish at dinner. Tinned oysters can be used and crab is an excellent alternative filling. The loaves should be crisp but not hard, so that the dish can be eaten with a fork.

Cut a small slice off the top of each roll and carefully scoop out all the crumb, so that a hollow shell remains. Deep fry these shells for about 2 minutes, pressing them into the hot oil if they float. As soon as they are a pale golden brown lift them out and drain on kitchen paper for a few minutes. Sprinkle the insides with a pinch of pepper, nutmeg, salt and cayenne. Then put in a low oven to keep hot until the filling is ready. Open the oysters and remove the beards. Save any liquor.
  Make a roux with the butter and flour. Add the liquor and then the cream. Bring just to the boil and stir in the oysters. Stir for 3 minutes, then lift out the oysters, cut them into dice and return them to the sauce. Stir again for 30 seconds. Put a small sprig of watercress into each hot roll, fill with the oysters and sauce and serve immediately.

Fillets of Duck with Mushrooms

2 ducks
1 lb (½ kg) mushrooms
½ bottle dry white wine
1½ cups (120 g) parsley, finely
  chopped
½ cup finely chopped shallots
¾ cup (90 g) flour
2½ cups (6 dl) strong brown
  stock
1¼ sticks (150 g) butter
1¾ cups (240 g) fresh
  breadcrumbs
Salt and pepper

This recipe comes from Richard Dolby, well known in the early nineteenth century as the head cook of the Thatched House Tavern in St James's. There is a similar recipe in a Kentish eighteenth-century manuscript from a manor house near Tenterden, but I give Dolby's recipe because it is much clearer.
  Serve plain boiled rice or creamed potato and green peas flavoured with mint with this dish.

Slice the mushrooms, stalks and all, and marinate them in the wine for 30 minutes or a little longer. Cut the fillets from the breast of each duck and cut the meat from the thighs into neat pieces. Mix the parsley and shallots into the flour. (The large amount of parsley is very important as it adds to the subtle flavour of the dish.)
  Pour off the wine from the mushrooms, add it to the stock, and boil until reduced by half. Meanwhile, roll the duck fillets and pieces in the flour, parsley and shallots mixture and fry them gently in half the butter until just golden on both sides.
  Lightly butter a large shallow ovenproof dish and place a layer of mushrooms on the bottom. On these place the duck pieces and over them a further layer of mushrooms. Season the reduced stock rather highly, using freshly ground black pepper, and pour over the duck and mushrooms. Cover the dish and place in a moderate oven, 350°F (180°C, Gas Mark 4), for 30 minutes.
  Take out the dish and scatter thickly with the breadcrumbs. Melt the remaining butter and spoon it over the breadcrumbs. Brown under a hot grill.

Wild Duck with Orange

2 ducks
½ stick (60 g) butter
1¼ cups (3 dl) good stock
Juice and zest of 1 large or 2
  small oranges plus 1 orange
  cut into slices
2 tablespoons (15 g) flour
Salt and pepper

Serve with brown or wild rice and a green salad.

Fry the ducks in 3 tablespoons (45 g) of the butter until they are brown all over. Then place them in a casserole with the stock and seasoning and sprinkle the grated orange zest over them. Cover the casserole and cook at 400°F (200°C, Gas Mark 6) for 40 minutes. When the birds are done, transfer them to a dish and keep hot while making the sauce. Reserve the gravy.

In a saucepan melt the remaining butter and stir in the flour. Cook for a few seconds, then stir in the orange juice and strain in the reserved gravy. Bring to the boil and cook for 2 minutes. Place the orange slices around the ducks and pour the sauce over all.

Goose Braised with Plums

1 two-year-old goose or gander
  about 11 lb (5 kg), or 1
  Michaelmas goose about 8 lb
  (4 kg), rubbed all over with
  seasoned flour
1 tablespoon (15 g) butter
2 large onions, finely chopped
1 tablespoon finely chopped
  parsley
½ teaspoon finely chopped
  thyme
1 teaspoon finely chopped sage
1¼ cups (3 dl) stock
1¼ cups (3 dl) dry white wine or
  cider
3 lb (1½ kg) ripe plums,
  Victorias or golden dessert
  plums are best
Sugar
Salt and pepper

A large, rather old goose is very good for a supper party if cooked in this way and served with rice. A large fish kettle is necessary, as the goose must be closely covered. The plums are just about ripe at Michaelmas when a young goose was sometimes cooked in this way in Kent. A young goose requires about two-thirds the cooking time of an older one.

Grease a fish kettle, which must be large enough to take the goose comfortably, with the butter and put half the onions in the bottom. Mix the herbs with salt and pepper and sprinkle half of them on top of the onions and put the remaining onion and herbs inside the goose. Lay the goose, breast downwards, in the fish kettle. Mix the stock with the wine or cider and pour it all round the goose. Cover the kettle with foil and then with its lid. Bring just to the boil and then put in the oven at 350°F (180°C, Gas Mark 4) for 3 hours if an old bird or 2 if young.

Meanwhile, stone all the plums, cutting them in half. Sprinkle with a very little sugar and leave in a colander to drain.

After 3 (or 2) hours remove the fish kettle from the oven and lift out the goose on to a board or clean dish. Turn the oven heat up to 400°F (200°C, Gas Mark 6). Let the goose drain for a minute and spoon out any liquid from inside the carcass, adding it to the rest in the kettle. Skim as much fat as possible from the liquid in the kettle, check the flavour and add more salt and a sprinkling of pepper, if necessary. Put half the plums inside the goose and put it back in the liquid, breast upwards. Put the remaining plums in the stock around it and return to the oven, uncovered for a further 45 minutes for a large bird or 30 minutes for a smaller one.

When the goose is cooked lift it out on to a dish and surround with the plums from inside the bird. The breast and thighs should be nicely browned. Keep hot while you skim the gravy and lift out some of the plums to add to those around the goose. Pour all the gravy, with any remaining plums, into a sauceboat and serve separately.

Pork with Nuts

*4 to 5 lb (2 to 2½ kg) top leg of
 pork
¼ cup (30 g) seasoned flour
1½ cups (120 g) walnuts, finely
 chopped
½ cup (90 g) almonds, finely
 chopped
⅝ cup (90 g) fresh fine brown
 breadcrumbs
2 tablespoons (30 g) butter
Salt and pepper
2½ lb (1¼ kg) potatoes, peeled
 and halved*

This delectable and unusual roast is an easy and
successful version of the ancient New Forest dish of
pork roasted over shelled beech nuts. It is very good
indeed made with pine kernels but as these are
difficult to obtain and expensive, it is usually made
with a mixture of chopped walnuts and almonds.
(Hazelnuts give a slightly musty flavour.) The nuts
are delicious with the crisp crackling of the pork.
Serve with red-currant or crab-apple jelly and runner
beans.

Rub the pork over with seasoned flour. Mix the nuts
with the breadcrumbs and ½ teaspoon of salt. Butter
a large baking tin thickly, and pour the nut mixture
down the centre, working it up with your hands to
form a loose, flat cake. Put a rack over this and set
the pork on it. Roast at 400°F (200°C, Gas Mark 6)
for 2 hours.
  Meanwhile, parboil the potatoes in salted water for
10 minutes. After the pork has roasted for 30
minutes, remove the baking tin from the oven, baste
the pork, and put the parboiled potatoes in the
baking tin. Return the baking tin to the oven. The
nuts which slip from the main cake will adhere
deliciously to the potatoes.
  When ready to serve, remove the pork to a warm
flat dish and the potatoes to a vegetable dish. Lift
the nuts with a slice, keeping them in a cake as far
as possible and put in a separate small dish. Keep all
hot while you make the gravy in the baking tin.

Beef Steak Pudding

*1 lb (½ kg) suet crust
1 tablespoon flour
1½ lb (¾ kg) rump steak, cut in
 thin small slices, about 2 by 4
 inches (5 cm by 10 cm), well
 trimmed of all fat
4 shallots or 1 medium onion,
 skinned and finely chopped
¼ lb (120 g) mushrooms, sliced
⅝ cup (1.5 dl) red wine
Salt and freshly ground black
 pepper*

Such puddings were made all over England but this
eighteenth-century recipe, using good steak and
plenty of red wine, makes for very tender beef in rich
gravy. The recipe is from Lewes in Sussex.

Roll out the suet crust ¾ inch (2 cm) thick. Line a
medium-sized bowl, so that the crust stands up about
¼ inch (0.5 cm) above the top. Roll out a circle for the
top.
  Season the flour with salt and pepper and dip the
steak slices in it. Put half the meat in the bowl, add
the shallots or onion and pile on the rest of the steak
with the mushrooms on top. Mix the wine with ⅝ cup
(1.5 dl) of water and fill up to within ½ inch (1 cm) of
the top of the bowl. Moisten the edge of the crust
and press the lid on it. Cover with foil and then with
a plate or saucer.
  Stand the bowl in a saucepan of boiling water (the
water should come about halfway up the sides of the
bowl). Cover the saucepan and simmer for 3 to 4
hours, adding a little boiling water to the pan
occasionally.

China Chilo

1½ lb (¾ kg) best mince (beef or
lamb but lamb is preferable)
¾ stick (90 g) butter
1 large lettuce, or Chinese
cabbage, finely chopped
1 lb (½ kg) shelled (2 lb/1 kg
unshelled) peas, fresh or
frozen
2 large onions, chopped
¼ teaspoon cayenne pepper
¼ teaspoon turmeric
1 teaspoon salt
1 teaspoon black pepper
½ lb (240 g) long-grain rice

Traditional in the families of certain nineteenth-
century sailors who, returning from a voyage to the
China seas, described a Chinese dish. This was the
nearest their wives could get to what they wanted.
There are several versions from different ports, called
by different names. This one comes from
Southampton but is almost identical to one given by
Mrs Rundell (1809) from London.

Melt the butter in a large casserole. Put in half the
lettuce, then half the mince, half the peas and half
the onions. Add all the spices and seasoning and
then repeat the layers of mince and vegetables,
finishing with the onion. Pour in ⅝ cup (1.5 dl) of cold
water. Cover closely and cook in a medium oven,
350°F (180°C, Gas Mark 4), for 2 hours.
  Meanwhile, cook the rice. Make a border of the rice
on a shallow dish and pour the chilo in the middle.

Mushroom and Potato Carole

1 lb (½ kg) young mushrooms
2 tablespoons (30 g) butter
Salt and pepper
4 tablespoons cream
8 slices lean bacon
1½ lb (¾ kg) mashed potatoes
2 egg yolks
2 tablespoons (30 g) toasted
breadcrumbs

This dish should be made with freshly picked wild
mushrooms but can, of course, be made with young
button mushrooms. The potato carole is also very
good filled with fish or chicken in a white sauce.
Carole was an old English word for chest or coffer.

Wipe and peel the mushrooms and remove the stalks.
Chop the stalks finely and mix them with the butter,
1 teaspoon salt and ½ teaspoon pepper. Fill the
mushrooms caps with this mixture and arrange them
side by side in a buttered heatproof casserole, in 2
layers, if necessary. Pour the cream over the
mushrooms, tightly cover the casserole and put it in
a moderate oven, 350°F (180°C, Gas Mark 4), for 30 to
40 minutes.
  Roll each slice of bacon, impale on skewers and
grill or bake in the oven. Meanwhile, mix the
mashed potatoes with the egg yolks (leaving a little
of the yolk for brushing over) and a little salt and
pepper. Grease a round cake tin thoroughly with
butter and scatter with breadcrumbs. Press the
potato mixture into the tin, so that it forms a deep
tart shape, smooth round the top edge and brush
over with the reserved egg yolk. Bake at 400°F
(200°C, Gas Mark 6) for 30 minutes.
  When the potato crust is baked turn it out by
placing a hot plate over it and turning it upside
down. If necessary loosen the sides with the blade of
a knife. Fill the crust with the mushroom mixture
and serve very hot with the bacon rolls.

Sussex Pond Pudding

¾ lb (360 g) suet crust
1 stick (120 g) butter (unsalted
  if possible), well chilled, plus
  1 tablespoon (15 g) butter,
  softened
⅞ cup (180 g) demerara sugar
1 lemon (large and juicy)

This is the best of all suet puddings. There are
Kentish recipes, using sugar and butter and omitting
the lemon; a Hampshire recipe, substituting an
orange (which becomes rather bitter with cooking)
and another which has a handful of soaked raisins
squeezed together with the butter moulded round it.
They are all good but the lemon is the best. None of
the others is called "pond" pudding, although the
butter and sugar also forms a pond on the dish when
it is cut. There seems to be no North or West
Country recipe of this kind.

Butter a large pudding bowl with the softened butter.
Roll out the suet crust about ¾ inch (2 cm) thick and
line the bowl with it. Reserve a circle for the lid.
  Cut the butter into 8 pieces and put 4 of them into
the bowl with half the sugar. Prick the lemon with a
sharp skewer or knife point so that the juice can
escape and press one end into the butter and sugar,
so that it stands vertically. Press the rest of the
butter and sugar around and over it. Dampen the
crust around the edge of the bowl and press the lid
down well, so that the lemon and filling are quite
enclosed by the crust. Cover closely with foil and put
a saucer over the foil.
  Put about 3 inches (8 cm) of water into a large
saucepan and bring to the boil. Stand the pudding in
it and put on the lid. Keep just boiling for 3 hours;
when the water gets low, pour in more boiling water.
The water must never go off the boil.
  To serve, lift the bowl out of the water, take off the
foil and invert on to a rather large shallow dish. Lift
off the bowl and stand the pudding in a low oven to
dry off for a few minutes.

Marigold Pudding

2½ cups (6 dl) marigold petals,
  chopped. Reserve a few whole
  ones for decoration
1 cup (120 g) shredded suet
4 tablespoons (60 g) clear honey
¼ cup (60 g) sugar
The crust from a large crusty
  white loaf, finely grated
  (about 1½ cups/240 g of crumbs)
⅝ to 1¼ cups (1.5 to 3 dl) milk

The earliest recipes for this pudding occur in
fourteenth-century manuscripts. This one comes from
Arundel. Flowers were used in cooking for their
colour and flavour in the Middle Ages as a matter of
course. Rose petals, violets, borage, cowslips and
marigolds were all used as an integral part of
various creams and tarts. Nasturtium flowers and
striped carnation petals were used for decoration on
salads and cold creams. Serve the gloriously orange
Marigold Pudding (which is lighter than the usual
flour and suet pudding) very hot, with plenty of thick
cream. The marigolds give it a very subtle flavour.

Mix all the ingredients except the milk well together,
then stir in only just enough milk to bind. Put the
pudding in a well-buttered bowl and cover closely
with foil. Stand the bowl in a saucepan of boiling
water (the water must come about halfway up the
sides of the bowl) and steam for 3 hours. Never let
the water go off the boil. Fill up with boiling water
from time to time.
  Turn out and sprinkle the reserved marigold petals
on top.

Kentish Pudding Pie

1 quart (9 dl) milk
1 cup (120 g) ground
  rice
½ lb (240 g) short pastry
1 stick and 1 tablespoon (135 g)
  butter
¼ cup (60 g) castor sugar
3 eggs
⅓ cup (60 g) raisins, currants or
  sultanas, or a mixture
¼ teaspoon nutmeg
2 tablespoons cream

A recipe with a very long history. A recognizable version was served at more than one medieval feast at Canterbury. It contained rosewater, nutmeg, cinnamon, "raisins of the sun", 20 eggs and some four pints of cream for the very large quantity required. The rice was ground in a mortar. Serve with a pitcher of good, thick cream.

Put the milk in a saucepan and stir in the ground rice. Bring to the boil and stir for about 10 minutes until the mixture thickens. Allow to cool for 15 minutes.

Meanwhile, line a pie dish with the pastry, turning the crust over the edge of the dish and marking it with a fork.

Cream 1 stick (120 g) of the butter and the sugar and beat in the eggs. Stir into the ground rice, add the dried fruit and nutmeg and beat well. Then add the cream and stir in gently. Pour the mixture into the pastry-lined dish and dot with the remaining butter. Bake in the middle of the oven at 350°F (180°C, Gas Mark 4) for 35 minutes. Serve hot or cold.

Rice and Apple Pudding

¼ lb (120 g) short-grain
  rice
2½ cups (6 dl) milk
½ stick (105 g) castor sugar
½ stick (60 g) butter
1½ lb (¾ kg) cooking apples
⅝ cup (1.5 dl) single cream
1 egg, well beaten
⅝ cup (1.5 dl) fairly dry white
  wine

A very good form of enriched rice pudding traditional in Sussex at least since the fifteenth century. It was a rich man's dish when rice was fashionable but not plentiful. Sometimes the top was sprinkled with nutmeg and sometimes raisins were added to the apples.

Gently simmer the rice in the milk and ⅝ cup (1.5 dl) of water with 2 tablespoons (30 g) of the sugar, stirring frequently for 30 to 35 minutes or until the rice is quite tender and has thickened so that it can only just be stirred.

While the rice is cooking butter a wide, shallow fireproof dish. Peel, core and slice the apples and lay them in it. Cover with the remaining sugar.

Add the cream and then the egg to the thickened rice and beat well. Pour the rice mixture over the apples and bake at 400°F (200°C, Gas Mark 6) for 30 minutes.

Melt the remaining butter so that it does not colour and slowly add the wine to it, beating all the time. Pour into a small pitcher or sauceboat, stir well and serve with the pudding.

Creamed Codlin Tarts

2½ lb (1¼ kg) large cooking
  apples (about 4)
½ cup (120 g) castor sugar
Juice of ½ lemon
1 lb (½ kg) short pastry
⅝ cup (1.5 dl) double cream
Butter
6 dates, stoned

Codlins, or Codlings, were a favourite cooking apple until the early part of the twentieth century.

Core the apples and score round the skins. Fill the centres with sugar and bake the apples in a buttered baking tin at 350°F (180°C, Gas Mark 4) for about 40 minutes or until the apples are quite soft. Remove the apples from the oven, cut them through and scrape all the pulp into a bowl. Stir in any remaining sugar and the lemon juice and leave to cool.

Roll out the pastry to about ⅛ inch (0.25 cm) thick and line 6 individual, buttered soufflé dishes with it. (Ordinary patty pans or tartlet tins are too shallow.)

When the apple pulp has cooled put it through a food mill, or purée in a blender, with the cream. Taste in case more sugar is required. Spoon the mixture, which should be fairly stiff, into the prepared soufflé dishes, put a small piece of butter on each and bake low in the oven at 425°F (220°C, Gas Mark 7) for 15 minutes. Place a date on each tart 5 minutes before the end. Allow to cool in the dishes for 2 to 3 minutes and then slip the little tarts out on to a flat dish and serve hot or cold.

Dr Venner's Cherry Pudding

1 lb (½ kg) good dessert cherries,
  white or black
½ cup (120 g) sugar
1 stick (120 g) butter
8 very thin slices of bread,
  crusts removed

Dr Venner lived in Bath in the early seventeenth century and was well known for his treatise *Via Recta ad Vitam Longam*. He gives a recipe for this pudding, which was served to him when he visited Kent and which he never forgot because of its simplicity and deliciousness. Serve with cream.

Stew the cherries gently with 1 tablespoon of water, half the sugar and 2 tablespoons (30 g) of the butter, until they are soft and have made some juice. Allow the cherries to cool a little and then stone them.

Butter the bread. Put 4 slices, butter side down, in a shallow fireproof dish. Pour in the cherries and their juice. Sprinkle with 2 tablespoons (30 g) of the remaining sugar. Put the 4 remaining slices of bread butter side down over the cherries. Sprinkle with the remaining sugar and dot with the remaining butter. Bake at 400°F (200°C, Gas Mark 6) for 15 minutes. Serve immediately.

Cherries Hot

¾ lb (360 g) stoned ripe cherries,
  white or black
1 egg
1¼ cups (3 dl) milk
¼ cup (60 g) castor sugar
4 slices bread from a large
  white loaf, each about ¼ inch
  thick
3 tablespoons (45 g) butter

Panperdy (a corruption of *Pain Perdu*, lost bread) was made from Norman times. Cherries Hot derives from it.

Beat the egg into the milk with 1 tablespoon (15 g) of the sugar. Cut the bread slices in half and soak in the egg and milk for 5 minutes, changing the top slice to the bottom after 2 or 3 minutes so that they all take up the egg mixture evenly.

Put the cherries in a small saucepan with 2 tablespoons (30 g) of the sugar and heat slowly until almost boiling, then leave the pan over very low heat so that the cherries remain hot but do not continue to cook.

Heat the butter in a large frying-pan until just foaming. Put in the bread and fry on both sides; it should be crisp on the outside and soft in the middle. Quickly place 4 pieces of the fried bread on a warmed dish and, using a perforated spoon, lift a quarter of the cherries on to each. Place the remaining four pieces of bread on top. Sprinkle each hot sandwich with the remaining sugar and serve the cherry juice separately as a sauce.

Hazelnut Cream

Serves 6 to 8

$\frac{1}{2}$ lb (240 g) hazelnuts
$\frac{1}{2}$ cup (120 g) castor sugar
$3\frac{1}{2}$ tablespoons (30 g) cornflour
  or arrowroot
4 eggs
3 cups (7 dl) milk
5 drops vanilla essence
$\frac{5}{8}$ cup (1.5 dl) double cream

This is not a frozen ice-cream but a chilled cream, rather like the Italian "semi-freddo". The original recipe, which dates from the late eighteenth century, used the cob nuts or filberts specially grown for market in Kent.

Shell, skin and chop the hazelnuts finely. Put them in a bowl with the sugar and cornflour or arrowroot and add the well-beaten eggs. Bring the milk to just under boiling point and then stir the hazelnut mixture into it. Stir over a very low heat until the mixture thickens, but do not let it boil again. Remove the pan from the heat and stir in the vanilla essence. Allow to cool for 20 minutes and then stir in the cream. Pour the mixture into a mould and put in the refrigerator overnight or in the freezer for 1 hour. Turn out to serve.

Stone Cream

Serves 6

12 teaspoons apricot jam
Juice and grated rind of $\frac{1}{2}$
  lemon
$\frac{1}{2}$ cup white wine
$\frac{1}{4}$ cup (60 g) castor sugar
Two $\frac{1}{4}$-oz packets (15 g)
gelatine, melted in a little
warm water
$2\frac{1}{2}$ cups (6 dl) cream (double or
  single)

This dish is mentioned in a seventeenth-century description of cold sweets. I obtained the following recipe from Hampshire. It should be made several hours before it is required and kept in the refrigerator until wanted. The combination of the cream and the sharp juice is excellent.

Put 2 teaspoons of jam in each of 6 wine glasses or glass custard cups. Mix the lemon juice, grated rind and the wine and put a little into each glass on top of the jam until all is used.

Mix the sugar and gelatine into the cream and bring slowly to the boil, stirring all the time. As soon as it begins to boil, remove from the heat. Allow to cool, stirring from time to time. When almost cold pour it gently into the glasses, so that the lemon juice and wine rise as little as possible up the sides of the glass.

Cinnamon Doughnuts

3 tablespoons (45 g) butter
$\frac{5}{8}$ cup (15 g) granulated sugar
2 eggs, well beaten
$\frac{3}{4}$ lb (360 g) self-raising flour
$\frac{5}{8}$ cup (1.5 dl) milk
Oil for deep frying
2 teaspoons ground cinnamon
12 cinnamon sticks, cut into 1
   inch (2.5 cm) lengths – they
   are made of the rolled leaves,
   rather like cigars, but very
   thin (optional)

These doughnuts were sold piping hot in baskets on the quayside at Ventnor, Isle of Wight, in the nineteenth century and were extremely popular with those who had been sailing or fishing. Traditional doughnuts are made with yeast; this is a local variation. The cinnamon sticks were eaten with the doughnuts but may be considered rather strong today.

Cream the butter into $\frac{3}{8}$ cup (90 g) of the sugar, stir in the well-beaten eggs and then the flour, adding just enough of the milk to make a soft dough which comes away clean from the bowl.
   Divide the dough and roll into ping-pong-sized balls. They will almost double their size as they cook. Drop them into very hot oil and deep fry for 3 to 4 minutes until brown all over. Turn them out on to a piece of foil, which has been spread with the remaining sugar mixed with the ground cinnamon, and roll them in it lightly. If cinnamon sticks are to be used, make a tiny hole in each doughnut with a skewer and insert a stick in it, allowing about $\frac{1}{2}$ inch (1 cm) to stick out. Put in a warm dish and serve quickly.

Mothering Sunday Wafers

$\frac{1}{2}$ cup (60 g) flour
$\frac{1}{4}$ cup (60 g) sugar
4 tablespoons double cream
1 tablespoon orange-flower
   water

These were traditionally served with jelly or trifle for tea on Mothering Sunday in Hampshire.

Beat all the ingredients together for 30 minutes. (This may be reduced to 5 minutes if an electric beater is used.) The long beating is important to the final result.
   Grease 2 or 3 baking sheets well. Spread the mixture very thinly on the trays in rounds about 4 inches (10 cm) in diameter. Bake in a hot oven, 425°F (220°C, Gas Mark 7), for 10 minutes or until they are beginning to brown. While still hot, roll the wafers round the handle of a wooden spoon. As they cool, they will dry and become crisp. They can be served plain or filled with whipped cream immediately before serving.

Oast Cakes

$\frac{1}{2}$ cup (120 g) lard
1 lb ($\frac{1}{2}$ kg) flour
$\frac{1}{2}$ teaspoon salt
$\frac{2}{3}$ cup (120 g) currants
4 tablespoons sweet wine or
   sherry
Oil for deep frying
$\frac{1}{4}$ cup (60 g) castor sugar

These cakes were made in the Kentish hop gardens when hop-picking was at its height. The dough was mixed early in the day in the hut or encampment and made into small balls and fried over the camp fire at the afternoon break. This was, of course, shallow frying in lard but the little cakes are crisper if deep fried. They must be eaten very hot.

Cut and rub the lard into the flour and salt. Scatter in the currants and mix to a stiff dough with the wine and 4 tablespoons water. Form into balls and deep fry in very hot oil until golden brown. Roll in castor sugar and serve at once.

Pokerounce

$\frac{3}{8}$ *cup (120 g) pure, thick honey*
  (honeycomb is best of all, but
  is expensive unless bees are
  kept)
$\frac{1}{2}$ *teaspoon ground ginger*
$\frac{1}{2}$ *teaspoon ground cinnamon*
$\frac{1}{4}$ *teaspoon grated nutmeg*
4 large, thick slices of bread,
  crusts removed
2 tablespoons (30 g) butter
$\frac{5}{8}$ *cup (60 g) pine kernels or*
  blanched, split almonds
  toasted on a tray in the oven
  for 10 minutes

This fourteenth-century recipe for a "spread" or "enriched" toast comes from Kent. The origin of the name is obscure. Honeycomb was made very hot, sprinkled with cinnamon, nutmeg and ginger, stirred well and spread on toasted trenchers. Sometimes butter was stirred in too and pine kernels or split and toasted almonds "planted" in the honey. Such toasts were considered a delicacy and four or more slices were served on a large platter at dinner as one of the dishes of the second course. This slightly adapted recipe makes a warming, heartening and delicious dish.

Put the honey in a small, heavy saucepan over low heat. As soon as it is hot (it should not quite boil), stir in the spices and continue to heat for 20 to 30 minutes.

Meanwhile, make the toast and butter it while it is hot. Spread the spiced honey thickly over the toast, sprinkle with pine kernels or almonds, and serve.

Manchet Bread

$1\frac{1}{2}$ *lb ($\frac{3}{4}$ kg) strong white flour*
2 teaspoons salt
3 teaspoons sugar
Four $\frac{1}{4}$ oz packets (30 g) dried
  yeast, mixed according to
  directions on packets
$\frac{5}{8}$ *cup (1.5 dl) warm milk mixed*
  with $\frac{5}{8}$ cup (1.5 dl) water
Extra milk or 1 egg white,
  optional

Manchet bread was the finest quality of bread made in all great households from the Middle Ages until the seventeenth century. In royal residences, castles and fine houses, it was served only to the lord and his lady and a few of their well-born attendants and their grown-up offspring. It was not usually served in the nursery. Manchet loaves were always moulded by hand (hence the name) and were never very large. This recipe is adapted from the instructions laid down at Eltham Palace.

Put the flour into a large bowl and mix in the salt and sugar. Make a hollow in the centre and pour in the yeast mixture, knocking a little of the flour over it. Cover with a folded tea towel and set in a warm place for 1 hour to prove.

Remove the cloth and pour in the milk and water, which should be just blood heat, working the liquid in all the time and kneading in the flour from the sides into the centre. When all the liquid is in, knead for several minutes on a board. Return the dough to the bowl. Cut a deep cross in it, cover and leave for another hour. Remove it from the bowl to the board, knead it again, cut it into quarters and mould each quarter into a round, fairly flat shape.

Put the 4 manchets well apart on a large, flat baking tin, cover lightly with a single cloth and leave in a warm place for a further 20 minutes. Bake at 400°F (200°C, Gas Mark 6) for 30 minutes. Take out, turn upside down and tap the bottoms which will sound hollow if fully baked. Turn the loaves the right way up and put on a rack. Leave for 1 hour in a warm place, as this makes the crust crisper.

Manchet loaves were sometimes brushed over with milk, or with the white of an egg just before the end of the cooking time and put back into the oven for 2 to 3 minutes.

The Home Counties

Surrey, Berkshire, Buckinghamshire, Hertfordshire

People on horseback, people in carriages and coaches, people driving carts and wagons passed along the king's highways out of the city of London, going south over the river, north into Middlesex (now included in the county of Greater London) and Hertfordshire, east into Essex, west through the villages of Chelsea and Kensington into Surrey and north-west into Berkshire and Buckinghamshire. All these, with the exception of Essex, were known, until after World War II, as the Home Counties. The culinary traditions of Kent and Sussex have been considered as part of the South and South East of England and those of Essex as part of East Anglia.

A noble lord whose estates were wholly in Scotland, Northumberland, Devon or Cornwall, was obliged to live mainly in his London house, returning home three or four times a year, to spend a month or two at his family seat. If he resided mainly in the country and rarely visited the Tudor or Stuart courts, he might all too easily find everything changed when he did so; his friends turned against him, his lands confiscated, even his head in danger. A daughter at court as one of the Queen's ladies-in-waiting, or a young son being brought up as a page was some insurance, but life was much more difficult than it was for those whose estates were within two or three hours' riding of London, or who were rich and powerful enough to own estates in different parts of the country with one house at least near the capital.

From the Middle Ages to the eighteenth century most of the nobility and gentry permitted themselves a degree of relaxation in their country houses. There was hunting, riding and dancing, visits to the neighbours, improvements to be made to the houses themselves, time to see the children and to put matters in order with stewards and bailiffs. On the whole, partly because the wealthy loved and enjoyed their lands and could reach them easily and partly because farmers could supply London markets, there has always been a certain feeling of reasonable and cheerful prosperity in the Home Counties. In our own day, large areas of Surrey and Hertfordshire as well as the whole of Middlesex have disappeared into the maw of Greater London, but royal parks, greens and gardens, commons, inns, palaces and such houses as Syon House, the unparalleled Chiswick House and Ham House show what the countryside was once like.

This countryside began on the edge of present-day central London. In the sixteenth century, the Hospital of St James stood, isolated in open fields, on the site where St James's Palace stands today. The long

Italian garden of the first Somerset House (one of the most favoured palaces of James I and Charles I) led down to the Thames, where a water gate gave access to the river. William III bought Nottingham House in Kensington village, which was a *"pleasant place, standing in green fields with well-wooded hills set about"*, from the Earl of Nottingham and engaged Sir Christopher Wren to turn it into a kind of double house, with separate grand entries and two suites of formal rooms of equal grandeur, because William and Mary ruled jointly as king and queen. Queen Anne, who had disliked William, lived entirely in her sister's apartments when she stayed at Kensington after her accession. George I decided to make it into a true palace, albeit a small one. Kensington village had become the most sought-after residential site outside London and the palace itself was famous for its lovely and extensive gardens. William, who often worried about his health, had been pleased to find an old gravel pit near the house, as he considered a gravel soil important to his physical welfare. It was, however, very raw and ugly, and Queen Anne had it altered into a new part of the gardens. Addison wrote in the *Spectator, "It must have been a fine genius for gardening that could have thought of forming such an unsightly hollow into so beautiful an area."* George I improved the grounds still further. The famous Round Pond was made and six other ponds were dug out and joined to form the Serpentine and in 1731 two yachts were launched on it for the amusement of the royal family.

A little further from the city, in Surrey, England's monarchs built more country homes, hunting lodges and palaces than anywhere else in England. These royal dwellings close by the gentle Thames, most useful and frequented of waterways at a time when travel by barge or wherry was easier than travel by road, doubly affected the Surrey countryside. Frequent royal progresses and visits meant that everyone who had something to sell, from beef cattle to cabbages, could obtain cash for them, instead of the more usual barter. When the king was in residence, noble and often foreign visitors came by water or on horseback with their retinues and had to be immediately and honourably feasted. At such a time everyone who could bring food of any kind was welcome in the yard where the steward and his men were buying and paying out in pence and shillings, while cooks' boys came running from the kitchens to demand more of this or that and the head cook himself might emerge in a rage at the shortage or the quality of birds or fish. He might rank lower than the steward in the hierarchy of retainers, but he was entitled to his wrath if he was not supplied with the ingredients necessary to make *"a pretty dish to set before a king"*. All kinds of fish were caught and taken to the palace caterers; poachers as well as legitimate hunters snared all possible birds *"as small as the little lark and as large as the bustard"* and sold them for the royal tables; extra cooks were hired and women in the villages were sometimes ordered to make great pies at home and to bring them to be baked in the palace bread ovens. Farmers sold specially fattened stock and their wives fattened the poultry. Surrey chickens were famous in the London markets and, for special occasions, pullets were fattened on raisins and corn soaked in milk and candles were left burning in their houses so that they would eat during the night.

All along the Thames in Surrey stretched the royal manor of Sheen, which had belonged to the Crown since the eleventh century. On these estates, through the centuries, were built the palaces of Sheen, Richmond, Kew and an unfinished palace started by George III.

The earliest was Sheen Palace, which grew up around the old medieval manor house of Sheen and was loved and frequently lived in by both Edward III and Richard II. Richard ordered it to be pulled down on the sudden death from the plague of his queen, Anne of Bohemia, and never discovered that only her apartments had been demolished and the rest of the building left standing. Henry V restored the palace, erecting a curious and costly building on the site of Anne of Bohemia's apartments. He built a Carthusian monastery to the north of the palace and, on the opposite bank of the river, a nunnery, Syon House, which stands to this day, although much altered.

In 1498, Henry VII intended to keep Christmas at Sheen and was in residence on 21 December when fire broke out. The palace was gutted and costly furniture, tapestries and plate destroyed. Henry, undaunted, almost immediately decided to build a new palace in the Gothic style, all the apartments to be built around a paved court. It was finished within two years and he decided to discard the Anglo-Saxon name "Sheen", meaning a place of beauty, and rename it. He had been Earl of Richmond in the honour of Yorkshire before his accession and he named his new residence Richmond Palace.

Queen Elizabeth I liked this palace of her grandfather's, which she considered warmer in winter than either Whitehall or Greenwich. She referred to it as her *"warm winter box"*. James I stayed there frequently during his reign and Charles II lived there for a time before he became king. Under Cromwell it began to fall into decay and Charles I's queen, Henrietta Maria, on her return after the Restoration of the Monarchy, could not afford to put it in order. Finally, only the lodge and the gate house remained.

George II, as Prince of Wales, acquired the lodge in order to live separately from the king, his father. After he had become king himself, his own son, Frederick Prince of Wales, bought Kew House (sometimes called White Lodge), which was very close to Richmond Lodge, in order to annoy the King. After Frederick's death, his widow lived at Kew House, ornamenting the gardens with fantastic buildings – a mosque, a Roman triumphal arch, a Gothic cathedral and a pagoda, which still exists. On her death, George III and Queen Charlotte moved into Kew House and other houses on Kew Green were acquired, including the Dutch House. By 1780, however, George III had decided to move to Windsor and did not visit Kew again for eight years. When he did, the lovely, serene place attracted him as it had attracted so many of his royal predecessors and he decided to build a fantastic new palace. Before it was finished he became blind and insane and the building was abandoned and demolished. Only the Dutch House (built for a Dutch merchant in 1631) remains and is known as Kew Palace. Queen Victoria gave Kew Gardens to the nation and the botanical gardens became famous throughout the world. There are now no residences in royal use along the Thames, but, because there were once so many, some of this part of the Surrey countryside has been preserved as it was once, although its native wildness has gone.

On the other side of the river, Cardinal Wolsey built his great manor house of Hampton Court. Realizing too late the dangers inherent in his position of immense temporal and spiritual power, he presented his fine house and all its land to the king. Henry VIII, unmoved, accepted the enormous gift and installed himself on the first floor while rebuilding was still in progress. He had a new and prodigious Great Hall built, with a musicians' gallery, and a new second kitchen to serve it. Wolsey's kitchen was 48 feet long and would not suffice for Henry's cooks, who had sometimes to provide a feast for 3,000 at one time. He had Wolsey's insignia removed and replaced everywhere by the royal arms and the King's Beasts.

The palace of Oatlands was also acquired by Henry VIII. The house stood on rich arable land not far from Weybridge and the King wanted to join the northern boundary to the extreme south of his Hampton Court estates. In this house he married Katherine Howard, holding a great feast, at which the chickens and capons for which Surrey has been famous in all ages, and swans from the Thames at Richmond and Hampton Court, were served, as well as venison and pheasants from the huge royal parks, which were gradually encroaching on a large area of the countryside.

Oatlands, however, was too far from London (some 26 miles) and not large enough. After this marriage Henry spent only single nights there when hunting or on a royal progress. In the seventeenth century the house was given to Anne of Denmark on her marriage to James I and Inigo Jones was employed to improve it. There was already a grove of mulberry trees, grown for their fruit and for their beauty. These were of the species known as Black Mulberry which had been grown in England since Roman times. The fruit was much favoured in Tudor and Stuart times but began to go out of favour in the eighteenth century. It is now eaten only by those who happen to have a mulberry tree, as many old houses have, and who do not dislike the very slight turpentine flavour of the ripe fruit, which is similar in size and shape to a loganberry but much darker in colour. There are early recipes for mulberry and apple tarts and references to a dish of fine black mulberries from the mulberry gardens behind Buckingham Palace. Dolby's early nineteenth-century *Cook's Dictionary* gives recipes for mulberry preserve, mulberry brandy, syrup and wine; but there are no pies or tarts. The large trees tend to have enormous quantities of fruit, which ripens very suddenly, much of it dropping and making a kind of purple slime under the tree.

Queen Anne decided to breed silkworms and to make her own silk, and an elegant silkworm house of brick was built among the trees. It had a fine staircase with panelled walls and windows painted with the Queen's arms, but the silkworms, carefully observed and fed on mulberry leaves, died in their thousands, probably either of cold or of some epidemic. Queen Anne sadly gave up the insects and the palace.

Many of Surrey's most beautiful houses were not royal, although some of them were the envy of royalty. Perhaps the most notable of these is Ham House which, in the late seventeenth century, was the seat of the Duke and Duchess of Lauderdale. It would have taken the Duke two hours to ride to Ham House from Whitehall, while it would have taken his Duchess about three hours to get there in her coach. Indeed, they must often have made this journey, since their pride and pleasure was the extension (they doubled the central block of the house), the decoration and refurnishing of this house of which Lady Dysart, who married the Duke, was the heiress. There was a great deal of family money and it was well spent on Ham House in terms of the taste of the time. Everything was lavish and sumptuous, portraits by Lely; a ceiling by Verrio, who was working for the King at Windsor at this time; specially designed furniture made by Dutch craftsmen; wonderful hangings of damask and cut velvet and splendid tapestries. Much of all this remains today. Ham House represents the best that can be said of the Duke and Duchess, who appear as unpleasant in the cold light of history as they must have seemed terrifying to servants, friends and enemies alike in their own time. Of the Duke it was said that he *"was the coldest friend and the most violent enemy that ever was known"*. He was also extremely powerful at court and a member of the hated cabal. The Duchess was beautiful, intelligent and well educated, but her ambition knew no bounds and a contemporary said of her that she was *". . . of a most ravenous covetousness"*. If she fancied some family possession which she saw in a house she was visiting, she had to have it by whatever means, unless she could hear of a better example. She was not lightly entertained by other members of the court in their houses. Curiously, the aggressiveness of the Lauderdales appears to have been a general and lasting family characteristic for, some hundred years later when George III expressed a wish to see Ham House, the current Lord Dysart, replied: *"Whenever my house becomes a public spectacle, His Majesty shall certainly have the first view."* He seems to have got away with this piece of unparalleled rudeness to the Crown. Among the improvements to Ham House was the remodelling of the kitchens: the Lauderdale and Dysart food was reputed to be of the greatest elaboration, the finished dishes piled high and decorated to show off the gold and silver plate on which they were served.

A much smaller, although extremely elegant, Surrey house was Polesden Lacey, of the Carolingian period, which was bought by Sheridan in 1797. He was extremely pleased that he was in a position to afford such a country house and wrote touchingly to his wife: *"We shall have the nicest place, within a prudent distance of town, in England."* A hundred years later another extremely successful English dramatist was to buy a house in the Home Counties, *"a prudent distance from town"*. George Bernard Shaw settled at Ayot St Lawrence in Hertfordshire. With a typical touch of irony, he called the hideous Victorian house "Shaw's Corner". He attributed his health and his longevity to the fact that he was a vegetarian. He was, however, no epicure and those who visited him were well entertained by his wit but never by his food.

Hatfield House is also in Hertfordshire. In medieval times it had been a manor belonging to the bishops of Ely, maintained by a succession of bishops as a hunting lodge for the entertainment of royal guests. The hunting was good since most of the land round about was heath. In 1480, the manor house was partly rebuilt in brick. Orchards were laid out, a pleasance was made and a great park well-stocked with deer, which also flourished on the heathland outside the bounds of the park.

In the reign of Henry VIII, the See of Ely, alarmed by its own wealth, the King's anger with the Church and his covetousness of its property, leased Hatfield to the Royal Farrier, who found his house constantly used by the King as a hunting lodge. In 1538 Henry acquired the buildings and the park for himself through a somewhat forced transaction with the Bishop of Ely, who was allowed certain confiscated monastic properties in East Anglia in exchange for Hatfield. Henry had acquired nearby Hunsdon House some 18 years earlier and it was this house that was granted to Elizabeth I. After her accession she passed Hunsdon to her cousin Henry Carey, whom she created Lord Hunsdon. She still maintained her Palace of Hatfield although she rarely visited it. It naturally passed to James I, but he exchanged it for Theobalds (pronounced Tibbalds), which was about nine miles from Hatfield and belonged to Robert Cecil, Earl of Salisbury.

Earliest and grandest of all the royal homes of England, Windsor Castle has been the home of royalty for a longer period than any other building in the world. It was begun by William the Conqueror in about 1080 and is still lived in by the royal family, which is why the county in which it is situated is known as Royal Berkshire. This county, according to the first-century historian Asser, derived its name from a forested area called the Wood of Berroc, where *"the box-tree grows most plentifully"*. Alfred the Great, dividing England into shires, called this division Berrocscir, which became Berkshire. William the Conqueror built the central mound at Windsor to be the citadel of a strong fortress in this central part of southern England, although he did little to make it a convenient dwelling.

Edward III was born in the castle and, after his accession, had more comfortable apartments built and made other alterations, enlarging the chapel when he founded the Order of the Garter, which was to have its spiritual base there.

Henry VIII rebuilt the gateway at Windsor but made no improvements to the royal apartments. Compared with Nonsuch and with the Palace of Whitehall, the castle seemed a sad and cold place in which to live. The young Edward VI wrote: *"Methinks I am in a prison: here be no galleries nor gardens to walk in."*

Later kings and queens, however, transformed the castle. Charles II's architect, Hugh May, rebuilt the royal apartments and the Great Hall. Carvings by Grinling Gibbons, ceilings by Verrio and tapestries covering cold stone walls made it beautiful and new kitchens and other offices made it comfortable. Those staying at Windsor could ride and hunt in the Great Park or walk in the new gardens, and along the avenues. The castle was transformed again by George IV, whose architect Wyatville, greatly extended it, adding new apartments and renovating many existing ones. Queen Victoria made it her main residence after the death of Prince Albert, and she became known as the Widow of Windsor.

Today, although it is one of the homes of the royal House of Windsor, the public is admitted to a large part of the castle as well as to the Great Park, and conferences are held in Cumberland Lodge in the grounds.

A great Buckinghamshire house with a strange history is Chequers Court, near Princes Risborough, the official country house of the prime ministers of England during their terms of office.

The British king Caractacus had a stronghold on the site, in the first century AD, of which earthworks are still visible. Under Henry II, the

Clerk to the Exchequer held the manor and the name Chequers seems to have come from his office. The house acquired much of its present appearance when it was remodelled in 1565. In the eighteenth century, a splendid collection of portraits and relics of Cromwell were brought to the house by the Russell family, and are there to this day. The house was rebuilt in Strawberry Hill Gothic style in the nineteenth century, but later much of its Elizabethan appearance was restored. In 1917, the house was dedicated to its present purpose, a place where every English prime minister can entertain official as well as private guests in style.

From Princes Risborough and other villages and small towns in the neighbourhood come many special dishes, some of them originally made in the kitchens of Chequers and copied by staff who worked there.

Most of the traditional Home Counties dishes which have survived come from farms and from menus and kitchen books most of which have never been published. Records of feasts and menus are hard to come by in this part of England, which has been virtually swallowed by Greater London, but very good food was grown and sold and carefully cooked and presented, sometimes simply and sometimes with grandeur.

Spinach Tart

Serves 6

$\frac{3}{4}$ lb (360 g) short pastry
1 lb ($\frac{1}{2}$ kg) chopped spinach
  (frozen is excellent)
$\frac{5}{8}$ cup (1.5 dl) white sauce
$\frac{1}{4}$ teaspoon grated nutmeg
4 tablespoons double cream
$\frac{1}{4}$ lb (120 g) lean ham, cut in
  strips, $\frac{1}{2}$ inch (1 cm) wide and
  3 inches (8 cm) long
12 prunes, soaked for 1 hour,
  stoned and halved, but not
  cooked
$\frac{1}{2}$ cup (60 g) grated Parmesan
  cheese
3 tablespoons (45 g) butter
Salt and freshly ground black
  pepper

Until the late seventeenth century there was a tendency to serve spinach as a sweetened dish. After the eighteenth century there was no longer any question of serving a leaf vegetable as a sweet dish, with the exception of sliced fruit in salads and a little chopped apple with onions and sultanas added to baked cabbage.

This spinach tart comes from a lady whose family has lived for three generations in the neighbourhood of Osterley. It included a few prunes, which show its long pedigree and seem to go well with the spinach.

Roll out the pastry and line a 10 inch (25 cm) flan tin. Bake blind to a light golden brown.

Meanwhile heat the spinach in a heavy saucepan. When heated through, pour off all the liquid, pressing the spinach to get out a little more. The spinach should not be quite dry but separate liquid should not be visible. Stir in the white sauce, beating it in well with a wooden spoon. Add the nutmeg. Season well with salt and black pepper. Allow to cool a little and then beat in the cream. Keep warm but do not allow to boil.

When the pastry case is ready, put the ham strips in the bottom and then fill with the spinach, almost to the top. Smooth over and arrange the halved prunes around the edge, pressing them into the filling so that they are only just visible. Sprinkle the Parmesan over the tart, being careful that each prune has cheese over it. Dot with tiny knobs of butter about 1 inch (2.5 cm) apart and put a little butter on each prune.

Put the tart into a medium oven 350°F (180°C, Gas Mark 4) for 25 minutes. Serve immediately.

Green Peas in Cream

*1 lb (½ kg) shelled green peas
  (2 lb/1 kg unshelled)
3 to 4 spring onions
3 to 4 sprigs of mint
1 tablespoon finely chopped
  parsley
2 tablespoons (30 g) butter into
  which 2 teaspoons of flour
  have been worked
2 teaspoons sugar
1 teaspoon salt
¼ teaspoon nutmeg
⅝ cup (1.5 dl) double cream*

Fresh garden peas are much to be preferred for this eighteenth-century recipe from Weybridge but it is also a very good way of serving frozen peas.

This dish can be served as a starting course with hot toast. It is also excellent served with roast meat or with fish.

Put all the ingredients except the cream into a saucepan, placing the lump of butter and flour in the centre of the peas and the herbs on the top. Pour on ⅝ cup (1.5 dl) of boiling water. Cover closely and simmer gently for 30 minutes.

Stir well, take out the sprigs of mint and the onions and pour on the cream. Bring to the boil again and boil for 30 seconds only. Pour into a suitable dish and serve immediately.

To Braise a Salmon

*2 lb (1 kg) middle cut of salmon
2 tablespoons (30 g) butter
1 bunch parsley, thyme and
  fennel
1 onion, halved
12 peppercorns
2½ cups (6 dl) dry white wine
Salt and pepper*

The stuffing:

*2 hard-boiled eggs and 1 well-
  beaten raw egg
1 tablespoon finely chopped
  parsley
1 teaspoon finely chopped
  fennel
1 teaspoon finely chopped
  thyme
¾ cup (120 g) fresh fine white
  breadcrumbs
1 tablespoon finely chopped
  walnuts
1 small tin anchovy fillets
Salt and pepper*

An eighteenth-century recipe for a Thames salmon as it might well have been served at Kew Palace. Mrs Glasse gives a slightly different recipe of which she says, *"This is a fine Dish for a First Course."* Her recipe requires an eel for the stuffing, half a pound of butter and mushrooms, morels and truffles for the sauce. The following recipe, of much the same date, is a little simpler but still does honour to a fine fish.

Serve with green peas and stewed diced cucumber.

Make the stuffing by mixing together the finely chopped hard-boiled eggs, chopped herbs, breadcrumbs and walnuts with ½ teaspoon salt and ¼ teaspoon pepper. Chop the anchovy fillets finely (or cut small with scissors) and add them with the oil from the tin. Add the beaten egg and mix well.

Put the stuffing into the salmon and tie a string around the fish in 2 places. Lightly butter a piece of foil which should be 4 inches (10 cm) longer than the length of the salmon; lay the salmon on it and turn up each end of the foil closely against the cut ends of the salmon. This is to prevent the stuffing from oozing out during cooking. Turn up the sides of the foil, which need not fit so closely, and tie a string round the length only.

Lay the whole parcel in a casserole, if possible only just big enough to take the fish. Lay the parsley, thyme, fennel and onion on it. Add the peppercorns and a teaspoon of salt. Pour in ⅝ cup (1.5 dl) of cold water and the wine.

Put the uncovered casserole in a 400°F (200°C, Gas Mark 6) oven for 30 minutes. If the top skin of the fish is crisping, cover lightly with foil.

Lift out the fish very carefully on to a hot serving dish. Remove the herbs and onions from the cooking liquid and pour it over the salmon. Serve very hot.

Young Chickens with Peaches

4 small poussins, or 2 large
  poussins cut in halves
4 small peaches, blanched,
  peeled, halved and stoned
2 teaspoons castor sugar
$\frac{1}{4}$ teaspoon grated nutmeg
$\frac{5}{8}$ cup (1.5 dl) white wine
Seasoned flour
4 thin lemon slices
4 slices streaky bacon
1 stick (120 g) butter
8 mushrooms about 1 inch
  (2.5 cm) across the cap, stalks
  discarded
$\frac{5}{8}$ cup (1.5 dl) chicken stock
  (stock cube will do)
4 tablespoons double cream
Salt and pepper

This recipe comes from a manor house near Guildford in Surrey. It was written down in the early nineteenth century with a note that it was "very old" and had been made in that household every summer for several centuries.

The kitchen garden had small, violet-red Peregrine peaches fan-trained on its walls and these were used for this dish. Serve with green beans and rice.

Put the peach halves, cut sides up, in a flat, fireproof dish. Sprinkle with the sugar and nutmeg and pour over the wine. Leave standing for a few minutes.

Rub the chickens all over with seasoned flour. Lay a slice of lemon on the breast of each bird and cover it with a slice of bacon.

Put the chickens in a baking tin with half the butter cut into small pieces.

Bake at 400°F (200°C, Gas Mark 6) for 20 to 30 minutes, near the top of the oven. Put the peaches in at the same time on a lower shelf.

Meanwhile, sauté the mushroom caps in the rest of the butter. Heat the stock and keep warm.

Dish the chickens on to a large flat platter. Arrange the peach halves round them. Pour the wine and peach juice into the stock. Place a mushroom in the hollow of each peach. Keep hot.

Pour off the butter from the pan in which the chickens have been roasted. Stir the cream into the pan juices. Stir hard for 30 seconds and then slowly pour in the stock and wine mixture. Stir again and add a very little salt and freshly ground black pepper. Pour over the chickens and serve at once.

Spring Chicken

4 poussins, halved down the
  back
$\frac{3}{4}$ lb (360 g) long-grain rice
Seasoned flour
$\frac{3}{4}$ stick (90 g) butter
$1\frac{1}{2}$ lb ($\frac{3}{4}$ kg) carrots, scraped
  and grated
2 medium onions, finely
  chopped
1 cup (60 g) flaked almonds
$\frac{5}{8}$ cup (1.5 dl) highly seasoned,
  thick white sauce
2 tablespoons double cream
1 lemon, thinly sliced
1 tablespoon very finely
  chopped parsley
2 hard-boiled eggs, very finely
  chopped
Salt and pepper

This seventeenth-century recipe is from Ockley in Surrey. The original suggests: "Take 12 chickens, which have been fattened for a week. When they are plucked and drawn, split them in halves down the back so that you have two dozen halves for your dish. . . ." The dish is unforgettable, both for its appearance and because it is delicious, a fine dish for a dinner party.

Bring 5 cups (1.2 litres) of water to the boil, add $1\frac{1}{2}$ teaspoons of salt and put in the rice. Boil briskly for 20 minutes. Drain the rice and run water from the cold tap through it. Gently heat the rice, uncovered, so that it dries a little.

Rub the chicken halves with the seasoned flour. Lay them, cut side down, in baking tins. Put a knob of butter on each and roast at 400°F (200°C, Gas Mark 6) for 20 to 30 minutes, basting twice.

Meanwhile, cook the grated carrot in $1\frac{1}{4}$ cups (3 dl) of boiling salted water for 10 minutes. Drain. Mix with 1 tablespoon (15 g) of the butter and $\frac{1}{2}$ teaspoon pepper.

Fry the onions in 1 tablespoon (15 g) of the butter and when soft but not at all browned, stir it into the rice with the almonds, white sauce and the cream.

Stir until very hot. Pile the rice on to a large, flat serving dish and keep hot until the chickens and carrot are ready. As soon as they are cooked, arrange the chicken halves up the sides of the mound of rice, the leg of each half pointing upwards. Put small heaps of carrot between the chicken pieces and top each heap with a slice of lemon. The dish may be kept warm for a few minutes at this stage if convenient. When ready to serve, sprinkle the parsley and the chopped egg on top of the mound of rice.

Fricassée of Chicken

Serves 6 to 8

2 chickens, 2½ to 3 lb (1 to 1½ kg) each
2 onions, halved
2 carrots, halved
Bouquet garni
4 tablespoons flour
½ teaspoon ground nutmeg
1¼ sticks (150 g) butter
4 shallots, sliced
2 teaspoons thyme and marjoram mixed
2 anchovy fillets, finely chopped
½ bottle dry white wine
2 egg yolks
Salt and pepper

The forcemeat balls:

1 small onion, finely chopped
3 tablespoons (45 g) butter
¾ cup (90 g) fresh white breadcrumbs
2 teaspoons finely chopped parsley
1 teaspoon thyme
1 egg yolk

The garnish:

9 slices of bread, cut across into triangles and lightly fried
½ lb (240 g) button mushrooms, lightly sautéed
1 lemon, cut into 8 slices

This recipe, reduced to reasonable proportions, comes from a Reading manuscript dated 1765. It is extremely good and quite unlike other fricassées of chicken. In the garnish, I have replaced the original oysters with button mushrooms for economy, but you can use fresh or tinned oysters if you wish.

Cut the meat off the chickens 2 hours before you want to start cooking the dish. Put the chicken meat in the refrigerator while you make the stock. Put the chicken bones, carcasses and skin into a large saucepan with 5 cups (1.2 litres) of water, the onions, carrots and bouquet garni and bring to the boil. Simmer, partly covered, for 1½ hours, by which time the stock should have reduced to about 4 cups (9 dl). Strain the stock and put it to cool for a few minutes, then skim the fat from the top.

Lightly rub the chicken pieces with 3 tablespoons of the flour into which you have mixed the nutmeg, salt and pepper. Fry the chicken pieces in ¾ stick (90 g) of the butter for 3 minutes, turning them all the time, using tongs.

Put the chicken pieces in a saucepan with the shallots, thyme and marjoram and chopped anchovies. Mix the wine and stock and pour it over the chicken. Stew gently for 45 minutes.

While the chicken is cooking prepare the forcemeat balls. Soften the onion in the butter. Mix the onion with all the remaining ingredients. Shape the mixture into 12 balls and lightly fry them in the pan in which the onions were softened. Then prepare the garnish.

When the chicken is ready, transfer the pieces to a fairly flat ovenproof serving dish, using a perforated spoon, and keep hot. Strain the stock into a bowl. Melt the remaining butter in the saucepan and stir in the remaining flour. Gradually pour the stock on to this roux, stirring all the time so that the sauce is smooth. Boil for 3 minutes then remove the sauce from the heat and allow it to cool while you beat the egg yolks. Stir the egg yolks into the sauce and beat with a spoon for 1 minute, holding the pan above the heat and not resting it on the stove. Do not allow the sauce to boil or it will curdle. The sauce should have the consistency and almost the colour of a thin custard; pour it over the chicken and place the croûtons, mushrooms and lemon slices all around. Serve immediately.

Chickens as Lizards

2 chickens, 2½ to 3 lb (1 to 1½ kg)
  boned by cutting along the
  backs, drumsticks and wing
  tips cut off before boning
1 large onion, stuck with 8
  cloves
6 slices streaky bacon

The stuffing:

1 lb (½ kg) sausage meat
24 stoned green olives, chopped
¾ lb (360 g) sliced and lightly
  fried mushrooms
1⅛ cups (180 g) fresh fine white
  breadcrumbs
2 teaspoons dried thyme
1 tablespoon chopped parsley
1 teaspoon salt
½ teaspoon freshly ground
  black pepper
2 well-beaten eggs

The garnish:

6 artichoke hearts, tinned or
  fresh, or 1 unpeeled cucumber
4 currants, capers or black
  olives
⅝ cup (3 dl) green mayonnaise
2 cucumbers, thinly sliced
  without peeling, salted and
  left to drain for 1 hour
2 lettuces (Webbs or iceberg),
  the hearts cut in solid
  sections, about 8 from each
  lettuce
8 strips of fresh, sweet red
  pepper or tinned pimiento, or
  8 radishes cut into roses

This elaborate recipe is given as an example of the time and trouble, skill and imagination expected of English cooks to the royal family and the rich in producing a dish which was not only good to eat, but also of unusual and interesting appearance.

The desire to disguise one bird or animal as another, or to combine two, such as a hare and a chicken, to make a mythical creature, comes from Romano-British cookery. The element of slightly off-colour humour in making an acceptable chicken appear like a rather horrific cooked lizard appealed to the ancient Romans. The diners enjoyed finding out what the strange lizards really were and that the dish was excellent. There is a fifteenth-century manuscript which described chickens treated in this manner and Richard Dolby's *Cook's Dictionary*, written in 1832, gives a recipe which is late for this type of dish. The recipe given here is adapted from both. Anyone preparing this dish will be cooking, decorating and serving something considered rare, amusing and delicious by the English nobility in the fifteenth century and possibly earlier.

This was an ornamental and brightly coloured dish for a feast. It was intended to form a centrepiece and probably 20 or so chickens would have been cooked and dressed in this manner, being arranged on an enormous silver platter. For a vast royal feast at Hampton Court or Richmond such a dish would have been prepared for the high table only, for which three or four platters of lizard chickens would have been made, while lower tables would have had chickens served in a more usual fashion.

In Dolby's recipe the chickens are garnished with tiny coloured omelettes: red, yellow, green and white, presumably to represent scales. The little cold omelettes would be quite inedible, so here they have been replaced by cucumber slices. The chickens must be boned. If given a day's notice a butcher or poulterer will probably bone the birds for you. The drumsticks and wing tips must be cut off before boning and left whole. When filling the chickens, it will be worth while to sew up the tail and any other openings where the stuffing may ooze out. If you prefer you can make one big "lizard" by sewing the two chickens together, but you will need to remove the chicken legs completely, leaving just the wing tips to represent the lizard's legs. The completed dish may be brushed over with aspic and decorated with globe artichoke leaves.

First, put the wing tips, drumsticks and the onion into 4 cups (9 dl) of salted boiling water. Boil briskly. After about 40 minutes the stock should be reduced to about 2½ cups (6 dl). Strain the stock into a bowl and allow it to cool for at least 10 minutes before using.

Meanwhile, prepare the stuffing by mixing all the ingredients together. Open the chickens out and fill each of the 4 halves with the forcemeat. Clap the halves together. Mould the bodies to be as long as possible. Sew up the chicken halves along the backs and turn them so that the breasts are upwards. Pull down the thighs and the stumps of the wings, as these represent the short legs of the lizards.

Line the bottom of an oval casserole with bacon slices and lay the two long, headless lizards side by side on them. Pour in the stock, closely cover with foil and cook in the oven at 350°F (180°C, Gas Mark 4) for 45 minutes. Take off the foil and allow the chickens to brown for a further 15 minutes. Lift out the birds and allow to drain and cool.

Meanwhile make their heads. Skewer 3 artichoke hearts together for each chicken and stick the skewer into the breast end, or use unpeeled end pieces of cucumber. Make eyes of capers, currants, or halved black olives, pushing them into the piece of artichoke or cucumber nearest the body. Skewer on pieces of unpeeled cucumber to form the tails.

Spread the green mayonnaise on a large, flat dish and set the chickens on top. Decorate with thin overlapping slices of cucumber down the backs and tails of the birds to represent the scales. Put a thick border of the lettuce heart sections all around the edge of the dish, outside the mayonnaise. On each lettuce section arrange a radish rose, or a strip of red pimiento or fresh sweet red pepper.

Carve the chickens straight across just behind the head in ½ inch (1 cm) slices and serve with a section of lettuce heart and a little mayonnaise.

Serves 4 to 6

Pepper Pot

2 large onions, finely chopped
⅝ stick (75 g) butter
4 medium potatoes, peeled and cut into ½ inch (1 cm) cubes
2 packets chopped frozen spinach, defrosted
1 lettuce, very finely chopped
½ lb (240 g) cold roast chicken or lamb, cut in 1½ inch (3.5 cm) slices
½ lb (240 g) back bacon slices, rind removed, cut into ½ inch (1 cm) strips
Salt and white pepper
1 teaspoon cayenne pepper
12 small suet dumplings

This is an interesting recipe because the two most famous Pepper Pots are entirely different from this and from each other. Jamaica Pepper Pot cannot rightfully be made without cassareep (the juice of the bitter cassava) and includes crab or lobster, and Philadelphia Pepper Pot includes shredded tripe.

This eighteenth-century recipe from Hertfordshire is simple and good. All three versions probably have a common ancestry. The stew should burn the mouth, but not fiercely. Serve with thick slices of fresh brown bread and unsalted butter.

In a very large saucepan, fry the onions in ½ stick (60 g) of the butter until soft but not coloured. Put in the potatoes, sprinkle with 1 teaspoon of salt and ½ teaspoon of white pepper. Add the spinach and stir in a further ½ teaspoon of salt and a little more white pepper. Put the lettuce on top and then the chicken or lamb with a further ½ teaspoon of white pepper.

Fry the bacon strips lightly in the remaining butter and add them to the pan. Pour in enough water to come almost up to the level of the bacon. Sprinkle the bacon with ½ teaspoon cayenne pepper. Bring just to the boil over very low heat, cover the pan and simmer gently for 45 minutes.

Meanwhile make the dumplings. Drop them into the stew and cook for a further 15 minutes. Lift out the dumplings and keep hot on a small dish. Mix all the layers of the Pepper Pot well together and add the remaining cayenne pepper. Ladle or pour the whole stew into a wide serving dish and set the dumplings round the edge.

Berkshire Harvest Supper

4 pork chops or chicken joints
1 young pigeon, cut in quarters
  or ½ saddle of hare, quartered
½ lb (240 g) dried haricot beans,
  soaked overnight
1 quart (9 dl) stock (stock cubes
  will do)
½ teaspoon rosemary
½ teaspoon thyme
2 onions, sliced in rings
3 tablespoons (45 g) butter
A little flour
⅝ cup (1.5 dl) red wine
Juice of ½ lemon
Pepper and salt

The garnish:

4 dessert apples, peeled and
  cored
1 tablespoon brown sugar
2 tablespoons red-currant jelly
1 tablespoon (15 g) butter
4 thin lemon slices
1 tablespoon finely chopped
  parsley with 1 teaspoon finely
  chopped mint mixed with it

This eighteenth-century farmhouse dish is excellent and the recipe is interesting because it has a rather sophisticated sauce and garnish. This suggests that it was originally served at the harvest feast of a great house or at the home farm of a big estate, where the farmer's wife had seen dishes prepared for the tables of the wealthy. Most early farmhouse recipes do not suggest any form of garnish. The original dish was made with joints of rabbit and hare (both, no doubt, driven out of the stubble of the harvest field and snared or shot). It is suggested, however, that it may well be made with pigeons and chickens. In fact, any dark and light meat, such as pork chops with a pigeon, or chicken with beef give the character of the dish. The original recipe would have served about 20 hungry men.

Drain the beans and put them into a large, wide casserole with the stock, rosemary and thyme. Cover the casserole and put it into the oven at 350°F (180°C, Gas Mark 4) for 1½ hours.
  Meanwhile prepare the apple garnish. Put the apples in a small, buttered baking tin and sprinkle 1 teaspoon of sugar into each central hole. Melt the red-currant jelly and pour it over the apples, coating them and almost filling the centre holes. Put a small dab of butter in the top of each hole. Bake at the same temperature as the beans but low in the oven until the apples are just soft; they must hold their shape. Remove the apples from the oven when cooked and keep warm.
  Fry the onion rings in the butter until just soft and beginning to colour. Remove to a dish and keep warm. Flour the meat and fry on all sides in the pan in which the onions were cooked. Remove the beans from the oven; they will have absorbed most of the stock. Pour in the wine, add the lemon juice and seasoning to taste.
  Arrange the onions on the beans and put the meat on top. Return the casserole to the oven uncovered and cook for a further 1 hour.
  To serve, put the pork or chicken alternately with the pigeon or hare all round the edge of a large flat dish. Pour the beans and onions in the centre and arrange the glazed apples on top of the beans. Garnish with the lemon slices and parsley.

Turnip Pie

2 to 3 young turnips
½ stick (60 g) butter
2 gammon steaks
⅝ cup (1.5 dl) milk
⅝ cup (90 g) fresh fine
  breadcrumbs
¾ cup (90 g) grated Cheddar
  cheese
Salt and pepper

The turnips for this dish must be fairly young, each weighing about half a pound (240 g). The dish is served for supper, with fresh brown bread and plenty of butter. It has been made on a farm not far from High Wycombe for many years and is still served when turnips are just ready to lift.

Wash the turnips and put them (unpeeled) into a large saucepan of boiling salted water. Allow to boil for 30 minutes or a little longer if they are not fairly soft when pierced with a skewer.

Meanwhile melt half the butter in a frying-pan and fry the gammon steaks on both sides. Drain the steaks and cut them in $\frac{1}{4}$ inch (0.5 cm) cubes.

Drain the turnips, peel them and cut them in $\frac{1}{4}$ inch (0.5 cm) slices. Butter a pie dish. Put in a layer of turnips, sprinkle with pepper and scatter a few gammon cubes on top. Repeat the layers until the dish is full. Pour over the milk. Cover with the breadcrumbs and then with the grated cheese. Dot with the remaining butter and bake in a hot oven, 400°F (200°C, Gas Mark 6), for 10 to 15 minutes until the top is brown.

The Richmond Froise

Serves 4

6 slices streaky bacon, cut into
  fine strips
$\frac{3}{4}$ stick (90 g) butter plus $\frac{1}{4}$ stick
  (30 g) butter, melted
$1\frac{1}{2}$ cups (180 g) cooked white
  meat or chicken, cut into
  $\frac{1}{2}$ inch (1 cm) dice
36 quarter-inch (0.5 cm) cubes
  of bread
1 tablespoon finely chopped
  parsley
Pepper

The batter:

2 eggs
2 tablespoons cream
$\frac{5}{8}$ cup (1.5 dl) milk
$\frac{1}{2}$ cup (60 g) flour
Salt

Recipes for froise (or fraise) occur from medieval times until the eighteenth century, when the name seems to have died out. The dish is really a form of filled pancake, with the filling stirred into the batter, rather than enfolded. The batter is a little more solid than the usual pancake batter and the dish was often made large enough to serve 12 or more. A bacon froise was the most usual, but a froise of flaked fish was sometimes served on fish days and froises made with sugared raspberries or sliced plums or pears were also made. The Richmond Froise is a side-dish for a feast. The original quantities would have served 20. The crisp squares of fried bread are very good in the rich batter.

Make a batter with the eggs, cream, milk, flour and $\frac{1}{4}$ teaspoon of salt in the usual way. Set aside.

In a large frying-pan, fry the bacon lightly. When the fat begins to run, add half the butter. Add the meat or chicken, season well with pepper and fry lightly. Using a perforated spoon, remove all the meat and set aside.

Melt the remaining butter in the frying-pan and fry the bread cubes until crisp. Pour off excess fat and mix in the bacon and meat.

Pour the batter over the ingredients in the pan, working it gently away from the sides and shaking the pan to prevent sticking. When the bottom of the pancake is golden brown, place a large plate over the pan and turn upside down. Return the pan to the heat and pour in half the melted butter. Slide the froise, with the uncooked side of the batter downwards, back into the pan. Fry for a further 4 minutes. If preferred, the second side of the froise can be cooked under a preheated grill.

Slide the froise on to a hot serving dish, pour the remaining melted butter over the top, sprinkle on the parsley and serve at once.

Spring Lamb

Boned shoulder of lamb, about
  5 lb (2½ kg) before boning
⅝ cup (90 g) fresh fine white
  breadcrumbs
2 tablespoons shredded suet
1 tablespoon finely chopped
  mint
12 spring onions, finely
  chopped
1 teaspoon thyme
1 egg, well beaten
A little milk
1 tablespoon seasoned flour
⅜ cup (90 g) dripping or
  cooking fat
Salt and pepper

The first shoots of mint, spring onions and young sprigs of thyme were used for this spring dish. The first broad beans should be just ready in the garden to accompany it. It is best served with creamed potatoes or boiled new potatoes and freshly made mint sauce.

Mix the breadcrumbs, suet, mint, onions and thyme together. Season lightly and mix in the egg and a little milk. Work all together with your hand and fill the bone cavity in the lamb with this stuffing. Roll and tie securely. Rub the lamb all over with the seasoned flour.

Put the lamb on a rack in a baking tin with half the dripping on top of the meat and half under the rack. Roast at 400°F (200°C, Gas Mark 6) for 1½ hours. Reduce the heat a little after the first hour and put the lamb lower in the oven. Baste 2 or 3 times.

When the lamb is dished up, pour off most of the fat and make gravy in the pan in the normal way.

Christmas Spiced Beef

4 lb (2 kg) topside of beef
¾ cup (180 g) sea salt (table salt
  will do)
⅞ cup (180 g) demerara sugar
1 tablespoon white pepper
1 tablespoon black pepper
1 tablespoon ground cloves
2 teaspoons turmeric
⅜ cup (90 g) cooking fat or good
  dripping, just melted
3 lb (1½ kg) potatoes, peeled and
  halved or quartered
2 tablespoons honey
2 tablespoons butter

This is a Buckinghamshire recipe. The meat must marinate for about 12 days before it is cooked. It is an unusual recipe because the spiced and salted beef is not boiled, but roasted. It requires plenty of basting. The meat has a subtle flavour and is extremely tender but crisp outside. It should be served with cranberry sauce or red-currant jelly and accompanied by candied potatoes, brussels sprouts with chestnuts and a good brown gravy. The dish was often served on one of the later 12 days of Christmas.

Rub the beef with the salt and sugar. Lay it on a large dish and pile any remaining salt and sugar on top. Mix the pepper, cloves and turmeric and pour all over. Put the dish into the refrigerator. Turn the beef and spoon the marinade over it daily for 10 to 12 days.

At the end of this time, wipe the meat with a clean, dry cloth and discard the salt and spices. Put the meat on a rack in a baking tin, pour the melted fat over the meat and bake at 350°F (180°C, Gas Mark 4) for 2 hours.

Meanwhile, bring the potatoes to the boil in salted water and cook gently for 10 minutes. Drain and put into a lightly buttered baking tray.

In a small saucepan melt the honey with the butter. Stir and pour the mixture over the potatoes. Put the potatoes in the oven when the beef has been cooking for 30 minutes. When the beef is ready the potatoes should be candied and golden brown.

Jugged Steak

2 lb (1 kg) very good chuck
    steak or best stewing steak
2 large onions, with 6 cloves
    stuck in each
4 celery sticks, cut in 1 inch
    (2.5 cm) lengths
2 teaspoons mushroom ketchup
$\frac{5}{8}$ cup (1.5 dl) red wine
1 teaspoon red-currant jelly
1 teaspoon salt
$\frac{1}{2}$ teaspoon finely ground black
    pepper
1 tablespoon finely chopped
    parsley
1 lemon, quartered

This Berkshire recipe dates back to the Middle Ages, or even earlier, when an open fire was all that was available and food was either roasted or boiled in a great iron cauldron which would have several stone jars standing on a plank across its bottom. The steak would have been cooked in one of the jars while a pudding or a bag of dried peas might be tied to the handles and submerged to cook at the same time.

Steak is extremely good when cooked in this way as all the moisture and flavour are retained. A deep casserole is needed, preferably with a lid.

Cut the steak into 1 inch (2.5 cm) pieces, removing all skin and fat. Put the onions and celery into the casserole and put the steak on top of them. Sprinkle well with the salt and pepper. Stir the mushroom ketchup into the wine and then stir in the red-currant jelly, which need not dissolve completely. Pour this mixture all over the steak. Seal the casserole with a double layer of foil and then put the lid on top, or use a plate if it has no lid. Stand the casserole in a large, uncovered saucepan of boiling water (the water must come halfway up the sides of the casserole), and keep it boiling for $2\frac{1}{2}$ hours on top of the stove. Alternatively, put it in a baking tin of boiling water in a 300°F (160°C, Gas Mark 2) oven for 3 hours. The water must be replenished from time to time.

To serve, spoon the meat and gravy on to a flat serving dish and garnish with parsley and lemon quarters. There will be a small quantity of particularly delicious gravy and the meat will be very tender.

Velvet Cream

$\frac{1}{4}$ cup (60 g) castor sugar
Grated rind and juice of 1
    lemon
$\frac{1}{2}$ cup (1.2 dl) amontillado
    sherry
Four $\frac{1}{4}$ oz packets (30 g)
    powdered gelatine, just melted
    in a little warm water
2 cups (4.5 dl) double cream

This recipe, in slightly varying forms, goes back to the seventeenth century. Hartshorn was used in the days before gelatine was manufactured. In the nineteenth and early twentieth centuries, gelatine was sold in thin, transparent, rippled sheets, not easy to melt or measure.

The recipe given here comes from Hertfordshire.

Add the sugar, lemon rind and juice and the sherry to the gelatine and stir well. Whip the cream so that it just holds a peak but is not at all solid. Fold the gelatine mixture into it and stir gently with a spoon to make sure everything is properly blended.

Put into a mould if it is to be turned out, or into individual glasses and allow to set in the refrigerator for at least 2 hours.

Country Toffee Pudding

½ *large stale white loaf*
1¼ *cups (3 dl) milk*
⅔ *cup (240 g) Golden Syrup*
1¾ *cups (360 g) demerara sugar*
2 *sticks (240 g) butter*
⅝ *cup (1.5 dl) whipped cream*

This simple pudding is interesting because it comes from a recipe book belonging to a housekeeper to the Gresham family who built Osterley Park in 1577, in what was then the county of Middlesex. It is clearly a favourite nursery pudding, probably originally made upstairs by nanny for a treat, but it has been enriched with extra butter and whipped cream. A small amount is delicious.

Cut all the bread into ½ inch (1 cm) cubes and soak them in the milk. Drain. Heat the syrup, sugar and butter together in a saucepan, stirring all the time, until they are all amalgamated and a dark golden colour but quite liquid. Remove the pan from the heat and lightly stir in the soaked bread cubes. Heat again, stirring for 2 minutes. Turn out on to a heated dish and serve with the whipped cream.

Makes 1 cake

A Very Fine Chocolate Sponge

1¼ *stick (150 g) butter (fairly
    soft for creaming)*
⅜ *cup (90 g) sugar*
2 *eggs, separated*
3 oz *(90 g) bitter chocolate, very
    finely grated*
½ *teaspoon salt*
1¾ *cups (210 g) self-raising flour*
1 *tablespoon coffee essence*
1 *tablespoon lukewarm milk*
A *few drops vanilla essence*

This excellent chocolate sponge from a Hertfordshire manor house used to be made for tea parties after Christmas, when everyone was tired of fruit cake.

A round cake tin about eight inches (20 cm) in diameter and two to three inches (5 to 8 cm) deep is required. It should be lined with two thicknesses of greaseproof paper standing about one inch (2.5 cm) above the top of the tin.

Beat the butter and sugar until creamy. Beat the egg yolks well and add to the butter and sugar. Mix the chocolate, salt and flour together and stir into the mixture. Add the coffee essence and milk.

Beat the egg whites to a stiff froth, add the vanilla essence and fold into the mixture gently. Stir in 1 teaspoon of boiling water just before putting the mixture into the prepared tin.

Bake at 350°F (180°C, Gas Mark 4) for 45 minutes. Cool on a rack.

Makes 2 loaves

Keeping Bread

6 *cups (¾ kg) self-raising flour*
½ *cup (120 g) granulated sugar*
½ *teaspoon salt*
1 *cup (180 g) stoned raisins*
2 *eggs*
1¼ *cups (3 dl) milk*
½ *cup (180 g) Golden Syrup*

This nineteenth-century Middlesex farmhouse recipe is for loaves which will keep their flavour and moisture for at least a month, if kept in a tin. They were not cut for two days after baking, because to eat them while they were still crumbly was considered too wasteful. After that time they could be cut and "*buttered, into slices wafer thin, or as required for the menfolk*".

Mix the flour, sugar and salt together and add the raisins. Beat together the eggs and the milk and stir into the flour mixture. Add the syrup and beat all the ingredients thoroughly. Put into 2 well-greased bread tins and bake at 350°F (180°C, Gas Mark 4) for 1½ hours. Cool on a rack.

Simnel Cake

1½ sticks (180 g) butter
1 cup (240 g) castor sugar
3 large or 4 small eggs
2 cups (240 g) flour
1 cup (180 g) currants
⅜ cup (60 g) mixed candied peel

The almond paste:

¾ cup (90 g) ground almonds
¾ cup (180 g) castor sugar
1 small egg

The decoration:

Glacé cherries
Angelica

This cake, with its rich layer of almond paste through the middle as well as on top, was traditionally made for the fourth Sunday in Lent. It was intended to be eaten at a small family celebration on the Sunday afternoon, marking the fact that Lent was more than half over. The recipe comes from Berkshire.

Grease and line an 8 inch (20 cm) cake tin.

Make the almond paste by working the ground almonds, sugar and egg into a stiff paste. Roll the paste out into 2 thin rounds the size of the cake tin.

Cream together the butter and sugar until pale and light and add each egg separately. Fold in the flour, currants and peel and stir lightly.

Put half the cake mixture into the tin, cover with 1 round of almond paste and then put in the rest of the cake mixture.

Bake at 350°F (180°C, Gas Mark 4) for 50 minutes, then remove the cake from the oven and put the second piece of almond paste over the top. Put the cake back in the oven for 5 minutes, so that the almond paste melts on to the cake. Remove the cake from the oven and take it out of the tin. Decorate with glacé cherry halves and a pattern of angelica while the almond paste is still soft.

London

London has always been beloved above all the other cities of England. The centre of government, the great centre of the Empire's trade and wealth, the centre of England's intellectual and cultural life, great and poor alike converged upon her, irresistibly drawn by her world-famous markets and her entertainments.

The Thames, dividing her north and south, was, for centuries, her main thoroughfare, carrying her citizens, merchants and sailors to the crowded shops of London Bridge and the City, and on to the docks and the estuary. Up and down the river the state barges passed from Westminster to Hampton Court. Watermen waited with their boats at every water gate and landing stage to row passengers from bridge to bridge or to private houses in between.

In the sixteenth century Edmund Spencer, in his great marriage poem, sang, *"Sweet Thames, run softly till I end my song,"* and for the next two hundred years the river did indeed run softly, if not always sweetly, her banks lined with palaces and pleasure gardens, her water so full of fish, particularly salmon, that apprentices had it written into their articles that they should not be given salmon for dinner more than twice a week. The many churches of the City, 52 of them rebuilt by Sir Christopher Wren after the Great Fire, were famous and celebrated in the nursery rhyme:

> *"Oranges and lemons," say the bells of St Clement's.*
> *"You owe me five farthings," say the bells of St Martin's.*
> *"When will you pay me?" say the bells at Old Bailey.*
> *"When I grow rich," say the bells at Shoreditch.*
> *"When will that be?" say the bells of Stepney.*
> *"I'm sure I don't know," says the great bell at Bow.*

The great bell at Bow also addressed the discouraged apprentice, Dick Whittington, who had decided to give up and return to his home in the country. He had travelled as far as Highgate Hill and was resting there when Bow bells called to him across the meadows from the City:

> *Turn again Whittington*
> *Lord Mayor of London,*
> *Turn again Whittington*
> *Three times Lord Mayor.*

And three times Lord Mayor he did indeed become.

Shakespeare, leaving Warwickshire and his family, came to the city and understood her every aspect, as he understood everything that came his way. Marlowe, writing with passionate involvement, could not withstand her temptations, nor conceal the friendships and the beliefs which put him at risk and probably led to his contrived death in a tavern brawl. The slums were dark and filthy, their inns and taverns dangerous. Everthing was done for profit: no man stopped at anything that might better his circumstances. Dryden said bitterly:

> *So poetry, which is in Oxford made*
> *An art, in London only is a trade.*

But London made him the money to live in comfort, as she had made Shakespeare the money to build New House in Warwickshire, and if it is accepted that poetry in London was a trade, then trade produced some of the greatest poetry of the Western World.

"*When a man is tired of London, he is tired of life, for there is in London all that life can afford,*" said Dr Samuel Johnson in 1777, but he also called her "*The Great Wen*", seeing only too clearly her dangers, her dirt and the ruthlessness of men gathered in the close quarters of a great city.

Throughout the centuries food, like everything else in London, could be and often was the best obtainable anywhere. It could also be disgracefully and unnecessarily bad, through appalling ignorance and poverty.

There are many first-hand reports of bills of fare and menus from different periods and many descriptions of what was available at cookshops, taverns, coffee houses, restaurants and clubs. They tell very clearly the story of English cookery in an urban context and show the importance attached to quality of ingredients, sauces and accompaniments (in Middle English called *tracklements*) and the honour in which good cooks were held.

Before city food can be skilfully dressed, however, it has to be bought and the big food markets of London, each specializing in different kinds of food, go back for centuries, Billingsgate and Southwark to pre-Roman times. The setting up of markets and fairs was a prerogative of the king, and none could be held except by direct grant from the Crown or by such long tradition that it could be accepted that a royal grant had once been given.

Markets could be tough and shopping, particularly for food, was not for the gentry, although after the Great Fire shops were better built and became more luxurious, and merchants and shopkeepers were held in greater esteem and treated their apprentices in a more civilized manner, and a lady, writing in the reign of Queen Anne, could say that shopping had become "*as agreeable an amusement as a lady can pass three or four hours in*".

Smithfield, perhaps the most famous meat market in the world, originated as a cattle market known as the King's Market in the place called Smoothfield, close to the great hospital of St Bartholomew's. The market and the fair grew and prospered, becoming the greatest in London, immortalized by Ben Jonson in his comedy "*Batholomew Fair*". Smoothfield became the chief sports ground of the citizens of London: there were weekly contests in archery, wrestling and jousting and a special Court of Justice was set up, which was ruled by the Prior of St

Batholomew's, who was known as the Lord of the Fair. However, Smoothfield was also used for public punishments and executions, and during the reign of Mary Tudor 200 people were burnt to death there. The fairground became a *"rude, vast place"*, half-deserted and known as Ruffians Hall, until in 1615 it was re-ordered, fenced and paved as a proper market place for the sale of livestock.

By this time the place was known as Smithfield, and over the next 200 years it proved totally inadequate in size for the amount of livestock driven in for the daily markets. The drovers had little compassion: the animals were neither fed nor watered and were abominably treated. Finally the market pavements, drains and gutters broke down under the millions of hooves, and the mud and stench was so fearful that a decision was made to move the livestock market out of the city to Copenhagen Fields (now the Caledonian Road) in Islington and to make Smithfield into the new meat market.

This new market was very badly needed indeed for, by the mid-nineteenth century, much less of London's meat came in on the hoof. As the railway system developed, more and more was brought in as carcasses, all of which were handled in the nearby Newgate Market, a very small and inconvenient site. The new Smithfield had an underground railway station connecting with suburban lines and linking with the main lines all over the country.

Billingsgate, mentioned in early Saxon manuscripts, has always been London's principal fish market and it has never been moved from its original site, in the Pool of London. The origin of its name is not clear but is thought to go back to pre-Roman times, when a British king called Belin cut a hythe from the bank of the Thames, where the Walbrook once flowed into it, and made a wooden quay and a water gate, which came to be known as Belin's Gate, easily and permanently corrupted to Billingsgate. In the reign of Edward I the prices which might be charged in the market for different fish were proclaimed. The valuations are curious in today's terms, as the following selection shows:

> *A dozen of best soles, 3d; Best fresh cod or ling, 3d; Best conger, 1s 0d; Best turbot, 6d; Best fresh oysters, 2d a gallon; Best fresh salmon, Christmas to Easter, 4 for 5s 0d.*

Only English fishermen were allowed to bring their fish to Billingsgate, but William III gave a concession to two Dutch eel boats to sell their catch there. The eels had to be kept alive in special tanks with running water, and the moorings for the two eel boats had to be always occupied or the privilege would be lost. Therefore an empty eel boat always waited for its replacement before sailing down river.

As late as 1810 a fair proportion of the fish sold at Billingsgate came from the Thames itself. The Clerk of the Market in that year claimed that the owners of 400 fishing boats, who usually employed one other man, earned reasonable livings by fishing between Deptford and London Bridge. He claimed that he had seen a fisherman bring in ten salmon and 3,000 smelts, caught in his nets near Wandsworth. Twenty years later factories and gas-works built along the banks and discharging their waste into the river put an end to all successful London fishing.

Leadenhall Market, in the centre of the City, was famous primarily for the sale of game and poultry, though meat, fish, eggs and vegetables were also sold. It seems first to have become a market in the fifteenth century, when a mansion (with a fine leaded roof, which may account for the name) and its grounds were bought by the City Corporation under the direction of Sir Richard Whittington, Lord Mayor of London (as Bow bells had promised him when he was a penniless boy).

The mansion was at first used as a granary and kept well stocked to provide against famine, but the market as a whole became so full of merchandise and so prosperous that it became a show-place in Tudor and Stuart times. The Spanish Ambassador to the court of Charles II said to that monarch, *"There is more meat sold in your market than in all the kingdom of Spain."*

Perhaps the most famous, the best loved and certainly the most beautiful of all London's traditional markets was Covent Garden, now moved south of the river for much the same reasons of overcrowding and unmanageable traffic that had brought about the removal of the livestock market from Smithfield almost a hundred years earlier. By the sixteenth century, market gardens had been established for some time around London, particularly to the north-east, and a guild of market gardeners was formed in 1605. At first it had been traditional to sell fruit and vegetables near St Paul's, but as that area became more congested with wagons, carts, carriages, riders and crowded market stalls, the stall-holders moved out to Covent (Convent) Garden. In the thirteenth century this garden had belonged to the monks of Westminster, who had claimed it as being a convenient distance from the Abbey *"for burying their dead out of sight"*, but about 1630 it had become the property of the Earl of Bedford. The piazza and the church of St Paul's, Covent Garden, were designed by Inigo Jones, for the fourth Earl of Bedford, as a square with a portico on two sides. The market gardeners took over the south side and in 1670 the Earl obtained a licence to hold a market in the piazza. The Earl received various levies from the traders, and as time went on these amounted to a substantial fortune for his family. From 1670 until 1975 Covent Garden was the fruit and vegetable market of London. With its fine church and piazza and the flowers, fruit and vegetables piled everywhere against the grey stone, it was a pleasant place. There was a coffee house, visited by Pepys and, in later years, by Dryden, who was attacked there because of a satirical poem. Later, more coffee houses and wine cellars were opened and Pope, Fielding, Johnson, Garrick and Hogarth all frequented the market quarter.

Spitalfields, near Bishopsgate and Stepney, had originally been a pleasant, green place where a hospital was dedicated to the Virgin Mary and known as "St Mary Spittle [hospital] without Bishopsgate". The hospital, a wooden building, contained 180 beds; being a religious foundation it was taken over in 1537 by Henry VIII and destroyed, although it was "a hospital of great relief". Not until the reign of Charles II was one John Balch and his heirs allowed to hold two markets a week near Spittle Square in the parish of Stepney.

Spitalfields market grew slowly from this beginning. Only in the late nineteenth century did the market begin to handle spectacular quantities of fruit and vegetables from East Anglia and the south-east of England and not until 1920, when it was bought by the Corporation of the City of London, did its full potential begin to be realized. Spitalfields became world famous, specializing in imported fruit and vegetables and in particular the handling, ripening (in special buildings) and distribution of bananas throughout London and to many other English cities.

One great London market has existed south of the Thames since pre-Roman times. This is at Southwark (where Chaucer's Canterbury pilgrims rested at the Tabard Inn) and was known as Southwark Market and later as Borough Market. Southwark was a flourishing township when the Romans reached the Thames. A fair and market were held there on the bank of the river opposite Billingsgate, but there was no bridge to link the two. The Thames could only be crossed in coracles or on rafts, so the Romans built the first London Bridge, which was made of wood. A second wooden bridge is recorded as having been built by the Saxons in the tenth century, the Roman bridge having presumably collapsed, and a third, of great strength, was erected at the beginning of the thirteenth century. Thirty years later Southwark stall-holders extended their market on to the bridge, but carts and wagons were involved in traffic jams and so stalls on the bridge were made illegal. It was also illegal for citizens of London to cross the bridge to buy cattle in Southwark instead of in Smithfield on their own side. They continued to do so, however, believing that they found exceptional bargains in Southwark, and the market flourished and spread over neighbouring areas on the south bank.

In 1327 Southwark was incorporated as a borough of the City of London. The annual fair and continuous market grew because all travellers coming from the south in coaches or wagons had to cross London Bridge to come into the city. The inns in Borough High Street became a natural overnight stop and were frequented by rich merchants and travellers from abroad. Players crossed the river to entertain them and in 1600 the Globe theatre was built, and Londoners came across by barge and wherry from Limehouse Steps, Westminster Steps, Wapping Old Stairs and other water gates to see the plays of Shakespeare and Marlowe.

All these were, and still are, London's greatest food markets. Naturally there were hundreds of smaller street markets, but many of the stall-holders bought their supplies from the markets already described. The housewife relied on these smaller markets for all her fresh food, as did the stewards and cooks of the great town houses and of the palaces. We hear from Pepys: "*My poor wife rose by five o'clock in the morning before day and went to market and bought fowles and many other things for dinner, with which I was highly pleased. . . .*"

For tea, coffee, sugar and spices, shoppers might go straight to Mincing Lane. From the sixteenth century, all ships carrying imported goods of this kind, including wines, unloaded in the Pool of London and warehouses had been built in Mincing Lane, Mark Lane and the surrounding area. In general, factors and brokers bought direct at the warehouses and sold from shops and stalls and by direct delivery to regular private customers. After the Great Fire, the city granaries were rebuilt and the distribution of grain regulated throughout the city. In 1747 the Corn Exchange was established in Mark Lane. Imported corn was stored in bonded granaries near Commercial Docks.

This, very briefly, is how the raw materials for feeding the citizens of London were collected, organized and sold, so that the farmer or market gardener, the transporter, the market porter, the market owner (the Crown or in later years usually the Corporation of the City) and the retailer all made a profit. It was little wonder that those who moved into London from the country often found wages sadly low and the proper feeding of their families difficult.

In contrast to these difficulties was the fact that life in the city was busy and exciting, full of variety and interest unknown to young men who had always lived on a farm or in a small village. Above all, London life from the Middle Ages onwards has always been noisy and, contrary to general belief, is perhaps less so today than it was in earlier centuries, at least in the streets near the great markets.

In the poorest and most crowded quarters of medieval London cooking facilities were impossibly limited, an open hearth on the ground floor of each wooden or wattle-and-daub house having, of necessity, to serve all the inhabitants. Cookshops, therefore, were a feature of daily life and excited admiration and appreciation, not only from the citizens but from those who came from the country to buy and sell and from visitors abroad. The Mayor and Aldermen of the city regulated the prices and their officers, called beadles, kept a watch on whether the rates were adhered to. In the second half of the fourteenth century "best" roast heron cost 18 pence, which was twopence more than the bird cost when bought raw from the poulterer. Geese, ducks or cockerels cost one penny for roasting and for a penny ten small birds roasted or 12 raw could be bought.

The cookshops also sold pottages of beef, mutton or goose and sometimes of partridge or pigeon. An ordinance of Richard II also controlled the price of pies. The best capon in a pasty cost eight pence and the best hen five pence. Small pies were made and sold by street traders as well as in the cookshops. The street traders carried large wooden trays, piled with hot pies, covered with a cloth, and cried their wares as they went, as the nursery rhyme about Simple Simon records.

William FitzStephen, describing London in the twelfth century, wrote:

> Moreover there is in London upon the river's bank . . . a public cookshop. There daily, according to the season, you may find viands, dishes roast, fried and boiled, fish great and small, the coarser flesh for the poor, the more delicate for the rich, such as venison, and birds both big and little. . . . Those who desire to fare delicately need not search to find sturgeon or 'Guineas-fowl' or 'Ionian Francolin', since all the dainties that are found there are set forth before their eyes. Now this is a public cookshop, appropriate to a city and pertaining to the art of civic life.

Other cookshops were not so highly regarded. Rotten meat was cooked in rancid grease. One, near Smithfield, was described in the seventeenth century by a visitor to London as having "a smell so bad and so putrid that we could not enter the door but withdrew at once. Yet the rooms were crowded with porters and drovers and wherrymen so used to the stink of the market that they could smell nor taste nothing amiss."

Taverns and coffee houses generally served an "ordinary", which was a dinner served at a fixed time in the middle of the day and sometimes a supper at night. Some establishments were known for a particular dish served on certain days. "Gammon and Peas" or "Gammon and Beans", "Beef Steaks", "Hotch potch of Goose" and "Pottage of Beef" were all typical dishes of the ordinary. Often oysters were available for those who wanted them before the main dish. The Castle Ordinary, off Paternoster Row, was frequented by booksellers and writers from the mid-fifteenth century until it was burnt down in the Great Fire of 1666. It was rebuilt as Dolly's Chop House, kept by a formidable lady whose "ordinaries" were considered excellent and were served by pretty maids instead of by men. Fielding, Defoe, Steele, Congreve, Smollett, Richardson, Swift, Dryden, Pope, Gainsborough and Handel all went there to eat chops and steaks. It was finally pulled down in 1885. A few city chophouses remain to this day, however, or have been rebuilt and rechristened in recent years by their earliest names.

Dr Johnson frequented the Cheshire Cheese and the Rainbow in Fleet Street, and records that he had a good dinner of two or three courses for seven pence. Pontack's, a very grand ordinary according to Defoe, charged four or five shillings for dinner and it was possible to spend up to a guinea. Locket's (which now has a restaurant in Westminster called after it) was famous for its entrées and ragouts. At the other end of the scale, it was possible to go to a "dive" where, among footmen, chairmen, and serving men, a meal was served at about two and a half pence. Alternatively, you could have a good, well-made and seasoned sausage at a "farthing fry".

In the seventeenth century it became fashionable to go by water to Greenwich to eat whitebait. Several taverns and hostelries along the waterfront served the whitebait with proper respect and ceremony to distinguished and merry company. In the reign of William III a very simple fish soup or stew called Water Souchet was introduced from Holland as a compliment to the King and his Dutch followers. This dish was taken up by the Greenwich taverns because it could be prepared in advance and served piping hot immediately the customers arrived, while the newly caught whitebait were fried to crisp perfection.

Discriminating London seized with enthusiasm on some of the delicacies that came in small quantities from the Colonies, brought in on the sugar ships. Pineapples were a truly expensive luxury. Lady Bessborough, an inspired letter-writer, bewails her fearful debts, describing the extravagances and, in particular, the gambling that caused them and says that at least she has decided on one economy – she will no longer have pineapples bought for her dinner parties, but will instruct her head gardener to grow them in her hot-houses. Dickens wrote, *When I had no money, I took a turn in Covent Garden and stared at the pineapples in the market.* The other imported luxury that London took to its heart was turtle, which became an essential part of the Lord Mayor's banquet and of the banquets given by many of the merchant guilds.

The turtles were brought back alive on the sugar ships from the Caribbean, and Mrs Glasse, whose great cookery book was first published in 1747, gives careful and detailed instructions on how to kill, prepare and cook a turtle of about 60 pounds in weight. At many of the city banquets the aldermen were served with thick, followed by clear, turtle soup: the next course consisted of calipash, the back, and calipee, the undershell (some diners preferred one and some the other), made into thick, glutinous stews with balls of minced turtle and veal added. The fins were served in a separate clear broth.

Real, live turtles were rare and very expensive, since they often died on the long voyage from the West Indies. They became extremely fashionable, however, and a specialist firm called Painters in Leadenhall Street made and sold such excellent turtle soup that Abraham Hayward, author of *The Art of Dining* (a kind of gourmet's guide, which was published in 1852 and went into several editions), describes it as, *"decidedly the best thing that can be had in this or any other country"*.

What could the mayors and aldermen of lesser cities serve at their banquets when the essential turtle was unobtainable? What could Londoners serve at banquets less important and luxurious than the Lord Mayor's? Mock turtle soup was invented – Mrs Lizzie Heritage in her cookery book of 1894 says: *"This is the staple soup of English life. . . . As its name implies it is an imitation of Turtle soup. . . . The essential point must, therefore, be the 'lumpy delight' furnished by calf's head. . . ."* She goes on to say that the preparation is lengthy, but if done properly produces a soup *"almost as good as real turtle, indeed by some people preferred"*.

"Soup of the evening, beautiful Soup!" sang the Mock Turtle, sadly. That was Lewis Carroll, laughing at them all, the true gourmets and the mock gourmets and at himself as well.

Rich Victorian London, prospering on the spoils of her vast empire, had not only the best raw materials available but the best chefs in the world to cook them. French chefs were engaged by royalty and nobility and came willingly to London because wages were higher, master chefs were held in great esteem and materials were superlative. Ude, a fine chef, worked devotedly for the Earl of Sefton, though he refused to stay with the Duke of Wellington who could not, or would not, differentiate between a perfectly cooked meal and a half-ruined one; he also cooked for the Duke of York, Crockfords Club and the United Services Club. Francatelli cooked celestially for Queen Victoria, who preferred plain food and indulged her preference when she was at Balmoral, thereby depressing her court, which had to sit shivering in the icy dining-room without even the comfort of a well-chosen menu. Escoffier cooked for Edward VII, who was well aware that he was being slowly killed by his chef's irresistible dishes. All these foreigners, however, were expected to understand and produce the traditional dishes of the English cuisine. No formal menu was acceptable without roast beef, game pie, a ham, turtle soup or whitebait, though, since French was the polite language of food, some of these dishes might be referred to in French.

Alexis Soyer was, in many ways, the greatest chef of nineteenth-century England. French by birth, he became entirely anglicized and married an English girl. His wife gained a reputation as a painter and the marriage was extremely happy until her sad death in childbirth at the age of 29. Soyer had his own house in London. From there he drove in a hansom cab to the Reform Club, which his very real genius, not only as a cook but as an organizer and inventor, made the gastronomic centre of London.

Soyer was by nature a kind and gentle man, although as Master Chef in his vast kitchens at the Reform Club his authority was absolute and he had no mercy for any incompetence on the part of his staff. His kindness and his high general intelligence gave him a rare percipience in his field. Even before he began to cook a dish, he could almost taste in his mind the exact flavouring, seasoning or consistency that would cause one of his great patrons to sing his praises yet again. It was said in London that when Soyer himself had once cooked for you, you were never satisfied until he had done so again.

His patrons, to whom he dedicated his huge book *The Gastronomic Regenerator*, included seven royal princes, and over 60 members of the nobility. Sometimes more than a dozen members of the aristocracy dined at the Reform Club on one evening and Soyer would personally cook for each nobleman, having first recommended which dishes he thought his client would find most pleasing.

Soyer entirely redesigned the kitchens of the Reform Club, which were considered the most up-to-date in the world and which many ladies came to see in the quiet afternoon period. In these kitchens on 9 May 1846, he cooked the most recherché dinner he had ever prepared. *"Mr G."*, who ordered it, wished Soyer *"to get him a first-rate dinner and spare no expense in procuring the most novel, luxurious and rare edibles to be obtained at this extravagant season of the year"*. There were more than 30 dishes, of which Soyer says that the most expensive were the mullets, the salmon, the Chickens à la Nelson, and *"above all, the crawfish which, when dressed, cost upwards of seven guineas"*.

Soyer preferred salmon from the Severn to any other. The large one for this dinner was brought to him alive, having come up in a tank of water on the afternoon train from Gloucester. It arrived at 7 pm, was immediately killed and boiled and was ready for garnishing à la Mazarine – with a hollandaise sauce, flavoured with lobster spawn and anchovy – just ten minutes before dinner was served. It was, therefore, Soyer says *"eaten in its greatest possible perfection"*.

Soyer adds to his account of this dinner that he had proposed a dish of ortolans, which the host had accepted, but which he was unable to get from Paris *"on account of a change in the weather"*. He describes what he would have done with the 24 tiny birds. He had already procured 12 large, fine truffles and, *"it was my intention to have dug a hole in each into which I should have placed one of the birds, and covered each with a piece of lamb or calf's caul, then to have braised them . . . in stock with ½ pint of Lachrymae Christi."* He says he would then have drained them, built them into a pyramid on a serving dish and surrounded them with a border of poached forcemeat. Next, he would have puréed the pieces of truffle that he had dug out to make room for the birds, added the reduced stock in which the truffles and birds had cooked, and poured this sauce over the pyramid. Finally, he would have roasted the remaining 12 ortolans and placed them all round the dish as garnish. Quite a dish to have missed.

He had, however, a serious side and could be ferocious when faced with incompetence and wanton waste. It was Soyer, and Soyer alone, who, during the Crimean War, reformed the previously appalling methods of allocating and cooking army rations, both for the fighting soldier and for the sick or wounded in hospital.

Three of Soyer's recipes, all cooked for the first time at the Reform Club, are given in this book.

Abraham Hayward wrote: "*It is allowed by competent judges that a first-rate dinner in England is out of all comparison better than a dinner of the same class in any other country: for we get the best cooks, as we get the best singers and dancers, by bidding highest for them, and we have cultivated certain national dishes to a point which makes them the envy of the world.*" This bold assertion is backed, moreover, by the unqualified admission of Ude, who wrote: "*I will venture to affirm that cookery in England, when well done is superior to that of any country in the world.*"

Hayward mentions by their plain English surnames several of the great English cooks of the nineteenth century. They all worked at their masters' London establishments, transferring to their country estates in the summer and at Christmas. Farmer was head cook to the Earl of Bathurst and was said to be the "*very first English artist of his day*". Pratt cooked for the Duke of York and Huggins followed a series of French chefs at Carlton House, the Prince Regent's London residence. Although many gourmet members of the nobility still had French cooks, and in some cases Italian pastry cooks, all the chefs working in London eagerly produced traditional English dishes as part of their repertoire. Hayward quotes the Earl of Dudley as saying, "'*A good soup, a small turbot, a neck of venison, ducklings with green peas or chicken with asparagus and an apricot tart is a dinner for an emperor,*'" and adds, "*such a dinner can be better served in England than in any other – or, more correctly speaking, there is no other country in the world where it could be served at all.*"

It is of some interest here to see how carefully a promising young English cook (who, by fortunate chance, was living in the servants' quarters of a great house that prided itself on its food) was trained in the seventeenth century.

Robert May published his book *The Accomplish't Cook* in 1660. He was indeed an accomplished cook himself and a brilliant one and he dedicated his book to his distinguished patrons, Lord Dormer, Lord Montague, Lord Lumley and Sir Kenelm Digby (whose own cookery book was published in 1669), and explains his education as one of the greatest cooks of his time. He was first taught by his father, himself a talented cook in charge of the kitchens of Lady Dormer. The young Robert so impressed the Dormer family that the Dowager Lady Dormer sent him to France to the household "*of a noble peer and first president of Paris*". When he came back, he was articled as an apprentice cook to "*Mr Arthur Hollinsworth in Newgate Market, one of the ablest workmen in London, cook to the Grocer's Hall and Star Chamber*". If you cooked for the Star Chamber you had to be good, for their menus were considered the most elaborate in London. When Robert May's apprenticeship was finished (in about 1610), Lady Dormer sent for him to cook under his father, who ruled over five undercooks, his son making the sixth.

Lower in the social scale of London, but very far from its bottom notes, we hear in the eighteenth and nineteenth centuries the memorable utterances of many a dedicated but untitled gourmet. Charles Lamb, in his *Essays of Elia* (1823), devoted a whole essay to the pleasures of eating roast pig, by which, of course, he meant sucking pig.

Dr Johnson, who had been poor enough to be very hungry as a young man, took his food very seriously.

"*Some people*", said the Doctor, "*have a foolish way of not minding or pretending not to mind what they eat. For my part, I mind my belly very studiously, and very carefully; for I look upon it that he who does not mind his belly, will hardly mind anything else.*"

Rough and eccentric, except in the elegant flow of his English sentences, he sometimes entertained a friend to "*a plain dinner*" at his home in Fleet Street and gave him "*a veal pie or a leg of lamb and spinach and a rice pudding*". When dining out himself, he was very displeased if the dishes he was offered did not do him due honour. "*A good dinner enough to be sure, but it was not a dinner to ask a man to,*" was his comment on one disappointing menu. But either his palate was very unusual or he was hardly discerning over his food, for his long-standing mistress and faithful nurse-companion, Mrs Piozzi, recorded that his favourite dishes were a leg of pork "*boiled till it dropped from the bone, a veal pie with plums and sugar and the outside cut of a salt buttock of beef*". She adds that she had known him, when the second course was on the table, to ask for the return of the lobster sauce from the first course and to pour all that remained over the plum pudding, eating the result with gusto.

Dickens, according to one of his letters, considered a leg of lamb with oysters a capital dish, though he makes Sam Weller say: "*Poverty and oysters always seem to go together.*" A far cry indeed from the situation today. Mr Jingle, also from *The Pickwick Papers*, says diffidently: "*Not presume to dictate, but broiled fowl and mushrooms – capital thing!*"

One great innovation in English upper-class life is supposed to have been started by the Duchess of Bedford. She had chanced to take some tea with her when she went on a long, idle visit to Belvoir Castle. The gentlemen being away hunting or shooting, she invited other female house-guests to drink it with her in her room, in the afternoons. The ladies enjoyed this so much that when she returned to London she continued to invite them to tea in the drawing-room of her town house.

By the late nineteenth century the "cup of tea" had become an elaborate meal, sometimes with a menu written in French (although the French have never served afternoon tea). The ladies took this meal to refresh themselves after their afternoon carriage exercise. They changed into special long, loose dresses, known as "tea-gowns", and left their drawing-rooms only when the dressing bell went and they returned to their bedrooms to make their more formal toilettes for dinner. No lady could enter a coffee shop, but in 1717 Thomas Twining, the well-known tea-merchant, opened the first tea-shop for ladies in Devereux Court, London. In 1732 Vauxhall Pleasure Gardens became a tea garden and after this tea gardens were opened in many places around the city. Concerts, sports and entertainments were provided as well as tea.

The high tea, so important in the industrial north of England, was not customary with the lower middle classes and the labourers of London. Those who had come from the North probably still had their high tea (defined by Mrs Beeton as "*where meat takes a prominent part and signifies really, what it is, a tea-dinner*"). Londoners born and bred had supper if they had taken a packed lunch to work, or a simple tea if they had had a hot dinner in the middle of the day. They might or might not have a snack before going to bed.

In Victorian London the pubs were the working men's clubs. Indeed, they were the natural place for an East End labourer to spend his evenings, since there was little enough to keep him at home. After his evening meal he joined his mates and drank till his money ran out, in order to escape from the discomfort and hopelessness of his life.

Hogarth's engraving of Gin Lane shows the sign above the Gin Shop: *"Drunk for a penny; dead drunk for 2d; clean straw for nothing."* Of course, the straw was seldom clean and late at night the wife might go in search of her husband leaving the children alone, or she might send a child to look for him. *"Please sell no more drink to my father,"* wails the Victorian song, *"It makes him so strange and so wild. Heed the prayer of a heartbroken mother, And pity the poor drunkard's child."*

Heavy drinking was a feature of all urban life in England, and of London in particular. In the houses of the rich only the appetite of the drinker was affected, but in the houses of the poor, the more the breadwinner drank the less there was to eat. There are reports of girls of 13 or 14 who went on the streets to earn money for food. They spent their earnings on pies and sausages and cakes, because eating their fill of food they considered delicious was their greatest pleasure.

Life in a London slum provided very few pleasures and very few opportunities, compared even with poverty in the country which, though cruel enough, at least left available the pleasures and profits of the natural world. The country family, even in dire poverty, might have enough garden to grow a few vegetables. There were wild foods to be searched out, among them young dandelion leaves and nettles, mushrooms, berries, the first hawthorn leaves, which were known to children as "bread and cheese", and crab apples. It was possible, if dangerous, to poach all kinds of game, in spite of the fearful penalties of the game laws.

In London there were filthy tenement staircases and pavements to play on, and mud where lanes and alleys were unpaved. Children could sometimes scrounge or steal refuse from the markets and women could take in washing or sewing. There were traditional street games to be played and time could be passed in neighbourly gossip while fetching water from the local pump or buying a screw of tea or sugar. On the whole, however, the poor in London had simply not enough to do. It was impossible to get more work. While the man of a family spent his evenings in his local pub, his wife gossiped with her relations and her neighbours and his children played in the street. Conditions improved very slowly.

We have an interesting example of the extreme contrast between high and low living at the very beginning of our own century in the menus for the coronation of King Edward VII and Queen Alexandra.

The coronation banquet of 1902 had to be postponed because the King had appendicitis, but 14 courses were already prepared, or their ingredients collected, when the King became ill. These included vast amounts of foie gras, sturgeon, asparagus and caviare. Two thousand quails, 300 legs of mutton and 800 chickens had been ordered, and vast quantities of strawberries and other fruits for the desserts. Cold storage could not be found for some of the food and it was distributed by the

Sisters of the Poor to the poorest families in Whitechapel and all over the East End. It is not known whether those who received the more exotic ingredients enjoyed them. However, the menu provided by the authorities *"for 50,000 of the King's poorest subjects in London in the Borough of Fulham in order that they might have the opportunity to celebrate his coronation"* was extremely plain and solid English fare. At least it was realized that celebration, no matter how loyal the subjects, was not possible on empty bellies and they were given:

Roast Beef and sauce, Potatoes, Bread ad lib, Plum Pudding, Cheese.
The menu for the coronation banquet attended by their majesties was very different:

> *Oeufs à l'Impératrice (Cotelettes elaborately dressed with caviare), panées Grillées, sauce mayonnaise, Canetons à la Rouennaise, Poulardes rôties au cresson, Homards au naturel, sauce rémoulade, Les Viandes froides à la gelée, Salade des Quatres Saisons, Courges au Gratin, Pommes de terre à la serviette, Röod Gröod [a scandinavian dish in compliment to visiting royal relations], Compôte des pêches à la Cardinal, Pâtisserie Parisienne.*

This was served as a luncheon at Buckingham Palace and the Master Chef was J. Menager.

At the same time a banquet was served at Marlborough House for the Prince and Princess of Wales, with other royal guests. Rather strangely since, unlike his father, the future King George V was not a gourmet, this menu, prepared under a Master Chef called H. Cedard, seems a little more light-hearted than the one prepared for the new king. It began with lobster salad, followed by salmon dressed with caviare, tiny cutlets of lamb, centre fillet steaks à la Cumberland, an elaborate dish of chickens and tongues, cold beef and roast beef, and a dish of splendid ham. The meal ended with Gâteaux Marignan, little gâteaux, tutti frutti champagne (which must have been a light and refreshing relief), iced coffee, gooseberry or raspberry water ice and lemonade or orangeade. The future Queen Mary was always imaginative and perhaps had some say in the lighter and more refreshing banquet with its traditional emphasis on the sweet course.

The dinner menus for the King and his court at Buckingham Palace were almost as elaborate as his coronation banquet. One includes quails stuffed with caviare, served cold with a chaudfroid sauce, and a haunch of venison from Sandringham served with aigredoux sauce, which goes back to the Middle Ages.

In Queen Victoria's day, dinner at the palace took one and a half hours and was still divided into two parts by the serving of a sorbet, a refreshing, soft water ice. This habit was dropped, except on certain occasions, in the next reign, as the King did not like his exquisite meals to take so long. In the reign of his mother, a curry was made every day by Indian servants (who were allowed a corner of the royal kitchens for this work) in case a visiting rajah might prefer it to the ordinary menu.

Edward VII, as Prince of Wales and in the first years of his reign, attended Ascot and Goodwood and from time to time the opera at Covent Garden. On all such outings his lunch, dinner or supper was prepared at the Palace. At the Covent Garden Opera House supper was served to the King in an interval that was extended to an hour. Tables in the room behind the royal box were set with gold plate and a cold supper of eight or nine courses was served. One menu consisted of consommé, lobster, trout, duck, lamb cutlets in aspic, plovers' eggs, chicken and a savoury jelly containing strips of ham and tongue, served with tiny assorted sandwiches, fresh fruit and pâtisserie.

These royal menus were emulated at many of the noble houses where the King was entertained and, indeed, at some which would have wished for his visits. As an epicure, Edward VII spurred on the culinary imagination of the English upper classes, but he was not particularly interested in traditional dishes, even at shooting-party luncheons or on board the royal yacht. His only exceptions seem to have been roast beef, about which he was extremely particular, and grilled lamb chops, which he liked plain but of exquisite quality.

London has always had a special tradition of City banquets held by the Lord Mayor in the Mansion House and by the trade guilds in their own fine halls. Such banquets were more traditional and less exotic than the royal menus and often followed a standard pattern. For many years, for example, it was unthinkable not to serve turtle soup at the Lord Mayor's banquets.

The following menu is for the Lord Mayor's banquet of 1892, exactly ten years before Edward VII's coronation banquets. The main ingredients are entirely English (no caviare or foie gras here) but several of the dishes were, in fact, as elaborate and as complicated as those prepared in the palace:

Turtle soup, Fillets of Turbot, Mousse of Lobster Cardinale, Sweetbreads with truffles, Baron of beef, Salads, Partridges, Mutton Cutlets royale, Smoked Tongue, Orange Jelly, Italian and Strawberry Creams, Maids of Honour, Pâtisserie Princesse, Meringues.

The total cost was £2,000 and this worked out at about two guineas a head. In 1978, the dishes set before the guests at one of the Lord Mayor's banquets were shown on television and the dinner consisted of only the following dishes with accompanying vegetables: two soups, neither of them turtle (apparently the fish course was omitted) a baron of beef, breasts of pheasants and trifles. A moderate menu indeed compared with the earlier one, but even so causing a certain outcry against greed and extravagance in an England less rich than ever before and more conscious of famine and poverty in other parts of the world.

Certain things are lost to those who buy in London's markets today. It is impossible to buy sturgeon, fresh truffles (white or black), cockscombs and, thankfully, most of the small birds and the waterbirds that our ancestors unthinkingly decimated. It is also difficult to find veal kidneys, and the price of oysters and lobsters, let alone Beluga caviare is often prohibitive.

On the other hand, all year round we can buy and afford the fruit and vegetables that earlier cooks could only buy in summer, and we can keep superb dishes for days or weeks without immuring them in coffins of pastry. The whole experience of English gastronomy is open to us and the special dishes of London through the centuries remain as special as they ever were.

Water Souchet

2 whole whiting, cleaned
1 lb (½ kg) whiting fillets or
large fresh sardines, also
filleted
½ tablespoon (8 g) salt
12 peppercorns
½ bottle white wine
¾ lb (360 g) parsley, including
the roots
2 lemons

Originally called *Sootje*, this dish was introduced from Holland in the time of William III. It is a very simple, refreshing dish and a fish dinner of Water Souchet followed by whitebait is unbeatable, particularly if it ends with a very good salad and cheese. Hot, thick, buttered toast is good with the Souchet.

Put the whole fish in a large saucepan with 5 cups (1 litre) of water to which is added the salt and the peppercorns. Add the wine and bring to the boil. Cover the pan and simmer gently for 20 minutes.

Meanwhile, wash the parsley and trim the roots, keeping as much of them as possible as they add to the flavour. Chop it all finely and, reserving 1 tablespoonful for the garnish, throw the rest into the saucepan to simmer for a further 40 minutes. Pour the stock through a fine strainer, reserving all the liquid. Put any nice flakes of the whole fish back into the clear green broth.

Put the fish fillets into a shallow pan, pour a little of the broth over them, just to cover, and poach uncovered for 5 minutes.

Have ready 4 heated soup bowls. Lift the fillets and lay 2 or more in each bowl. Pour the broth in which they cooked into the saucepan with the rest of the broth. Add the juice of 1 lemon and bring to the boil. Pour through a strainer to fill up each bowl. Drop a slice of the second lemon into each bowl, add a sprinkling of parsley and serve quickly.

Coldstream Eggs

6 kipper fillets, lightly poached
1¼ cups (3 dl) single cream
6 eggs
Salt and black pepper
Hot buttered toast

A breakfast dish served in the Officer's Mess of the Coldstream Guards about 100 years ago. It is very good as a starting course today.

Mash the kipper fillets. Mix in the cream, reserving 2 tablespoons. The mixture should have a very soft purée consistency. Put the mixture into individual soufflé dishes, filling them only half-full, and carefully break an egg into each. Sprinkle with a little black pepper.

Season the reserved cream with salt and pepper and put a little on top of each egg. Bake in a moderate oven, 350°F (180°C, Gas Mark 4), for 7 minutes or until the eggs are just set. Serve with slices of hot buttered toast.

Cream Omelette

4 eggs
1¼ cups (3 dl) single cream
1 tablespoon fresh fine white
  breadcrumbs
1 tablespoon finely chopped
  parsley
3 shallots, very finely chopped
1 tablespoon (15 g) butter
Salt and freshly ground black
  pepper

Richard Dolby's recipe, 1832. This flat cream omelette is quite out of the ordinary and makes a splendid light dish. Serve with brown bread and butter.

Bring the cream to the boil in a saucepan. Stir in the crumbs, parsley, shallots and seasoning. Simmer, stirring, until the mixture is quite thick. Remove the pan from the heat and allow to cool a little.

Beat the eggs well, stir them into the cream mixture and beat well.

Melt the butter in a large frying-pan and when it is very hot, pour in the mixture, stirring as it cooks. It will take a little longer than an ordinary omelette. Hold the omelette under the grill to finish—Richard Dolby would have used a salamander.

Lift the omelette flat on to a hot dish and serve.

Serves 4

Fried Celery

1 head celery
1 egg
½ cup (60 g) flour
1¼ cups (3 dl) milk
Salt and pepper
Oil for deep frying

This recipe is from *Adam's Luxury & Eve's Cookery*, published in 1744.

Remove the strings from the celery and cut the stalks into 1½ inch (3.5 cm) pieces. Boil the celery for 30 minutes, then cool slightly.

Beat the egg yolk and white separately. Beat the flour and the egg yolk, salt and pepper into the milk. Fold in the stiffly whisked egg white. Dip the celery pieces in the batter and deep fry until golden brown.

Serves 4

A Side-dish of Vegetables

2 cauliflowers, outer leaves and
  stalks trimmed
1 lb (½ kg) brussels sprouts,
  small and firm, with outer
  leaves removed
1¼ cups (3 dl) white sauce
½ stick (60 g) butter
1 egg yolk, well beaten
2 tablespoons double cream
Salt and pepper
1½ lb (¾ kg) potatoes, cooked
  and mashed with plenty of
  butter and a little milk

Soyer served this dish as a side-dish at several Reform Club dinners in about 1846. The sauce is very subtle and delicious.

Put the cauliflowers into a large saucepan of boiling water with 2 teaspoons of salt. The water should just cover them. Boil, covered, for 20 minutes. If not tender continue to boil for another 5 minutes and test again with a skewer. When tender lift the cauliflowers carefully to avoid breaking and put to drain in a colander.

Meanwhile, put the brussels sprouts in about 2½ cups (6 dl) of boiling salted water and boil for 15 minutes or until just tender. Lift and drain very well.

While the vegetables are cooking bring the sauce to just below boiling point, melt the butter and stir it in. Whisk in the egg yolk and then the cream, adding a little salt and pepper. On no account let it boil. Stand it on the side of the stove while arranging the potato in a border around the edge of a warmed, large, flat dish. Put the brussels sprouts in groups of five at intervals on the potato border. Place the cauliflowers in the middle. Pour the sauce over the cauliflowers and serve immediately.

Macaroni Cheese

½ lb (240 g) macaroni (short or
 long)
1¼ cups (3 dl) cheese sauce
Butter
⅔ cup (60 g) grated Cheddar or
 Parmesan cheese
Salt

It is unexpected that macaroni is traditional in
English cooking, but it was first prepared at the
court of Richard II in about 1390 and served more or
less as the dish we call Macaroni Cheese. The early
recipe, which does not inspire confidence, is:
"*Macrows. Take and make a thin foil of dough, and
carve it in pieces, and cast them on boiling water, and
seeth it well. Take cheese and grate it and butter cast
beneath and above . . . and serve forth.*"

C. Anne Wilson, historian and author, says that
macaroni had been invented only a short time earlier
in Italy. The recipe probably reached the English
court because Richard II was known to be a great
gourmet. Although there seem to be no recipes for
Macaroni Cheese in English cookery books for the
next 400 years, there are one or two references to
"Maccharoni". By the early nineteenth century
macaroni had become a sophisticated London novelty
and was used with chicken or shellfish to make small
moulds, turbans and a very fine pie.

With the exception of vermicelli, which was used in
clear soups and consommés, macaroni is the only
form of pasta which became a part of traditional
English cooking.

Bring 1 quart (9 dl) of water to the boil. Add 1
teaspoon of salt and plunge in the macaroni (if the
macaroni is the quick-cooking short kind, boil it for
10 minutes; if it is long, break it into short lengths
and boil for 20 minutes). Drain the macaroni well
and stir it into the cheese sauce.

Butter a shallow fireproof dish and pour the
macaroni into it. Sprinkle the cheese on top. Put the
dish under a hot grill or at the top of a hot oven,
425°F (220°C, Gas Mark 7), for about 10 minutes for
the cheese to melt and slightly brown.

Macaroni Pie

1 lb (½ kg) short macaroni,
 boiled until just tender
1¼ cups (3 dl) double cream
⅝ cup (1.5 dl) well-seasoned
 white sauce
2½ lb (1¼ kg) roast chicken,
 skinned and chopped into ½
 inch (1 cm) pieces
¼ lb (120 g) cooked tongue,
 finely chopped
¼ lb (120 g) cooked lean ham,
 finely chopped
¼ lb (120 g) mushrooms, sliced
 and lightly fried in butter
½ cup (60 g) plus ¼ cup (30 g)
 grated Parmesan cheese
1 tablespoon (15 g) butter
16 triangles made from ½ lb
 (240 g) puff pastry and kept hot

There is an eighteenth-century recipe for this hot
macaroni pie which differs very little from the
slightly simpler nineteenth-century one given here. It
is a quite outstanding dish for a dinner party and is
best with a plain dressed lettuce salad.

Bring the cream just to the boil and stir it into the
white sauce. In a large pie dish, put a layer of
chicken and sprinkle some tongue, ham and
mushrooms on top. Put in a spoonful of the sauce
and a sprinkling of the cheese. Cover with a thick
(about 1 inch/2.5 cm) layer of macaroni. Pour on to
this about 2 tablespoons of sauce, sprinkle with
cheese and repeat the layers twice more, ending with
macaroni. Pour all the remaining sauce on top and
sprinkle with the rest of the ½ cup (60 g) of the
cheese.

Stand the dish in a baking tin filled with enough
hot water to come halfway up the sides of the dish.
Bake at 350°F (180°C, Gas Mark 4) for 1 hour.

Ten minutes before serving, remove the dish from the oven and sprinkle the browned top with the remaining ¼ cup (30 g) of cheese and the butter in small dabs. Put the dish back in the oven to finish making the cheese crust.

Put the hot pastry triangles on a separate dish and serve 2 with each helping of pie.

Turban of Shellfish and Macaroni

Serves 6

¾ lb (360 g) macaroni (long macaroni, broken into 1½ inch/3.5 cm lengths)
Butter
2 frozen lobster tails, thawed, or 1 small, fresh, boiled lobster
½ lb (180 g) frozen prawns, thawed
⅝ cup (1.5 dl) double cream
1¼ cups (3 dl) white sauce
1 cucumber, diced and lightly fried in butter
Salt and white pepper
1 tablespoon finely chopped parsley

You will require a ring mould for this dish.

Boil the macaroni. Grease a ring mould with butter. Chop the lobster and reserve 3 or 4 neat pieces and 12 prawns for decoration.

Stir all the rest of the shellfish into the macaroni and mix in 2 tablespoons of the cream. Turn the mixture into the ring mould and stand it in a baking tin containing 1 inch (2.5 cm) of water. Cover the whole tray with foil and bake at 350°F (180°C, Gas Mark 4) for 25 minutes.

Meanwhile make the white sauce and stir in the rest of the cream and the cooked cucumber. Season highly with salt and white pepper. Keep warm.

Take the ring mould out of the oven and unmould. Pour the sauce into the centre of the ring. Sprinkle the parsley lightly all round the top of the ring but not on to the sauce.

Place the reserved shellfish around the top of the ring on the parsley and serve immediately.

Smoked Haddock Soufflé

Serves 4

1 large smoked haddock, about 1½ lb (¾ kg) fillets, fresh or frozen, will not give quite such a distinctive flavour
¾ stick (90 g) butter
½ cup (60 g) flour
1¼ cups (3 dl) single cream
¼ teaspoon freshly ground black pepper
4 eggs, yolks and whites separated and both well beaten

The sauce:

¼ lb (120 g) mushrooms, very finely chopped
2 tablespoons (30 g) butter
3 tablespoons dry sherry
⅝ cup (1.5 dl) double cream
Salt and pepper

White's Club was started in 1693 as White's Chocolate House and it cost two pence to enter. It was frequented by Beau Brummel and, as a club during the Regency, was noted for the high play at its tables. This haddock soufflé was usually served as a late supper dish.

Poach the haddock gently in a pan of boiling water for 10 minutes. Lift it out and flake the flesh finely, discarding all skin and bone.

Melt the butter and stir in the flour to make a roux. Cook, stirring, for 1 minute but do not allow it to colour. Stir in the single cream and add the pepper. Stir in the haddock and the egg yolks and beat for a minute with a wooden spoon. Fold in the egg whites, which should be stiff enough to hold a peak.

Turn the mixture quickly into a buttered 1 quart (9 dl) soufflé dish. Stand the dish in a baking tin half-filled with boiling water and cook in a hot oven, 400°F (200°C, Gas Mark 6), for 20 minutes.

Meanwhile, make the sauce. Sauté the mushrooms in the butter. Stir in the sherry. Add a little salt and pepper. When hot slowly add the cream, stirring all the time.

Turn out the soufflé and pour the mushroom sauce over it. Or serve immediately in the dish with the sauce in a sauceboat.

Stewed Carp with Forcemeat Balls

2 to 3 lb (1 to 1½ kg) carp
2½ cups (6 dl) chicken stock (a
  stock cube will do)
1¼ cups (3 dl) medium dry
  sherry
2 bay leaves
12 peppercorns
1 teaspoon salt
⅝ cup (1.5 dl) good brown
  sauce, rather thick
Juice of ½ lemon
¼ teaspoon cayenne pepper

Forcemeat balls:

1 cup (120 g) minced raw veal
  or chicken
1 medium onion, very finely
  chopped
1 teaspoon dried tarragon
2 teaspoons chopped parsley
  (fresh or dried)
4 tablespoons (60 g) fresh fine
  white breadcrumbs
1 egg
Salt and pepper
Fat for frying

An early recipe which occurs in various manuscripts from the days when all great houses and monasteries had their own fishponds. Carp were highly considered. In large ponds or lakes they grow to a good size over several years and have a delicate flavour and consistency. This is an adaptation of a recipe from Richard Dolby, who was head cook at the fashionable Thatched House Tavern in St James's Street in about 1820. It can also be made with pike or with two large trout. London fishmongers will usually get a carp if the order is placed a day or two before it is required. The brown sauce is delicate enough for the fish and does not disguise its flavour, which contrasts well with the forcemeat balls.

Trim the fins from the cleaned carp and make 3 cuts across the back. (This is known as crimping; it allows the fish to cook more quickly and prevents the skin splitting.)
  Lay the fish in a flat stew pan and pour over the stock and sherry. Add the bay leaves, peppercorns and salt, bring to the boil and simmer very gently, covered, for 30 minutes. (If two smaller fish are used, they will only require about 15 minutes cooking.)
  Meanwhile make the forcemeat balls by mixing all the dry ingredients in a bowl and stirring in the egg to bind. When well worked together, divide the mixture into 12 small pieces, roll into balls and fry in fat for about 5 minutes until golden brown on all sides. Lift, drain well and keep hot.
  When the fish is cooked, lift on to a flat serving dish and keep hot. Boil the stock and wine (in which it has been cooking) fiercely for 5 minutes, then reduce the heat and stir in the brown sauce, a little at a time, beating well. Add the lemon juice and cayenne. Check the seasoning. Pour the sauce over the carp and lay the forcemeat balls around the edge of the dish.

Greenwich Whitebait

2 lb (1 kg) whitebait
½ cup (60 g) seasoned flour
1 lemon, cut in quarters
8 very thin slices brown bread,
  buttered

In the seventeenth century the best whitebait in the world were caught at Greenwich in July and August. Special whitebait dinners were given in Greenwich taverns and parties of Londoners would go by water or by road to spend the day by the Thames where it widened to the estuary. They watched the ships, strolled along the river bank and in the park and ate whitebait, often preceded by Water Souchet, for which a recipe is also given.

Have ready a deep-fryer half-filled with clean frying oil, which must reach at least 400°F (200°C) before the whitebait go in.
  Lay a large double piece of kitchen paper on a flat dish. Spread a clean tea towel on your working surface. Shake the seasoned flour all over the middle of the cloth and pour the whitebait on to it. Gather up the corners of the cloth and gently shake the

little fish about until they are dry and coated with flour. Do not hold too tightly or shake too violently as the fish must not be bruised or broken.

Turn the whitebait into the frying basket and plunge it into hot oil for 1 minute. They should just have time to crisp but not brown. After 30 seconds, plunge them in again for a further 1 minute, this time to brown as well as crisp.

Turn the whitebait out on to the kitchen paper to drain for only a second, then pull the paper out from under them and serve immediately with the buttered brown bread and lemon quarters.

Savoury Rice with Chicken or Lamb

Serves 4

6 oz (180 g) short-grain rice
1 small onion, finely chopped
Pinch of dried thyme
Pinch of dried rosemary
$3\frac{3}{4}$ cups (9 dl) stock
1 chicken or small leg of lamb
$\frac{1}{2}$ stick (60 g) butter, for roasting
Salt and pepper

This nineteenth-century recipe from Bethnal Green makes a very good and unusual dish.

Put the rice mixed with the onion, herbs and seasoning in a wide fireproof dish. Pour over the stock. Cook, uncovered, at the bottom of the oven at 350°F (180°C, Gas Mark 4) for $1\frac{1}{2}$ hours.

After 1 hour put the lamb or chicken to roast near the top of the oven. When the rice has cooked for $1\frac{1}{2}$ hours, put the chicken or lamb on top of it and pour the juice and fat from the pan over all. Put the meat and rice back in the oven for as long as it takes to cook the joint, which should be at least 30 minutes, but may be longer without harming the rice.

White Devil

Serves 2

The breast of a roasted chicken, skinned, boned and divided in half
Butter
Four 2-inch (5 cm) puff pastry triangles, previously baked and reheated

The devil:

$\frac{1}{4}$ teaspoon turmeric
$\frac{1}{4}$ teaspoon cayenne pepper
$\frac{1}{4}$ teaspoon white pepper
1 teaspoon dry English mustard
$\frac{1}{2}$ teaspoon salt
$1\frac{1}{4}$ cups (3 dl) double cream

This dish was sometimes served in a silver chafing dish at Romano's in the Strand to gentlemen who had taken one of their private rooms for a late and very intimate supper.

Lightly butter a small, shallow, ovenproof dish and lay the 2 chicken breast halves in it.

Prepare the devil by mixing all the spices and the mustard and salt into the cream; beat it a very little so that it is just beginning to thicken.

Pour the devil over the chicken and put it in a hot oven, 400°F (200°C, Gas Mark 6), for 8 to 10 minutes or until just beginning to brown; it should not actually bubble.

Serve with the puff pastry triangles.

Chicken with Almond Stuffing

2 chickens, about 1 lb (½ kg)
  each in weight, cleaned and
  cut in halves
¾ stick (90 g) butter, melted
Flour
⅝ cup (1.5 dl) dry white wine
1 tablespoon brandy or whisky
⅝ cup (1.5 dl) chicken stock (a
  stock cube will do)
1 cup (60 g) flaked almonds
Juice of ½ lemon

The stuffing:

⅝ cup (90 g) fresh fine white
  breadcrumbs
1 cup (60 g) almonds, finely
  chopped (ground almonds will
  not do)
1 teaspoon dried tarragon
1 teaspoon finely chopped
  parsley
1 egg, well beaten
¼ teaspoon salt
Pinch of freshly ground black
  pepper
2 tablespoons (30 g) butter, just
  melted

A nineteenth-century recipe from a London cookery book. The chickens weighed about 1 pound (¾ kg) each and were simply cut in half down the back, allowing half per person. They were served with a rather thin sauce, sharpened with lemon juice. Rice and french beans are good with this dish.

First make the stuffing by mixing all the ingredients together in a bowl, adding the melted butter last, and stirring very well.

Grease a baking tin with a little of the butter. Flour the uncut sides of the chicken halves and lay them, cut sides upwards, in the baking tin. Put a quarter of the stuffing on to each half and mould it to a smooth filling. Spoon about a tablespoon of wine over each, reserving the rest. Then pour on the remaining melted butter. Put the chicken halves in the oven at 350°F (180°C, Gas Mark 4) and bake for 30 minutes.

Meanwhile simmer together the remaining wine, the brandy or whisky and the stock until reduced by about one-third. Five minutes before the chickens are done, take them from the oven, baste them with the stock and wine and sprinkle with the flaked almonds. Baste over the almonds and put the chicken halves back in the oven for 5 minutes so that the almonds brown delicately.

Lift the chicken halves on to a heated, flat serving dish. Pour off all but 2 teaspoons of the butter and juices from the baking tin and put it over heat. Stir in 2 teaspoons flour. Add the wine and stock and the lemon juice, pouring slowly. Check the seasoning. Pour a little of the sauce around the chickens when you are ready to serve and put the rest in a sauceboat.

The Cavalier's Broil

3½ to 4 lb (1¾ to 2 kg) shoulder
  of lamb
¾ stick (90 g) butter or ⅜ cup
  cooking fat
¾ lb (360 g) mushrooms
Juice of ½ lemon mixed with
  ½ teaspoon salt and a pinch of
  pepper
1 teaspoon cayenne pepper
1 teaspoon ground ginger
½ teaspoon ground coriander
1 teaspoon freshly ground
  black pepper
1 teaspoon salt

This recipe belongs to Royalist tables of the seventeenth century. A simplified version is quoted by Eliza Acton, but the original recipe dates from a hundred years or so before her day. The shoulder of lamb would probably have been expected to serve only two gentlemen. In our day it is enough for more than double that number. It is extremely good if served with green peas cooked with mint, creamed potatoes and red-currant jelly.

Put the lamb with about two-thirds of the butter or fat into a baking tin and roast in a hot oven, 400°F (200°C, Gas Mark 6), for 40 minutes.

Meanwhile slice the mushrooms finely and sauté them in the remaining butter or fat. When almost done add the lemon juice. Set aside and keep hot.

Heat the grill. Remove the joint from the oven and put it on a fireproof serving dish. With a sharp, heavy knife score the meat down to the bone, 3 times on each side.

Mix the spices and seasonings together and spoon them well into each scored cut. Put the joint on the grill pan. Keep the serving dish, and the juices that came from the meat when it was scored, hot.

Grill the meat, turning it 2 to 3 times until it is done. This should take about 20 minutes, when the meat should be pink near the bone while the skin is very brown and crisp.

When the meat is ready, put the joint back on the hot serving dish and pour over any gravy collected in the grill pan. Pour the mushrooms over the joint and serve.

Mutton Pie à la Reform

Serves 6 to 8

12 lamb chops, boned
¼ lb (120 g) home-cooked ham, chopped
¼ lb (120 g) mushrooms, chopped
½ teaspoon dried thyme
½ teaspoon grated nutmeg
1 teaspoon salt
½ teaspoon black pepper
¾ lb (360 g) rough puff or flaky pastry

The sauce:

1 onion stuck with 6 cloves
2½ cups (6 dl) stock (a stock cube will do)
1 tablespoon (15 g) flour
2 tablespoons (30 g) butter
⅝ cup (1.5 dl) red wine
3 teaspoons red-currant jelly

This pie was served at the Reform Club in the middle of the nineteenth century. The recipe was probably devised by the great chef Alexis Soyer, at the request of one of the members. The pie must be made in two stages and takes at least one hour to prepare, apart from the pastry, but it is a most impressive and worthwhile dish for a special occasion. Nothing should be offered with it except a green salad served on a separate plate to each guest.

First make the sauce. Put the onion in the stock and boil until the liquid is reduced by about one-third. Remove the onion and thicken the stock using the flour and butter to make a brown roux. Add the red wine and stir in the red-currant jelly. Keep hot.

Remove the centre round of meat (the eye) from each lamb chop. Cut the rest of the meat finely and mix with the ham, mushrooms, dried herbs and seasonings.

Lay half of the meat rounds in a pie dish. Cover with half the ham mixture. Lay the remaining meat rounds on top and cover with the rest of the ham mixture. Pour over the hot sauce. Cover the dish with a piece of foil and allow to get almost completely cold before putting on the pastry. (By covering, none of the flavour and aroma are lost and the lamb is slightly impregnated by the hot sauce.)

Cover the pie with the pastry and bake in a very hot oven, 450°F (230°C, Gas Mark 8), for 10 minutes. Reduce the heat to 350°F (180°C, Gas Mark 4), put the pie on a lower shelf and cook for a further 30 minutes, covering the pastry with foil to prevent over-browning, if necessary.

Boiled Calf's Head

1 calf's head, boned and
  cleaned
2 large onions, quartered
2 to 3 carrots, halved
1 celery stick, cut in pieces
Sprigs of thyme and marjoram
A few sage leaves
2 to 3 bay leaves
12 peppercorns
2 teaspoons salt
Juice of 1 lemon
$\frac{1}{2}$ cup (60 g) flour
Brown, caper or parsley sauce

After the Restoration of the Monarchy, some of the younger Republicans used to meet once a year at a London inn, where they celebrated the anniversary of the death of Charles I on 30 January 1649. The main part of the dinner consisted of calves' heads, some crowned with garlands of parsley. The bitterly discontented men drank derisive toasts to the monarchy and eventually went in procession to a courtyard, where they built a great fire. One, masked and carrying an axe, represented the executioner; a second carried a calf's head on a napkin, representing the fine Stuart head of Charles I. The rest waved handkerchiefs stained with wine to represent blood. The head was thrown into the fire amid ribald cries and songs.

They called themselves simply The Calves' Head Club and presumably hoped that loyalists would assume that they met because they considered calf's head one of the greatest dishes in the world. Until the beginning of the nineteenth century, their descendants ate calf's head at home on 30 January each year.

If preferred, the head may be cut in pieces after cooking and served in a brown sauce with hard-boiled eggs, mushrooms and olives. There is a fine, elaborate, seventeenth-century recipe which required cockscombs, kidneys and crayfish in addition.

Put the vegetables, herbs, seasoning and lemon juice in a saucepan of boiling water. Sprinkle in the flour (which later keeps the head white) and boil for 10 minutes, without the head. Then lower the head into the bouillon and simmer for $1\frac{1}{2}$ hours or until perfectly tender.

Lift out the head and drain; trim the tongue and serve with the chosen sauce.

Ragout of Ham

2 lb (1 kg) piece of gammon
$\frac{1}{4}$ cup (60 g) brown sugar
2 tablespoons (30 g) butter
$\frac{1}{4}$ cup (30 g) flour
$\frac{3}{8}$ cup (1.5 dl) red wine
1 teaspoon castor sugar
$\frac{1}{2}$ teaspoon ground cinnamon
$\frac{1}{2}$ teaspoon freshly ground
  black pepper
Juice and zest of 1 large
  orange

This is a delicious eighteenth-century recipe from Dr Johnson's London.

Boil the gammon in water with the brown sugar and when it is cooked allow it to get cold in the liquid. It is often convenient to do this the day before.

Lift out the gammon and discard the liquor in which it cooked. Carve it into 12 rather thick slices and trim them of all fat and skin. Melt the butter in a saucepan, lay the gammon in it and turn the slices frequently over a low heat until they are heated through.

Lay the gammon slices in a fireproof dish and keep warm.

Stir the flour into the butter to make a roux, add the wine, stirring well, and then stir in the sugar, cinnamon and pepper. Finally stir in the orange juice and zest. Check the seasoning: the sauce should be of the consistency of fairly thick cream, slightly sharp and a little sweet and spicy. Pour it over the ham and serve at once.

Apples with the Vestal Fire

12 very small baked tart shells made with short pastry
Apricot jam
2½ lb (1¼ kg) Cox's Orange apples or Golden Delicious. 6 of these must be evenly sized to about 2 inches (5 cm) in diameter
Juice of 3 lemons
1 cup (240 g) castor sugar
½ cup (120 g) short-grain rice
3 cups (7.5 dl) milk and a little more
½ stick (60 g) butter
2 eggs, well beaten
Brandy
4 tablespoons double cream

This was a full-dress sweet for a Reform Club dinner. It is grand and complicated, but the ingredients are simple and it is not very difficult to make for a dinner party. The effect of the blue flame burning on each little altar of apple and pastry, and the sea of blue flame round the bottom of the creamy rice is very pretty and surprising. The burnt brandy adds a very subtle flavour to the whole.

The tarts: the little tarts can be made several hours in advance or the day before they are wanted. They must be very small, coming only halfway up the smallest tart tins. Just before using, spread the inside of each with a little apricot jam and put in a low oven to warm through.

The apples: peel all the apples thinly. Reserve 6 whole apples in water and add the juice of 1 lemon to prevent discoloration. Cut the remainder into slices about ⅛ inch (0.25 cm) thick, and place in a heavy saucepan with about half of the sugar, ⅜ cup (1.5 dl) of water and the juice of 2 lemons. Simmer gently, until the apple slices are quite soft, but keep their shape. Drain them, reserving the liquid, and put on a dish to cool.

Add ⅜ cup (1.5 dl) of water, 1 tablespoon of apricot jam and 4 tablespoons (60 g) of the remaining castor sugar to the reserved liquid and stir well. Cut the 6 whole apples across in half and dig out a little of the core from the centre of each half with a pointed knife. Place the apples in the syrup. A flat skillet may be necessary as they should cook in a single layer. Simmer very gently, covered with a lid or foil, for 20 to 30 minutes until the apples halves are soft but hold their shape. When they are cooked, remove them from the syrup and allow to cool. Reserve the syrup.

The rice: put the rice in a heavy saucepan which has been rinsed out with cold water and left wet. Pour on the milk and stir until it comes to the boil. Cover and simmer very gently, stirring from time to time. Test after 15 minutes and if the rice is not quite tender, add a little more milk. As soon as the rice is cooked add the remaining castor sugar, the butter and the eggs. Stir very well over low heat until quite thick. It must not boil or it will curdle and may burn. Turn the rice out into a pudding bowl, stir in the lightly whipped cream and leave to get cold.

The presentation: when the rice and apples are cold, turn the rice out on to a flat dish. Scoop 3 tablespoonfuls from the middle of the top and fill the hole with the cooked apple slices. Put the scooped out rice on top and smooth with a spatula to form a pyramid. On each half-apple put one of the little tartlets and arrange the 12 halves to stand out from the sides of the rice pyramid by sticking one side a little way into the soft rice. Pour the syrup in which the apples cooked all over the pyramid. Chill in refrigerator for 2 to 3 hours but not much longer.

Just before serving pour a teaspoonful of brandy into each tart and 2 tablespoonfuls in the dish and set it alight.

Cabinet (or Chancellor's) Pudding

½ lb (240 g) stale Madeira cake
  or Victoria sandwich
3 eggs
⅝ cup (1.5 dl) milk
Vanilla essence
⅓ cup (60 g) currants
⅓ cup (60 g) sultanas
Glacé cherries
Small pieces angelica
Jam sauce or hard sauce

This pudding was supposed to have been traditional at Westminster. It requires no added sugar as it is sweetened by the cake and the dried fruit.

Crumble the cake into a bowl. Whisk the eggs. Heat the milk slowly. Add the hot milk, with the vanilla, to the eggs and pour gently over the cake. Stir in the currants and sultanas. Cover the bowl and leave the cake crumbs to soak until quite cold.

Grease a small pudding bowl and put a round of greased paper or foil in the bottom. Arrange pieces of glacé cherries and angelica on the paper or foil. Pour the pudding mixture over the top. Cover the bowl tightly with foil and place a saucer on top of it.

Steam the pudding gently for 45 minutes to 1 hour or until firm. Turn the pudding out of the bowl and remove the paper or foil from what is now the top. Serve with jam sauce or hard sauce.

Fried Camembert

1 piece Camembert cheese
  (about 6 oz/180 g) or 4 portions
  wrapped Camembert
¼ teaspoon cayenne pepper
1 egg, well beaten
⅝ cup (90 g) fresh fine white
  breadcrumbs
4 thin fingers dry hot toast,
  without crusts

This hot savoury was occasionally served to follow a cold grouse or partridge, either for lunch or for dinner. It probably came originally from the Reform Club, but it is mentioned in the list of savouries at other London clubs.

The Camembert retains its texture inside the crisp cover and the cayenne gives it a little bite. It is best if the cheese is prepared and the toast cut before the meal and the cooking done when the main course is finished. It should take only 3 to 4 minutes if the deep-fryer is preheated and kept waiting on the side of the stove.

Fried Camembert is particularly good if red wine is being served.

Have some clean cooking oil heated to 400°F (200°C) ready in a deep-fryer.

Cut the Camembert into 4 triangular pieces, but do not cut off the rind. Sprinkle each piece with cayenne pepper and then dip in the egg. Cover with breadcrumbs, pressing them in well.

Put the Camembert gently in the frying basket and fry for 2 minutes or until a light golden brown. While they fry, make the toast. Serve on very small, heated plates immediately the cheese is ready.

Bibliography

Eliza Acton, *Modern Cookery in all its Branches*, Longmans, London, 1845. See also *The Best of Eliza Acton*, Penguin Books, Harmondsworth, 1974.

Samuel & Sarah Adams, *The Complete Servant*, Knight & Lacey, London, 1825.

Mary L. Allen, *Breakfast Dishes*, J. S. Virtue, London, 1894.

Dorothy Allhusen, *Book of Scents and Dishes*, Williams and Norgate, London, 1926.

Anon, *Adam's Luxury & Eve's Cookery*, R. Dodsley & M. Cooper, London, 1744.

Anon, *Complete Family Piece*, A. Bettersworth & C. Hitch, London, 1737.

Anon, *Court and Country Confectioner*, G. Riley & A. Cooke, London, 1770.

Anon, *The Court and Kitchen of Elizabeth, commonly called Joan Cromwell*, 1664.

Apicius, *The Roman Cookery Book*, translated by Barbara Flower & Elizabeth Rosenbaum, Harrap, London, 1958.

Thomas Austin, *Two 15th Century Cookery Books*, edited in 1888, manuscripts in British Library, British Museum.

Mary Aylett & Olive Ordish, *First Catch your Hare*, Macdonald, London, 1965.

Marchioness of Bath, *Before the Sunset Fades*, Longleat Estate Co., Warminster, 1951.

Mrs Beeton, *The Book of Household Management*, S. O. Beeton, London, 1861. Facsimile of 1861 edition published by Cape, 1968.

Anne Blencowe, *Receipt Book 1694*, Guy Chapman, London, 1925.

Andrew Boorde, *A Compendyous Regymen or a Dyetry of Helth*, John Gowghe, London, 1542.

John Boys, *A General View of the Agriculture of the County of Kent*, Board of Agriculture, London, 1794. Board of Agriculture, London, 1813.

Fernand Braudel, *Capitalism and Material Life 1400–1800*, translated by Miriam Kochan, Fontana, London, 1974.

Dame Alice de Bryene, *The Household Book 1412*, Harrison, London, 1931.

Edward A. Bunyard, *The Anatomy of Dessert*, Dulan, London, 1929. Chatto & Windus, London, 1933.

John Burnett, *A History of the Cost of Living*, Penguin Books, Harmondsworth, 1969. *Plenty and Want*, Nelson, London, 1966.

H. E. Butler, editor, *The Chronicle of Jocelin de Brakeland*, Nelson, London, 1949.

Charles Cooper, *The English Table in History and Literature*, Sampson Low, London, 1929.

Joseph Cooper, *The Art of Cookery Refin'd and Augmented*, R. Lowndes, London, 1654.

Rt. Hon. J. W. Croker, *The Journals of J. W. Croker*, edited by Lewis J. Jennings, Murray, London, 1884.

Nicholas Culpeper, *Culpeper's English Physician and Complete Herbal*, Peter Cole, London, 1652.

Mary Day, *Farmhouse Fare*, Hulton, London, 1954.

Sir Kenelm Digby, *The Closet of the Eminently Learned Sir Kenelm Digby, Knight, Opened*, 1669, reprinted by Philip Lee Warner, London, 1910.

Margaret Dods, *The Cook and Housewife's Manual*, Oliver Boyd, Edinburgh, 1826.

Richard Dolby, *The Cook's Dictionary*, Colburn & Bentley, London, 1832.

Joyce Douglas, *Old Derbyshire Recipes and Customs*, Hendon Publishing, London, 1976.

Sir Jack Drummond & Anne Wilbraham, *The Englishman's Food*, Cape, London, 1939.

Helen Edden, *County Recipes of Old England*, Country Life, London, 1929.

F. G. Emmison, *Tudor Food and Pastimes*, Ernest Benn, London, 1964. *Elizabethan Life*, Essex Record Office, Chelmsford, 1978 (publications no. 71).

Celia Fiennes, *Journeys of Celia Fiennes* (seventeenth century), Cresset Press, London, 1947.

F.J. Furnival, editor, *The Babees Book*, Early English Text Society: London, 1868, Chatto & Windus, London, 1908. *Early English Meals and Manners*, Early English Text Society, London, 1939.

Mark Girouard, *Life in the English Country House*, Yale University Press, New Haven and London, 1978.

Hannah Glasse, *The Art of Cookery made Plain and Easy*, first folio 1747. S. R. Publications, 1972.

Louis Golding and André Simon, *We shall Eat and Drink Again*, Hutchinson, London, 1944.

Maud Grieve, *A Modern Herbal*, Cape, London, 1931. Peregrine, London, 1976.

Mrs Groundes-Peace, *Old Cookery Notebook*, David & Charles, Newton Abbot, 1971.

John Hampson, *The English at Table*, Collins, London, 1944.

Dorothy Hartley, *Food in England*, Macdonald, London, 1954. Macdonald & Jane, London, 1975.

George Hartman, *Excellent Directions for Cookery*, A. & J. Churchill, London, 1682.

Abraham Hayward, *The Art of Dining*, J. Murray, London, 1852.

William C. Hazlitt, *Old Cookery Books and Ancient Cuisine*, Book Lover's Library, London, 1886.

Nell Saint John Heaton, *Traditional Recipes of the British Isles*, Faber & Faber, London, 1951.

W. M. Hendy, *Gourmet's Book of Food & Drink*, Bodley Head, London, 1933.

Lizzie Heritage, *New Universal Cookery Book*, Cassell, London, 1894.

Brian Hill, *The Greedy Book*, Hart-Davis, London, 1966.

Lady Agnes Jeckyll, *Kitchen Essays* (reprint from *The Times*), Nelson, London, 1922.

Walter Jerrold, *The Heart of London*, Blackie & Son, London, 1924.

Auguste Kettner, *Book of the Table*, Dulam, London, 1877. Centaur, London, 1968.

The Rev. Francis Kilvert, *Kilvert's Diaries* (1870–1879), edited by W. Plomer, Cape, London, 1944. Penguin Books, Harmondsworth, 1977.

William Kitchiner, *The Cook's Oracle*, Samuel Bagster, London, 1817. Houlston & Wright, London, 1860.

Patrick Lamb, *Royal Cookery or The Complete Court Cook*, Abel Roper, London, 1710.

Louis Lémery, *A Treatise of All Sorts of Foods*, T. Osborne, London, 1745, (Macadam collection, Edinburgh.)

Elizabeth Lothian, *Country House Cookery from the West*, David & Charles, Newton Abbot, 1978.

W. M., *The Queen's Closet Opened*, Nathaniel Brooke, London, 1655.

Gervase Markham, *The English Hous-wife*, 1649.

Agnes B. Marshall, *Mrs A. B. Marshall's Cookery Book*, Simpkin and Marshall, London, 1890. *Fancy Ices*, Marshall's School of Cookery, London, 1894.

Robert May, *The Accomplish't Cook*, Nathaniel Brooke, London, 1660.

M. F. Misson, *Memoires et Observations*, translated by Mr Ozell, D. Browne, London, 1719.

Judy Moore, *Sussex Recipes*, James Pike, London, 1976.

Richard Morris, editor, *Liber Cure Cocorum*, taken from Sloane manuscript no. 1986, Philological Society, London, 1854.

Mrs Napier, *A Noble Boke of Cookery*, 1480, MS in Holkham Collection, Holkham Hall, Norfolk. National Trust Guide, 1979, Cape, London.

W. J. Passingham, *London's Markets*, Sampson Low & Co., London, 1935.

Thomas Percy, editor, *Northumberland Household Book*, printer unknown, London, 1770. Also published 1905, printer unknown.

Joan Poulson, *Old Cotswold Recipes*, *Old Northern Recipes*, *Old Lancashire Recipes*, *Old Yorkshire Recipes*, *Old Thames Valley Recipes*, Hendon Publishing, London, 1975–77.

Philippa Pullar, *Consuming Passions*, Hamilton, London, 1970. Sphere, London, 1972.

Nancy Quennell, *The Epicure's Anthology*, Golden Cockerel Press, London, 1936.

Elizabeth Raffald, *The Experienced English Housekeeper*, privately printed, Manchester, 1769. Henry Mozley, Derby, 1825.

J. Rey, *The Whole Art of Dining* (translated from the French), Carmona & Baker, London, 1921.

Mrs Maria E. Rundell, *A New System of Domestic Cookery*, J. Murray, London, 1809. T. Allman, London, 1838.

V. Sackville-West, *Knole and the Sackvilles*, Heinemann, London, 1926. Ernest Benn, London, 1958.

André Simon, *A Concise Encyclopaedia of Gastronomy*, Wine and Food Society, London, 1939–48. Collins, London, 1952.

Alexis Soyer, *The Gastronomic Regenerator*, Marshall, London, 1846.

Elizabeth Steele, *Northumbrian Country House Recipes*, Hendon Publishing, London, 1977.

Reay Tannahill, *Food in History*, Eyre Methuen, London, 1973.

Mary Tillinghast, *Rare and Excellent Receipts*, privately printed, 1678.

Gabriel Tschumi, *Royal Chef*, William Kimber, London, 1954.

Thomas Tusser, *Five Hundreth Points of Good Husbandry*, R. Tottel, London, 1573, J. Tregaskis, London, 1931.

Louis Eustache Ude, *The French Cook*, John Ebers, London, 1813.

Alison Uttley, *Recipes from an Old Farmhouse*, Faber & Faber, London, 1966.

Tobias Venner, *Via Recta ad Vitam Longam*, E. Griffin for R. Moore, London, 1620.

A. W., *A Booke of Cookerie*, published privately, London, 1594.

Isaak Walton, *The Compleat Angler*, Richard Marriot, London, 1655. A. & C. Black, London, 1978.

Edward Ward, *The London Spy*, London, 1699, privately published, Edinburgh. 1823.

The Rev. Richard Warner, *Antiquitates Culinariae*, R. Blamire, London, 1791.

Florence White, *Good Things in England*, Cape, London, 1932. *Good English Food*, Cape, London, 1952.

Hannah Wolley, *The Queen-like Closet*, private press, London, 1670.

Women's Institute, *Poultry and Game*, edited by Rachel Ryan, National Federation of Women's Institutes, London, 1960.

James Woodforde, *Diary of a Country Parson 1758–1802*, Humphrey Milford, London, 1924. Oxford University Press, 1978.

Wynkeworthe de Worde, *The Book of Kervynge*, Quarto, 1508.

Glossary

British terms used
in this book

ANCHOVY ESSENCE use
pounded salted anchovies
as a substitute

BAKING BLIND baking an
empty pastry shell

BEETROOT beets

BEST END OF NECK the
choicest (the rib-chop)
part of the lamb, between
the shoulder and loin

BILBERRIES blueberries

BLOOD HEAT body
temperature (about 98°F)

BOUDOIR SPONGE FINGERS use
ladyfingers

BRACE (as, OF PHEASANTS) a
pair of birds, properly a
male and female

BROAD BEANS also known
as fava beans or windsor
beans (lima beans can
sometimes be used instead,
but are not the same)

CASINO FINGERS use
ladyfingers

CASTOR SUGAR white sugar
roughly equivalent to
superfine

CHINE backbone
containing spinal column
of butchered animal,
sometimes removed (v., to
chine) to facilitate carving

CLARET red Bordeaux

CORNFLOUR cornstarch

COS LETTUCE romaine

DEMERARA SUGAR raw
sugar; coarse amber-
colored crystals (roughly
midway between
granulated white sugar
and dark brown sugar)

DOUBLE CREAM heavy
whipping cream

DRIPPING fat from roasted
meat

DRY CIDER hard cider

FISH SLICE spatula

FORCEMEAT stuffing
mixture for meat or fish

FRENCH BEANS green beans

GAMMON similar to ham,
but, unlike ham, is not
separated from the rest of
one side of the animal
before the curing process

GAS MARK low-to-high dial
markings on British ovens

GOLDEN SYRUP trade name
for a thick, refined sugar
syrup (light corn syrup is
the nearest equivalent)

GREASEPROOF PAPER use
wax paper

GRILL broiler; thus v., to
grill means to put under
(not over) source of heat

HAND OF PORK fresh pork
arm roast

ICING SUGAR equivalent to
confectioners' sugar

JELLY a flavored gelatin
dessert in addition to
meaning a smooth sweet
spread made of fruit, as in
the USA

JOINT piece of meat,
usually of a size to serve
several people

JUG pitcher

MINCE OR MINCED MEAT
ground meat

MINCER grinder

MOTHERING SUNDAY the
original Mother's Day

MUSHROOM KETCHUP a
piquant sauce; use steak
sauce

MUSTARD AND CRESS
misnomer for a salad cress
sold growing in small
boxes; it was originally
marketed with two plants
mingled, but these days
mustard is not included

OX KIDNEY beef kidney

PASTY turnover, usually
with meat or vegetable
filling

PIE DISH deep baking dish

PIG'S TROTTER pig's foot

PINE KERNELS pine nuts

PIPS seeds

PLAICE flatfish of the
flounder family

POUSSIN very young
chicken, usually about 1lb
in weight

PRAWNS medium-size or
large shrimp

RAISED PIE PASTRY a hot-
water crust

RATAFIA BISCUIT a sort of
miniature macaroon

ROUGH PUFF PASTRY use any
shortcut puff pastry recipe

SADDLE (as, OF HARE) the
two loins and connecting
backbone

SALAMANDER disc of metal
with a handle, to be made
red hot and then held over
food to provide a fast blast
of heat, e.g. to caramelize
the sugar on a crème
brûlée

SCALLOPS use sea scallops

SEETHE boil

SELF-RAISING FLOUR self-
rising flour

SILVERSIDE OF BEEF a round
or rump roast, usually
salted

SINGLE CREAM light cream

SKIRT OF BEEF a coarse-
grained cut from the
diaphragm of the animal

SLICE (as in FISH SLICE)
spatula-like lifting utensil

SOFTEN cook gently until
soft

SPRING ONIONS scallions

STONED seed removed

STREAKY BACON use thinly
sliced regular bacon

STRONG FLOUR flour made
from hard-grained wheat
rather than soft-grained;
use all-purpose flour

SUCKING PIG suckling pig

SUET CRUSTS most
commonly used for meat
pies; made by combining
equal amounts of flour
and shredded suet with a
little salt, adding cold
water slowly until a firm
dough is formed, which is
then rolled out on a
floured surface

SUET DUMPLINGS dumplings
made with suet

SULTANAS raisins from
seedless yellow grapes

TEA in some cases, the
evening meal rather than
a late afternoon between-
meals refreshment; in the
north of England the meal
is called "high tea"

TOPSIDE OF BEEF a rump
roast

TRAIL entrails

TREACLE use molasses

TRENCHER a piece of bread
used as a plate in
medieval times

WEBBS LETTUCE use any
iceberg lettuce

WHITEBAIT tiny fish, (as
many as 200 to the pound),
usually herrings and
sprats

General Index

A

Apicius, 6
Arlington Court, 118
Athelhampton, 122
Austen, Jane, 157

B

Barrington Court, 122
Beans, 57
Beaulieu Abbey, 155
Beaver, 59
Bedfordshire, 91
Bell, Kenneth, 88
Berkshire, 179
Billingsgate, 194
Birds, wild, 39, 86
Birmingham, 83
Borough Market, 196
Boys, John, 145–6
Bread, 59–60, 149
Brighton Pavilion, 150–2, 153
Bristol, 119–20
Bryene, Dame Alice de, 37
Buckinghamshire, 179
Burford, 85
Butter, 58, 59

C

Cabbage, 58
Cambridge, 40, 41
Cambridgeshire, 7, 34, 39
Carême, Marie-Antoine, 13, 151–2
Cauldrons, 9
Celtic food, 6
Cheddar cheese, 120
Cheeses, 11–12, 36–7, 41, 120
Chequers, 179–80
Cherries, 145–6
Cheshire, 120
Chophouses, 198
Christmas, 60, 88–9, 114
Cider apples, 146
Coaching, 111–12, 125
Cockles, 61
Coffee houses, 197–8
Colchester, 37
Compton Castle, 115–16
Cookshops, 197
Cooper of Peterhouse, 40
Cornwall, 113–15
Cotswolds, 84–5
Covent Garden, 195
Cowes Week, 153–4
Cranborne Manor, 121
Cream, clouted, 113, 115
Cromwell, Elizabeth, 41
Cumbria, 56

D

Dark Ages food, 7
Deer hunting and poaching, 34–5, 85, 155, 156
Derbyshire, 120
Devonshire, 115–16, 117–18, 120
Dickens, Charles, 13, 150, 198, 202
Dietary laws, 7, 36, 37, 58–9
Dorset, 120–3
Drinking, 203

E

East Anglia, 18–19, 34–55
East Quantoxhead, 123
Easter eggs, 37
Eels, 39, 86, 123, 152, 194
Eggs, 37
Eltham Ordinances, 149
Eltham Palace, 148–9
Ely, 39
Epping Forest, 34–5
Escoffier, 13, 199
Essex, 34–7, 174
Essex cheeses, 36–7
Evesham, 89
Exeter, 118
Exotic foods, 57, 120, 198

F

Fast days, 37
Feasts, 13, 14, 38, 40, 60, 84–5, 88–9, 114, 118, 147, 156–7, 177
Fens, 34, 38–40
Fiennes, Celia, 12, 112–13
Fish, 59, 86–8, 113, 146, 151–2, 154, 192, 194, 198; see also individual fish
Fish days, 7, 36, 59
FitzStephen, William, 197
Fox hunting, 89–90
Francatelli, 13, 199
Fruit, 7, 89, 145–6, 195–6; see also Cherries, Cider Apples, Mulberries

G

Game, 38, 64, 85, 177, 195; see also Venison
Game Dinner, 64–5
Georgian food, 12–13, 202
Glasse, Mrs, 198
Glastonbury Abbey, 61, 119
Gloucestershire, 84–9
Gravy, 9, 33
Gypsy food, 156

H

Hadrian's Wall, 56–7
Ham House, 177–8
Hampshire, 153–7
Hampton Court, 176–7
Hams, 11, 112
Hardy, Thomas, 120–1
Hartley, Dorothy, 116
Harvest Suppers, 40, 60
Hatfield House, 178–9
Hayward, Abraham, 201
Heritage, Lizzie, 199
Herrings, 37–8
Hertfordshire, 174, 178–9
Heveningham Hall, 38
High tea, 64, 202
Home Counties, 28–9, 174–91
Hop picking, 145
Hunting food, 89–90
Hunting forests, 34–5, 37, 39, 85, 121
Huntingdon, 7, 40–1

I

Ice, 118
Industrial Revolution and eating habits, 13, 62–3
Ingatestone Hall, 35–6
Inns, 12–13, 112–13, 125, 197–8
Ireland, 8–9
Isle of Wight, 153–4

J

Johnson, Dr Samuel, 193, 198, 202
Jonson, Ben, 148

K

Kensington Palace, 175
Kent, 7, 145–50, 174
Kew House, 176
Kinder, Philip, 59
King Edward VII, 203–5
King George V, 204
Kitchens, 116, 119, 122, 123, 151
Knole, 146–7

L

Lamb, Patrick, 91
Lampreys, 87
Lancashire, 61–2
Leadenhall Market, 194–5
Leeks, 58
Leicestershire, 7, 41, 89, 90
Lent, 7, 37, 59, 87

Recipe Index